# The Egyptian Book of Gates

LIVING HUMAN HERITAGE PUBLICATIONS, ZURICH

Studies from the

RESEARCH AND TRAINING CENTRE
FOR DEPTH PSYCHOLOGY
ACCORDING TO C. G. JUNG AND MARIE-LOUISE VON FRANZ

# The Egyptian Book of Gates

Translated by Erik Hornung
in collaboration with Theodor Abt

Living Human Heritage Publications, Zurich

2014

Second, improved edition 2022
First edition 2014
Living Human Heritage Publications
Münsterhof 16, 8001 Zurich, Switzerland
info@livinghumanheritage.org
www.livinghumanheritage.org

ISBN 978-3-9525713-0-9



FRONTCOVER: Final Scene from the Book of Gates
from the alabaster sarcophagus of Seti I

LAYOUT: Pınar Tuncer and Theodor Abt

COLOUR SEPARATION, PRINTING AND BINDING:
MAS MATBAACILIK A.Ş.
Hamidiye Mahallesi Soğuksu Caddesi
No:3 34408 Kağıthane, İstanbul / Türkiye
T. +90 212 294 10 00 (pbx) F. +90 212 294 90 80
book@masmat.com.tr

# Contents


| | |
|---|---|
| 1. Introduction | 7 |
| 2. The collated Book of Gates in images, hieroglyphs, transcription and English | 11 |
| The First Hour | 17 |
| The Second Hour | 28 |
| The Third Hour | 56 |
| The Fourth Hour | 96 |
| The Fifth Hour | 144 |
| The Sixth Hour | 194 |
| The Seventh Hour | 234 |
| The Eight Hour | 270 |
| The Ninth Hour | 304 |
| The Tenth Hour | 334 |
| The Eleventh Hour | 368 |
| The Twelfth Hour | 408 |
| 3. Bibliography | 458 |
| 4. List of Illustrations | 459 |
| 5. General Index | 460 |

# 1. Introduction

Following the *Amduat*, *The Book of Gates* is the second great Book of the Netherworld of the New Kingdom. Composed shortly after 1400 B.C., it already shows influences of the Amarna Period, the Age of Akhenaten. In twelve parts, corresponding to the hours of the night, it follows in word and image the journey of the Sungod through these hours, until he is rejuvenated every morning.

The first complete version of the book was engraved by Seti I on his alabaster sarcophagus and painted in turquoise, but some of its hours had already been depicted by king Horemheb on the walls of his burial chamber. Before him, the burial chamber used to be decorated with the *Amduat*. Nearly all the Royal Tombs and sarcophagi of the Ramesside Period in the Valley of the Kings included *The Book of Gates* for their decoration, and a non-royal person, the priest Tjanefer under Ramses III, also used some of the scenes in his tomb (Theban Tomb 158). A complete but now partially destroyed version can be found in the Osireion in Abydos, decorated by king Merenptah. All versions of the New Kingdom are available in the edition by Erik Hornung, with German translation and commentary (*Das Buch von den Pforten des Jenseits*, 2 vols, Geneva 1979/1984). Another transliteration and translation has been published by J. Zeidler (*Pfortenbuchstudien*, 2 vols, Wiesbaden 1999).

After the end of the New Kingdom (1070 B.C.) we can find quotations from *The Book of Gates* on several coffins and papyri, and whole sections again in certain tombs of the Saite Period (26th dynasty, 664-525 B. C).

In this volume, we basically follow the version on the alabaster sarcophagus of Seti I, which is now in the Sir John Soane's Museum in

The barque of the Sungod who is accompanied by *Sia* (Percipience) and *Heka* (Magic). Scene from the tomb of Seti I.

London. An excellent copy of it was published back in 1864 by J. Bonomi and S. Sharpe. Errors and omissions are corrected with the help of the other versions, as the hieroglyphic writing on this alabaster sarcophagus is often very concise due to lack of space.

An original title is not attested, but it may be the title mentioned in the judgement hall (33rd scene) as "Book of protecting Osiris among those of the Netherworld". The title now used is based on the prominent depiction of gates concluding the section of every night hour. These gates are mentioned but not yet represented in the *Amduat*, but we also know them from the Egyptian *Book of the Dead.*

Each hour is divided into three registers (horizontal sections), with the sun barque placed in the middle one, as in the *Amduat*, but with a reduced crew. Exceptions are the judgement hall and the final representation, which is also a summary of the daily course of the sun and its permanent renewal. The deities (or blessed dead) often have no individual names, but are summed up into collective groups, usually of nine or twelve. As the text belonging to each scene is showing the beginning and the end of it – mostly ending with a remark about their supply – we can distinguish exactly one hundred scenes.

A psychological interpretation of *The Book of Gates* by Theodor Abt, based on a series of lectures given at the Research- and Training Centre for Depth Psychology, Zurich during the years 2009-2011, will be published on the basis of this volume. This interpretation work gave rise to various questions with regard to the English translation of various terms; these could later on be discussed and the translation accordingly revised.

For her careful and competent documentation of the hieroglyphs, we are grateful to lic. phil. Alice Matheson. Her corrections and suggestions to improve the translation were also valuable. We also thank the Theban Mapping Project, especially Prof. Dr. Kent Weeks and Lori Lawson, for providing us with different pictures. For a careful language wash we are grateful to David Roscoe. Encouraging seed-money was provided by the Marie-Louise von Franz Foundation for Analytical Research in Zurich. For the final publication, we thank the Foundation of the Research- and Training Centre for Depth Psychology, Zurich.

Basle and Istanbul, May 2013 Erik Hornung and Theodor Abt

# 2. The Collated Book of Gates in Images, Hieroglyphs, Transcription, and English Translation

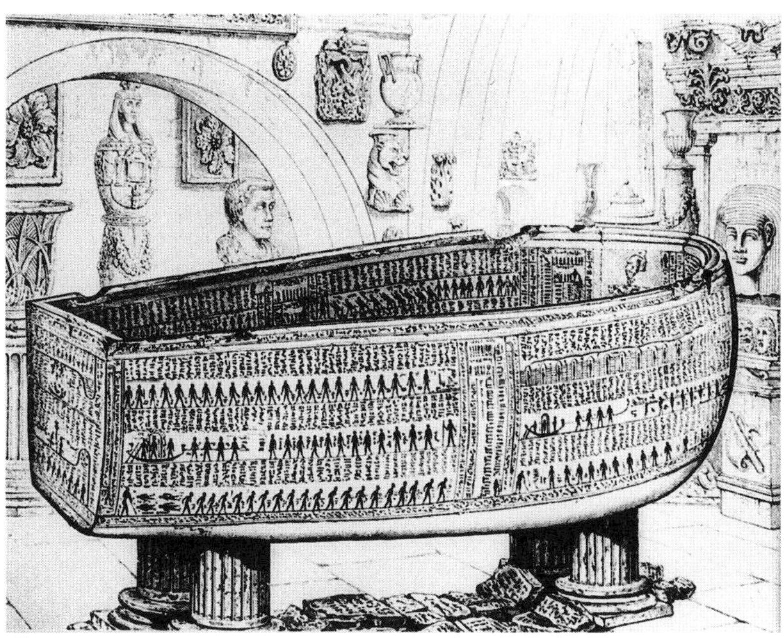

In this volume, we basically follow the version on the alabaster sarcophagus of Seti I, which is now in the Sir John Soane's Museum in London. We can see on the outside the 1st, 2nd and 3rd hour, on the inside part of the 9th hour, below the sarcophagus some broken fragments from the lid.

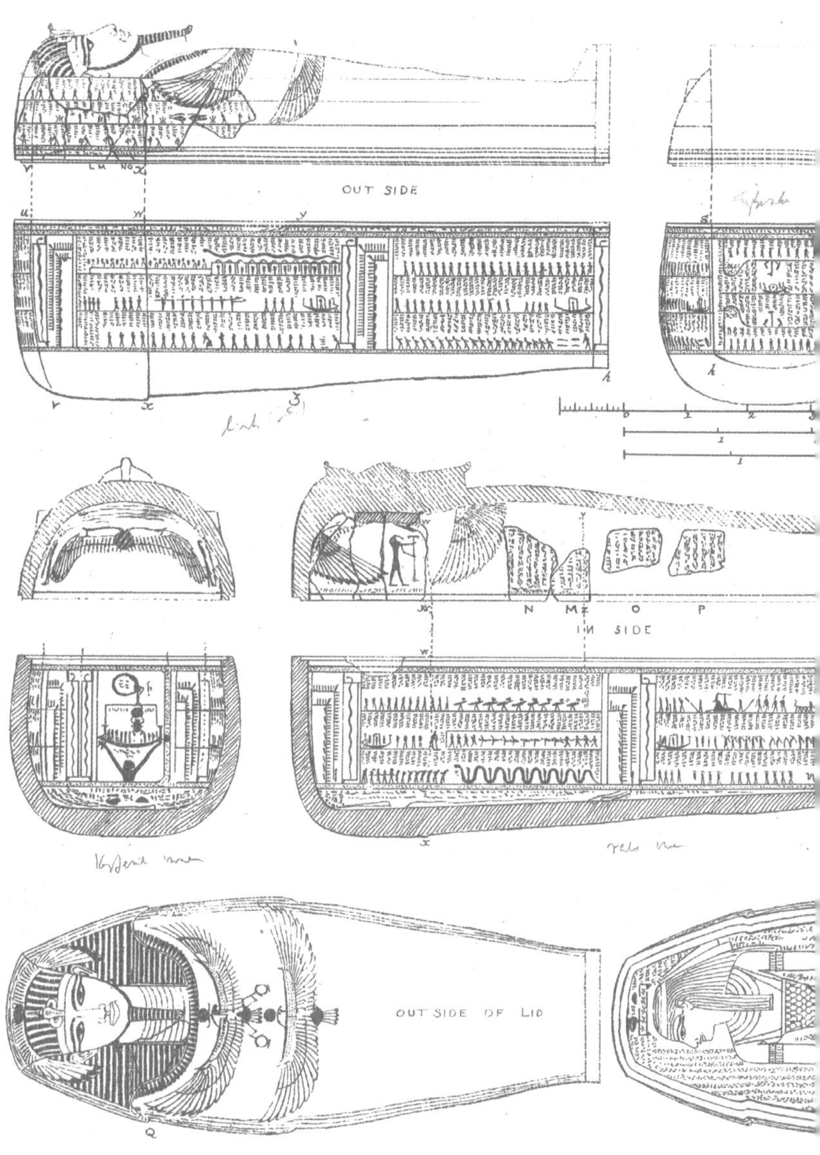
OUT SIDE
IN SIDE
OUT SIDE OF LID

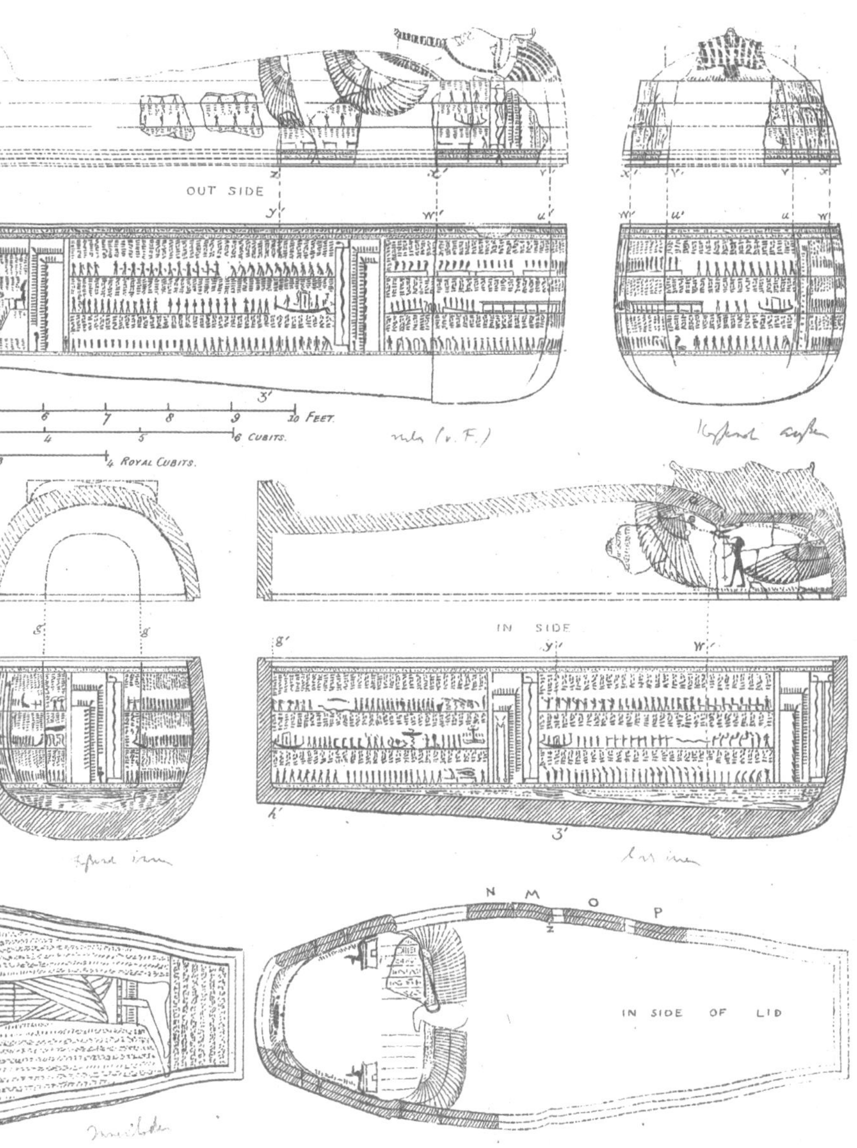
OUT SIDE
6
7
8
9
10 FEET.
4
5
6 CUBITS.
3
4 ROYAL CUBITS.
IN SIDE
N
M
O
P
IN SIDE OF LID

From the Tomb of Ramses V/VI.

# First Hour

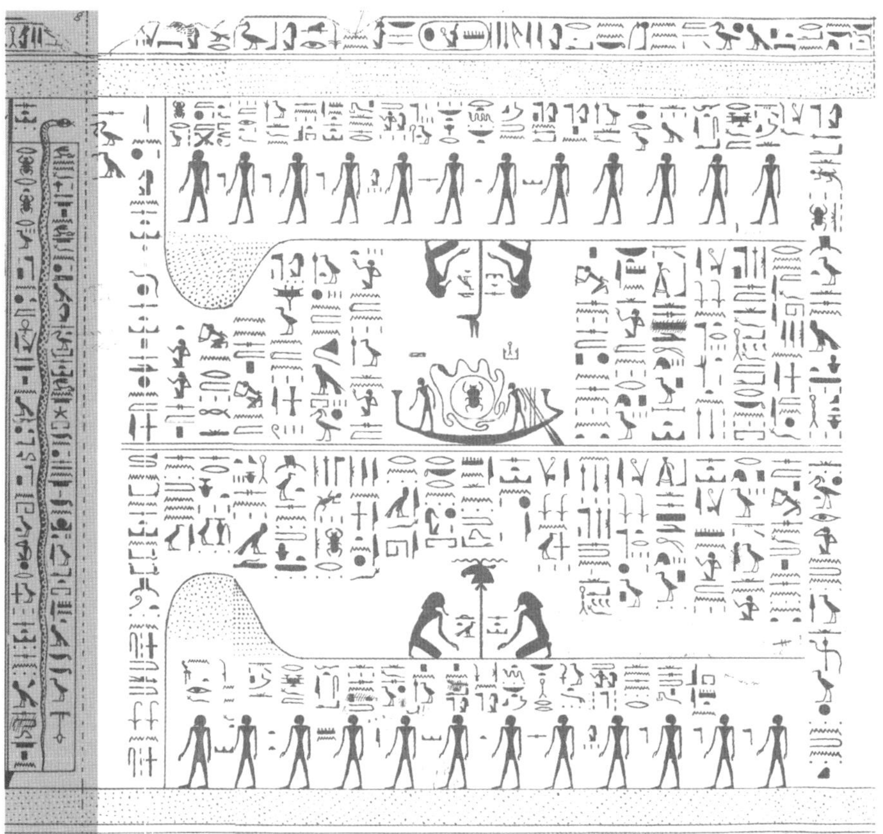

## Upper Register

### 1st Scene

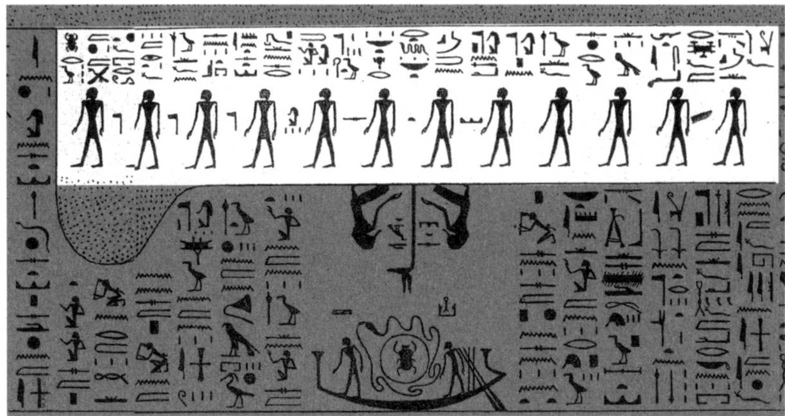

On a mountain range in the desert are twelve gods without attributes. They are called collectively "Gods of the Western Desert" and represent the blessed dead. The inscription reads:

*nṯrw zmjt*

"Gods of the Western Desert",

*ḫprw m rꜥw m ꜣḫt.f*

those who emanated from Re, from his brilliant eye,

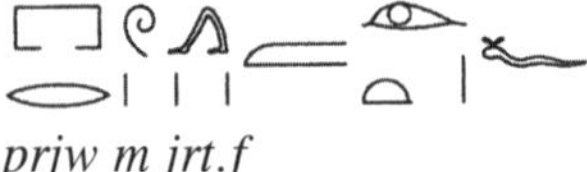

*prjw m jrt.f*

who came forth from his eye.

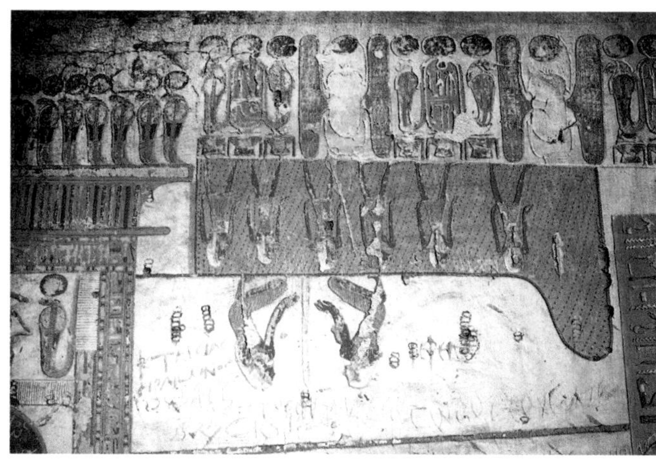

From the Tomb of Ramses VII.

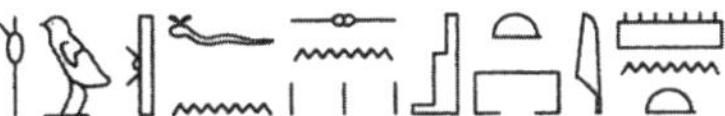

*wḏ.f n.sn st jmnt*

He has assigned to them the Hidden Place

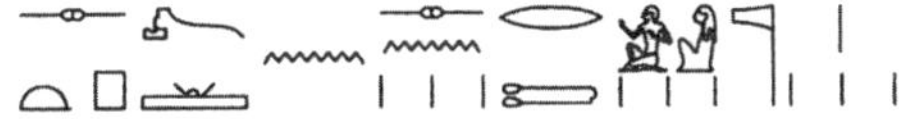

*sṯp n.sn rmṯw nṯrw*

to whom humans and gods have been removed,

*ʿwt nbt ḥrrt nbt qmꜣwt nṯr pn ʿꜣ*

as well as all (other) living beings which this great god has created.

*nṯr pn wḏ.f sẖrw*

This god, he takes care of them (all)

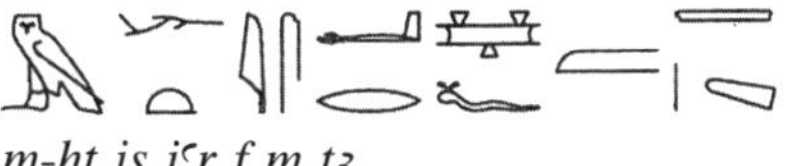

*m-ḫt js jʿr.f m tꜣ*

after he has approached them in the earth

*qmꜣn.f n wnmt.f*

which he has created for his Right Eye.

## Middle Register

### 2nd Scene

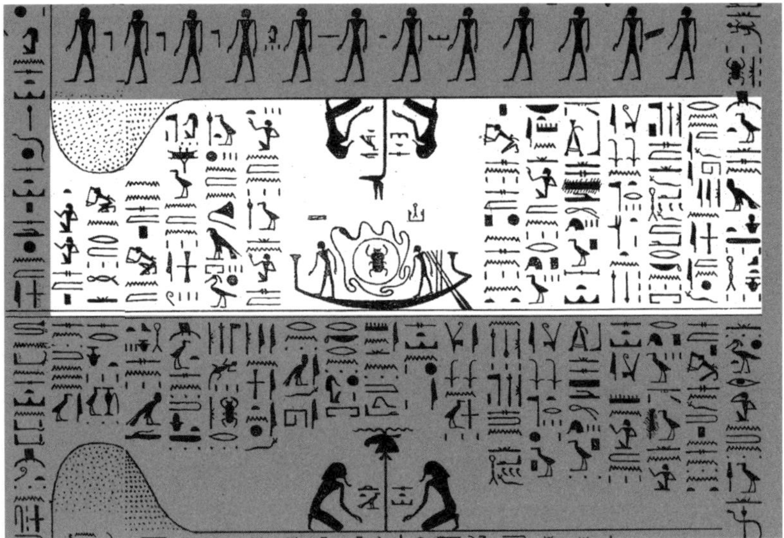

The barque of the Sungod moves along in the centre. The Sungod is depicted as a scarab beetle inside the sun disk, while the serpent bent back in itself is coiled around the disk. At the prow of the barque stands the god *sjꜣ* (Sia, percipience), at the stern the god *ḥkꜣ* (Heka, magic). Above, a jackal-headed pole is placed in the desert mountain, flanked by two kneeling gods, *dwꜣt* (Duat, Netherworld) and *zmjt* (Zemit, desert). The accompanying text reads:

*jn rꜥw n zmjt*

Re says to the desert:

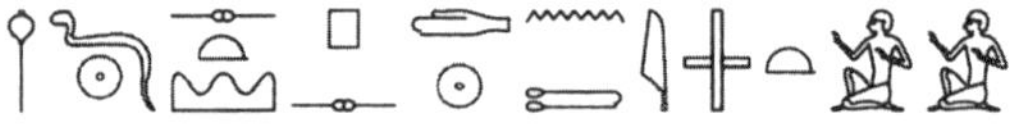

*ḥḏ zmjt psḏn.ṯ jmjt.j*

«Lighten up desert, as for you shines that which is in me!

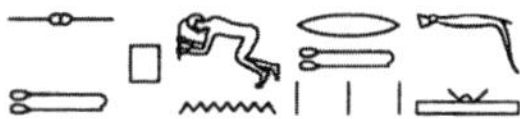

*sṯpn rmṯw mḥw*

Humans have removed the filled (eye),

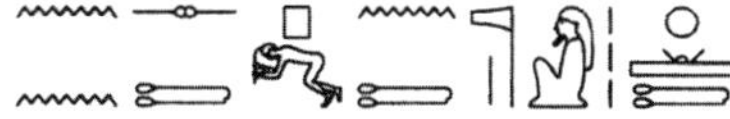

*nn sṯp n.ṯ nṯrw jrt(.ṯ)*

(but) the gods will not remove your eye for you.

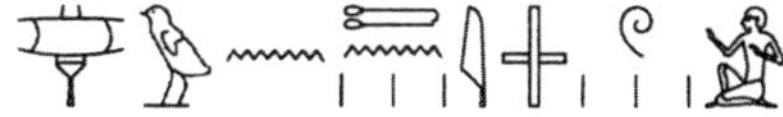

*ṯ3w n.ṯn jmyw.j*

Breath belongs to you, among whom I am,

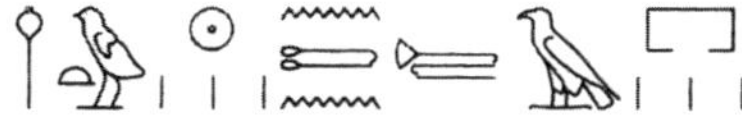

*ḥḏwt n.ṯn dw3tyw*

light belongs to you, you from the Netherworld!

*3ḫt.j n.ṯn wḏn.j sṯp.sn*

My brilliant eye belongs to you, to whom I have ordered that they be removed,

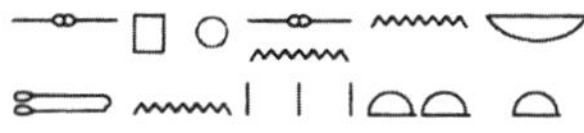

*sṯp n.sn ntt nbt*

to whom all [beings] will be removed.

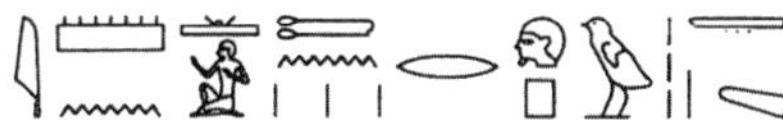

*jmn.j.ṯn r tpyw t3*

I have hidden you from those upon earth

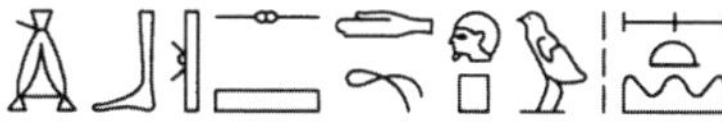

*ḏb3w ssd tpyw zmjt*

adorned with the headcloth, those upon the desert.»

*jn nn nj nṯrw*

These deities say:

*wsrt tn wḏ-mdw nṯr ꜥꜣ sṯ(n)j.f ḥꜥw.f*

«This neck is the order of the great god, when he raises his body.

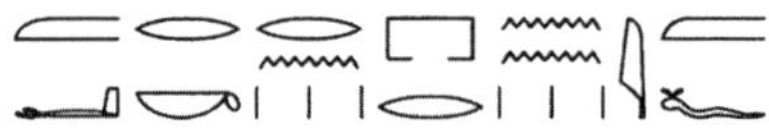

*my rk r.n prjw n.n jm.f*

Come to us, who have come forth from it (the body)!

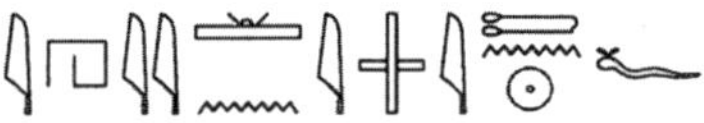

*jhy n jmy jtn.f*

Hail to the one who is in his sun disc,

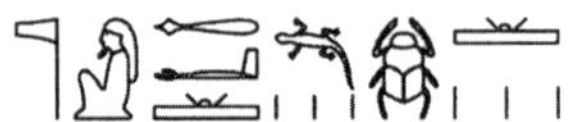

*nṯr ꜥꜣ ꜥšꜣw ḫprw*

the great god with many manifestations.»

*ꜣwt.sn m tꜣ ḥnqt*

Their sacrificial food consists of bread and beer.

## 3RD SCENE

A ram-headed pole is placed in the desert mountain. It is a counterpart of the jackal-headed pole of the second scene. Again, two kneeling gods, *dwꜣt* (Netherworld) and *zmjt* (desert) flank the pole. The text is to a large extent similar to that of the 2nd scene (the next seven lines go in the opposite direction):

(Re says to the desert:)

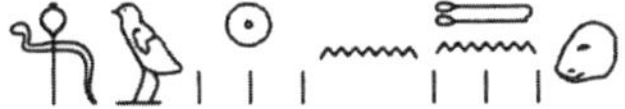

*ḥḏwt n.ṯn ḫntjw (dwꜣt?)*

«Light belongs to you, who are in the Netherworld.

*ꜣḫt.j n.ṯn wḏn.j stp.sn*

My brilliant eye belongs to you, to whom I ordered that they be removed,

*stp n.sn ntt*

to whom all [beings] are removed.

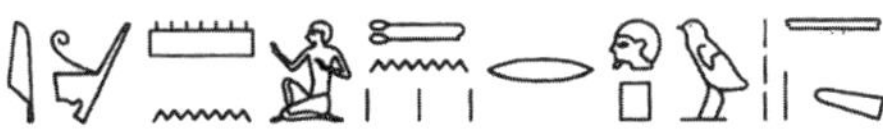

*jmn.j.ṯn r tpyw tꜣ*

I have hidden you from those who are upon earth,

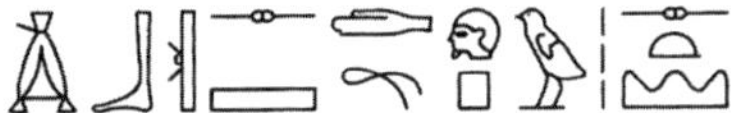

*ḏbꜣw sšd tpyw zmjt*

adorned with the headcloth, those upon the desert.»

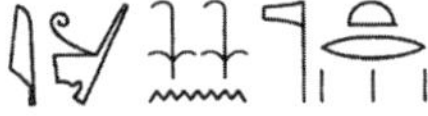

*jn nn nj nṯrw*

These deities say:

*tp pn wḏ-mdw nṯr ꜥꜣ sṯnj ḥꜥw.f*

«This head is the command of the great god, when he raises his body.»

*jn nn jmyw zmjt n r ꜥw*

Those who are in the desert say to Re:

*j jmnw.n my rk r.n*

«O you who have hidden us, do come to us,

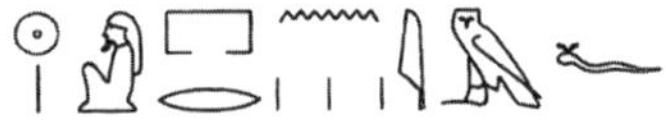

*rꜥw prjw.n jm.f*

Re, from whom we have come forth!

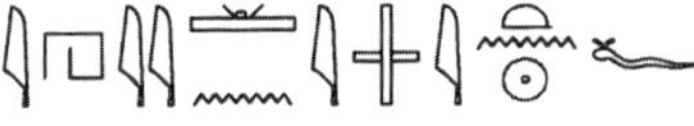

*jhy n jmy jtn.f*

Hail to the one who is in his sun disc,

*nṯr ꜥꜣ ꜥšꜣw ḫprw*

the great god with many manifestations.»

*ꜣwt.sn m tꜣ*

Their sacrificial food consists of bread,

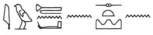

*ḥnqt.sn m ḏsrt*

their beer is Djeseret,

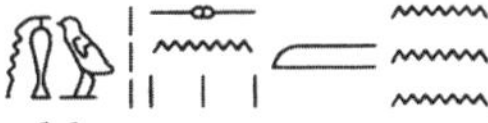

*qbḥw.sn m mw*

their refreshment is water.

*jw wdnw n zmjt (t)n*

Who makes sacrifices to this desert

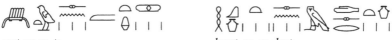

*ddw ꜣwt n jmyw.s*

and gives offerings to those who are in it,

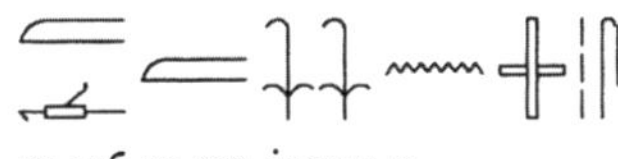

*m wꜥ m nn jmyw.s*

is one of these who are in it.

Part of 1st Hour on the Sarcophagus of Neshutefnut.

## Lower Register
## 4th Scene

This scene is identical with the first scene of the middle register. So is the inscription.

## First Gate

This first gate is, in contrast to the other gates, shown in abbreviated form. Only one leaf of the door is visible and fills the entire height of the picture. It is guarded by a giant serpent which is called *zꜣw zmjt* "Who Guards the Desert". The beginning of the text written on the leaf of the gate refers to this serpent-shaped guardian:

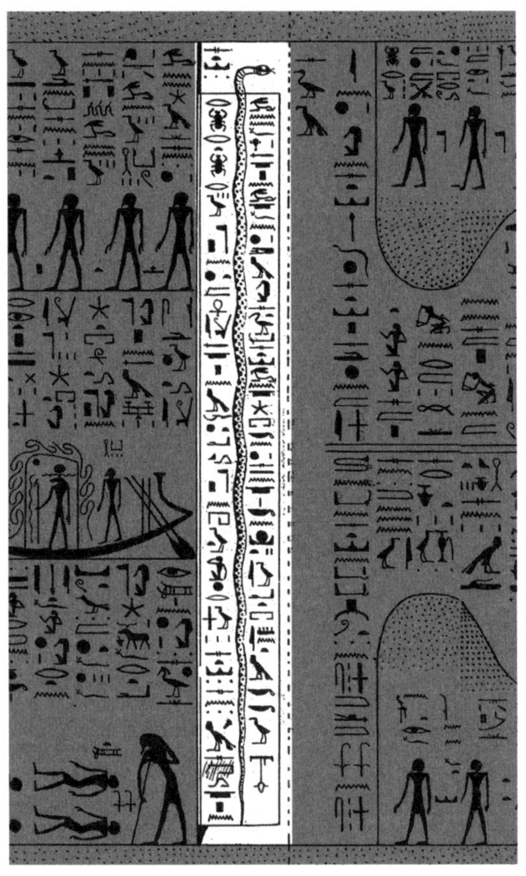

*wnn.f ḥr ꜥꜣ pn*

He is upon this door-leaf,

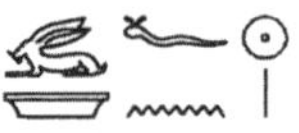

*wn.f n rꜥw*

he opens for Re.

*sjꜣ n zꜣw zmjt*

Sia (says) to "Who Guards the Desert"

*wn sbꜣ.k. n r ꜥw*

«Open your gate for Re,

*zn ꜥꜣ.k n ꜣḫty*

open your door for Akhty (He of the horizon)!»

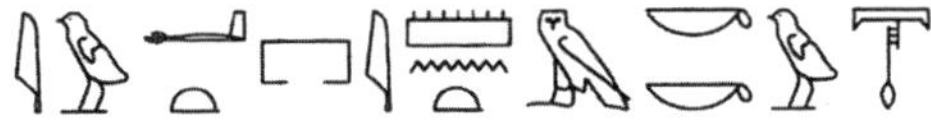

*jw ꜥt jmnt m kkw*

The hidden region is in darkness

*r ḫprt ḫprw nṯr pn*

until the manifestation of this god emerges.

*ḫtm jn ꜥꜣ pn*

Then this door is closed

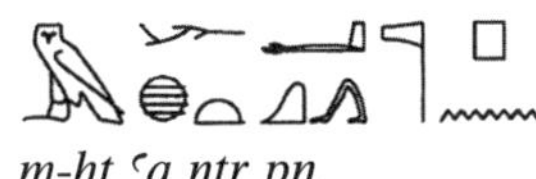

*m-ḫt ꜥq nṯr pn*

after this god has entered.

*hwt ḫr jmyw zmjt.sn*

Then those who are in their desert wail

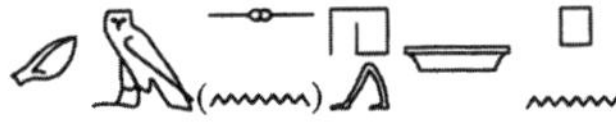

*sḏm.sn hꜣꜣ ꜥꜣ pn*

when they hear this gate being closed.

# SECOND

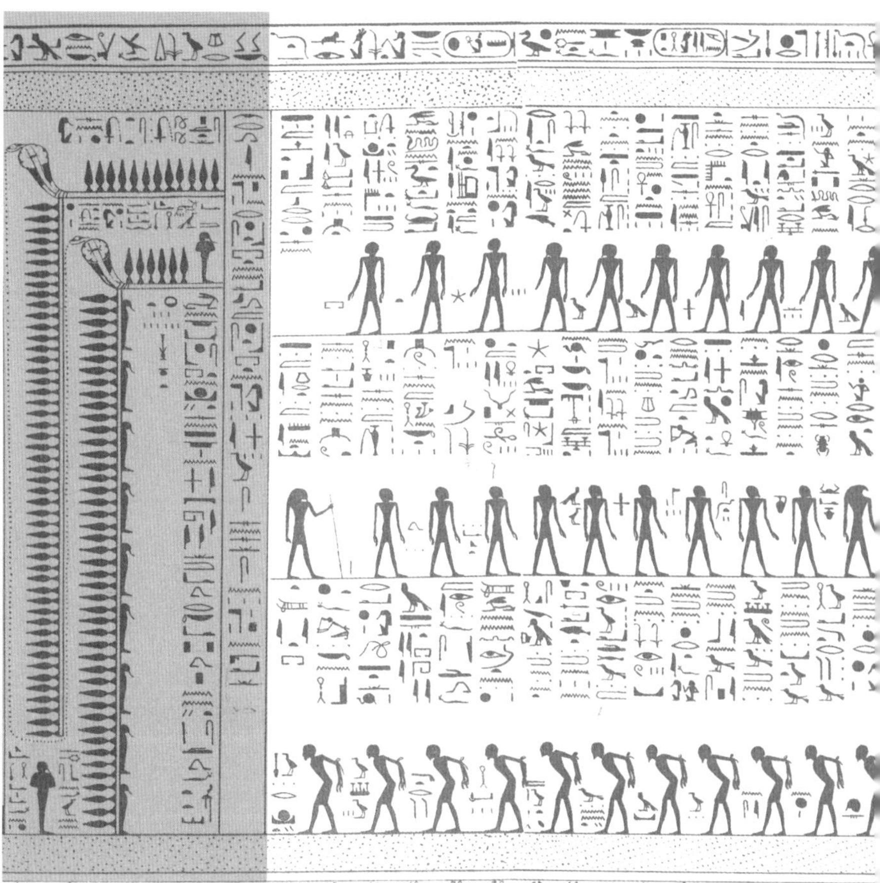

# HOUR

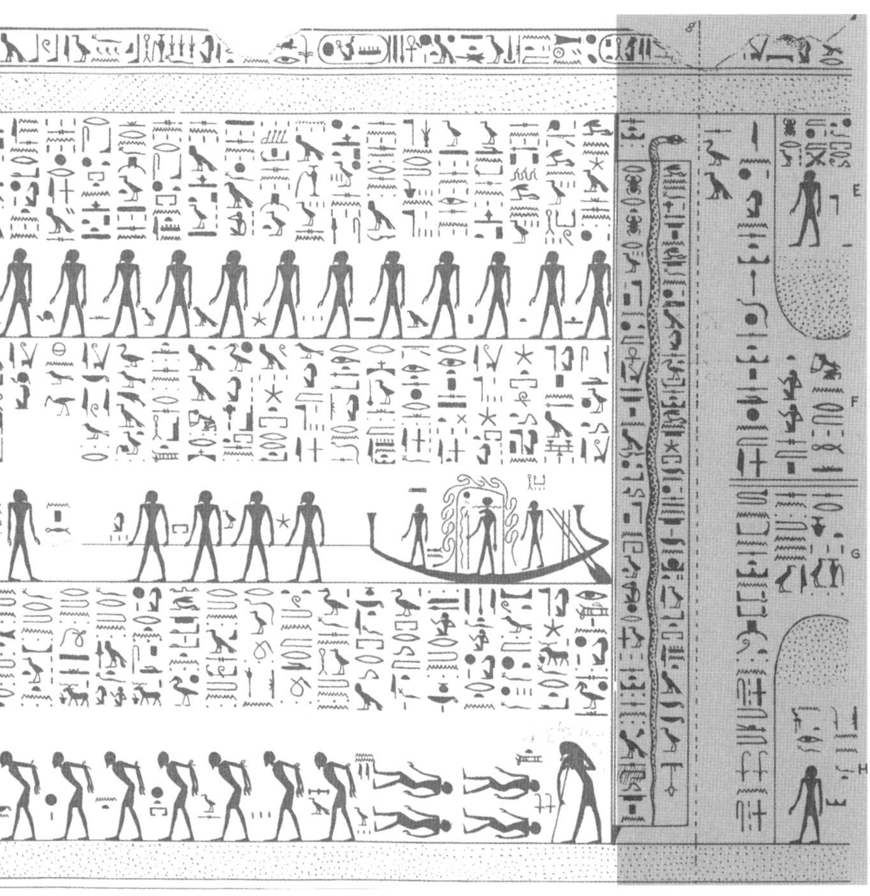

# SECOND HOUR FROM THE

The hour is depicted around one corner of the burial chamber of the tomb of Pharoh Ra

# TOMB OF RAMSES IV

34.

## Upper Register

### 5th Scene

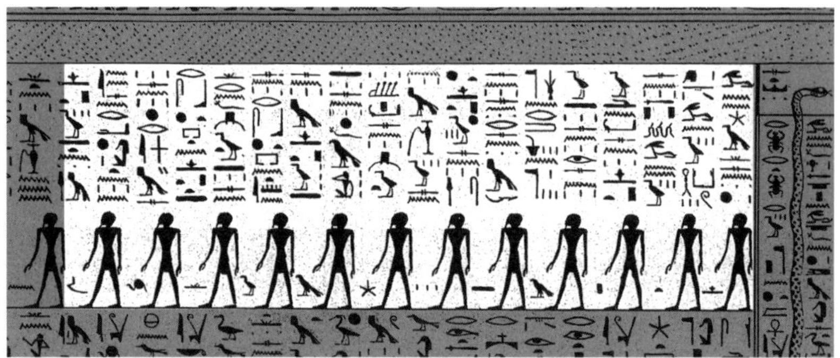

Twelve gods without attributes are named collectively, the text being written between the twelve gods, *ḥtptyw dwꜣw rꜥw* "Who are supplied with offerings, who have adored Re". The text of this scene refers to the provisioning of these gods (i.e. blessed dead!) with all the necessary oblations.

*wnn dwꜣ.sn rꜥw tp tꜣ*

They have adored Re on earth,

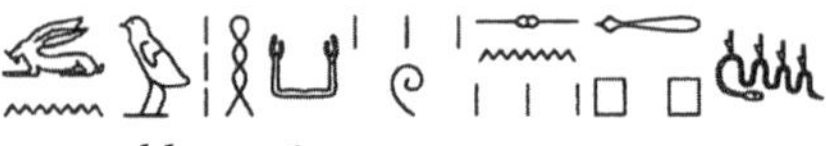

*wnnw ḥkꜣ.sn ꜥꜣpp*

(and) have enchanted Apopis,

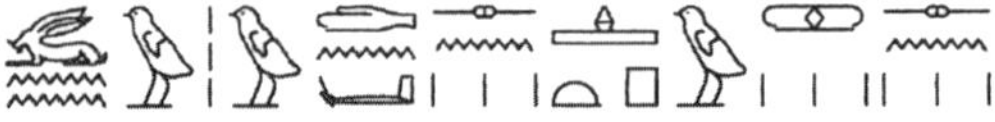

*wnnw wdn.sn ḥtpw.sn*

they bestow their offerings,

*jry.sn snṯr n nṯrw.sn*

they offer incense to their gods.

*sn r.sn m-ḫt ḥtpw.sn*

They are behind their offerings,

*sḫm.sn m qbḥw.sn*

they take hold of their refreshments;

*šzp.sn ꜣwt.sn*

they receive their oblations,

*ḫfꜣ.sn m ḥtpw.sn*

and they nourish themselves from their offerings

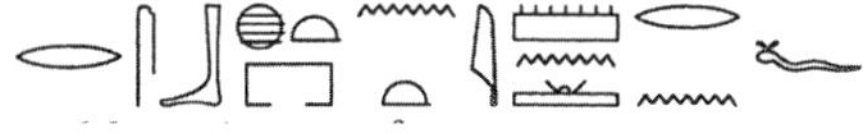

*r sbḫt nt jmn-rn.f*

at the gate of (the god) “with hidden name”.

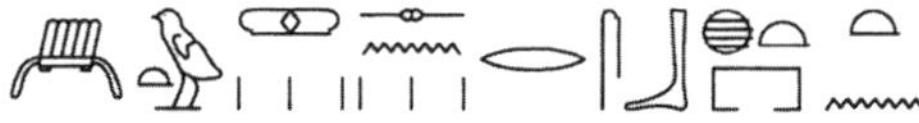

*ꜣwt.sn r sbḫt tn*

Their oblations are at this gate,

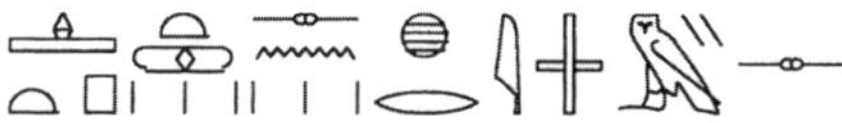

*ḥtpwt.sn ḫr jmy.s*

and their offerings with him who is in it.

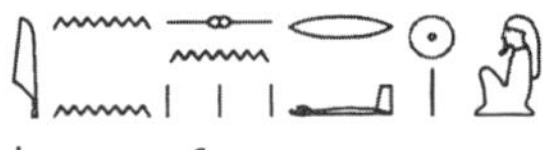

*jn n.sn rʿw*

Re says to them:

*ṯn n ḥtpw.ṯn sḫm.ṯn m qbḥw.ṯn*

«You belong to your offerings; you take hold of your refreshment!

*n stp bꜣw.ṯn n sk ꜣwt.ṯn*

your *Ba*-souls are not removed, your oblations are not destroyed.

*ntṯn dwꜣw.wj trjw n.j ʿꜣpp*

(For) you are those who adore me, (and) who finish off Apopis for me.»

From the tomb of Pharoh Ramses IV.

## 6TH SCENE

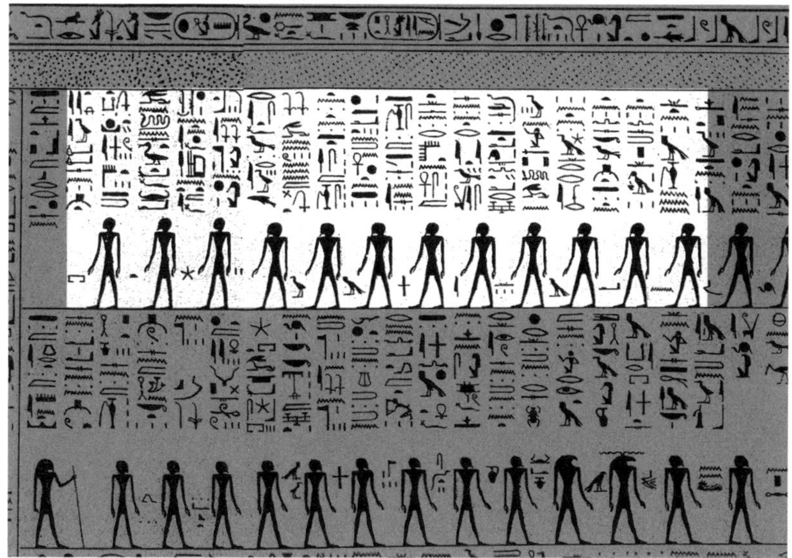

Twelve deities without attributes: *mꜣꜥtyw jmjw dwꜣt* “The justified who are in the Duat”. They are again blessed dead who followed the laws of Maat on earth.

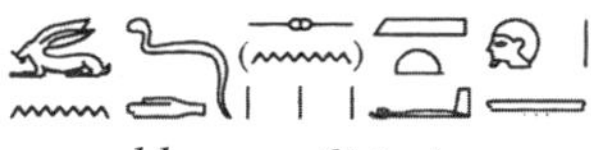

*wnw ḏd.sn mꜣꜥt tp tꜣ*

Those who have spoken Maat on earth,

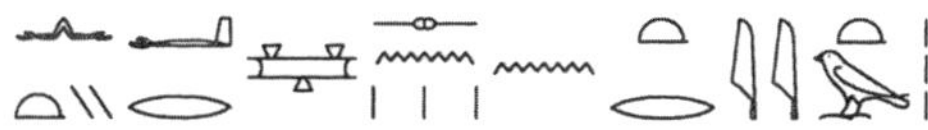

*jwty jꜥr.sn n tryt*

who have kept afar from doing wrong.

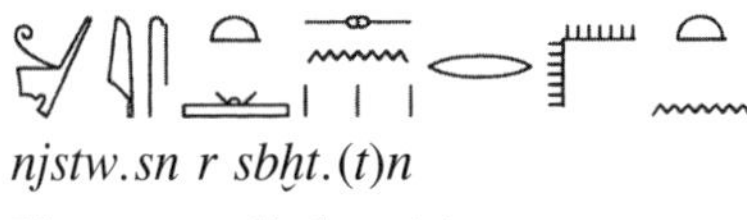

*njstw.sn r sbḫt.(t)n*

They are called to this gate,

*ꜥnḫ.s(n) m mȝꜥt*

they live from Maat,

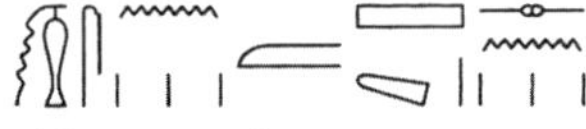

*qbḥw.sn m š.sn*

their refreshment is in their lake.

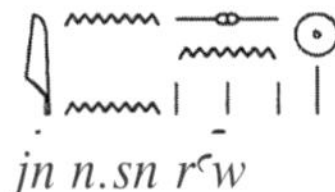

*jn n.sn rꜥw*

Re says to them:

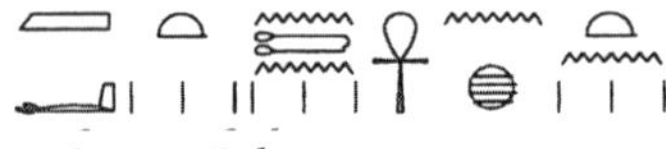

*mȝꜥt n.ṯn ꜥnḫ.ṯn*

«Maat belongs to you that you live,

*ḥtpw.tn (n).tn (n) mȝꜥt*

your offerings belong to you because of Maat.

*sḫm.s(n) m qbḥw.s(n)*

They take hold of their refreshment,

*nn wnnw mw m sḏt*

(although their) water is fire

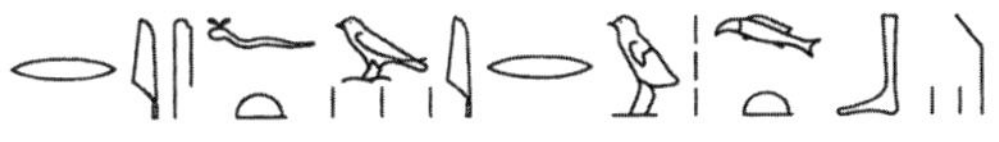

*r jsftyw jryw ḫ3bt*

for the sinners who have committed wrong.»

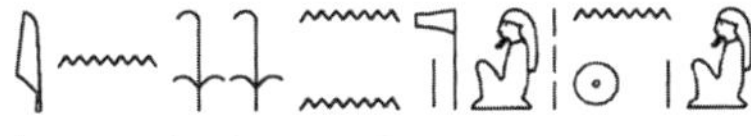

*jn nn nj nṯrw n rʿw*

These gods say to Re:

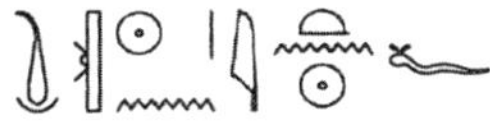

*mn rʿw n jtn.f*

«Enduring is Re because of his disc,

*sḫm k3r nty jm.f*

powerful is the shrine, and who is in it!

*wn mḥn n z3wt.f*

Mehen cares for his protection,

*wḥʿ tk3w 3ḫty jmyw sbḫt št3yt*

and the torches of Akhty liberate those who are in the gate of the Shetit (the Beyond).»

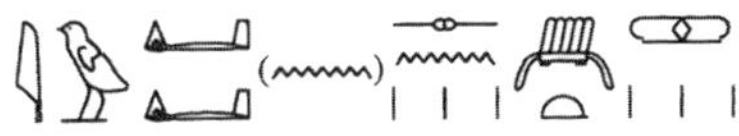

*jw ddw (n).sn 3wt*

He who gives oblations to them

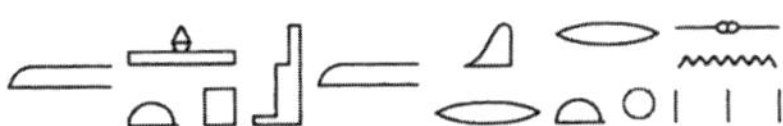

*m ḥtpw st m qrrt.sn*

is one who takes a place in their cavern.

## Middle Register, 7th Scene

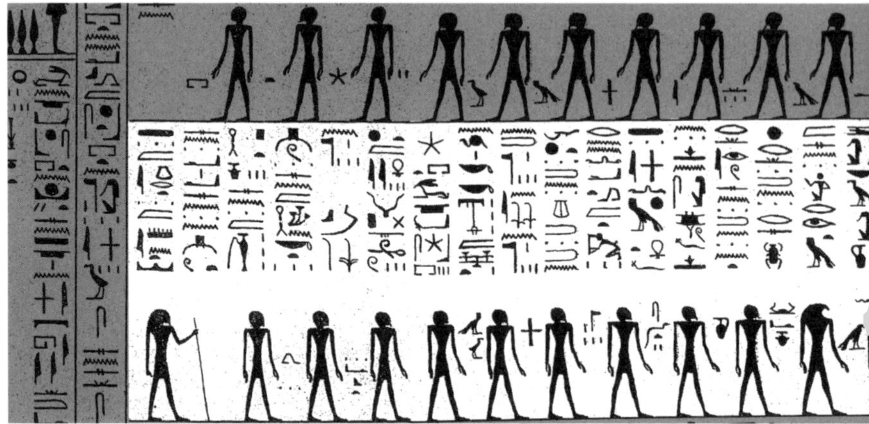

From now on the barque of the Sungod has its permanent shape: In a shrine in the centre stands the ram-headed god, holding the *was*-sceptre and the *ankh*-sign in his hands. The *Mehen*-serpent protectively curls around the shrine. At the prow stands the god *sjꜣ* (Sia, percipience) who is the spokesman of the Sungod; in front of the rowing gear stands the god *ḥkꜣ* (Heka, magic). The figure of the nocturnal Sungod is called *jwf rꜥw* (Flesh of Re).

Four blessed dead called collectively *dwꜣtyw* (Those of the Underworld) hold the towrope of the barque. A procession of fourteen deities moves towards him. Three of them are distinguished by their attributes – the third is ram-headed, the fourth falcon-headed, and the last one carries a long staff in his hand as a sign of his status.

Only the first seven deities have individual names:

1. *npn*
Grain

2. *nn-ꜥ*
Without Arms (?)

3. *bꜣ*
Ram

4. *ḥrw*
Horus

5. *wḥꜥ-jb*
The Sensible One

6. *ẖnmw*
Khnum

7. *sḏtj*
Child

The deities 1-7, from the tomb of Pharaoh Horemheb.

The subsequent six figures are collectively called

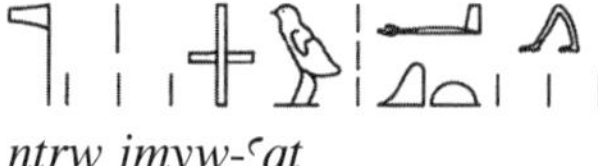

*nṯrw jmyw-ꜥqt*

"Deities who are at the entrance (of the Netherworld)".

The god carrying a staff at the end of the register appears to be called *mdwj* (He with the staff).

The accompanying text refers to the entire register:

*sqdwt jn nṯr pn ꜥꜣ m wꜣwt dwꜣt*

Proceeding by this great god on the ways of the Duat.

*stꜣ nṯr pn jn nṯrw dwꜣtyw*

Towing of this god by the gods of the Netherworld,

*r jryt psšt jmyt tꜣ*

to distribute what is in the Earth,

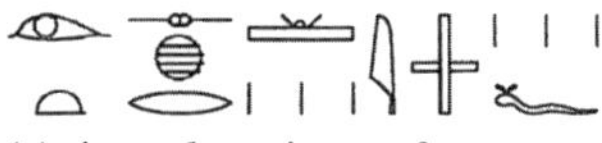

*(r) jryt sḫrw jmyw.f*

to take care of those who are in it,

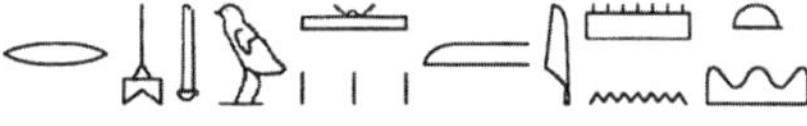

*r wḏꜥ-mdw m jmnt*

to hold judgement in the West,

*r jryt ꜥꜣ r nḏs*

to make a great one to a small one

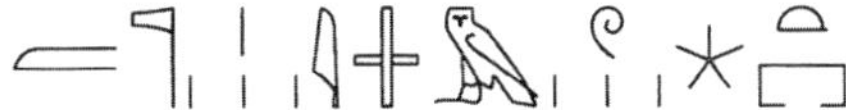

*m nṯrw jmyw dwꜣt*

among the gods who are in the Duat,

*r rdyt ꜣḫw ḥr st.sn*

to put the *Akhu* (Blessed) on their place,

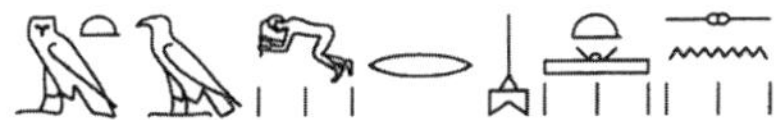

*mtyw r wḏꜥt.sn*

and the damned to their judgement,

*r sḥtm ḫꜣwt njkyw*

to destroy the corpses of those who are punished,

*r ḫnr bꜣ* [*ḥtmw*]

to confine the *Ba*-soul [of the annihilated ones].

*jn rꜥw*

Re says:

*j m.ṯn.wj ḏbꜣn.j sšd*

«Look, I have adorned myself with the headcloth,

*sḫm.kwy m kȝr jmy-tȝ*

I have taken possession of the shrine which is in the earth.

*sjȝ ḥkȝ ẖnm.sn.wj*

*Sia* and *Heka* have joined me

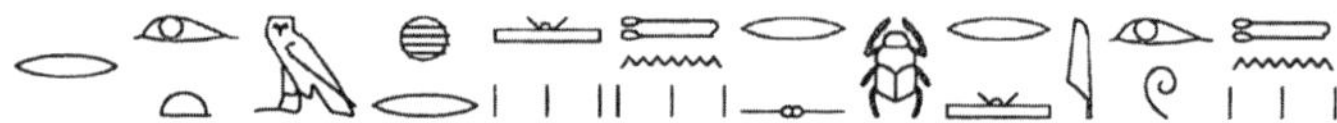

*r jryt mḫrw.ṯn r sḫpr jrw.ṯn*

to take care of you, to assign to you your functions.

*n ḫtm.f r.ṯn ṯȝw.f*

He does not cut his breath from you,

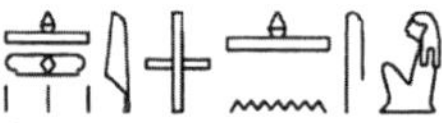

*ḥtpw jmyw (s)ḥtpn.s*

as well as the offerings which are in (this hour).

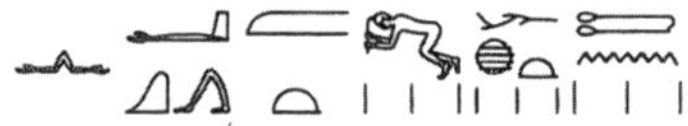

*n ʿq mtyw ḫtw.ṯn*

The damned do not enter after you,

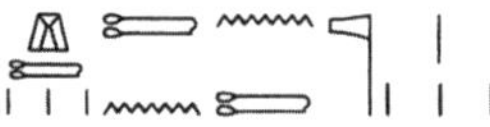

*ẖrt (n).ṯn nt nṯrw*

to you belongs what is due to the deities.»

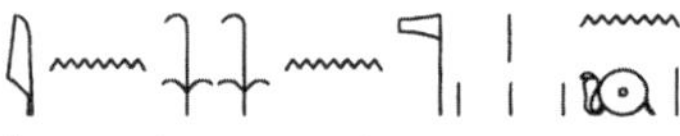

*jn nn nj nṯrw n rʿw*

These gods say to Re:

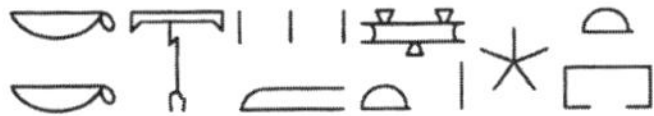

*kkw m w3t dw3t*

«Darkness reigns on the way of the Duat –

*wn sb3w ḫtmyw wpw-t3*

open the closed gates, opener of the earth,

*st̲3wn nt̲rw qm3w.sw*

whom the gods have towed, who created himself!»

*3wt.sn m ḥnkt ḥnqt.sn m qbḥw.sn*

Their offerings are donations, their beer is their refreshment.

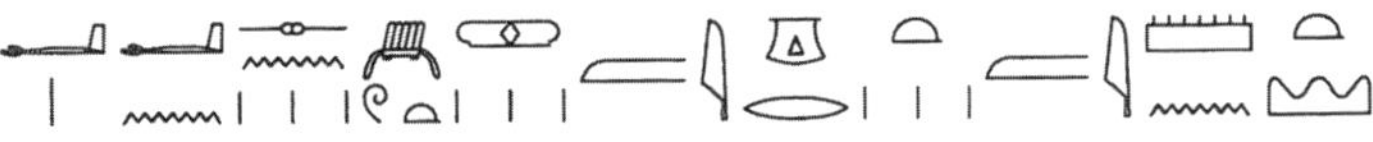

*(jw) ddw n.sn 3wt m jgrt m jmnt*

Whoever gives oblations to them (will be) in the Hereafter, in the West.

From the tomb of Pharoh Ramses IV.

## LOWER REGISTER, 8TH SCENE

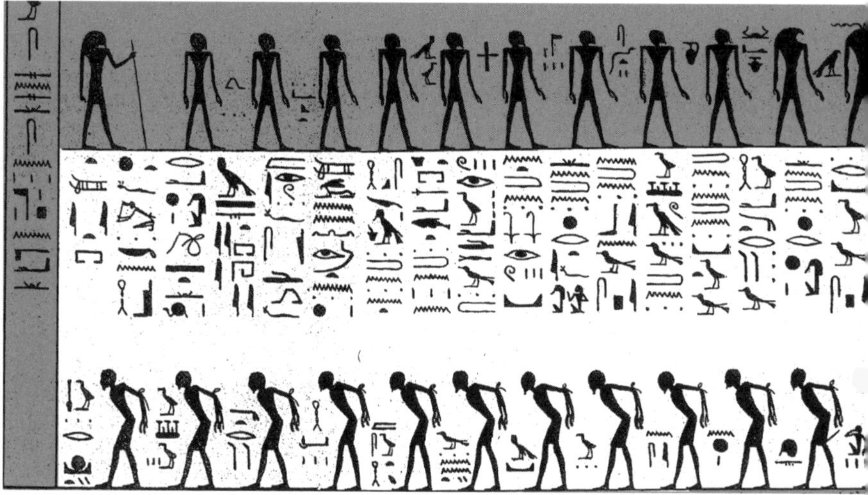

The god Atum, leaning on his staff, guards four outstretched human figures in front of him who are called *nnyw* "Inert ones", the embodiment of the four quarters of the world, kept in the Netherworld. The remaining register is filled with twenty enemies whose hands are fettered behind their backs.

The text between the 20 figures describes them collectively:

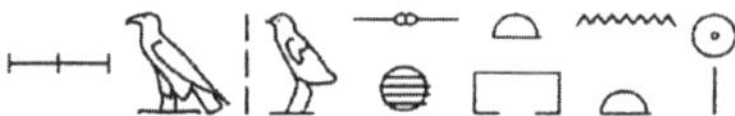

*zmytyw wsḫt nt rꜥw*

The desert-dwellers of the hall of Re,

*knyw tp tꜣ n rꜥw*

who have quarrelled on earth because of Re,

*njsw m ḏw n nty m swḥt*

who have cried evil against "Him who is in the Egg",

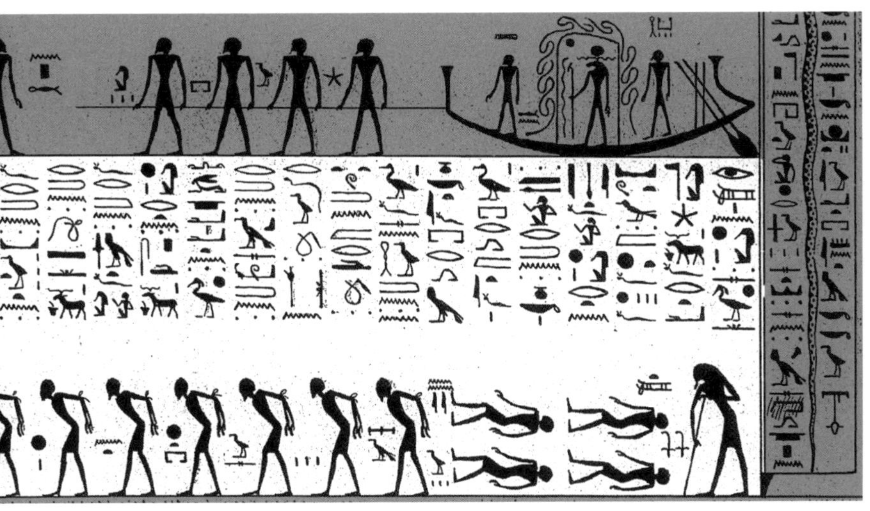

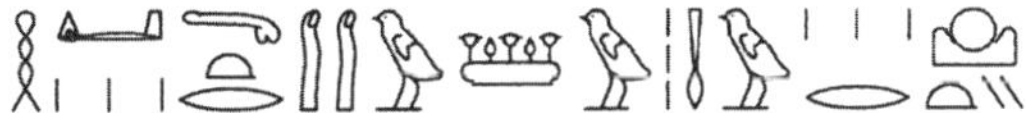

*ḥwjw mtrw wšȝw ḫrw r ȝḫty*

"The Witnesses who have offended Akhty".

The text of the register reads:

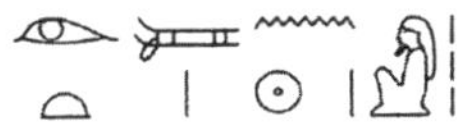

*jryt jtmw n rʿw*

What Atum has done for Re:

*sȝḫ(t) nṯr dwȝ bȝ.f*

to glorify the god, to adore his *Ba*-soul,

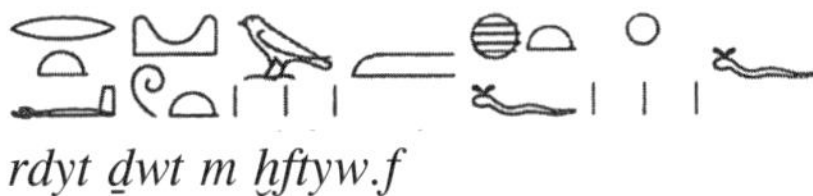

*rdyt ḏwt m ḫftyw.f*

to afflict evil on his enemies.

(Atum addresses the enemies:)

*mꜣꜥ-ḫrw jt.j rꜥw r.ṯn*

«My father Re is triumphant against you,

*mꜣꜥ-ḫrw.j r.ṯn*

I am triumphant against you!

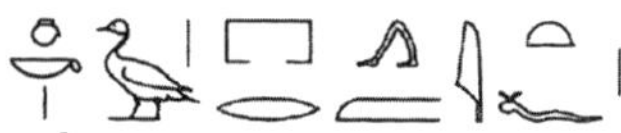

*jnk zꜣ pryw m jt.f*

I am the son who emanated from his father.

*jnk jt pryw m zꜣ.f*

I am the father who emanated from his son.

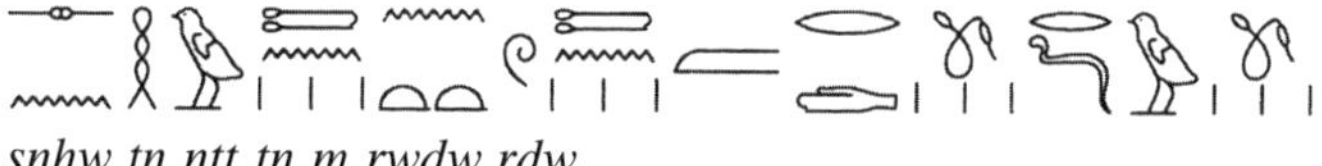

*snḥw.ṯn nṯṯ.ṯn m rwḏw rḏw*

You are fettered, you are bound with firm ropes.

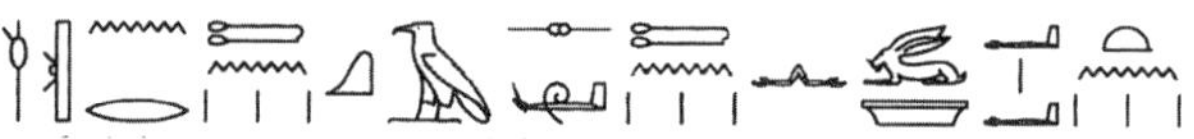

*wḏn(.j) r.ṯn qꜣsw.ṯn n(n) wn ꜥwj.ṯn*

I have ordered that you be fettered; your arms will not be opened!

*ꜣḫ rꜥw r.ṯn spd bꜣ.f r.ṯn*

Re's magic is against you, effective is his *Ba*-soul against you,

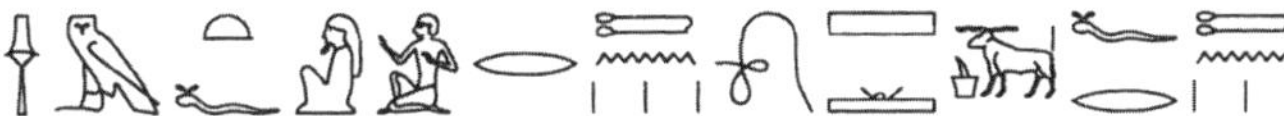

*sḫm jt.j r.ṯn wꜣš bꜣ.f r.ṯn*

powerful is my father against you, strong is his *Ba*-soul against you!

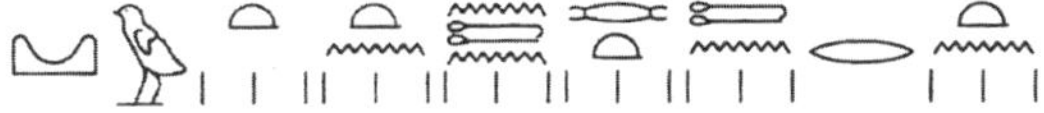

*ḏwt.ṯn n.ṯn ꜥḏt.ṯn r.ṯn*

Your evil belongs to you; your slaughtering is against you,

*knyw.ṯn n.ṯn (n)jsw.ṯn r ḏw(t)*

your punishment is upon you, you are summoned to evil!

From the tomb of Horemheb.

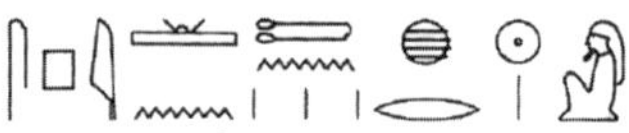

*sjpwn.ṯn ḫr rʿw*

You are condemned by Re,

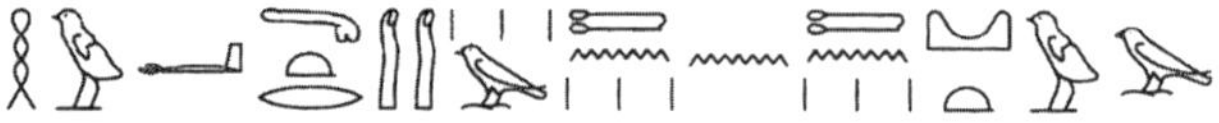

*ḥwy mtrw.ṯn n.ṯn ḏwt*

destroyed is your witness document for you, being evil,

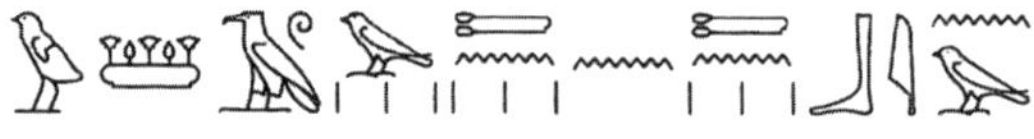

*wšꜣw.ṯn n.ṯn bjnw*

your calumny is upon you, since it is wicked,

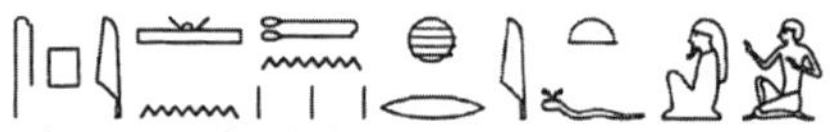

*sjpwn.ṯn ḫr jt.j*

you are condemned by my father!

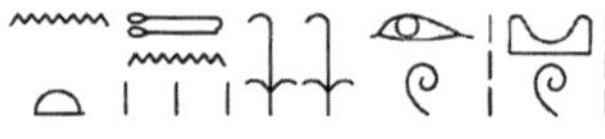

*ntṯn nn jryw ḏwt*

You are these who have committed evil,

*jryw ʿḏt m wsḫt ʿꜣt*

who have caused slaughter in the Great Hall!

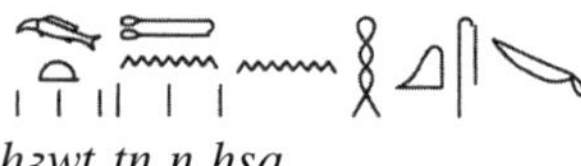

*ẖꜣwt.ṯn n ḥsq*

Your corpses are committed to beheading,

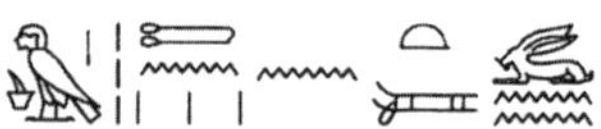

*bꜣw.ṯn n tm wnn*

your *Ba*-souls to non-being!

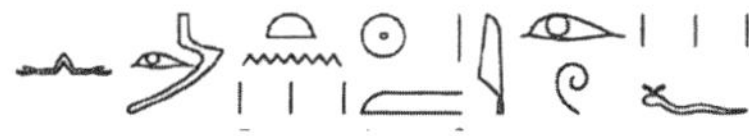

*n mꜣꜣ.ṯn rꜥw m jrw.f*

You shall not view Re in his manifestations,

*sqdi̓.f m štꜣyt*

when he sails in the *Shetit* (Beyond)!

*jhy rꜥw wꜣš.tj rꜥw*

Hail Re! You are strong, Re!

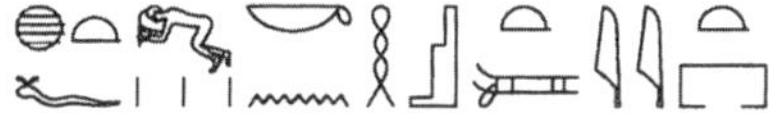

*ḫftyw.k n ḥtmyt*

Your enemies will belong to the place of destruction!»

From the tomb of Seti I.

## SECOND GATE

The gates between the areas of the respective hours of the night have their complete form from now on. Behind the leaves of the gate (as in the First Gate, above), are two walls topped with upright *ḫkr*-daggers. Each wall is guarded by an Uraeus-serpent rearing up and by a mummiform guardian. Inside the gate are nine mummies, one above the other, here referred to as 'The Second Group of Nine Gods' "The Second Ennead". They should, in reality, probably be seen as being side by side.

Text in front of the door:

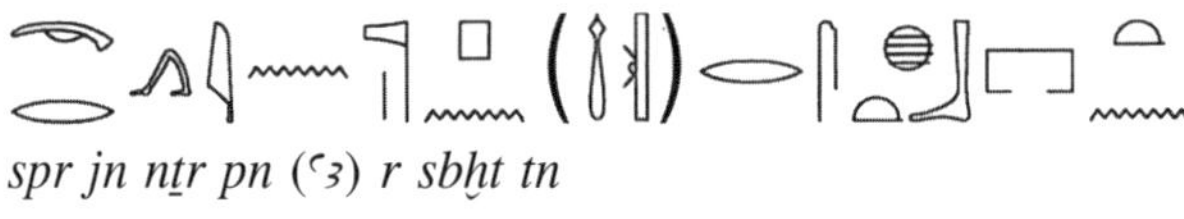

*spr jn nṯr pn (ꜥꜣ) r sbḫt tn*

Arrival of this great god at this gate,

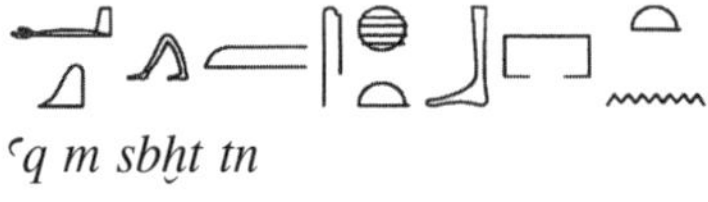

*ꜥq m sbḫt tn*

entering into this gate.

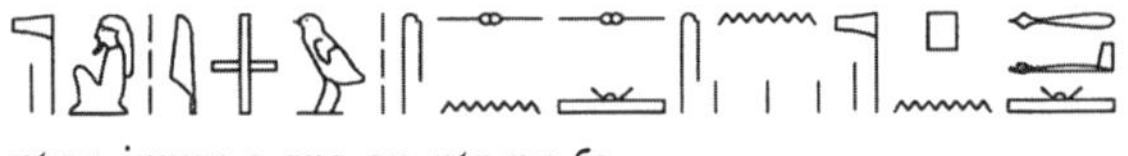

*nṯrw jmyw.s sns.sn nṯr pn ꜥꜣ*

The gods who are in it acclaim this great god.

Name of the gate:

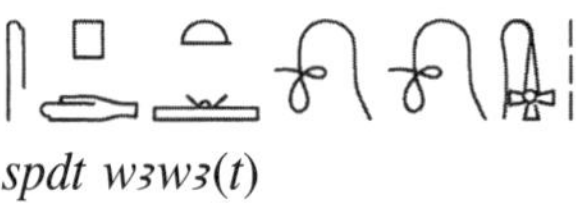

*spdt wꜣwꜣ(t)*

"With piercing blaze".

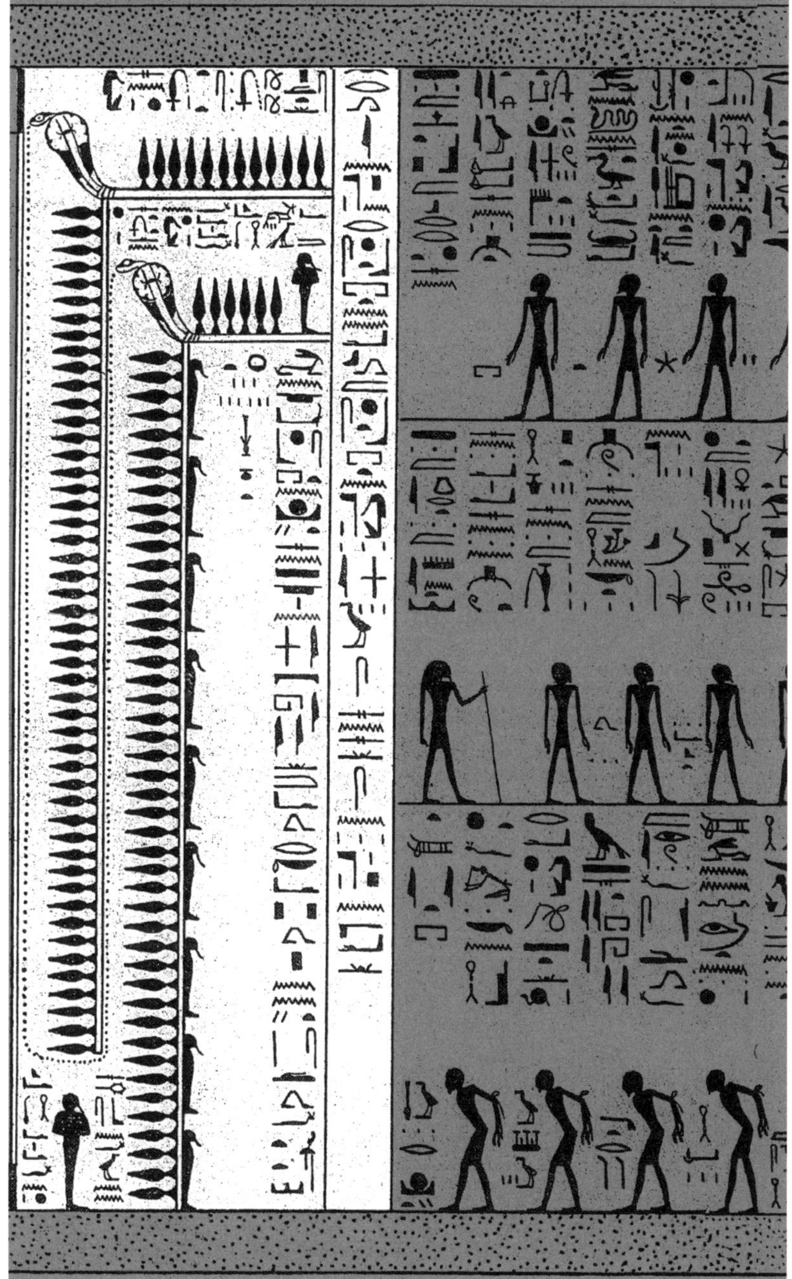

The two Uraeus-serpents on the wall:

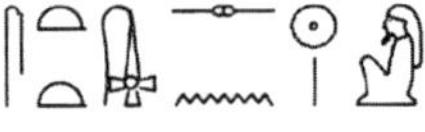

*stt.s n rʿw*

"She lights up for Re".

The two guardians:

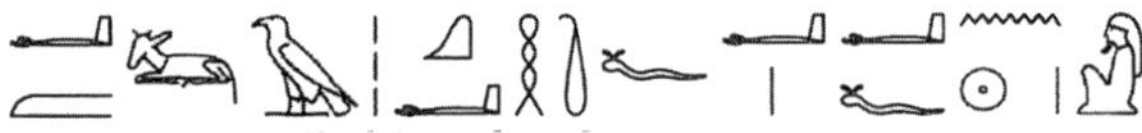

*ʿmw-jwtyw qʿḥ.f ʿwy.f(j) n rʿw*

"Who devours the non-existing". He bends his arms for Re.

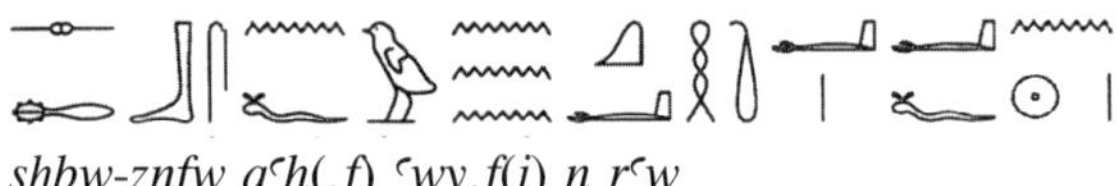

*sẖbw-znfw qʿḥ(.f) ʿwy.f(j) n rʿw*

"Who slurps blood". He bends his arms for Re.

The nine mummies:

*psḏt snwt*

"Second Ennead".

Text in front of the Ennead of mummies:

*wnw sbḫt n ꜣḫty*

Open is the gate for Akhty,

*znw ʿꜣ n jmy-pt*

open is the door for him who is in heaven.

*jhy my rk ʿppw pn nty sqdj.f jmntt*

Hail! Come, you moving one, who crosses the West!

The serpent upon the doorway:

*qꜣby*

"The coiled one".

*wnn.f ḥr ꜥꜣ pn*

He is upon this door,

*wn.f n rꜥw*

he opens for Re.

*sjꜣ n qꜣbjy*

Sia (speaks) to "the coiled one":

*wn sbꜣ.k n rꜥw*

«Open your gate for Re,

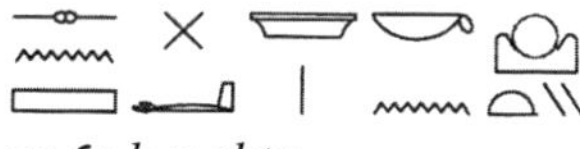

*zn ꜥꜣ.k n ꜣḫty*

open your door for Akhty!»

*jw.f sḥḏ.f kkw zmꜣw*

He lights up the Primeval Darkness,

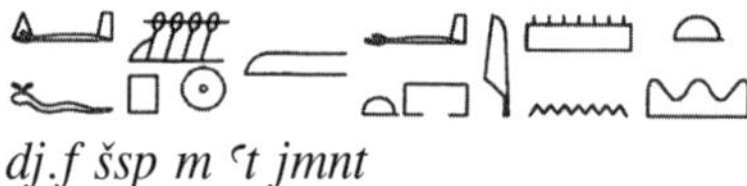

*dj.f šsp m ꜥt jmnt*

he gives light to the hidden region.

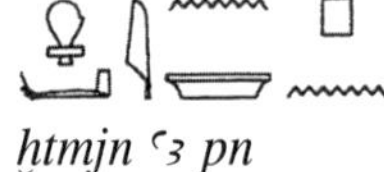

*ḫtmjn ꜥꜣ pn*

Then this door is closed,

*m-ḫt ꜥq nṯr pn ꜥꜣ*

after this great god has entered.

*hwtḫr jmyw sbḫt.sn*

Then those in their gate wail

*sḏm.sn hꜣꜣ ꜥꜣ pn*

when they hear this door being shut.

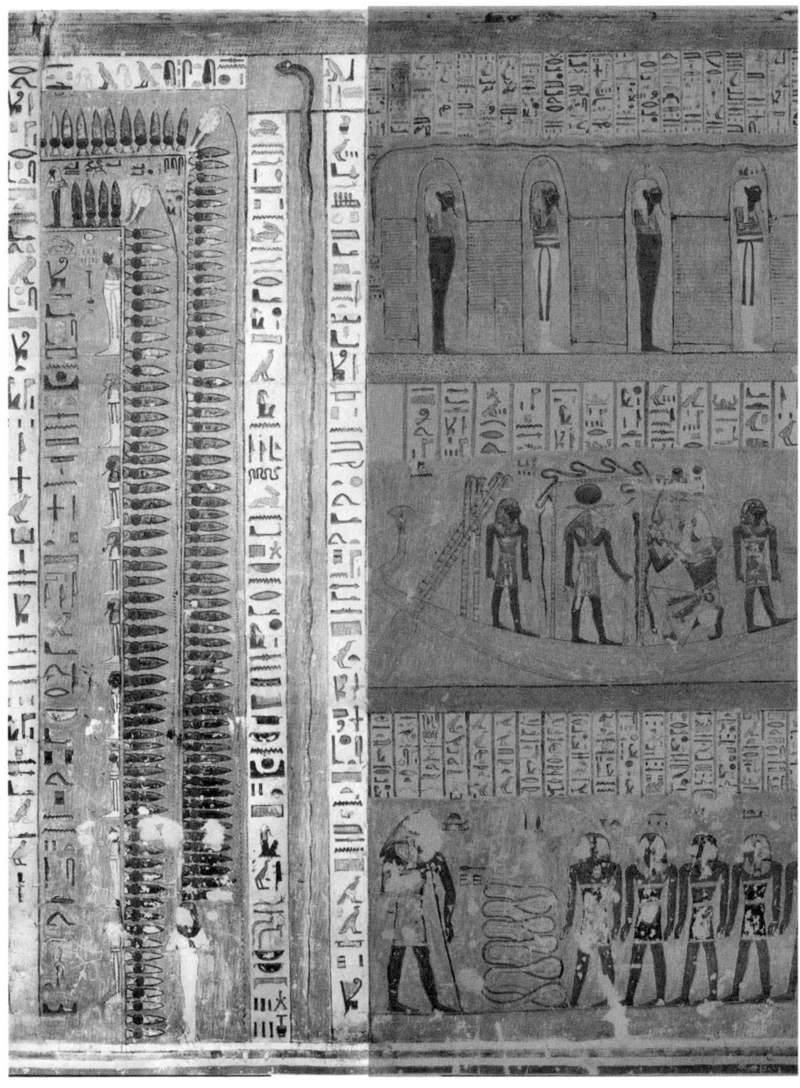

From the tomb of Ramses IV.

# THIRD

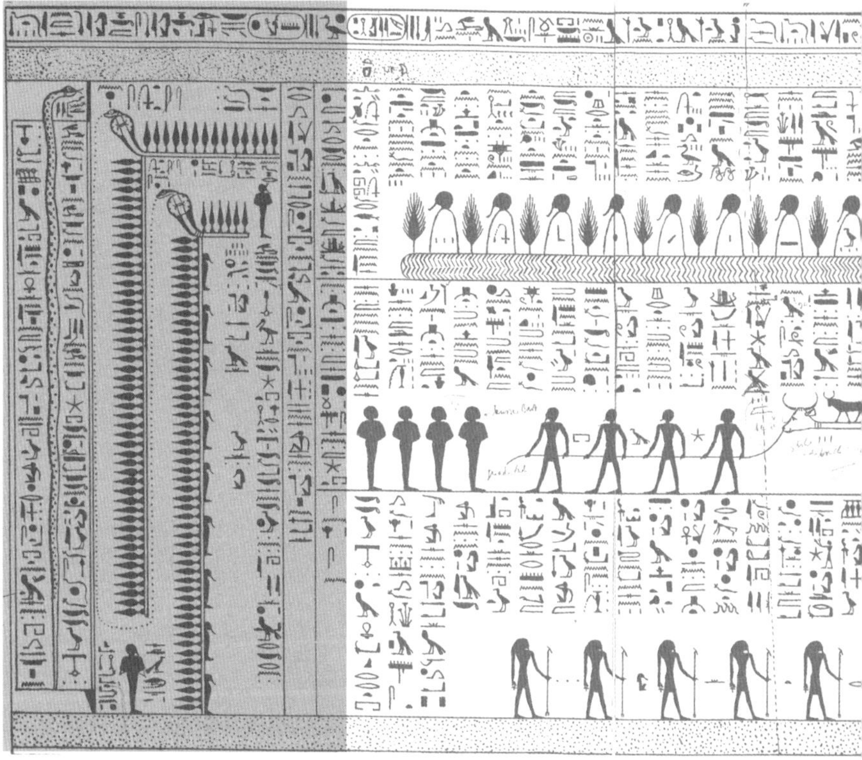

# HOUR

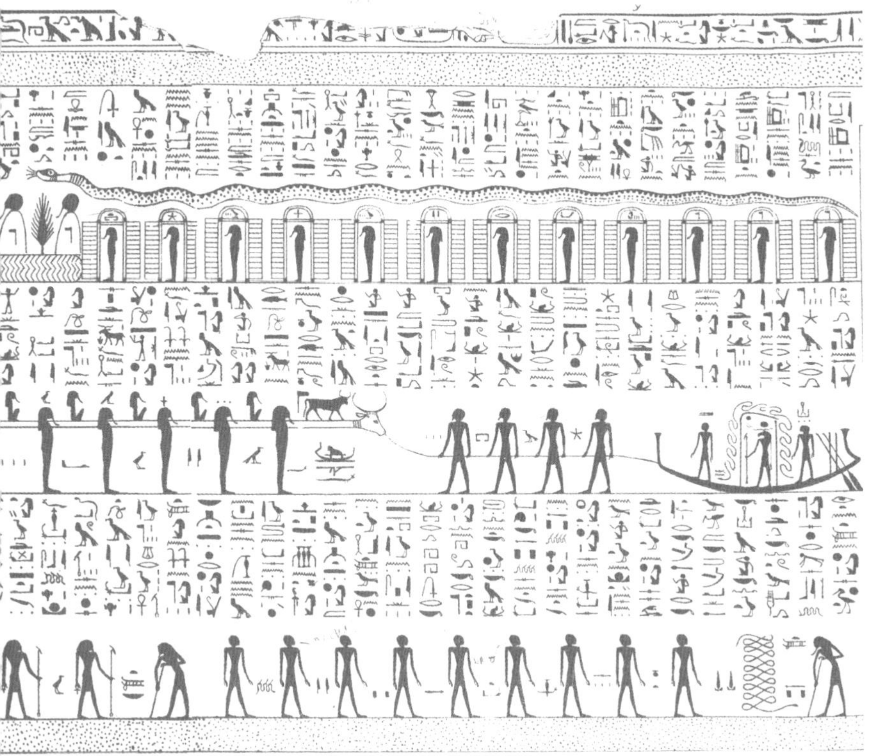

# Part of the Third Hour

# FROM THE TOMB OF RAMSES I

# Parts of the Third Hour

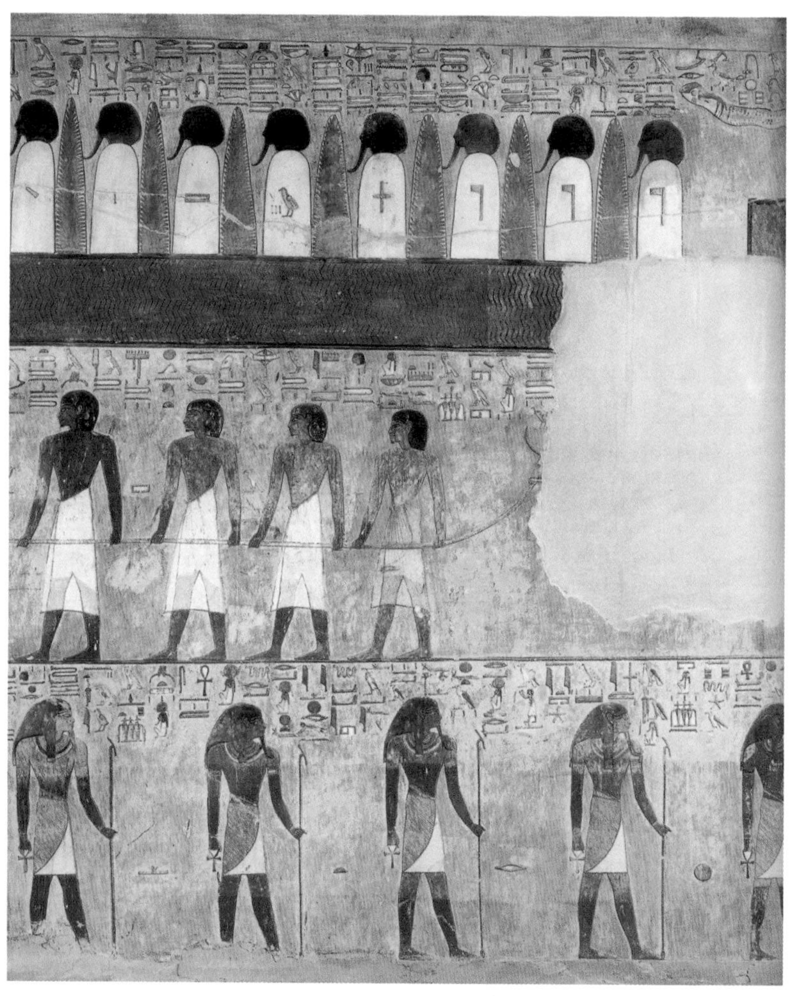

# FROM THE TOMB OF SETI I

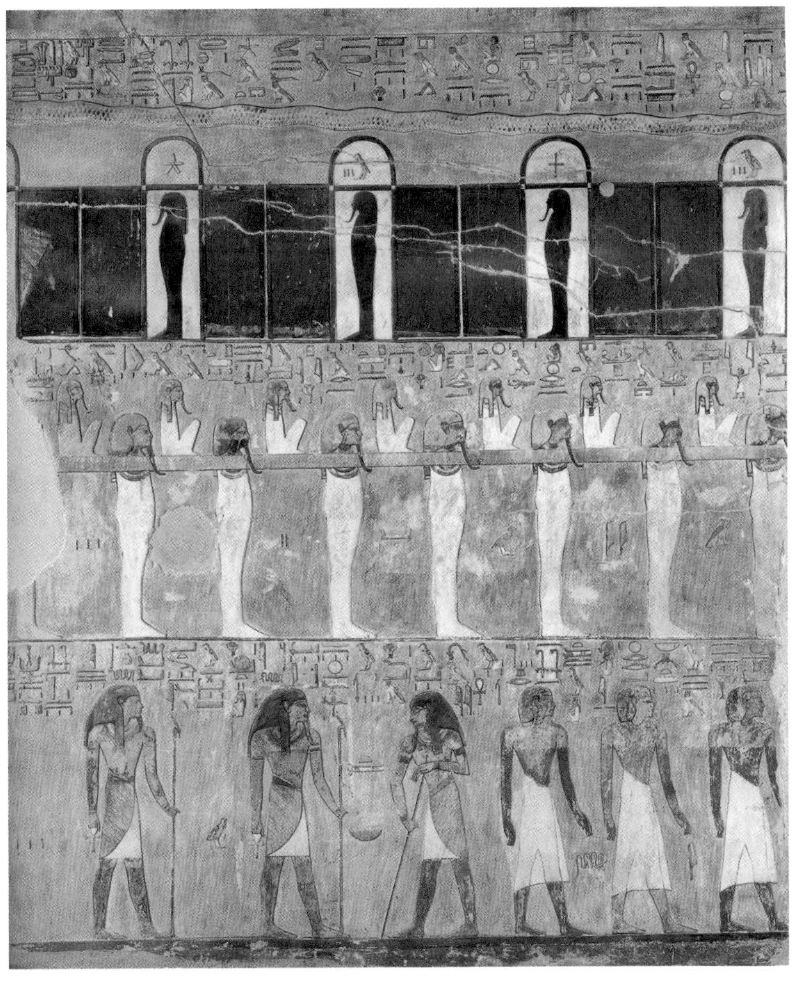

## UPPER REGISTER, 9TH SCENE

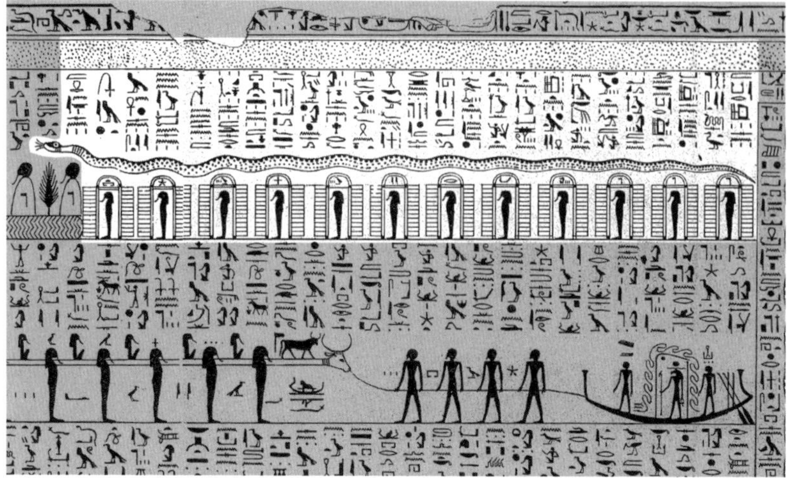

Twelve shrines with vaulted roofs and red (later yellow) doors shown open. In each shrine stands a mummy painted black. The huge serpent stretched over all the shrines has no name, but is called in the text *sty* "The flaming one".

*nṯrw ḏsryw jmyw dwꜣt*

Protected gods who are in the Netherworld (written above the mummies)

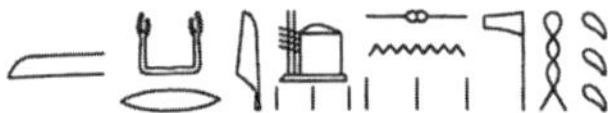

*m kꜣrw.sn ḥꜥw-nṯr*

in their shrines, divine bodies

*sty zꜣw.f kꜣrw.sn*

"The flaming one" guards their shrines.

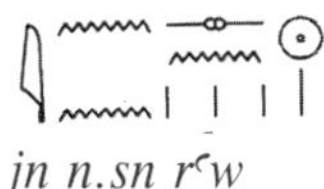

*jn n.sn rꜥw*

Re says to them:

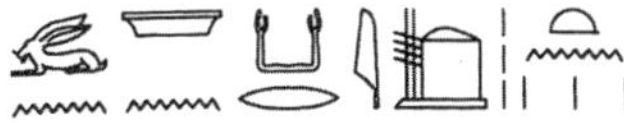

*wn n kꜣrw.ṯn*

«Opening be for your shrines,

*ꜥq ḥḏwt.j m snkw.ṯn*

so that my light may enter your darkness.

*gmjn. j.ṯn jꜣkb.tn*

I found you when you were mourning

*kꜣrw.ṯn ḫtmy ḥr.ṯn*

and your shrines were closed upon you.

*jw dy.j ṯꜣw n fnḏw.ṯn*

(But now) I give breath to your noses

*wḏ.j n.ṯn ꜣḫw.ṯn*

and I have assigned to you your blessed state.»

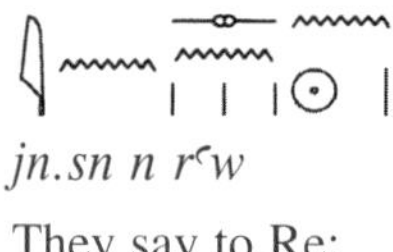

*jn.sn n rꜥw*

They say to Re:

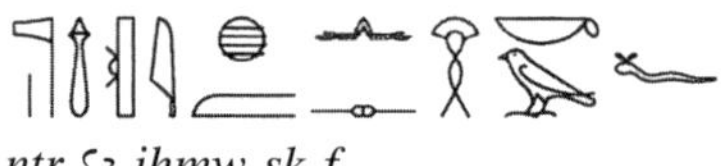

*jhy rꜥw my rk n.n*

«Hail Re! Come to us,

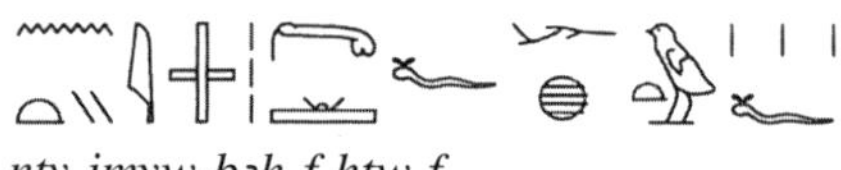

*nṯr ꜥꜣ jḫmw sk.f*

greatest god who knows no setting,

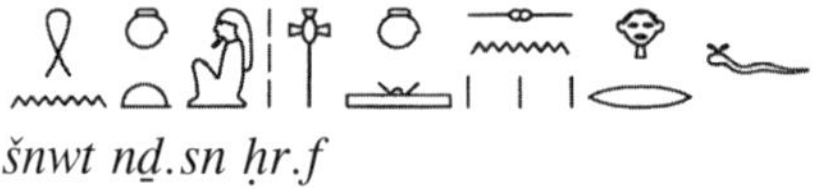

*nty jmyw-bꜣḥ.f ḫtw.f*

whom those who are before him and behind him,

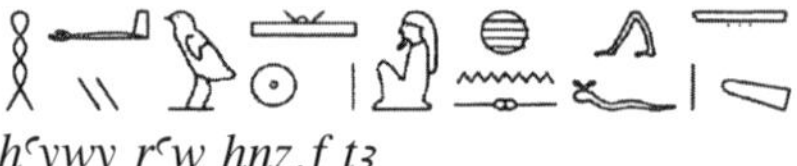

*šnwt nḏ.sn ḥr.f*

(his) retinue, are greeting!

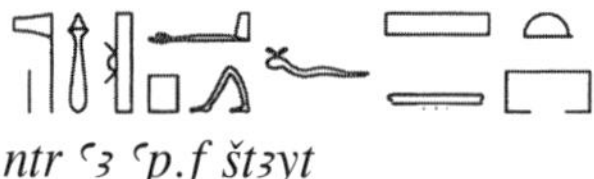

*ḥꜥywy rꜥw ḫnz.f tꜣ*

How joyful is it when Re passes the Earth,

*nṯr ꜥꜣ ꜥp.f štꜣyt*

when the great god moves through the Shetit (Beyond)!»

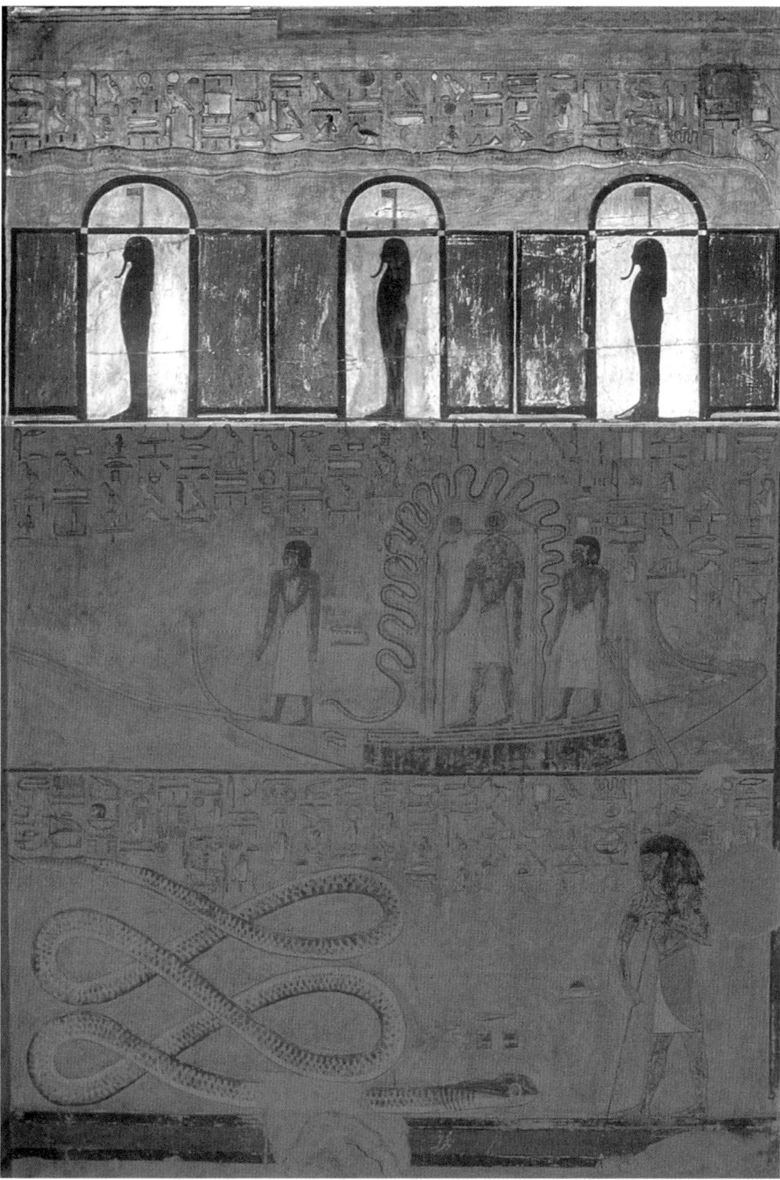

From the tomb of Pharaoh Seti I.

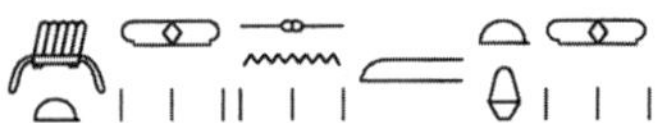

*ꜣwt.sn m tꜣ*

Their oblation is bread,

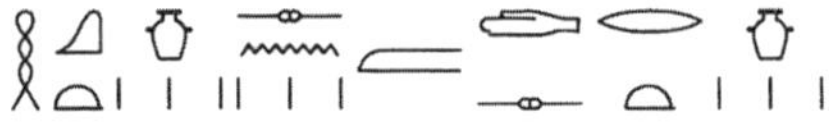

*ḥnqt.sn m ḏsrt*

their beer is Djeseret,

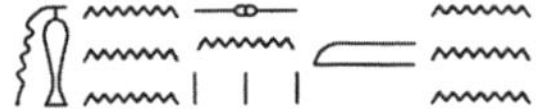

*qbḥw.sn m mw*

their refreshment is water.

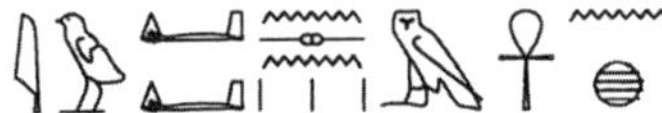

*jw ddw n.sn m ꜥnḫw*

He who makes an offering to them, he lives

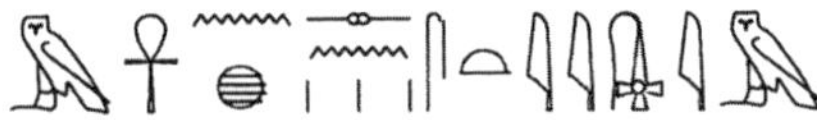

*m ꜥnḫw.sn sty jm*

on what they and «The flaming one» are living.

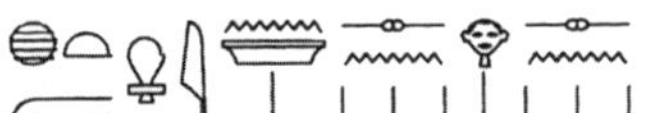

*ḫtmjn ꜥꜣw.sn ḥr.sn*

Then their doors are closed upon them,

*m-ḫt ꜥpp nṯr pn*

after this god has passed.

*hwtḫr.sn sḏm.sn hꜣꜣ ꜥꜣw.sn ḥr.sn*

Then they wail when they hear their doors being shut upon them.

From the tomb of Pharaoh Horemheb.

## 10th Scene

The "Lake of Fire" (in the older copies with water painted red), surrounded by twelve mummy-envelopes with human heads, each with large ears of barley (painted green, later yellow) before it. The hieroglyphs of their name are distributed between the twelve bodies:

*nṯrw jmyw š-ḫb(t)*

"Gods who are in the Lake of Fire".

The text reads:

*š pw wnn.f m dwꜣt*

That Lake is situated in the Netherworld

*dbnw.f m nn nṯrw*

and is surrounded by these gods.

From the tomb of Pharaoh Seti I.

*wnn.sn m ˁꜣtyw tpw.sn ḥꜣyw*

They are in their wrappings, but their heads are bare.

*š pn mḥw m kꜣmwtt*

This Lake is filled with barley,

*mw (nj) š pn m wꜣwꜣt*

(but) the water of this lake is fire.

*ḫpp ꜣpdw mꜣꜣ.sn mw.f*

The birds fly away when they see its water

*ssn.sn stj ntj jm.f*

and smell the odour of that which is in it.

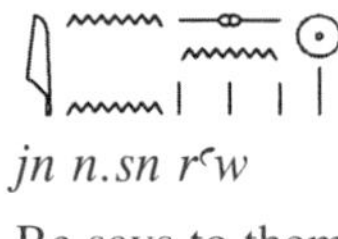

*jn n.sn rꜥw*

Re says to them:

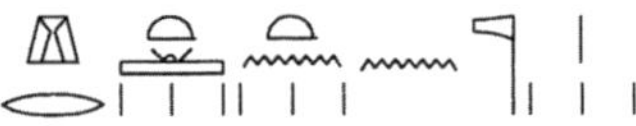

*ẖryt.ṯn n(t) nṯrw*

«Your divine provision

*m kꜣmwtt nt š.ṯn*

consists of the barley of your lake.

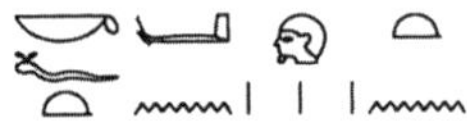

*kfꜣt n tpw.ṯn*

Unwrapping for your heads,

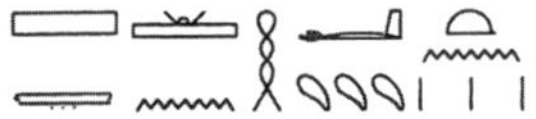

*štꜣw n ḥꜥw.ṯn*

covering for your limbs,

*ṯꜣw n fnḏw.ṯn*

breath for your noses!

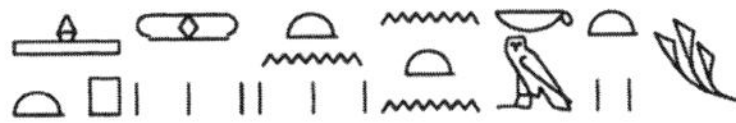

*ḥtpw.ṯn n.ṯn kꜣmwtt*

Your offerings belong to you, (i.e.) barley,

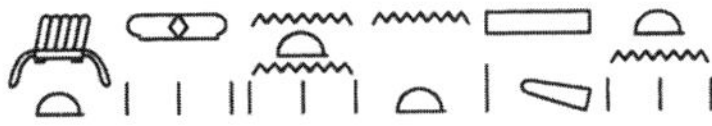

*ꜣwt n.ṯn nt š.ṯn*

oblations belong to you from your lake.

*mw.f n.ṯn jwty tꜣw.f r.ṯn*

Its water belongs to you, without its heat being against you,

*jwty hh.f r ẖꜣwt.ṯn*

without its fiery blast being against your bodies.»

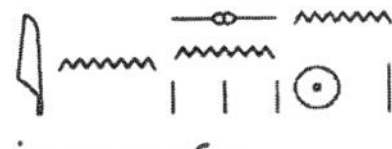

*jn.sn n rʿw*

They say to Re:

*my rk r.n ḏꜣy.f m wjꜣ.f*

«Come to us, who travels in his barque

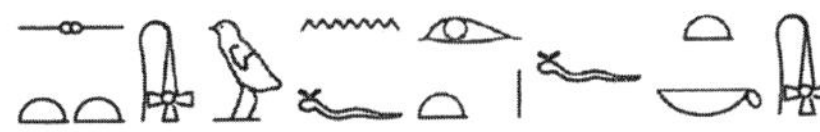

*sttw n.f jrt.f tkꜣ*

for whom his eye kindles the torch

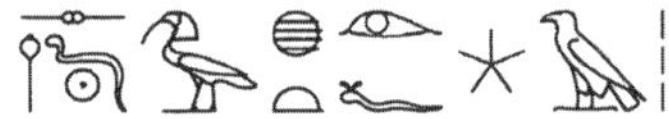

*sḥḏw 3ḫt.f dw3tyw*

and his brilliant eye illuminates those in the Netherworld!

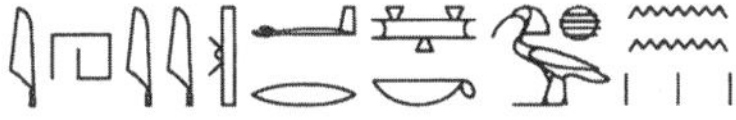

*jhy jʿr.k 3ḫw n.n*

Hail, when you approach, who is helpful for us,

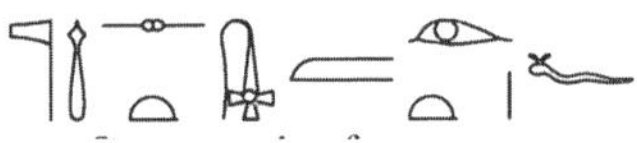

*nṯr ʿ3 sty m jrt.f*

great god who inflames with his eye.»

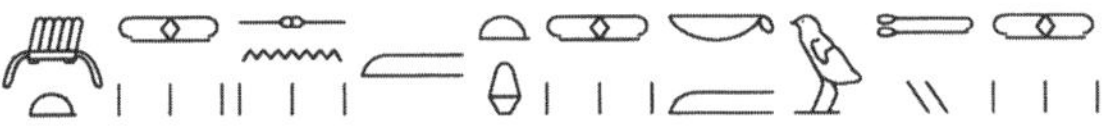

*3wt.sn m t3-k3mwtt*

Their oblations are barley-bread,

From the tomb of Pharaoh Horemheb.

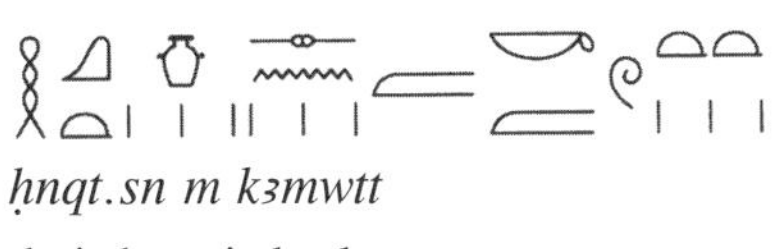

*ḥnqt.sn m k3mwtt*

their beer is barley,

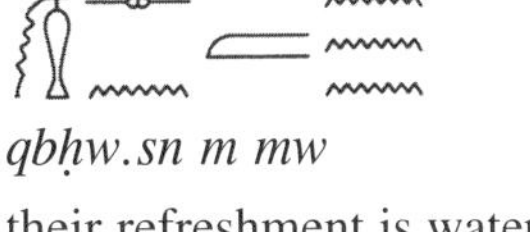

*qbḥw.sn m mw*

their refreshment is water.

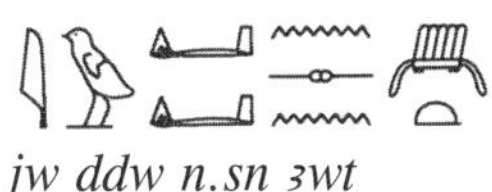

*jw ddw n.sn 3wt*

Whoever offers to them

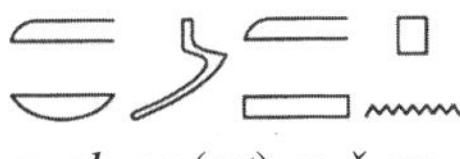

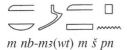

*m nb-m3(wt) m š pn*

is a master of renewal (or ears of barley) in this lake.

## Middle Register, 11th Scene

The sun barque is identical with that in the second hour, again pulled by four *dwꜣtyw* "gods of the Netherworld". The rope passes through a long-stretched object called *wjꜣ-tꜣ* «Barque of the Earth», beginning and ending with a bull's head. It is carried by eight mummiform *fꜣyw* "carriers". Upon this "Barque of the Earth" are placed seven *nṯrw jmyw* "Gods in (it)" between the bull's heads. Another four *dwꜣtyw* are pulling the rope out of it.

The scene is accompanied by the following text:

*sṯꜣw nṯr pn ꜥꜣ jn nṯrw dwꜣtyw*

This great god is being towed by the gods of the Netherworld.

*spr jn nṯr pn ꜥꜣ*

Arrival of this great god

*r wjꜣ-tꜣ dpw nṯrw*

at the Barque of the Earth, the ship of the gods.

From the tomb of Ramses I.

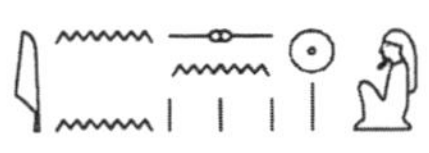

*jn n.sn rʿw*

Re says to them:

*j nṯrw ẖryw wjꜣ-tꜣ*

«O you gods below the Barque of the Earth,

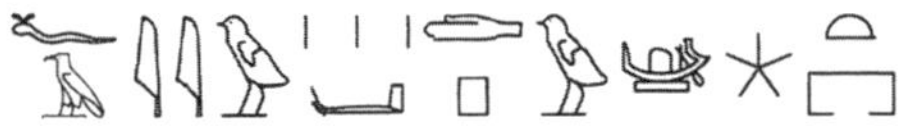

*fꜣyw dpw dwꜣt*

carrying the ship of the Netherworld –

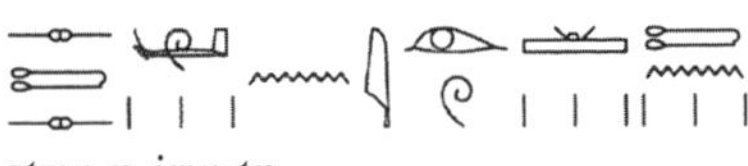

*sṯzw n jrw.ṯn*

Raising be for your manifestations,

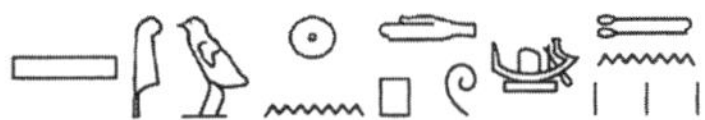

*šw n dpw.ṯn*

light for your ship,

*ḏsrw* (*n*) *ntt jm.f*

and protection (for) what is in it.

*wjꜣ-tꜣ ḥmw n.j*

The Barque of the Earth has receded before me,

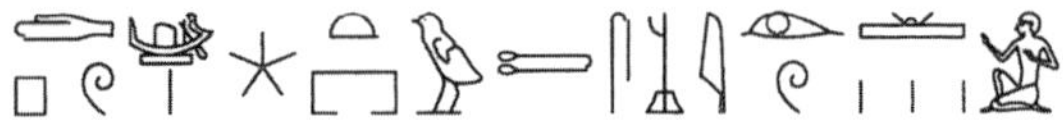

*dpw-dwꜣt wṯz*(*.f*) *jrw.j*

the ship of the Netherworld has raised my manifestations.

*mk.wj ꜥp.j štꜣyt*

Lo! I pass through the Shetit (Beyond)

*r jryt sḫrw ntyw jm.s*

to care for those who are in it!

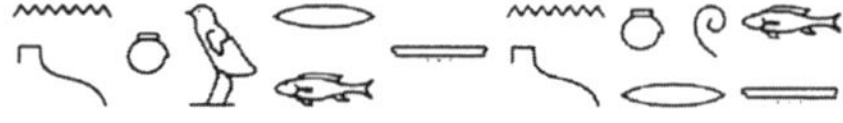

*nwr tꜣ nwr tꜣ*

The earth quakes, the earth quakes,

*wꜣš bꜣ njm kꜣwj*

strong is the *Ba*-soul, the Double-Bull rejoices.

*ḥtp nṯr m qmꜣ*(*t*)*n.f*

The god rests in what he has created.»

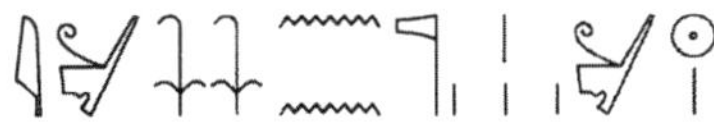

*jn nn nj nṯrw n rʿw*

These gods say to Re:

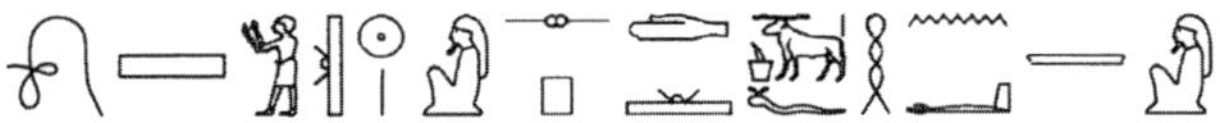

*wꜣš rʿw spd bꜣ.f ḥnʿ tꜣ*

«Strong is Re, effective is his *Ba*-soul together with the God of the Earth.

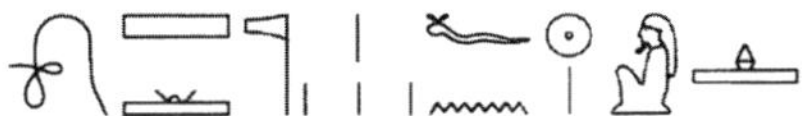

*wꜣš nṯrw.f n rʿw ḥtpw*

Strong are his gods for Re when he has gone to rest.

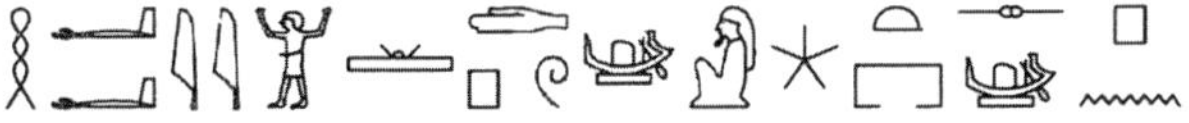

*ḥʿʿy dpw-dwꜣt sjw wjꜣ pn*

Acclaimed is the ship of the Netherworld, and praised is this barque.»

*hwtḫr.sn m-ḫt ʿpp rʿw ḥr.sn*

But then they wail, after Re has passed them.

*ḥtpw.sn (m) rnpyt*

Their offerings are fresh plants.

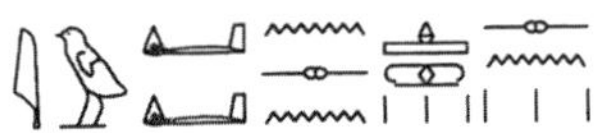

*jw ddw n.sn ḥtpw.sn*

Whoever gives to them their offerings

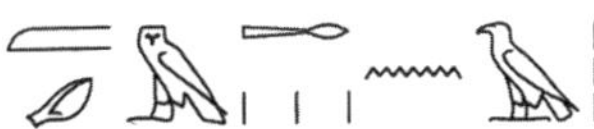

*m sḏm.w ḫrw ntyw*

is one who hears the voice of those existing (in the Netherworld).

## 12TH SCENE

Four wrapped gods with invisible arms confront the sun barque and its retinue. They are the *wtꜣw tꜣ* "Wrapped ones of the Earth". The text reads:

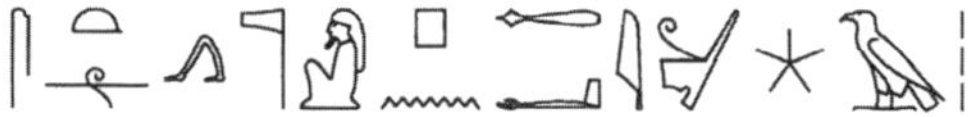

*sṯꜣw nṯr pn ꜥꜣ jn dwꜣtyw*

This great god is being towed by those of the Netherworld

*m wjꜣ ḏsr jmy tꜣ*

(out) of the protected Barque which is in the Earth.

*wḏ-mdw n wtꜣw jmnw-ꜥ*

Orders to the wrapped ones with hidden arms:

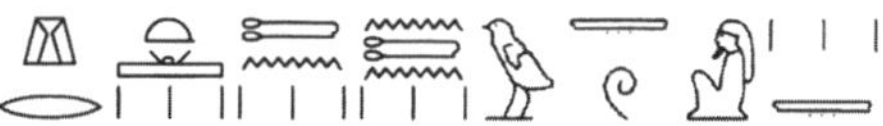

*ḫryt.ṯn n.ṯn wtꜣw tꜣ*

«Your provisions belong to you, "Wrapped ones of the Earth" –

From the tomb of Pharaoh Ramses I.

*hmhmt ḫnty-mnt.f*

the renown of Khentymentef (The Foremost of his thighs),

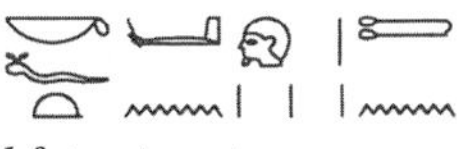

*kfꜣt n tpw.ṯn*

unwrapping for your heads,

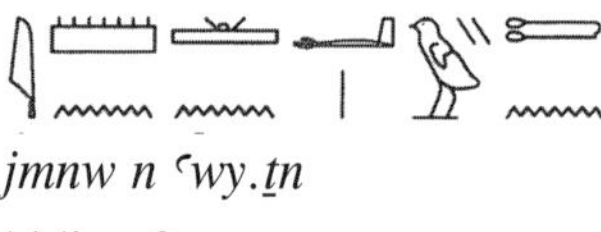

*jmnw n ꜥwy.ṯn*

hiding for your arms,

*ṯꜣw n fnḏw.ṯn*

breath be for your noses,

*snfḫfḫ n wtw.ṯn*

loosening for your wrappings!

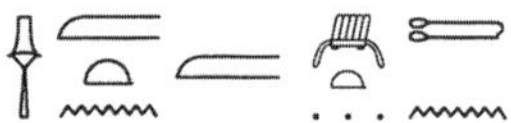

*sḫm.ṯn m ꜣwt.ṯn*

May you dispose of your oblations,

*ḥtpn.ṯn m qmꜣwn.j*

when you rest in (this) which I have created.»

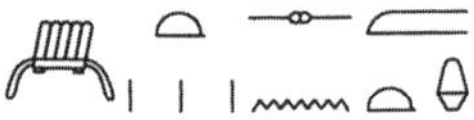

*ꜣwt.sn m tꜣ*

Their oblations are bread,

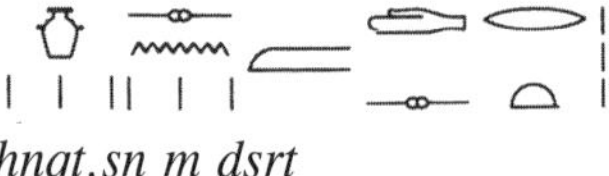

*ḥnqt.sn m ḏsrt*

their beer is Djeseret,

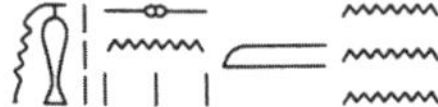

*qbḥw.sn m mw*

their refreshment is water.

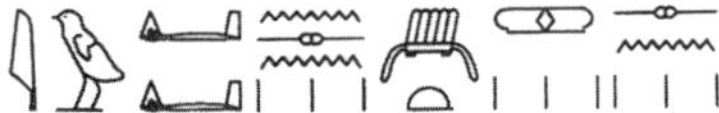

*jw ddw n.sn ꜣwt.sn*

Whoever makes an offering to them

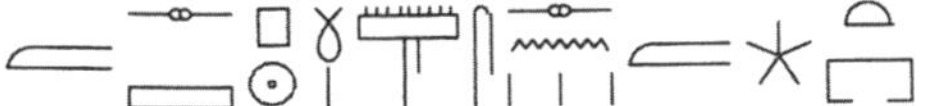

*m sšpw.sn m dwꜣt*

is among those with shining garments in the Netherworld.

From the tomb of Pharaoh Horemheb.

## LOWER REGISTER , 13TH SCENE

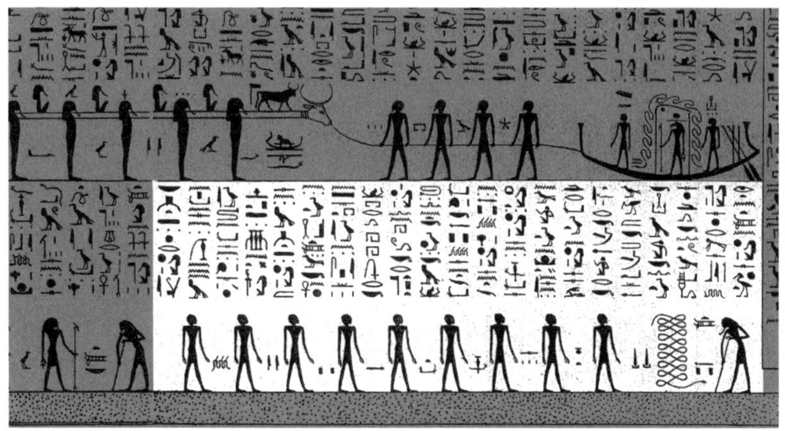

*Jtmw* Atum, again leaning on a staff, confronts the multi-coiled serpent *ꜥ3pp* Apopis and, before him, nine blessed dead, which are named:

*ḏ3ḏ3t ḫsft ꜥ3pp*

"The council that drives away Apopis".

The text reads:

*jrytn jtmw n rꜥw*

What Atum has done on behalf of Re:

*s3ḫt nṯr sḫrt sby*

to glorify the god, to overthrow the rebel.

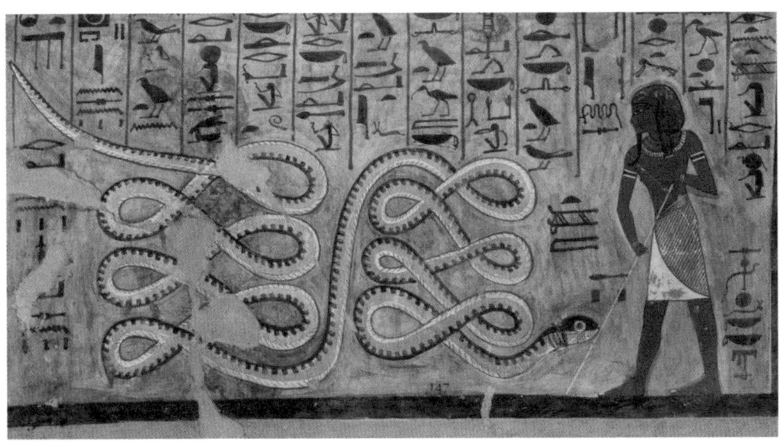

From the tomb of Pharaoh Ramses I.

(Atum speaks to Apopis:)

*sḫdw.k jwty ꜥḥꜥ.k*

«You are upside down, so that you cannot rise (again),

*ḥkꜣw.k jwty gmj.k.ṯ(w)*

you are bewitched so that you cannot find yourself!

*mꜣꜥ-ḫrw jt.j r.k*

My father has triumphed over you,

*mꜣꜥ-ḫrw.j r.k*

I have triumphed against you,

*dr.j.ṯw n rꜥw*

I have driven you away on behalf of Re.

*sswn.j.ṯw n ꜣḫty*

I have punished you on behalf of Akhty.»

*jn.sn psḏt-rꜥw*

They say, the Ennead of Re,

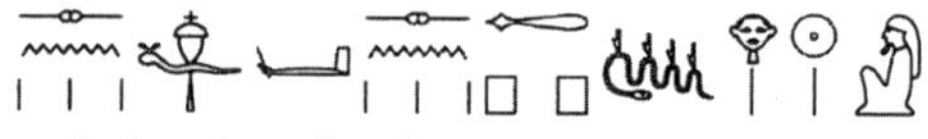

*sn ḫsf.sn ꜥꜣpp ḥr rꜥw*

when they drive away Apopis from Re:

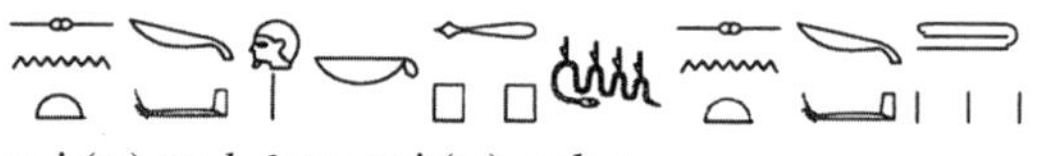

*znjt(w) tp.k ꜥꜣpp znjt(w) qꜣbw*

«Your head is cut off Apopis, the coils chopped up!

*nn tknw.k m wjꜣ rꜥw*

you will not come near to the barque of Re,

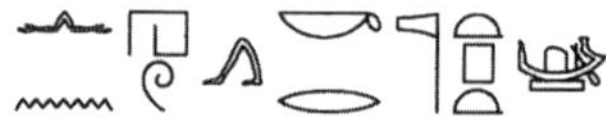

*nn hꜣj.k r dpt-nṯr*

you will not come near to the god's ship!

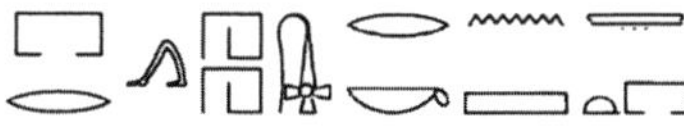

*pry hh r.k n(j) št3yt*

The fiery blast of the Shetit has gone forth against you,

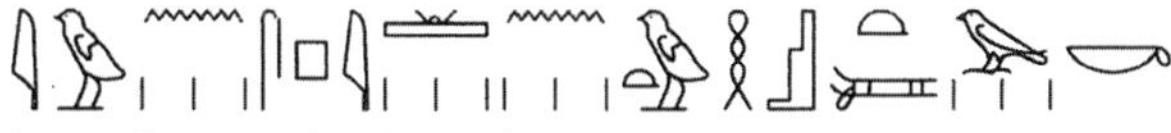

*jw.n sjp.n.ṯw (n) ḥtmw.k*

and we have condemned you to your destruction!»

*ʿnḫ.sn m 3wt rʿw*

They live on the oblations of Re

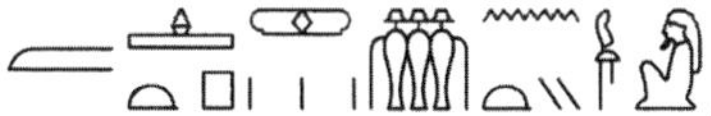

*m ḥtpw ḫnty-jmntyw*

and the offerings of the Foremost of the Westerners (Osiris).

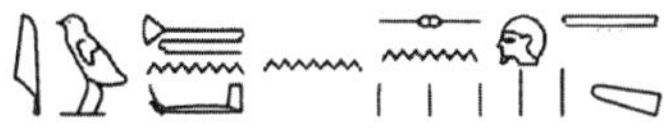

*jw wdnw n.sn tp t3*

Whoever makes an offering to them on earth,

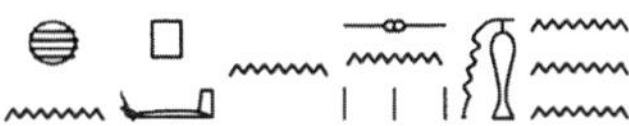

*ḫnpw n.sn qbḥw*

and lets them have cool refreshment,

*m nb 3wt ḫr rʿw*

is a master of oblations with Re.

## 14TH SCENE

A second, similar figure of Atum confronts nine gods carrying Ankh and Was, named *nbw-ẖrt* masters of provisions.

*jn jtmw n nn nj nṯrw*

Atum says to these gods:

*j nṯrw ẖryw ꜥnḫ wꜣs*

«O gods who carry Ankh and Was,

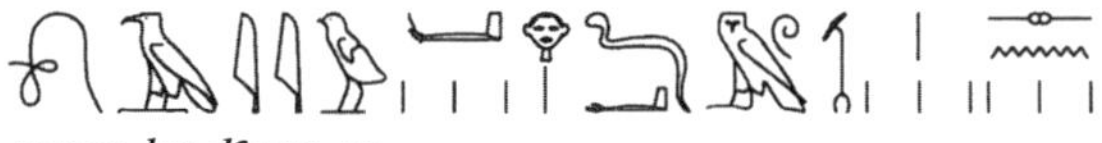

*wꜣyw ḥr ḏꜥmw.sn*

who lean upon their Djam-sceptres –

*ẖsf sby ḥr ꜣḫty*

Drive away the rebel from Akhty,

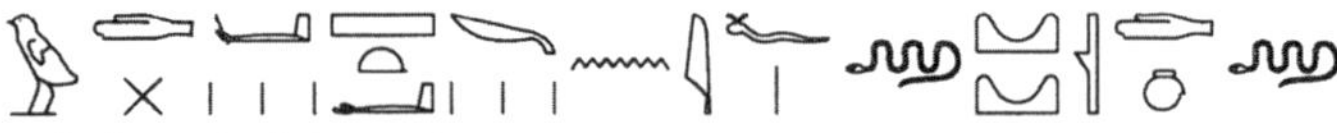

*wdy šꜥt n jwf ḏwy-qd*

hack up the flesh of the Wicked one!»

From the tomb of Pharaoh Ramses I.

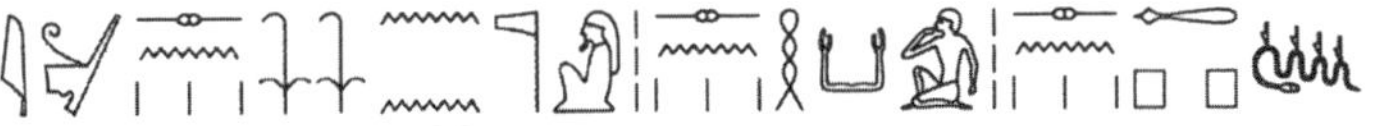

*jn.sn nn nṯrw sn ḥkꜣ.sn ꜥꜣpp*

These gods say, when they enchant Apopis:

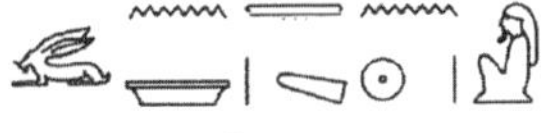

*wnw tꜣ n rꜥw*

«Open is the Earth for Re,

*ẖtmw tꜣ r ꜥꜣpp*

sealed is the Earth against Apopis!

*dwꜣtyw ḫnty-jmntyw jmyw štꜣyt*

You of the Netherworld of the Foremost of the Westerners, who are in the Shetit,

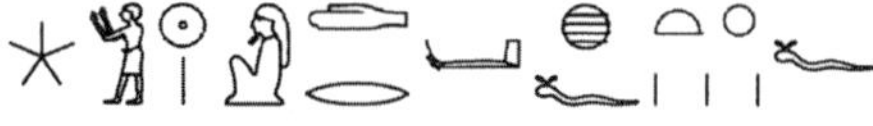

*dwꜣ rꜥw dr ḫftyw.f*

praise Re and drive away his enemies,

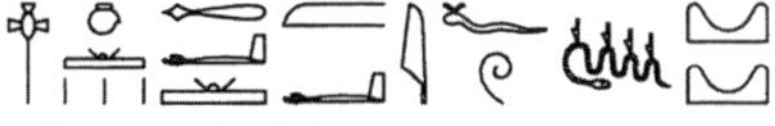

*nḏ ꜥꜣ m-ꜥ jwf ḏwy*

protect the Great one (Osiris) from the flesh of the Wicked one!

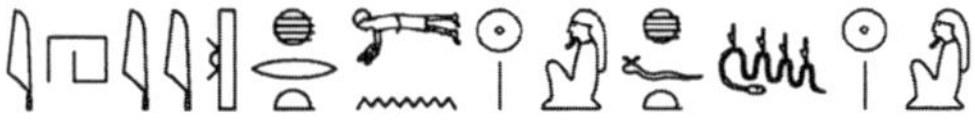

*jhy ḫrtw n rꜥw ḫfty rꜥw*

Hail, felled for Re is the enemy of Re!»

*ꜥnḫ.sn m ꜣwt rꜥw*

They live on the oblations of Re

*m ḥtpw ḫnty-jmntyw*

and on the offerings of the Foremost of the Westerners.

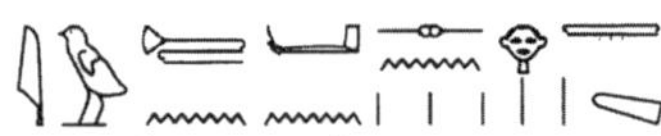

*jw wdnw n.sn ḥr tꜣ*

Whoever offers them on earth

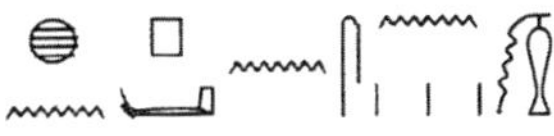

*ḫnpw n.sn qbḥw*

and lets them have cool refreshment,

*m mꜣꜥ-ḫrw m jmnt*

is one who is justified in the West,

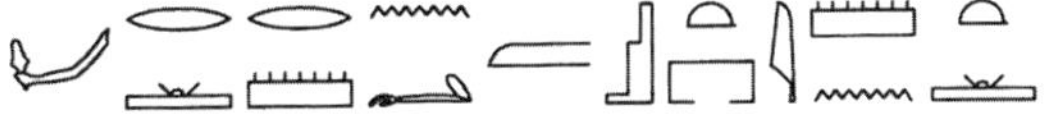

*ḏsrw rmn m st-jmnt*

with protected shoulder in the Hidden Place.

*sn hwt.sn n rꜥw*

They wail because of Re

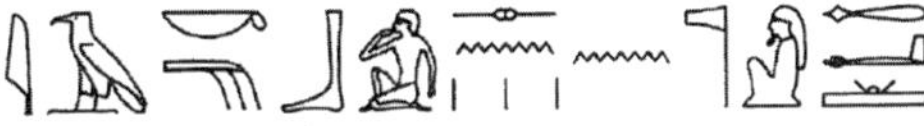

*jꜣkb.sn n nṯr ꜥꜣ*

and they lament because of the great god,

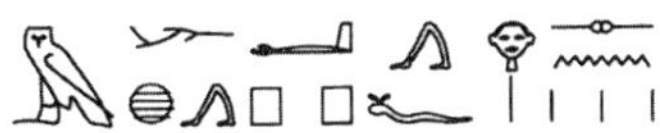

*m-ḫt ꜥpp.f ḥr.sn*

after he has passed them.

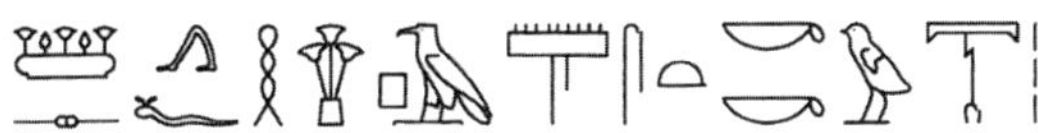

*šꜣs.f ḥꜥp.st kkw*

When he rushes away, darkness envelops them

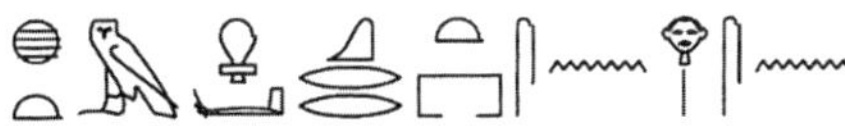

*ḫtmw qrrwt.sn ḥr.sn*

and their caverns are closed upon them.

## Third Gate

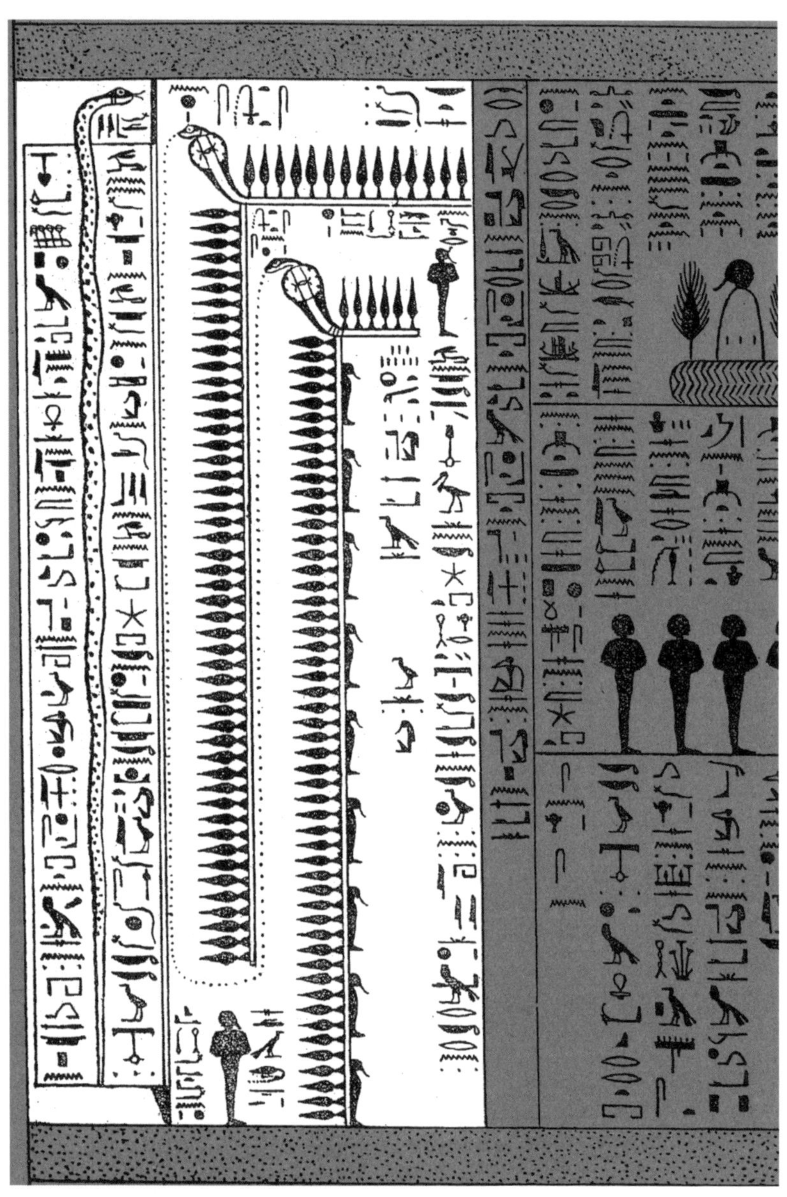

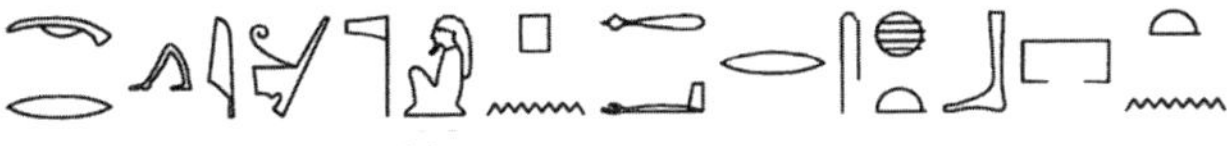

*spr jn nṯr.pn ꜥꜣ r sbḫt tn*

Arrival of this great god at this gate,

*ꜥq m sbḫt tn*

entering into this gate.

*nṯrw jmyw.s sns.sn nṯr pn ꜥꜣ*

The gods who are in it acclaim this great god.

The gate is called:

*nbt sḏfꜣw*

"Mistress of nourishment".

At the two Uraeus-serpents on the wall:

*stt.s n rꜥw*

"She lights up for Re".

The two guardians:

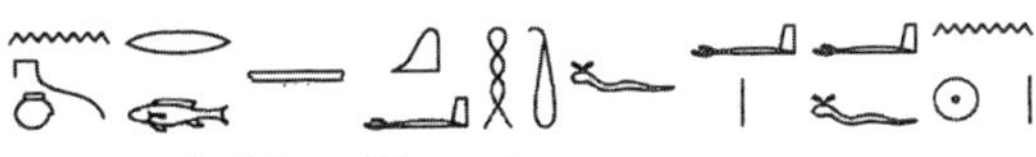

*nwr tꜣ qꜥḥ.f ꜥwy.f(j) n rꜥw*

"Earthquake". He bends his arms for Re.

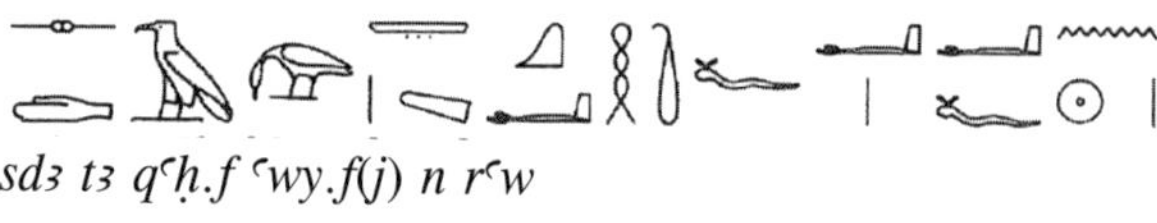

*sdꜣ tꜣ qꜥḥ.f ꜥwy.f(j) n rꜥw*

“Trembling of the earth”. He bends his arms for Re.

Nine mummies:

*psḏt ḥmt nṯr ꜥꜣ jmyw*

“Third Ennead of the great god which is in (it)”.

Text in front of the Ennead:

*wnw n.k tꜣ wbꜣw n.k dwꜣt*

«Open for you is the Earth, thrown for you open is the Duat,

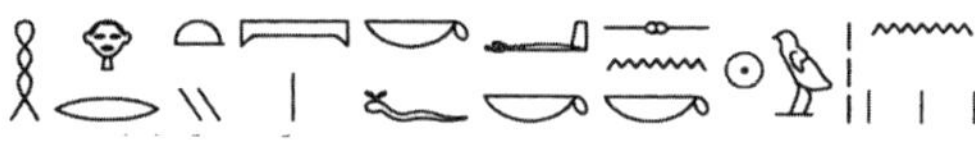

*ḥrty kfꜥ.k snkw.n*

you from heaven – you have uncovered our darkness.

*jhy rꜥw my rk r.n*

Hail Re! Come to us!»

The serpent upon the doorway:

*ḏdby*

“The piercing one”.

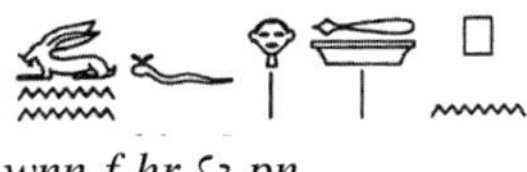

*wnn.f ḥr ꜥꜣ pn*

He is upon this door,

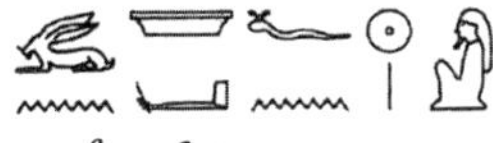

*wn.f n rꜥw*

he opens for Re.

*sjꜣ n ḏdby*

Sia (speaks) to “the piercing one”:

*wn sbꜣ.k n rꜥw*

«Open your gate for Re,

*zn ꜥꜣ.k n ꜣḫty*

open your door for Akhty!»

*jw.f sḥḏ.f kkw zmꜣw*

He lights up the Primeval Darkness,

*dj.f šsp m ꜥt jmnt*

he brings light into the Hidden Region.

*ḫtmjn ꜥꜣ pn*

Then this door is closed,

*m-ḫt ꜥq nṯr pn ꜥꜣ*

after this great god has entered.

*hwtḫr jmyw sbḫt.tn*

Then those in this gate wail

*sḏm.sn hꜣꜣ ꜥꜣ pn*

when they hear this door being slammed.

From the tomb of Pharaoh Ramses IV.

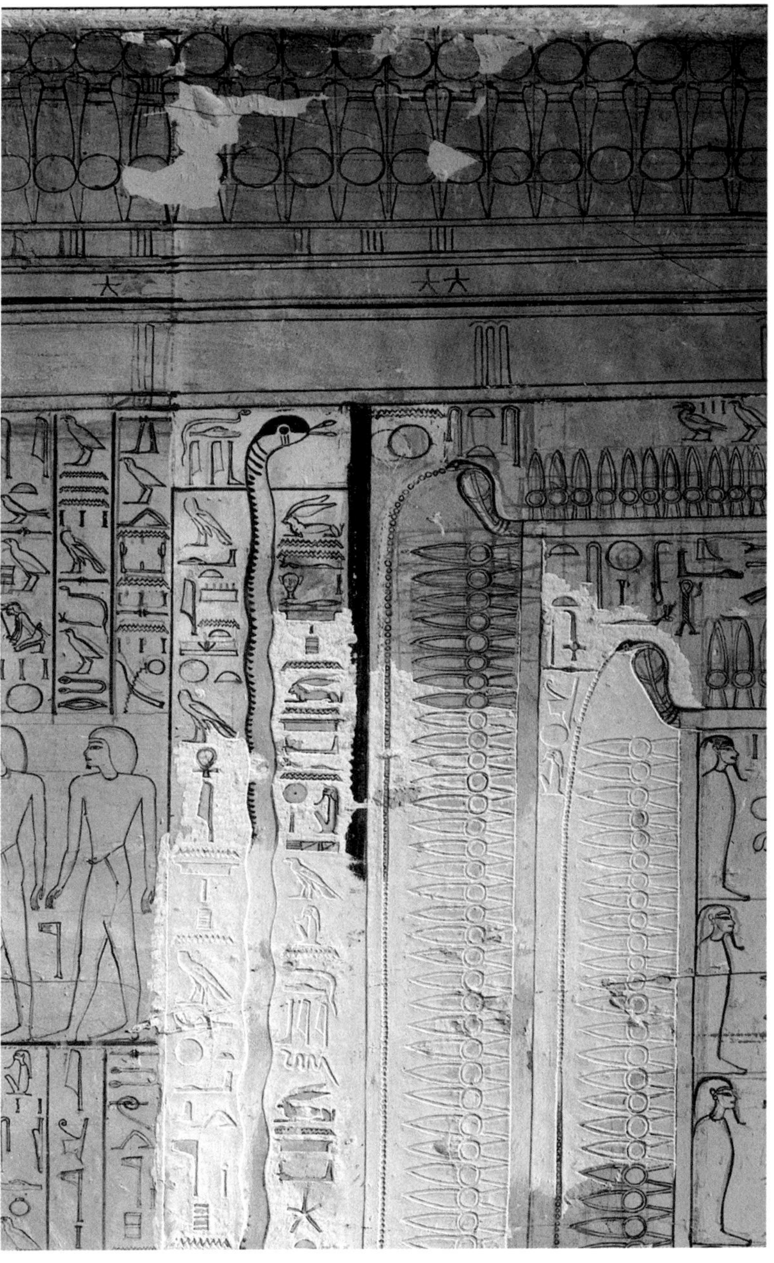

From the tomb of Pharaoh Horemheb, part of the high relief is already chisled out.

# FOURTH

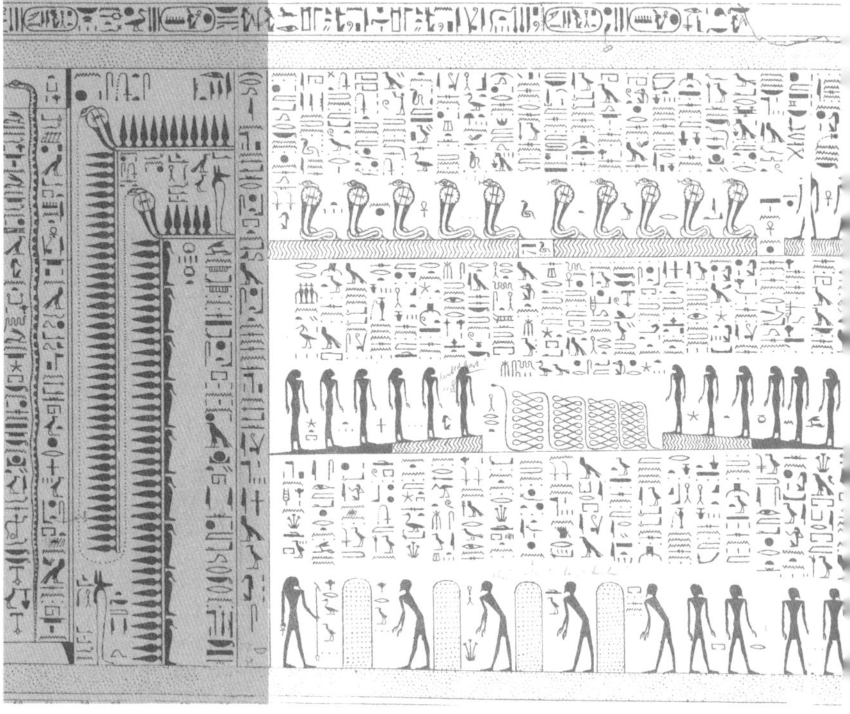

# HOUR

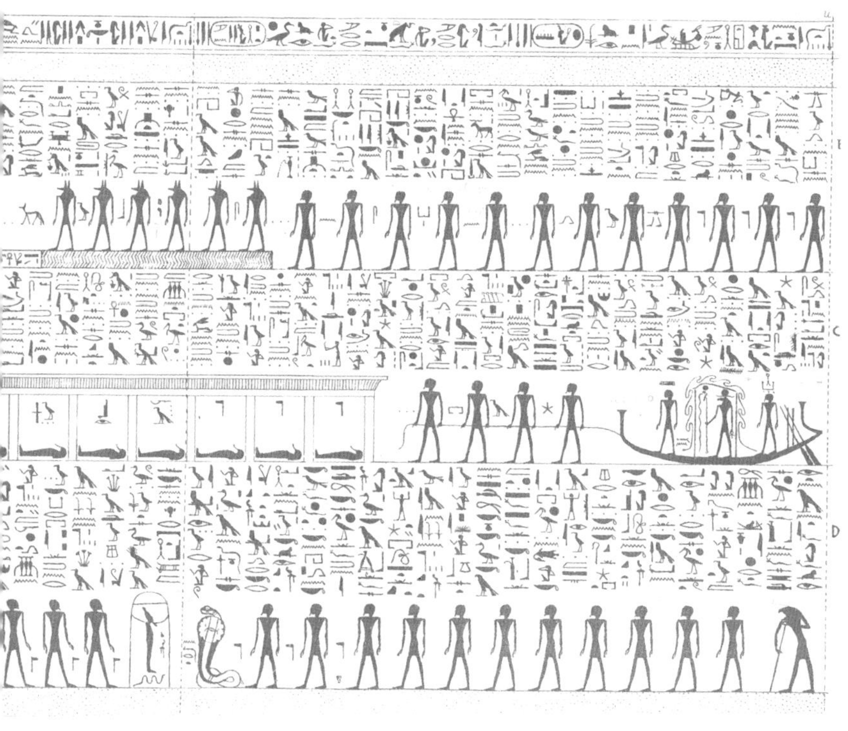

# Part of the Fourth Hour

# From the Tomb of Ramses I

# Part of the Fourth Hour

# FROM THE TOMB OF RAMSES IV

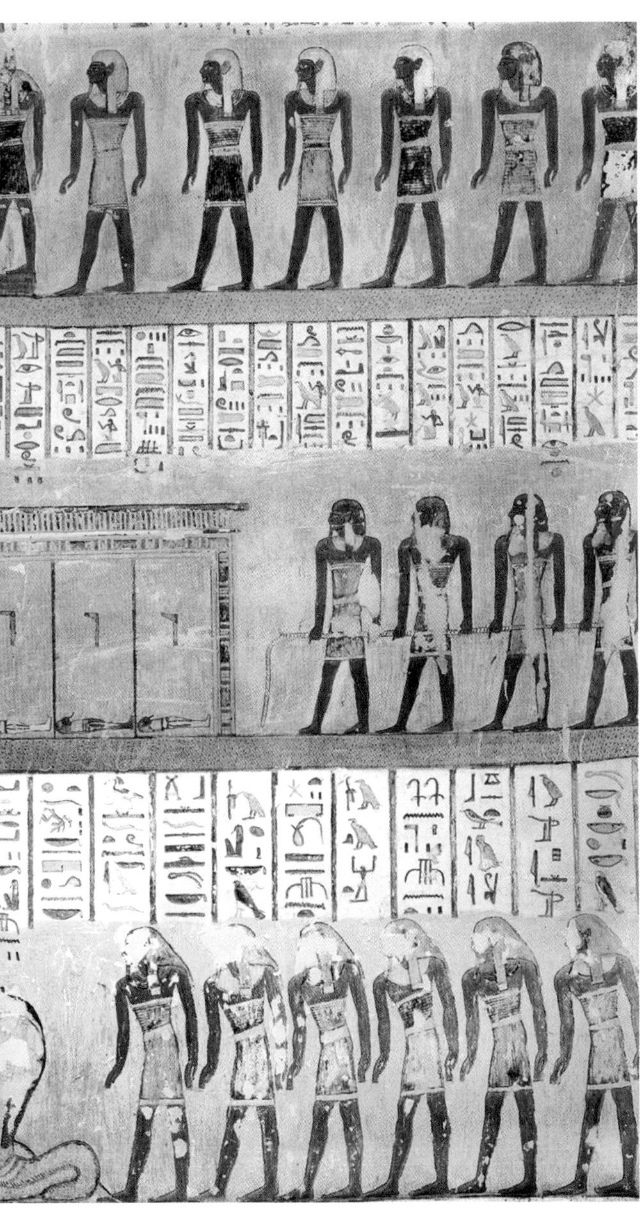

## UPPER REGISTER, 15TH SCENE

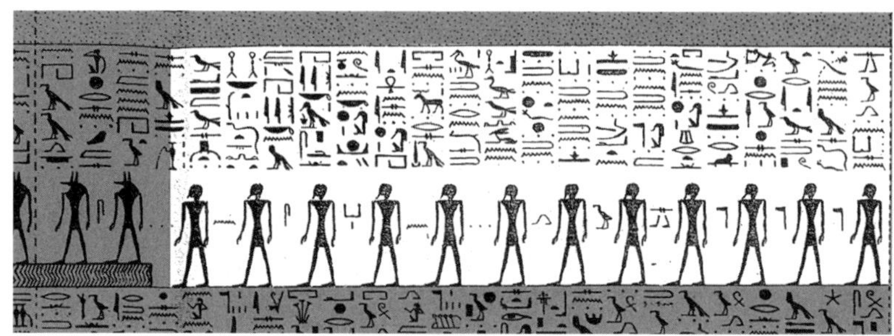

Twelve deities without attributes:

*nṯrw zbjw n kꜣ.sn*

"The gods who have gone to their *Ka*-energy".

The text reads:

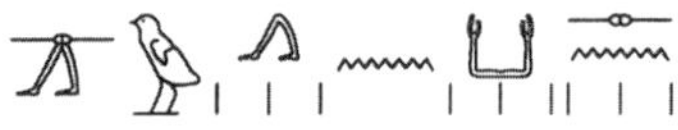

*zbjw n kꜣw.sn*

Those who have gone to their *Ka*-energies,

*wꜥbw m sḏfw-ṯryt*

who are purified by a solemn oath,

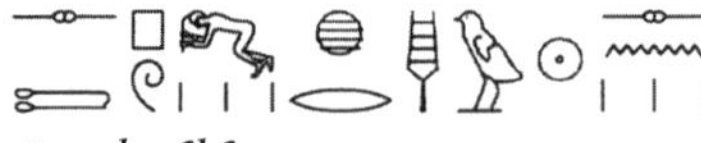

*stpw ḫr ꜥḥꜥw.sn*

who have been removed during their lifetime,

From the tomb of Pharaoh Horemheb.

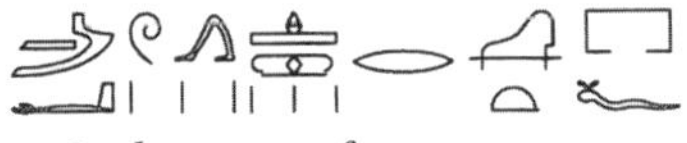

*mꜣʿw ḥtpw r st.f*

who guide the offering to its place.

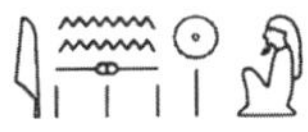

*jn n.sn rʿw*

Re says to them:

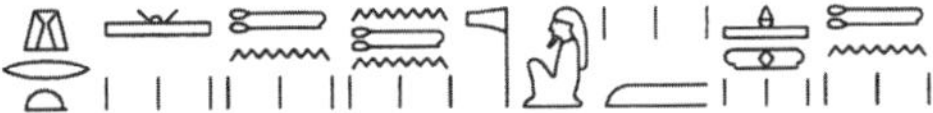

*ḫryt.ṯn n.ṯn nṯrw m ḥtpw.ṯn*

«Your provisions belong to you, gods, from your offerings!

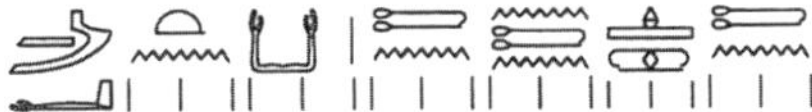

*mꜣʿ.ṯn kꜣw.ṯn n.ṯn ḥtp.ṯn*

You guide your nourishment to you, so that you are content.

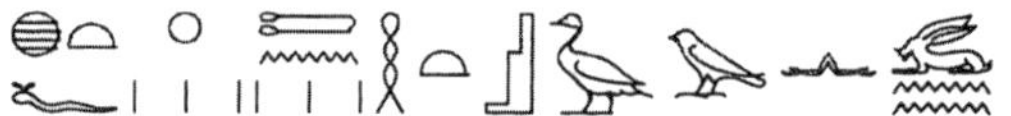

*ḫftyw.ṯn ḥtmw n(n) wnn*

Your enemies have been destroyed, without being,

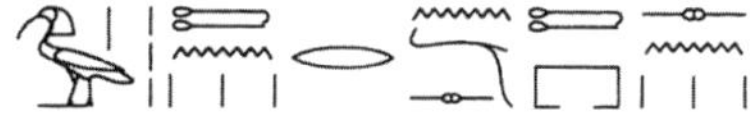

*ꜣḫw.ṯn r nswt.sn*

your *Akh*-spirits are at their thrones,

*bꜣw r sḏꜣyt*

the *Ba*-souls at what is concealed.»

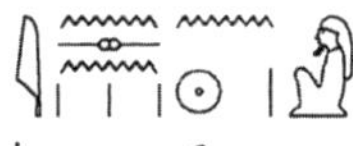

*jn.sn n rꜥw*

They say to Re:

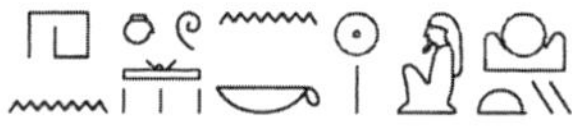

*hnw n.k rꜥw-ꜣḫty*

«Acclamation to you, Re-Akhty,

*hy (n).k bꜣ spdw m tꜣ*

«Hail to you, effective *Ba*-soul in the Earth!

*hy (n).k nḥḥ nb rnpwt*

Hail to you, Permanent one, Master of years.

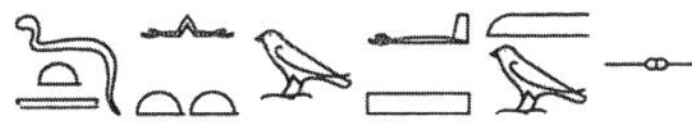

*ḏt jwtt ꜥšm.s*

Duration, which cannot be extinguished!»

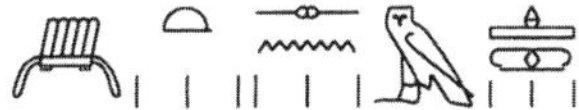

*ꜣwt.sn m ḥtpw*

Their oblations are the offerings,

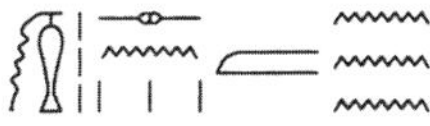

*qbḥw.sn m mw*

their refreshment is water.

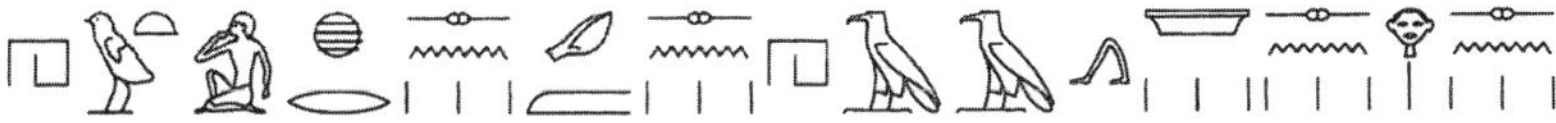

*hwtḫr.sn sḏm.sn hꜣꜣ ꜥꜣw.sn ḥr.sn*

Then they wail when they hear their doors being shut upon them.

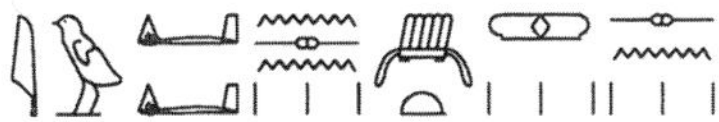

*jw ddw n.sn ꜣwt.sn*

Whoever offers to them their oblations,

*m sṯꜣw nḏrt-bꜣw*

is one who pulls the “Container of the *Ba*-souls”.

## 16TH SCENE

Twelve gods with jackal's heads surround a rectangular lake.

The lake:

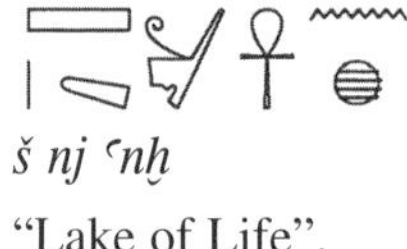

*š nj ꜥnḫ*

"Lake of Life".

The gods' name is written between the twelve jackals:

*zꜣbw jmyw š nj ꜥnḫ*

"Jackals who are in the 'Lake of Life'".

The text reads:

*sn m dbnw (nj) š pn*

They are in the surroundings of this Lake,

From the tomb of Pharaoh Horemheb.

*n jʿrn bꜣw mtyw r.f*

(but) the *Ba*-souls of the dead cannot approach it

*n ḏsrw wnn jm.f*

because of the taboo which is in it.

*jn n.sn rʿw*

Re says to them:

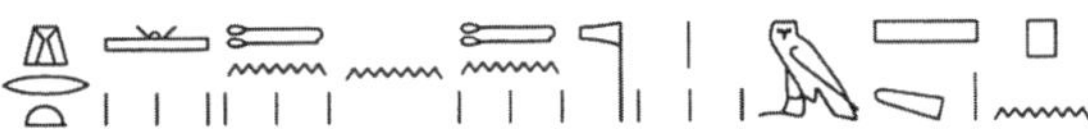

*ḫryt.ṯn n.ṯn nṯrw m š pn*

«Your provisions belong to you, gods, from this Lake!

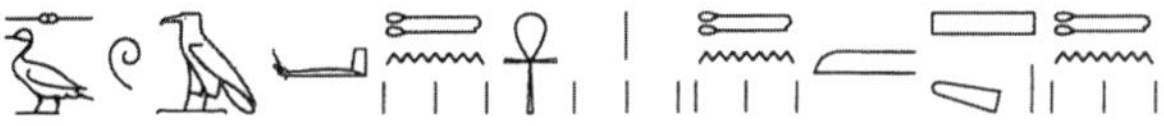

*zꜣw.ṯn ꜥnḫ.ṯn m š.ṯn*

You guard your life in your Lake.

*ḥtpw.ṯn m zꜣwt zꜣbw*

Your offerings are what the jackals guard,

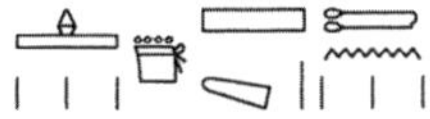

*ḥtpw ḏr š.ṯn*

who rest at your Lake.»

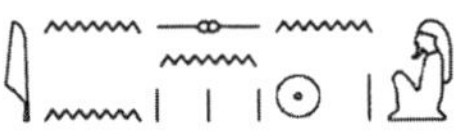

*jn.sn n rꜥw*

They say to Re:

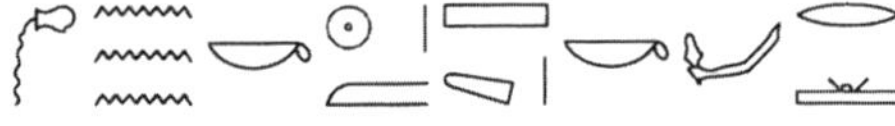

*wꜥbw.k rꜥw m š.k ḏsr*

«You are purified, Re, in your secluded Lake,

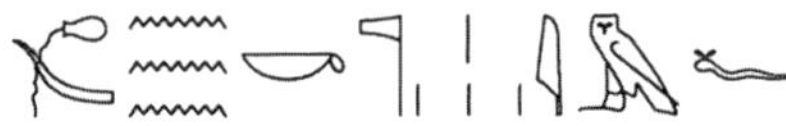

*ꜥby.k nṯrw jm.f*

in which you have purified the gods

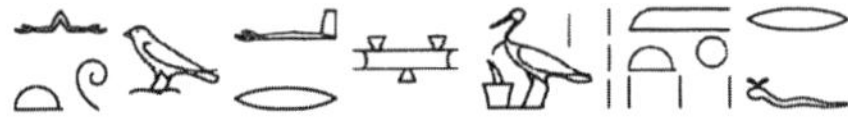

*jwty jꜥr bꜣw mtyw r.f*

and which cannot be approached by the *Ba*-souls of the dead,

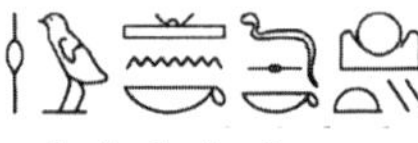

*wḏn.k ḏs.k ꜣḫty*

(as) you have decreed yourself, Akhty!»

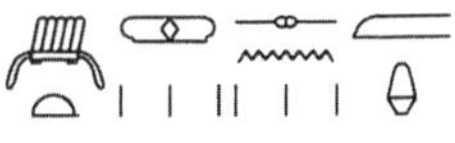

*ȝwt.sn m tȝ*

Their oblations are bread,

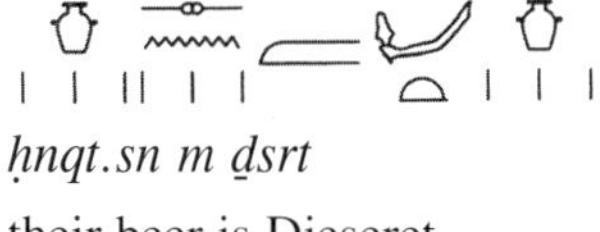

*ḥnqt.sn m ḏsrt*

their beer is Djeseret,

*mw.sn m jrp*

their water is wine.

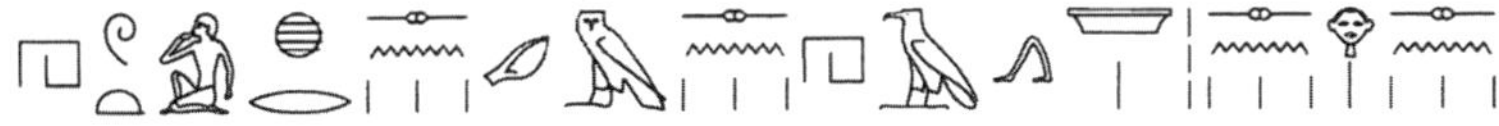

*hwtẖr.sn sḏm.sn hȝȝ ꜥȝw.sn ḥr.sn*

Then they wail when they hear their doors being shut upon them.

*jw ddw n.sn ȝwt.sn*

Whoever offers to them their oblations,

*m nb ḏȝt (j)m.sn*

is a master of the rest of them

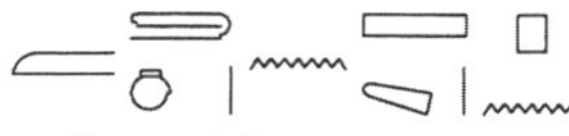

*m dbnw nj š pn*

in the surroundings of this Lake.

From the tomb of Pharaoh Ramses IV.

## 17TH SCENE

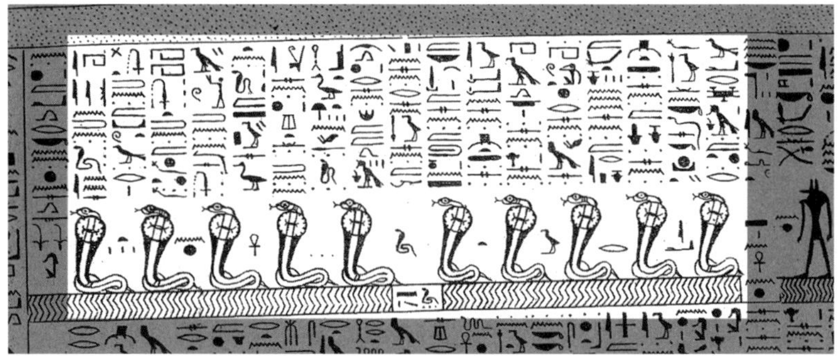

Another rectangular lake and ten Uraeus-serpents surrounding it.

The Lake is named:

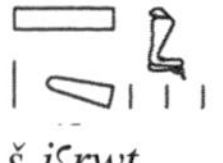

*š jʿrwt*

"Lake of Uraeus-serpents".

The ten cobras (uraei) rearing up are collectively named, with the name written in between them:

*jʿrwt ʿnḫwt*

"Living Uraeus-serpents".

The text reads:

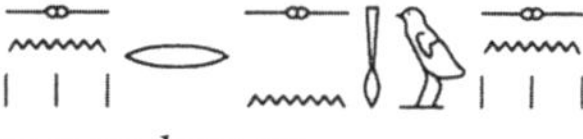

*sn r.sn ḫrw.sn*

They hiss

From the tomb of Pharaoh Merenptah.

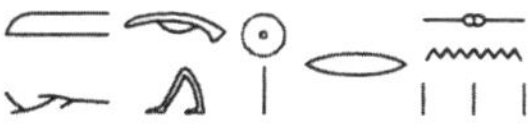

*m-ẖt spr rʿw r.sn*

after Re has reached them.

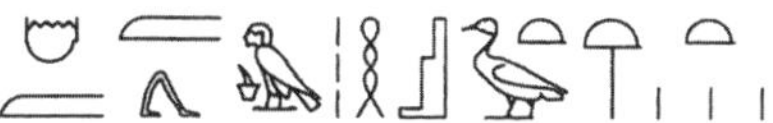

*ḥmm bꜣw ḫtmw šwwt*

The *Ba*-souls are repulsed and the shadows destroyed,

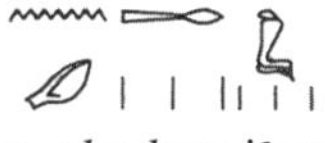

*n sḏm ḫrw jʿrwt*

when the voice of the Uraeus-serpents is heard.

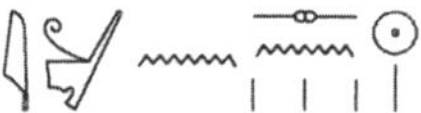

*jn n.sn rʿw*

Re says to them:

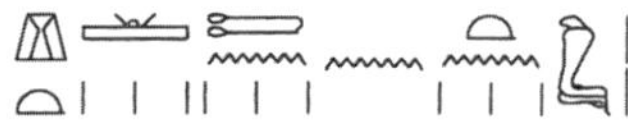

*ẖryt.ṯn n.ṯn jʿrwt*

«Your provisions belong to you, Uraei,

*m š pw zꜣꜣw.ṯn*

from that Lake which you guard.

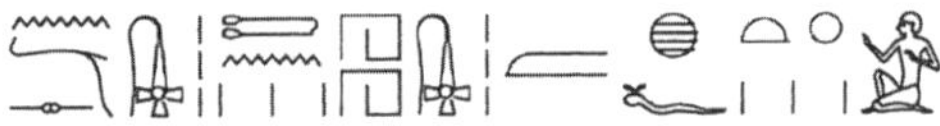

*nsw.ṯn hh m ḫftyw.j*

Your flames are a fiery blast against my enemies.

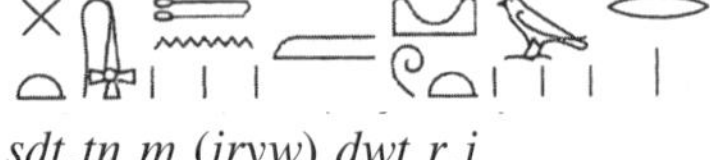

*sḏt.ṯn m (jryw) ḏwt r.j*

Your fire burns in those (who have done) evil against me.

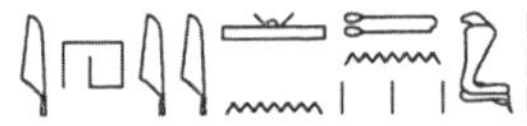

*jhy n.ṯn jʿrwt*

Hail to you, Uraei!»

From the tomb of Pharaoh Horemheb.

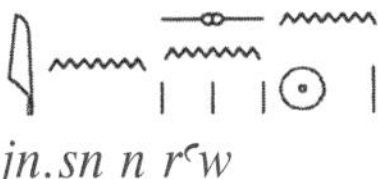

*jn.sn n rʿw*

They say to Re:

*my rk n.n ḫnzw tꜣ(ṯ)nn*

«Come to us, who traverses Tatenen,

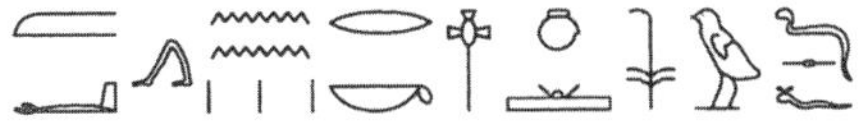

*my n.n rk nḏ.sw ḏs.f*

come to us, who guards himself!

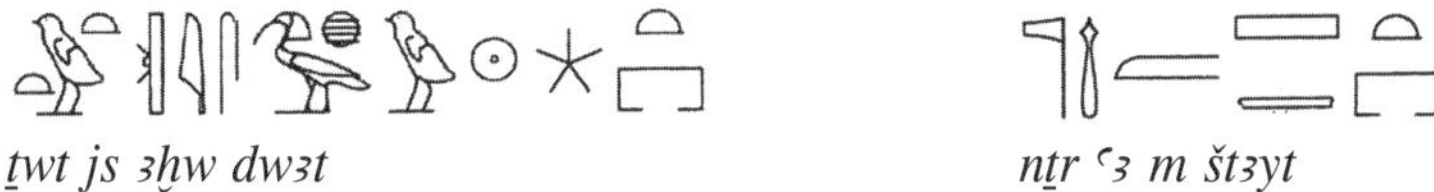

*ṯwt js ꜣḫw dwꜣt*

You are indeed the splendor of the Netherworld.

*nṯr ʿꜣ m štꜣyt*

Great god in the Shetit!»

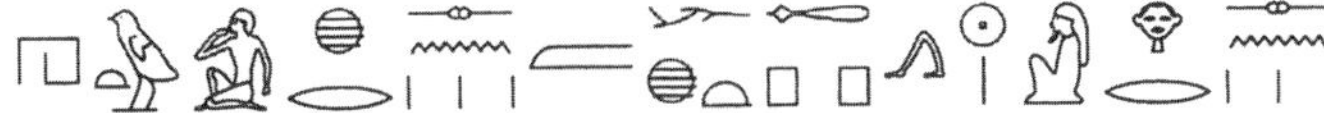

*hwtẖr.sn m-ḫt ʿpp rʿw ḥr.sn*

Then they wail after Re has passed them.

From the tomb of Pharaoh Ramses IV.

## Middle Register, 18th Scene

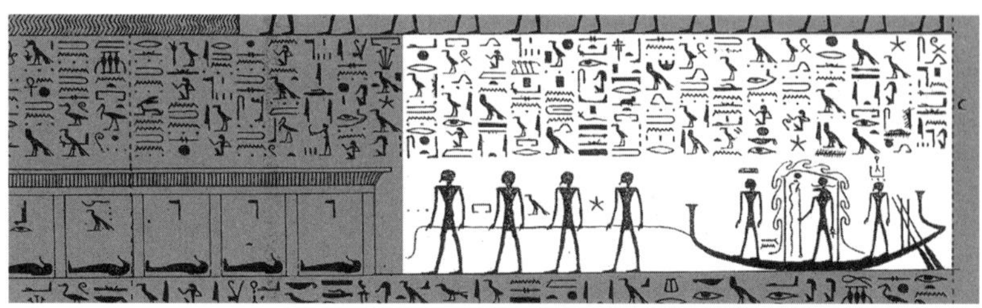

The sun barque, represented as usual and carrying the gods *sjꜣ* (Sia, percipience) and *ḥkꜣ* (Heka, magic) as well as *jwf rꜥw* (flesh of Re). It is pulled by four *dwꜣtyw* (gods of the Netherworld).The text reads:

*stꜣ nṯr pn ꜥꜣ jn nṯrw dwꜣtyw*

Towing of this great god by the gods of the Netherworld,

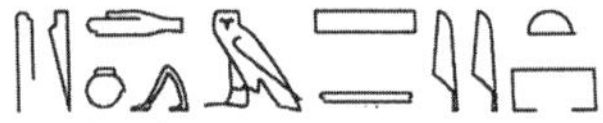

*sqdwt m štꜣyt*

sailing in the Shetit (Beyond)

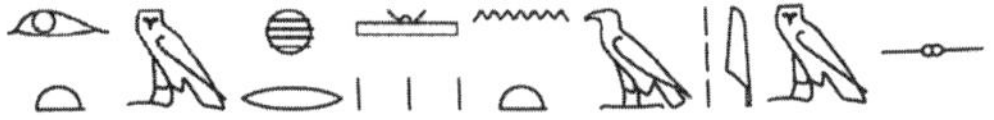

*jryt mḫrw ntyw jm.s*

caring for those who are in it.

(Re says:)

*sṯꜣw.ṯn.wj dwꜣtyw mꜣwn.j*

«Tow me, you of the Netherworld, whom I have viewed!

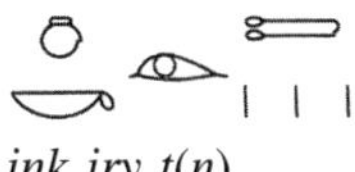

*jnk jry.ṯ(n)*

It is me who has created you!

*wdy ʿwj.ṯn sṯꜣw.ṯn.wj jm.sn*

Stretch your arms that you may pull me by means of them!

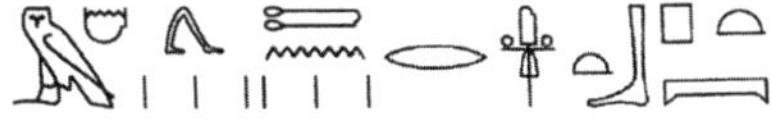

*ḥmw.ṯn r jꜣbt pt*

Turn away to the eastern side of heaven,

*r st wṯzt jry.sj*

to the place which raises its creator,

*ḏw pf sṯꜣ*

that mysterious mountain!

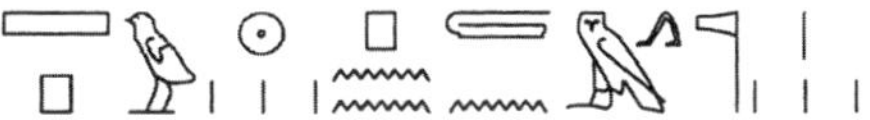

*špw pn n dbn(w) m nṯrw*

This light belongs to him who is surrounded by the gods.

*šzp.sn.wj pry.j*

They receive me when I go forth

*m tn m štꜣyt*

from this, from the Shetit (Beyond)

*sṯꜣw.wj jry.j mḫrw.ṯn*

Tow me, as I care for you,

*r sbḫt ḥꜣpt dwꜣtyw*

to the gate which hides those of the Netherworld.»

## 19TH SCENE

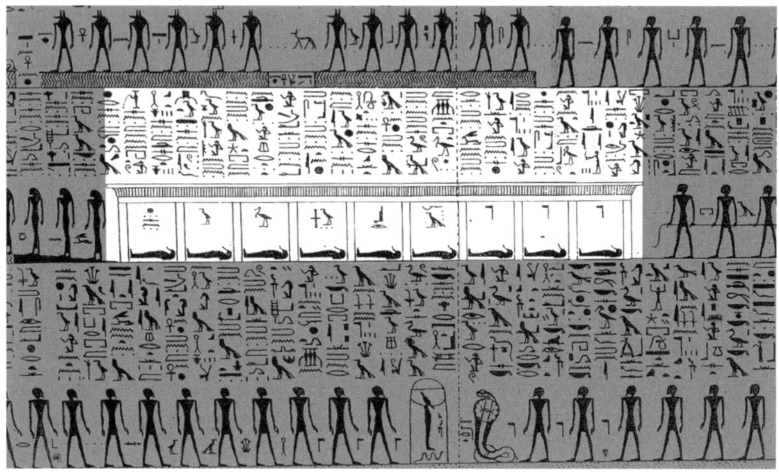

Nine mummies lying in shrines:

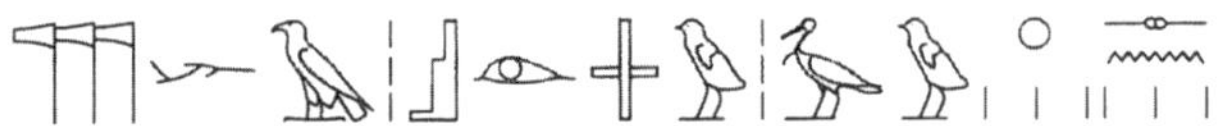

*nṯrw ḫtjw wsjr jmyw bꜣwt.sn*

"Gods (in) the following of Osiris who are in their cavities".

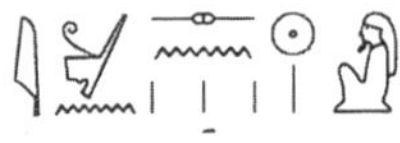

*jn n.sn rwʿ*

Ra says to them:

*mꜣn.j nṯrw*

«I have perceived the gods,

From the tomb of Pharaoh Seti I.

*jdyn.j ntyw m bꜣwt.sn*

I have applied force to those in their cavities.

*ṯzy.ṯn jr.ṯn nṯrw*

Raise yourself, gods!

*jw.j wḏ.j n.ṯn sẖrw.ṯn*

I care for you,

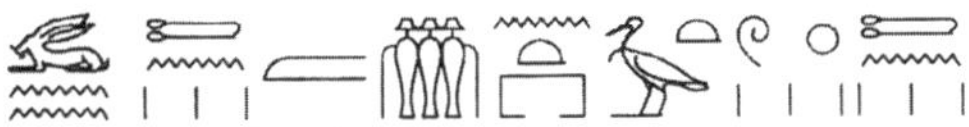

*wnn.ṯn m ẖnt bꜣwt.ṯn*

while you are in your cavities.

*n(t).ṯn zꜣꜣw bꜣw*

You are those who guard the *Ba*-souls,

*ꜥnḫ.ṯn m ḥwꜣt.sn*

you live on their rotting,

*srq.ṯn m jwtyw.sn*

you breathe through their putrefaction.

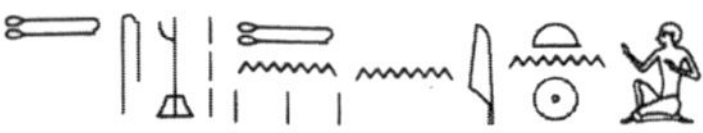

*ṯzy.ṯn n jtn.j*

Rise up with the help of my disc,

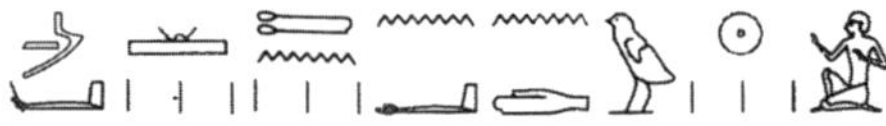

*mꜣꜥ.ṯn n ꜥnḏw.j*

stretch yourselves with the help of my splendor!

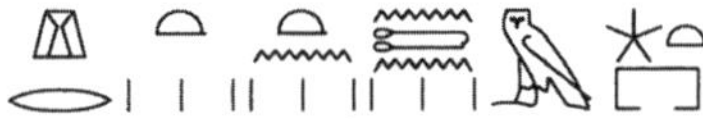

*ḫryt.ṯn n.ṯn m dwꜣt*

Your provision belongs to you in the Netherworld,

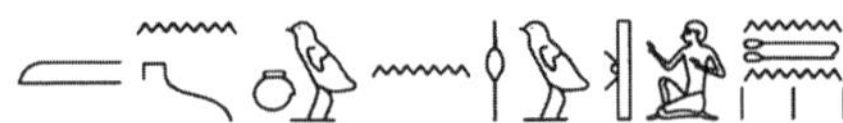

*m nw nj wḏ(n).j n.ṯn*

consisting of this which I have assigned to you.»

*ꜣwt.sn m jwf*

Their oblation is meat,

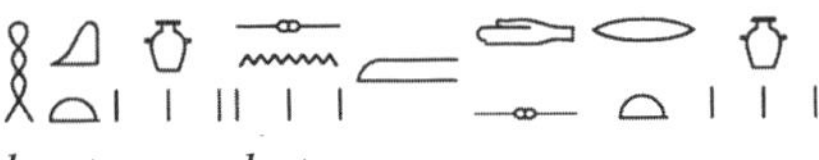

*ḥnqt.sn m ḏsrt*

their beer is Djeseret,

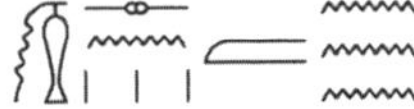

*qbḥw.sn m mw*

their refreshment is water.

*hwtẖr.sn*

Then they wail

*m-ẖt sḏm.sn hꜣꜣ ꜥꜣw.sn ḥr.sn*

after they hear their doors being closed upon them.

From the tomb of Pharaoh Horemheb.

## 20TH SCENE

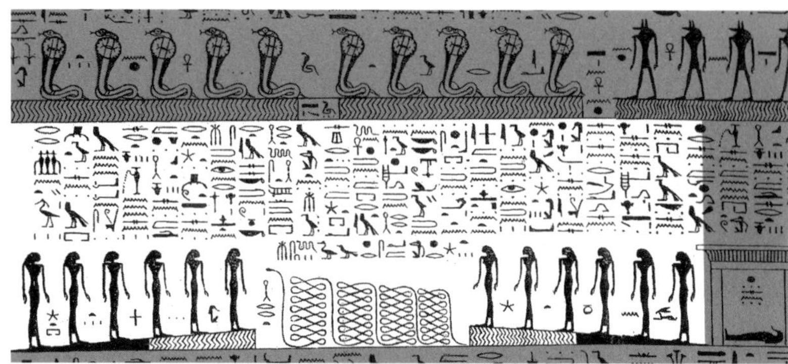

Twelve goddesses of the hours:

*wnwwt jmywt dwꜣt*

"The hours who are in the Duat".

*sn ꜥḥꜥw ḥr š.sn*

They are standing upon their lake,

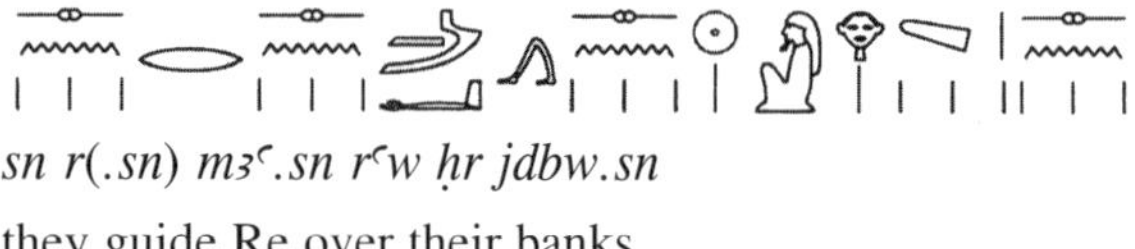

*sn r(.sn) mꜣꜥ.sn rꜥw ḥr jdbw.sn*

they guide Re over their banks.

Time as a serpent:

*(s)ḥrrt msy.(s) ḥfꜣw* 12

The removing one, she gives birth to twelve serpents,

From the tomb of Pharaoh Ramses I.

*ḥtmḫr.s ʿmḫr(.s) wnwt*

which she destroys and which she swallows afterwards, the hours.

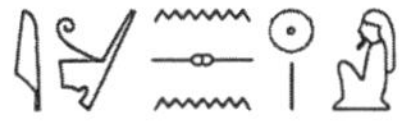

*jn n.sn rʿw*

Re says to them:

*sḏmw wnwwt ḏwyw n.ṯn*

«Hear, hours, what is cried out to you!

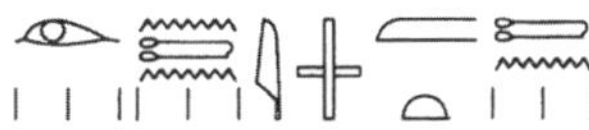

*jryn.ṯn jmyt.ṯn*

you have covered (the time) which you are,

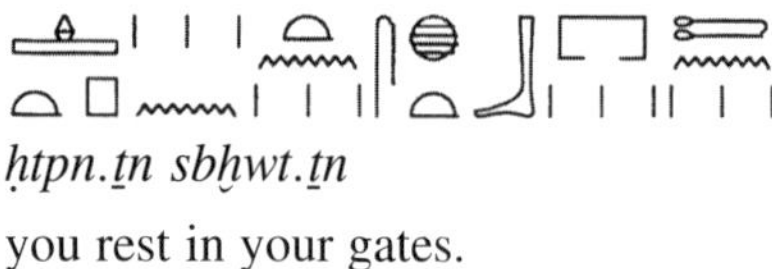

*ḥtpn.ṯn sbḫwt.ṯn*

you rest in your gates.

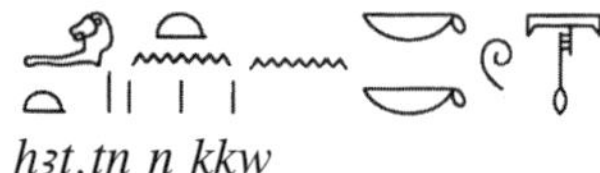

*ḥ3t.ṯn n kkw*

Your front belongs to darkness,

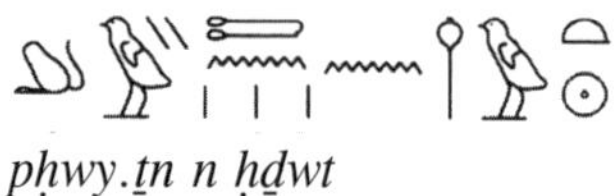

*pḥwy.ṯn n ḥḏwt*

your back to light.

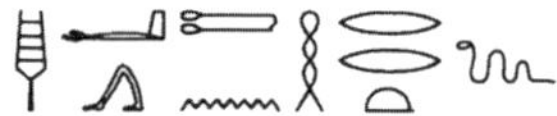

*ʿḥʿw.ṯn ḥrrt*

Your lifetime is "The one that takes away",

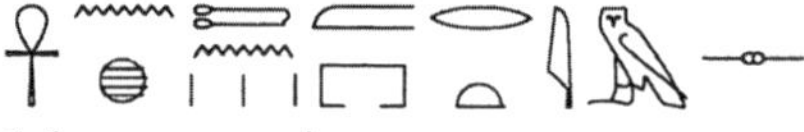

*ʿnḫ.ṯn m pryt jm.s*

you live upon that which comes forth from it.

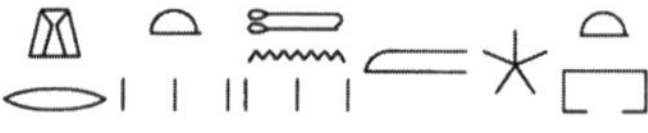

*ḫryt.ṯn m dw3t*

your provision is in the Netherworld.

*ʿm.ṯn msyw ḥrrt*

You swallow what "The Frightful one" has given birth to,

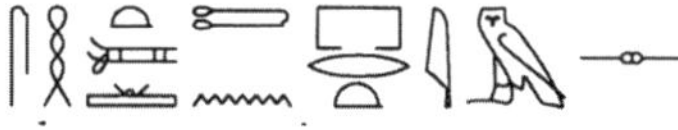

*sḥtm.ṯn pryt jm.s*

and destroy what comes out of it.

*sšm.ṯn.wj jnk msy.ṯn*

May you guide me, since I have given birth to you!

*jry n.j r nḏ-ḥr.j*

Act for me to greet me,

*ḥtp.ṯn r.ṯn wnwwt.j*

and so you will be content, my hours!»

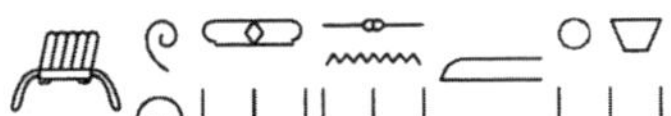

*ꜣwt.sn m tꜣ*

Their oblations are bread

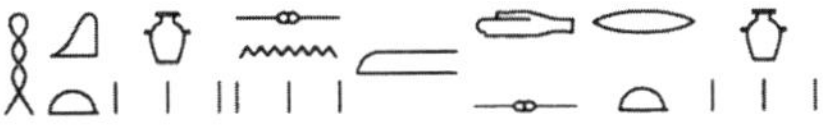

*ḥnqt.sn m ḏsrt*

their beer is Djeseret,

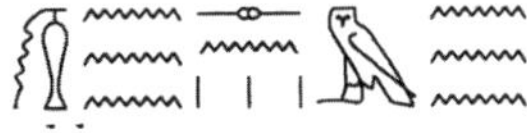

*qbḥw.sn m mw*

their refreshment is water,

*ddw n.sn ꜣwt.sn*

whoever offers to them their oblations

*m prrw ḫnty ꜣḫw*

is one who comes forth as the Foremost of the *Akh-spirits.*

From the tomb of Pharaoh Seti I.

## LOWER REGISTER, 21ST SCENE

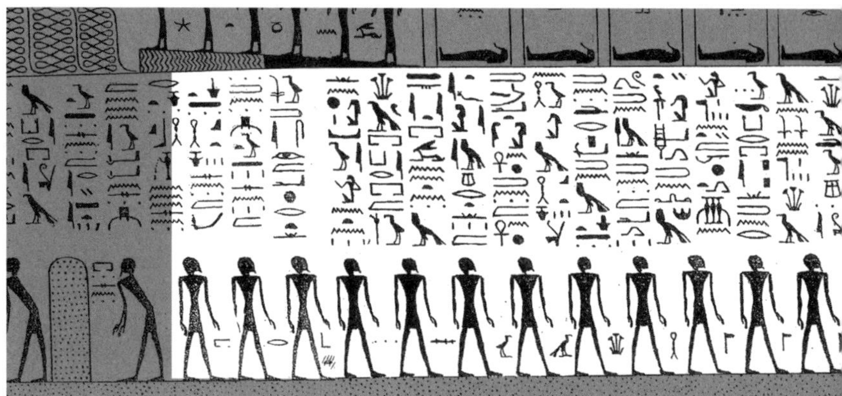

*ḥrw*

Horus

Eleven gods before the shrine of Osiris:

*nṯrw jryw sšd*

"Gods belonging to the headcloth".

Uraeus-serpent before Osiris:

*nsrt*

"Flaming one".

Osiris in the shrine, standing on a serpent:

*ḫnty-jmntyw*

Foremost of the Westerners.

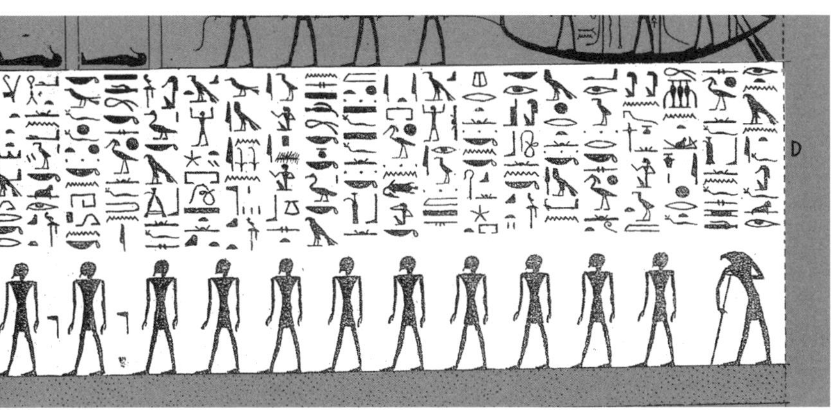

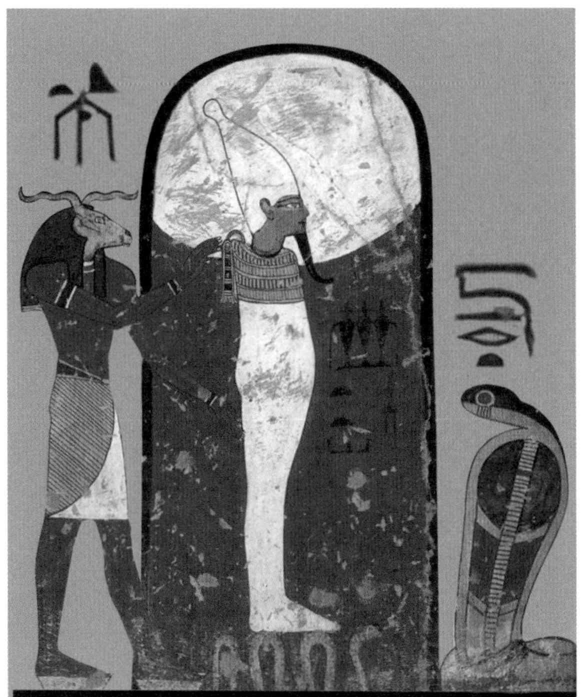

From the tomb of Pharaoh Ramses I.

Twelve gods behind the shrine (Text between the gods):

*nṯrw ḥ3w k3r*

"The gods who surround the shrine".

*jrytn ḥrw n jt.f wsjr*

What Horus has done for his father Osiris:

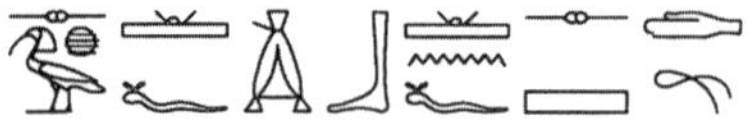

*s3ḫ.f ḏb3 n.f sšd*

To glorify him, to adorn him with his headcloth.

(Horus speaks:)

*ḫntj jb.j ḫr jt.j*

«My heart sails upstream to my father.

*m3ʿ jb.j jt.j*

My heart is honest, my father!

*nḏ.j.ṯw m-ʿ jryw r.k*

I protect you against those who have acted against you,

*s3ḫ.j.ṯw m ḫrt.k*

I glorify you with what belongs to you.

*sḫm n.k wsjr*

Power belongs to you, Osiris,

*bwꜣ n.k ḫntj-jmntyw*

Dignity belongs to you, Foremost of the Westerners.

*ḫryt.k n.k ḥqꜣ-dwꜣt*

Your provision belongs to you, Ruler of the Duat,

*qꜣw jrw m štꜣyt*

with high manifestation in the Shetit!

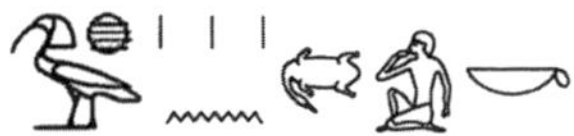

*ꜣḫw n snḏ.k*

The *Akh*-spirits are in fear of you,

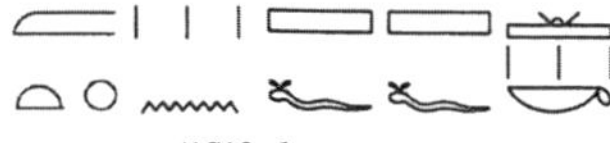

*mtyw n šfšft.k*

the dead are in awe of you.

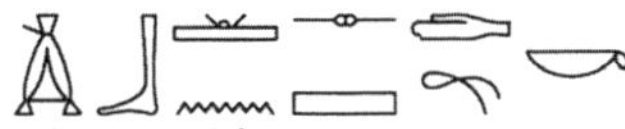

*ḏbꜣ n ssd.k*

Replacement be for your headcloth.

*jnk zꜣ.k ḥrw* *jw.j jp.j bgst jm*

I am your son Horus. I repair the damage in it.»

*jn nn nj nṯrw ḫnty jmntyw*

These gods of the Foremost of the Westerners say:

*qꜣy.tj dwꜣty*

«You are high, you of the Netherworld!

*wꜣš.tj ḫnty jmntyw*

you are strong, Foremost of the Westerners!

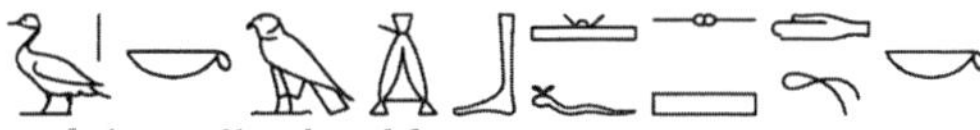

*zꜣ.k ḥrw ḏbꜣ.f sšd.k*

Your son Horus, he adorns you with your headcloth,

*sꜣḫ.f. ṯw njk.f ḫftyw.k*

he glorifies you and punishes your enemies.

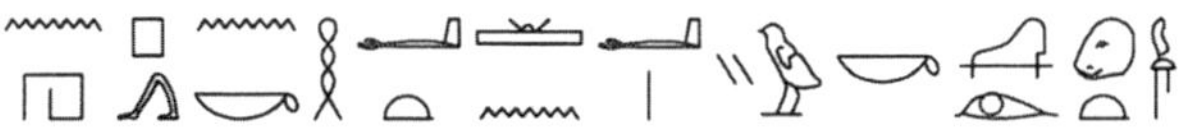

*nhp n.k ḥꜥwt ꜥwj.k wsjr ḫnty jmntyw*

Leap up, so that your arms rejoice, Osiris, Foremost of the Westerners!»

*jn ḫnty jmntyw*

The Foremost of the Westerners says:

*my rk r.j zꜣ.j ḥrw*

«Come to me, you my son Horus,

From the tomb of Pharaoh Ramses IV.

*nḏ.k.wj m-ʿ jrjw r.j*

that you may protect me from those who have acted against me!

*wḏ.k.sn n ḥry-ḥtmw*

You assign them to Him who is in charge of destruction—

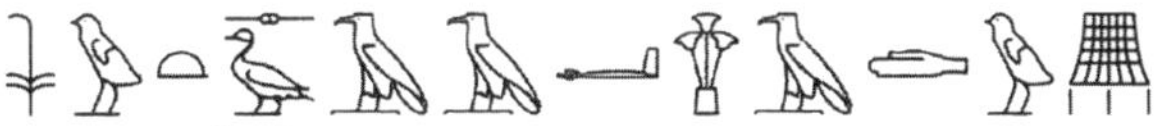

*swt zꜣꜣw ḥꜣdw*

it is he who guards the traps!»

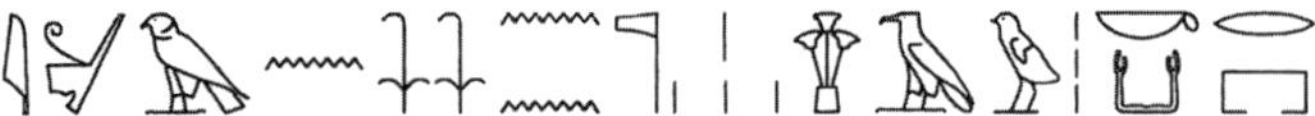

*jn ḥrw n nn nj nṯrw ḥ3w k3r*

Horus says to those gods who surround the shrine:

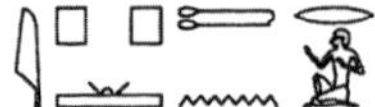

*jpp.ṯn r.j*

«You have been allotted to me,

*nṯrw ntyw m-ḫt ḫnty jmntyw*

gods who are in the retinue of the Foremost of the Westerners!

*ʿḥʿ.ṯn n ḥmw.ṯn sḫm.ṯn*

You stand up, you do not retreat, you are powerful!

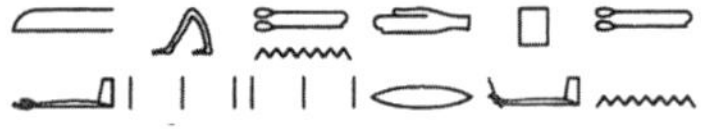

*my.ṯn drpw.ṯn*

Come, so that you are fed

*m t3 nj ḥw m ḥnqt nt m3ʿt*

with the bread of Hu and the beer of Maat!

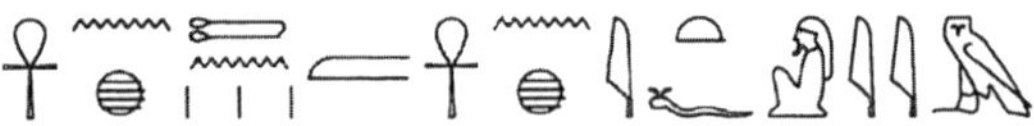

*ʿnḫ.ṯn m ʿnḫw jt.j jm*

You live upon what my father lives upon,

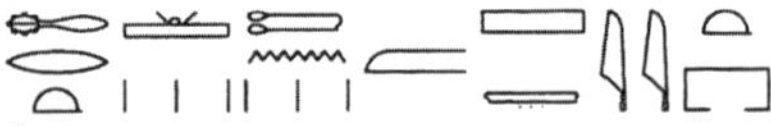

*ḫryt.ṯn m št3yt*

your provisions are in the Shetit.

*wnn.ṯn m ḥ3w k3r*

You are around the shrine,

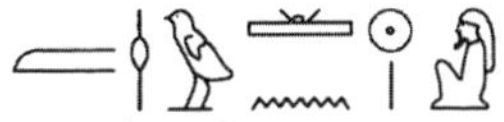

*m wḏ n rʿw*

by the order of Re.

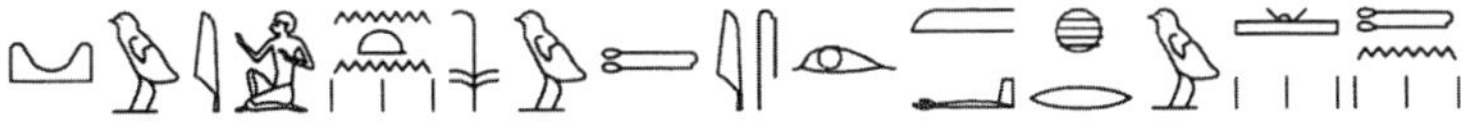

*ḏwy.j n.ṯn swt js jryw mḫrw.ṯn*

I call to you, but it is he who provides for you!»

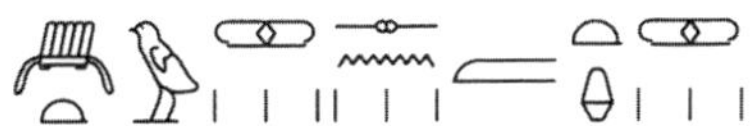

*3wt.sn m t3*

Their oblations are bread,

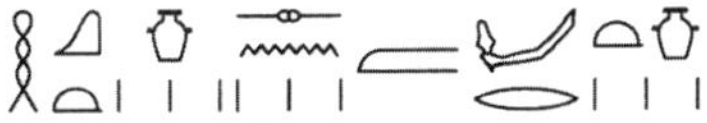

*ḥnqt.sn m ḏsrt*

their beer is Djeseret,

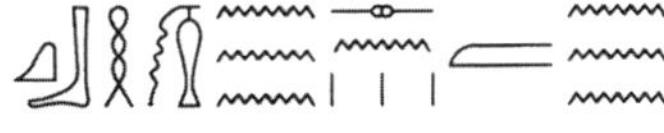

*qbḥw.sn m mw*

Their refreshment is water.

*jw ddw n.sn 3wt.sn*

Whoever offers to them their oblations

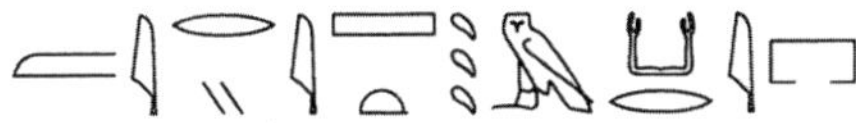

*m jrj jšt m k3r*

is entitled to meals in the shrine.

From the tomb of Pharaoh Seti I.

## 22ND SCENE

Four traps filled with red fire, and guarded by a demon.
They are named:

*ḥryw ḥ3dw.sn*
"Those who are over their traps".

A god at the end of the register, holding Ankh and Was, is named:

*ḥrj ḥtmw*
"Who is at the head of destruction".

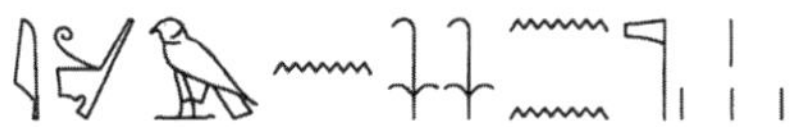

*jn ḥrw n nn nj nṯrw*
Horus says to these gods:

From the tomb of Pharaoh Seti I.

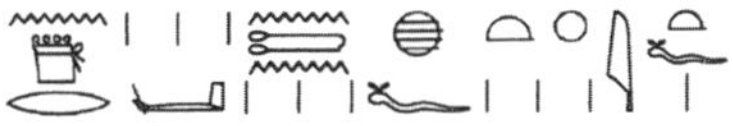

*nḏrw n.ṯn ḫftyw jt.j*

«Seize for you the enemies of my father,

*ḫn(p)wn.ṯn r ḥ3dw.ṯn*

whom you have dragged away to your traps

*ḥr nn mrw jrywn.sn*

on account of this pain they have inflicted

*r ꜥꜣ gmytw msy.wj*

against the Great One who has been found and who has given birth to me.

*ẖryt.ṯn n.ṯn m dwꜣt*

Your provisions belong to you in the Duat.

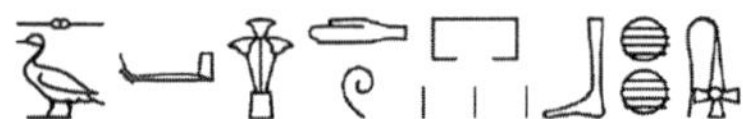

*zꜣw ḥꜣdw bḫ̮ḫ̮yw*

(to you who) guard the traps and the flames,

*m wḏwn rꜥw*

as Re has decreed.

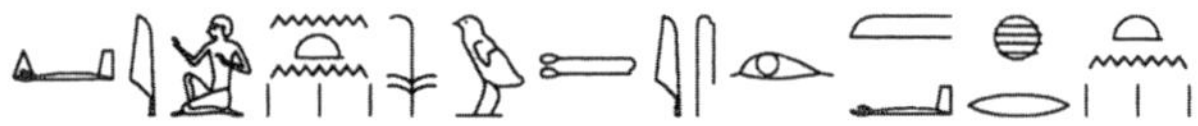

*ḏwy.j n.ṯn swt js jryw mḫrw.ṯn*

I call for you but it is He who provides for you.

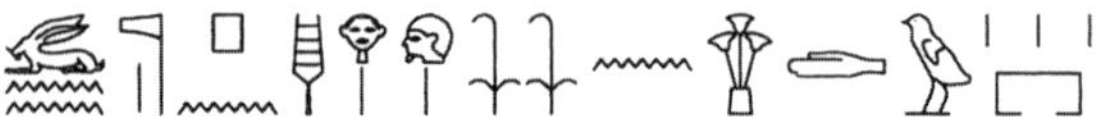

*wnn nṯr pn ꜥḥꜥw ḥr-tp nn nj ḥꜣdw*

This god pauses above these traps.

From the tomb of Pharaoh Ramses IV.

## Fourth Gate

From the tomb of Pharaoh Seti I.

Text in front of the door:

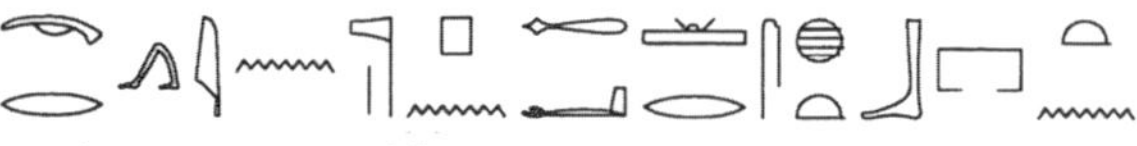

*spr jn nṯr pn ꜥꜣ r sbḫt tn*

This great god arrives at this gate,

*ꜥq m sbḫt tn*

entering into this gate.

*snsn nṯr pn ʿꜣ jn nṯrw jmyw.s*

This great god is acclaimed by the gods who are in it.

Name of the gate:

*jryt*

"Who does (her) duty".

Above the two Uraeus-serpents on the wall:

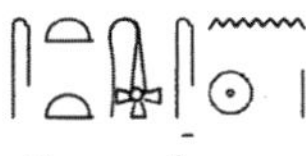

*stt.s n rʿw*

"She lights up for Re".

The first guardian:

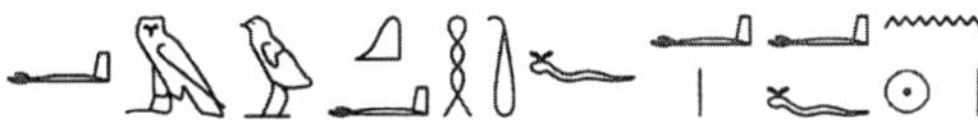

*ʿmw qʿḥ.f ʿwy.f(j) n rʿw*

"The devourer". He bends his arms for Re.

The second guardian:

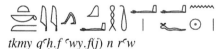

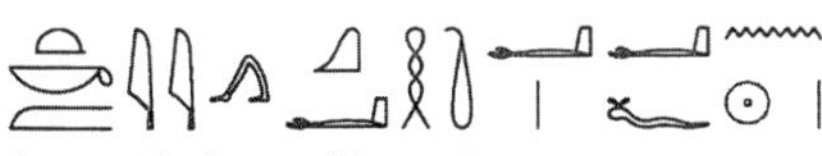

*tkmy qʿḥ.f ʿwy.f(j) n rʿw*

"Who draws near". He bends his arms for Re.

Nine mummies:

*psḏt* 4 *nwt*

"The fourth Ennead".

Text in front of the Ennead:

*wnw ꜥꜣw.n znw sbḫwt.n n rꜥw-ḥrw-ꜣḫty*

Open are our doors, open our gates for Re-Horakhty.

*jhy rꜥw my rk r.n*

Hail to you, Re. Come to us.

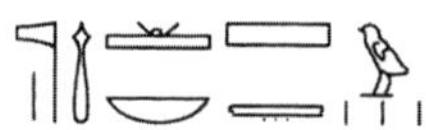

*nṯr ꜥꜣ nb štꜣw*

Great God, Master of mysteries!

The serpent upon the doorway:

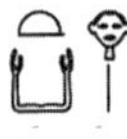

*tkꜣ-ḥr*

"With fiery face".

*wnn.f ḥr ꜥꜣ pn*

He is upon this door,

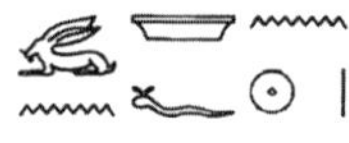

*wn.f n rꜥw*

he opens for Re.

*sjꜣ n tkꜣ-ḥr*

Sia (says) to him "with fiery face":

*wn sbꜣ.k n rꜥw*

«Open your gate for Re,

*zn ꜥꜣ.k n ꜣḫty*

unlock your door for Akhty!»

*jw.f sḥḏ.f kkw zmꜣw*

He illuminates the Primeval Darkness,

*dj.f šsp m ꜥt jmnt*

he throws light into the Hidden Region!

*ḫtmjn ꜥꜣ pn*

Then this door is closed,

*m-ḫt ꜥq nṯr pn ꜥꜣ*

after this great god has entered.

*hwtḫr jmyw sbḫt.tn*

Then those in this gate wail

*sḏm.sn hꜣꜣ ꜥꜣ pn*

when they hear this door being slammed.

# FIFTH

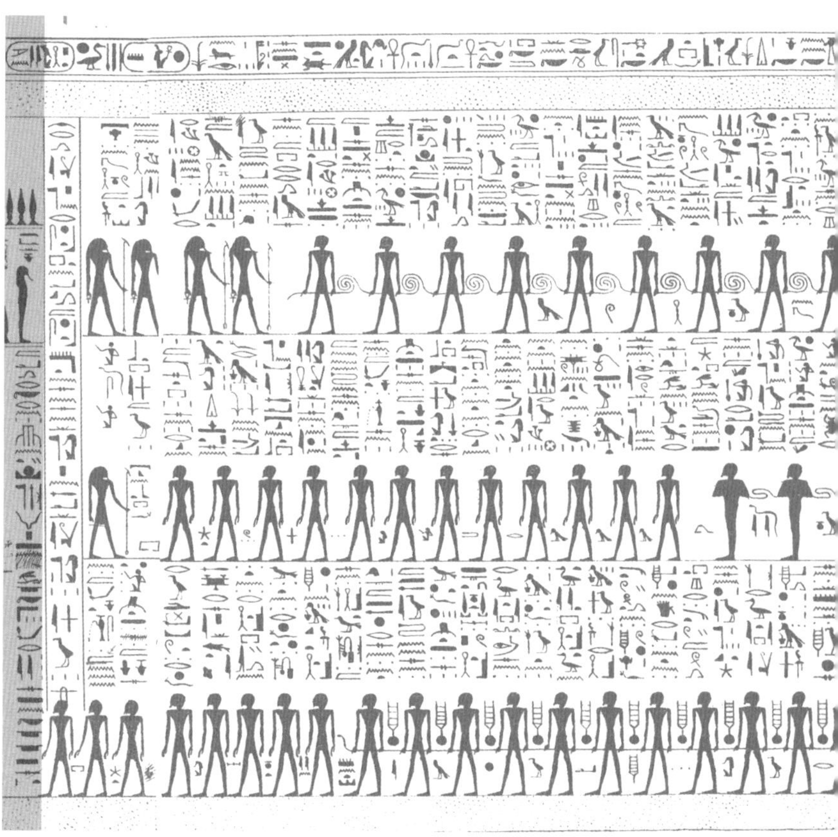

# Hour

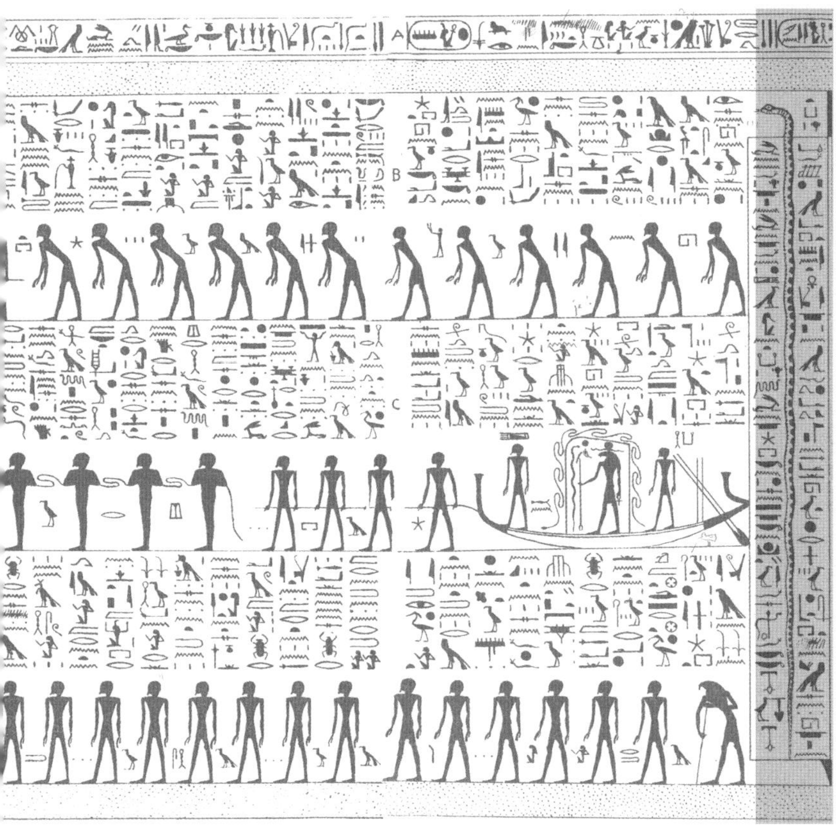

# Part of the Fifth Hour

# FROM THE TOMB OF SETI I

## 23RD SCENE

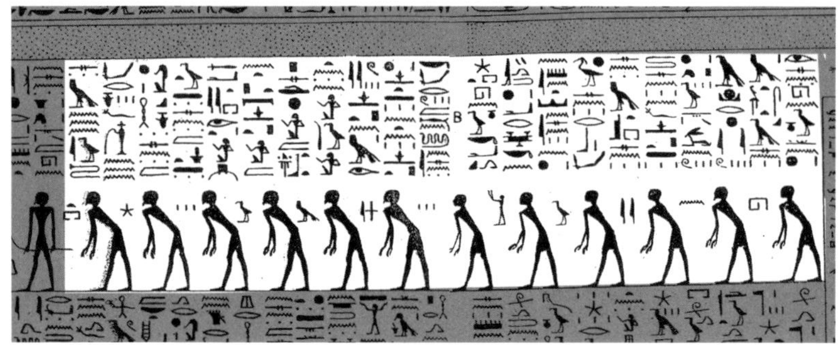

Twelve blessed spirits who are named (written between them):

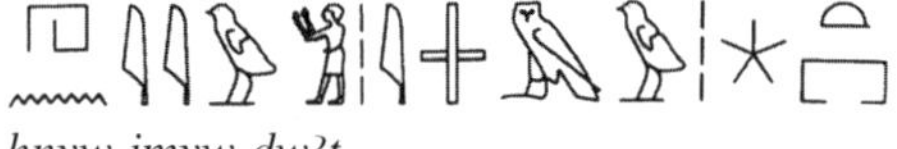

*hnyw jmyw dwꜣt*

"Acclaiming ones who are in the Duat".

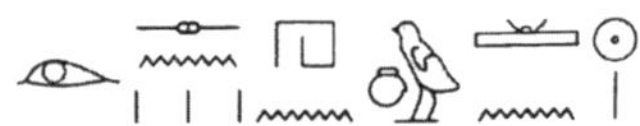

*jry.sn hnw n rʿw*

They make jubilation for Re

*m jmntt sqꜣy.sn ḥrw-ꜣḫty*

in the West, they celebrate Horakhty –

*rḫyw rʿw tpyw tꜣ*

(those) who have known Re (already) on earth,

From the tomb of Pharaoh Ramses IV.

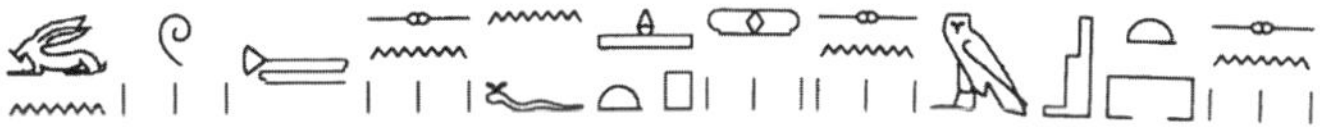

*wnw wdn.sn n.f ḥtpw.sn m st.sn*

who have presented their offerings wherever they were,

*ꜣḫw.sn r bw ḏsr nj jmnt*

their *Akh*-spirits are (now) in the protected place of the West.

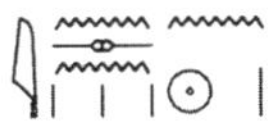

*jn.sn n rꜥw*

They say to Re:

*jy.tj rꜥw jꜥr.k n dwꜣt*

«Welcome, Re, when you approach the Duat!

*hnw n.k ꜥq.k ḏsrw m mḥn*

Jubilation to you when you enter the protection in Mehen!»

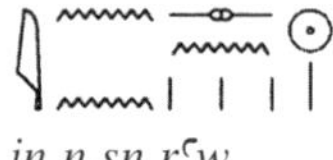

*jn n.sn rꜥw*

Re says to them:

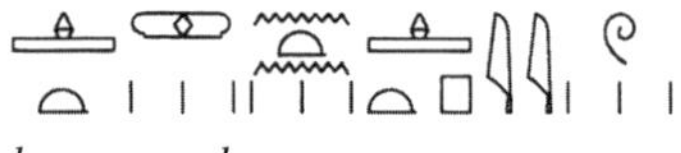

*ḥtpw n.ṯn ḥtpyw*

«Offerings are for you, offerers!

*ḥtpn.j m jrytn.ṯn n.j*

I was content with what you have done for me,

*ty.wj psḏ.j m jꜣbtt nt pt*

when I rose in splendour in the East of the sky,

*ḥtp.j m ꜥꜣyt jrt.j*

and when I set in the sanctuary of my eye.»

*ꜣwt.sn m ḥtpw rꜥw*

Their oblations are the offerings of Re,

*ḥnqt.sn m ḏsrt.f*

their beer is his Djeseret,

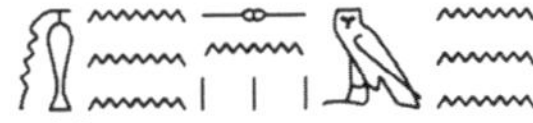

*qbḥw.sn m mw*

their refreshment is water.

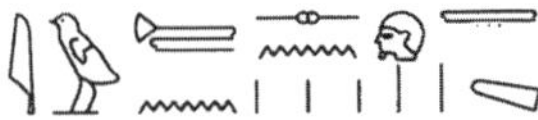

*jw wdnw n.sn tp tꜣ*

Whoever makes an offering to them on earth

*m hnyw ḫr rꜥw m jmnt*

is one who will be acclaimed with Re in the West.

From the tomb of Pharaoh Seti I.

## 24TH SCENE

Twelve gods carrying a measuring rope:

*ẖryw nwḥ m sḫwt dw3t*

"Those who carry the (measuring-)rope in the fields of the Duat".

(Re speaks:)

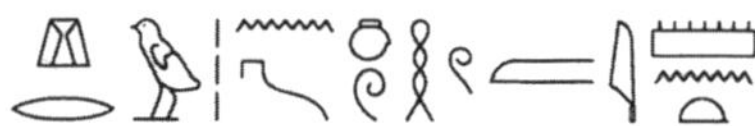

*ẖryw nwḥ m jmnt*

«You who carry the rope in the West,

*sšmyw 3ḥwt n 3ḫw*

who allocate plots to the blessed *Akh*-spirits,

*šzp n.ṯn nwḥ*

do receive for yourself the rope,

From the tomb of Pharaoh Seti I.

*nḏr n.ṯn sṯꜣyw ꜣḥt nj jmntyw*

seize hold of the measurer of those of the West!

*ꜣẖw.sn r nswt.ṯn*

Their *Akh*-spirits (stand) at your thrones,

*nṯrw r swt.ṯn*

the gods at your seats.

*ꜣẖw nṯry m ḥtp*

The *Akh*-spirits of the Divine (Osiris) are content,

*sẖt-ꜣẖ jptw m jmy-nwḥ*

the *Akh*-field is measured by what is in the rope.

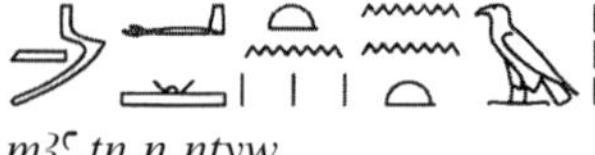

*m3ʿ.ṯn n ntyw*

You are right for those who exist,

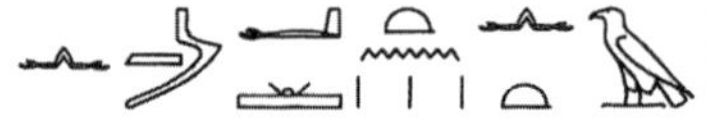

*nn m3ʿ.ṯn (n) jwtyw*

you are not right for those who do not exist!»

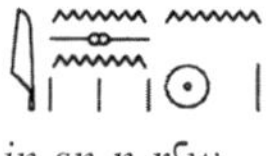

*jn.sn n rʿw*

They say to Re:

*m3ʿ nwḥ m jmnt*

«Stretched is the rope in the West.

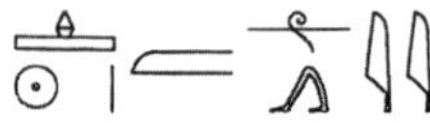

*ḥtp rʿw m sṯ3y*

Re is satisfied with the outstretched one.

*ẖryt.(n) n.ṯn nṯrw*

Your provisions belong to you, gods,

*psšwt.ṯn n.ṯn 3ḫw*

Your shares belong to you, *Akh*-spirits!

*m.ṯn rʿw jry.f 3ḥwt.ṯn*

Lo, Re creates your plots,

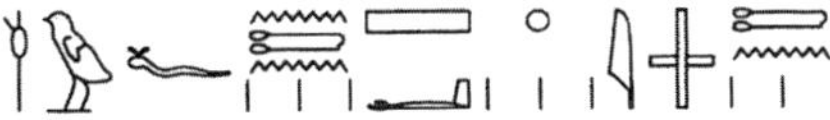

*wḏ.f n.ṯn šꜥw jmy.ṯn*

he assigns to you the estate in which you are.

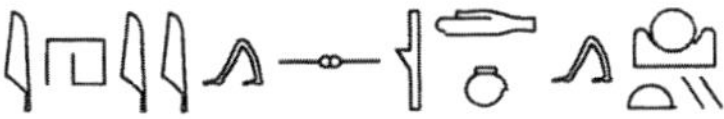

*jhy sqdw ꜣḫtj*

Hail to you, Moving one, Akhty!

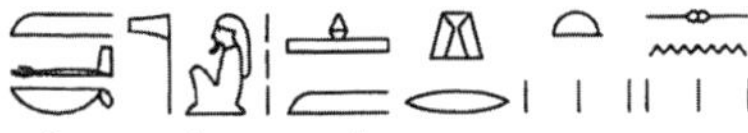

*mk nṯrw ḥtpw m ḫryt.sn*

Look, the gods are content with their provision,

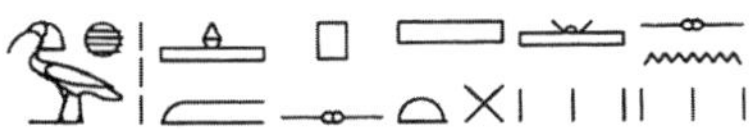

*ꜣḫw ḥtpw m psšwt.sn*

The *Akh*-spirits are content with their allotments!»

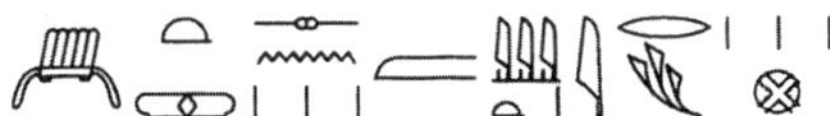

*ꜣwt.sn m sḫt-jꜣrw*

Their oblations are in the Field of Rushes,

*ḥtpw.sn m prrt jm.s*

their offering is that which comes forth from it.

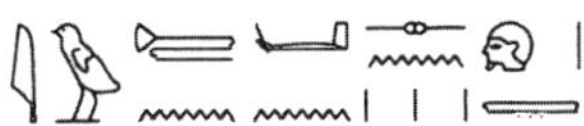

*jw wdnw n.sn tp tꜣ*

Whoever makes an offering to them on earth

*m ꜣḥt tn sḫt-jꜣrw*

(will be) on this ground, the Field of Rushes.

## 25TH SCENE

Four gods carrying Ankh and Was in their hands.

*ḥryw nwḥ m jmntt*

"Those who supervise the (measuring-)rope in the West".

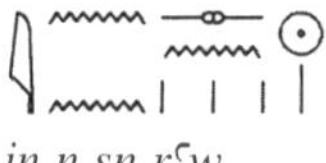

*jn n.sn rʿw*

Re says to them:

*ḏsrw n.ṯn ḥnbyw*

«Protection for you, land-measurers,

*ḥryw nwḥ m jmntt*

who supervise the (measuring-)rope in the West!

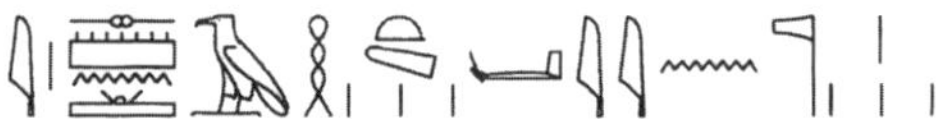

*j smn 3ḥt dyw n nṯrw*

O, confirm the allotment that has been given to the gods,

From the tomb of Pharaoh Seti II.

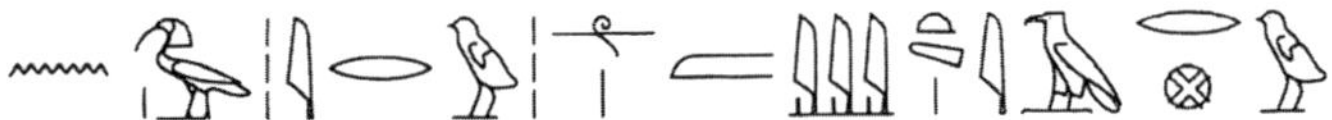

*n ꜣḫw jryw sṯꜣ m sḫt-jꜣrw*

and to the *Akh*-spirits who participate in measuring in the Field of Rushes!»

*ntsn ddw ꜣḥwt šꜥw*

They are those who distribute fields and estates

*n nṯrw ꜣḫw jmyw dwꜣt*

to the deities and the *Akh*-spirits who are in the Duat.

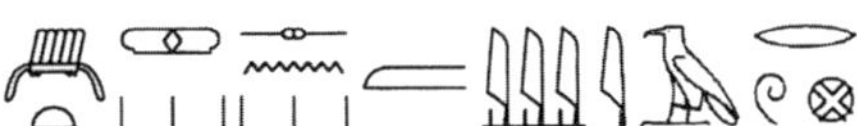

*ꜣwt.sn m sḫt-jꜣrw*

Their oblations are in the Field of Rushes,

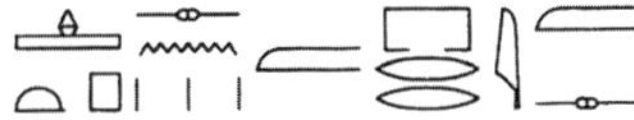

*ḥtpw.sn m prrw jm.s*

their offering is what comes forth from it.

## Middle Register

### 26th Scene

In the sun barque:

*sjꜣ mḥn jwf-rꜥw ḥkꜣ*

Sia, Mehen, flesh of Re, Heka

Four towing gods or deceased ones:

*dwꜣtyw*

"Those belonging to the Netherworld".

*sṯꜣw nṯr pn ꜥꜣ jn nṯrw dwꜣtyw*

Towed is this great god by the gods of the Duat,

*sqdwt m štꜣyt*

travelling in the Shetit.

(Re speaks:)

*sṯ3.ṯn n.j dw3tyw*

«Tow for me, you from the Duat,

*hnw.ṯn n.j ḫntyw sb3w*

make ovation for me, you in the gates!

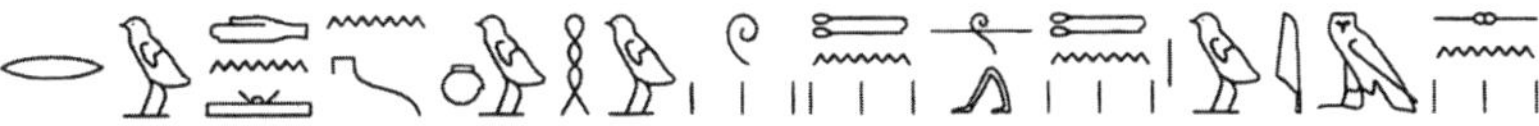

*rwḏn nwḥw.ṯn sṯ3.ṯn.wj jm.sn*

May your ropes be strong, that you tow me with them.

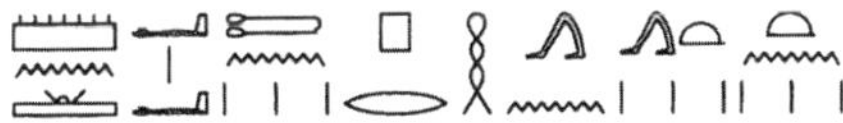

*mn ʿwy.ṯn pḥrn nmtt.ṯn*

May your arms be firm, may your steps be fast!

*3ḫ n b3w.ṯn*

May your *Ba*-souls be glorified,

*w3š n jbw.ṯn*

and your hearts be strong,

*wn.ṯn w3t nfrt r qrrwt št3(wt) ḫrt*

so that you open the perfect path to the caverns with secret content.»

## 27TH SCENE

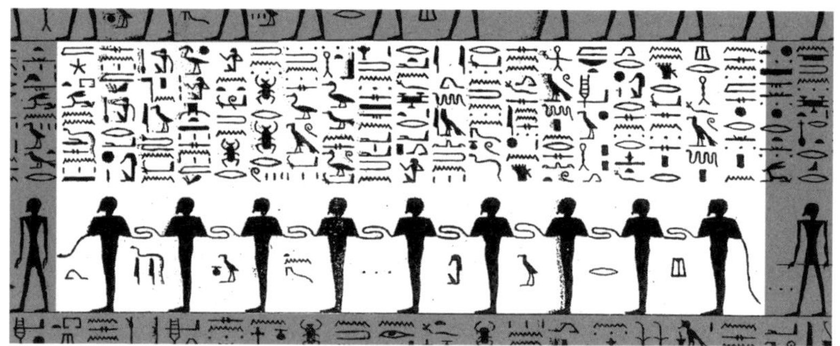

Nine gods with 'hidden' arms carrying a serpent:

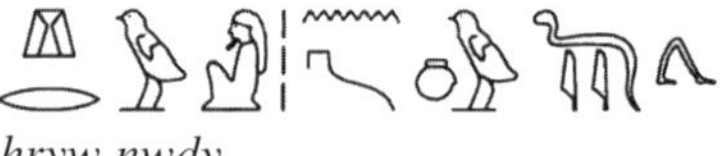

*ḫryw nwḏy*

"Those who carry 'The trembling one' (serpent)".

*wnn.sn m sḫr pn ḫr ḥfꜣw pn*

They are in this way carrying this serpent,

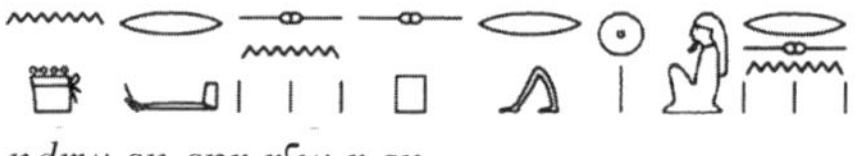

*nḏrw.sn spr rꜥw r.sn*

which they retain when Re reaches them,

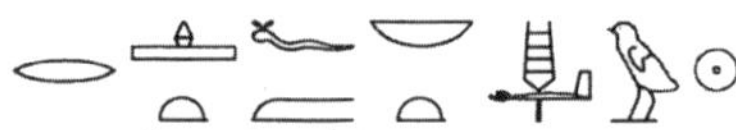

*r ḥtp.f m nbt-ꜥḥꜥw*

to rest in the (gate) "Mistress of Lifetime".

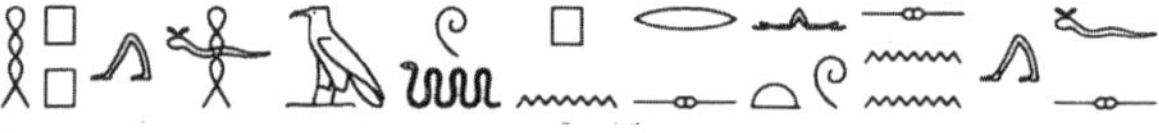

*ḥpp ḥfꜣw pn r.s jwty snn.f.sj*

This serpent is held back from it without being able to pass it.

From the tomb of Pharaoh Merenptah.

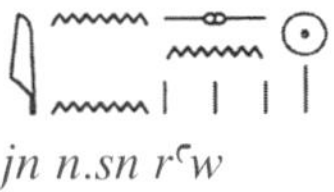

*jn n.sn rʿw*

Re says to them:

*nḏrw n.ṯn nwḏy*

«Detain for you "The recoiling one",

*jm.ṯn rdyt n.f w3t r ʿp.j ḥr.ṯn*

do not set him free, until I have passed you!

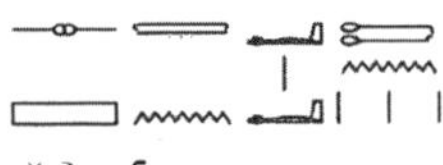

*sšt3 n ʿwy.ṯn*

Hiding be for your arms.»

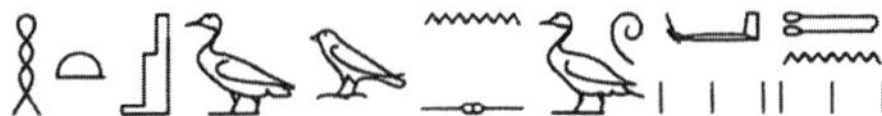

*ḥtm n z3w.ṯn*

Destruction for him whom you guard!

*z3w.ṯn ḫpr ḫprw.j*

You guard so that my manifestation can change,

*nṯt.ṯn ḫpr 3ḫw.j*

you fetter so that my magic power can manifest (itself)!»

From the tomb of Pharoh Seti I.

*ꜣwt.sn m sḏm ḫrw nṯr pn*

Their oblations consist in hearing the voice of this god.

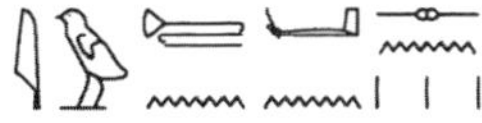

*jw wdnw n.sn*

Whoever makes an offering to them,

*m sḏmw ḫrw rꜥw m dwꜣt*

he will hear the voice of Re in the Duat.

From the corridor to the Osireion in Abydos.

## 28TH SCENE

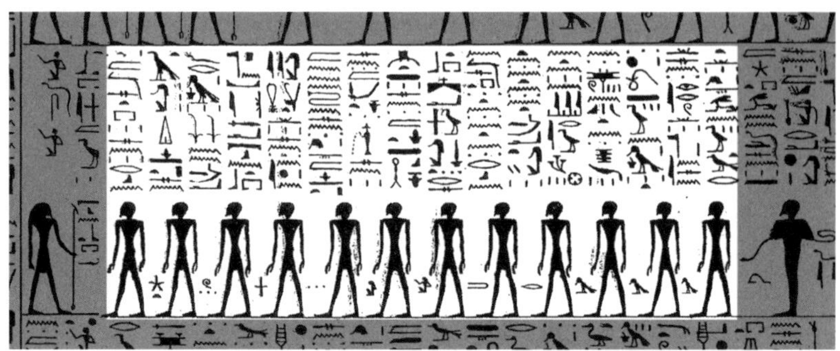

Twelve *Ba*-souls in human form:

*b3w rmṯw jmyw dw3t*

"The *Ba*-souls of human beings who are in the Duat".

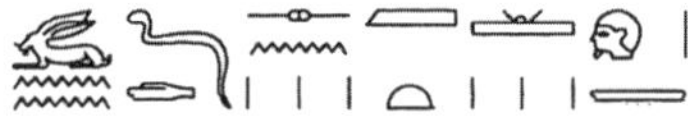

*wnw ḏd.sn m3ʿt tp t3*

Those who have spoken Maat on earth,

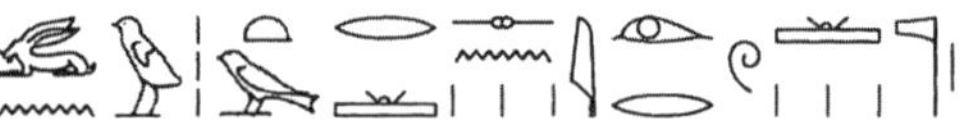

*wnw twr.sn jrw nṯr*

who have respected the essence of the god.

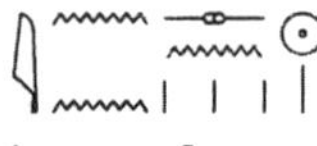

*jn n.sn rʿw*

Re says to them:

From the tomb of Pharaoh Seti II.

*w3š n b3w.ṯn*

«Strength for your *Ba*-souls,

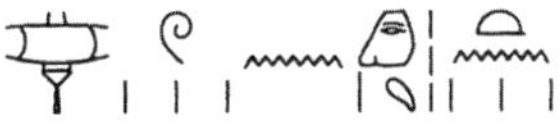

*ṯ3w n fnḏw.ṯn*

breath for your noses!

*š<sup>c</sup>w n.ṯn nj sḫt-j3rw*

estates belong to you from the Field of Rushes.

*ṯn n.ṯn ntyw m3<sup>c</sup>tyw*

For you are the truthful ones,

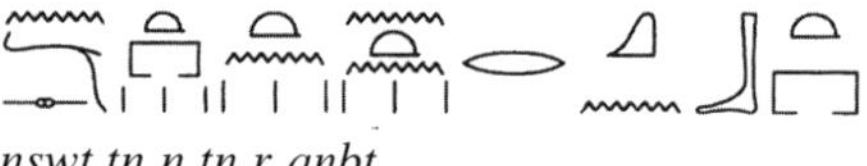

*nswt.ṯn n.ṯn r qnbt*

your thrones belong to you at the court,

*wḏʿwt jmyw.j mdw r.s*

in which those, among whom I am, pronounce judgement.»

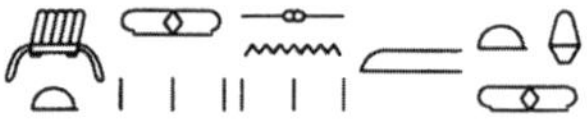

*ꜣwt.sn m tꜣ*

Their oblations are bread,

*ḥnqt.sn m ḏsrt*

their beer is Djeseret,

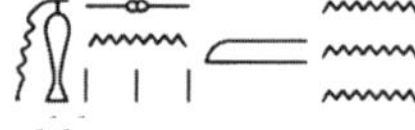

*qbḥw.sn m mw*

their refreshment is water.

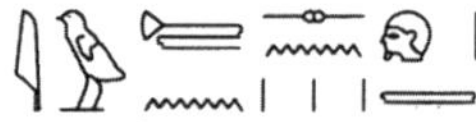

*jw wdnw n.sn tp tꜣ*

Whoever makes an offering to them on earth

*m ḥtpy (m) mjnt.sn*

is one who is content (with) their daily rations.

## 29TH SCENE

From the tomb of Pharaoh Seti II.

At the end of the register, a single god confronts the *Ba*-souls, holding Ankh and Was in his hands:

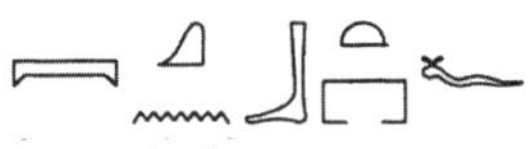

*ḥry qnbt.f*

"Who presides his law court".

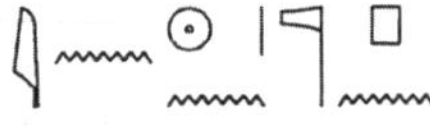

*jn rʿw n nṯr pn*

Re says to this god:

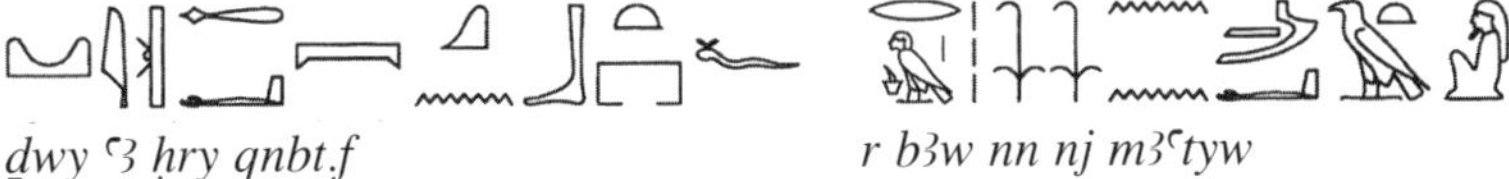

*ḏwy ʿ3 ḥry qnbt.f* *r b3w nn nj m3ʿtyw*

«Call, Great one who presides his law court, to the *Ba*-souls of these truthful ones!

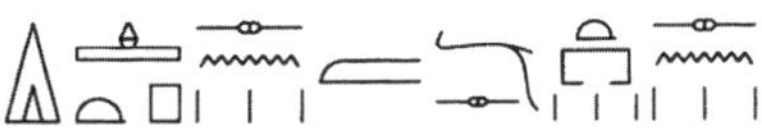

*dy ḥtp.sn m nswt.sn*

Let them rest upon their thrones

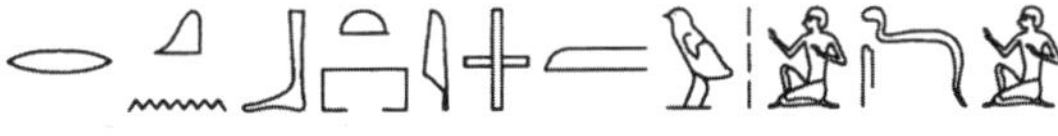

*r qnbt jmyw.j ḏs.j*

at the law court in which I am myself!»

## Lower Register, 30th Scene

Horus, falcon-headed and leaning on a staff, is standing in front of four representatives of each of the four human races.

*ḥrw*

Horus

*rmṯw*

The Egyptians:

*nḥsyw*

The Nubians:

*ꜥꜣmw*

The Asiatics (Syrians):

*ṯmḥw*

The Libyans:

From the tomb of Pharaoh Seti I, 1820.

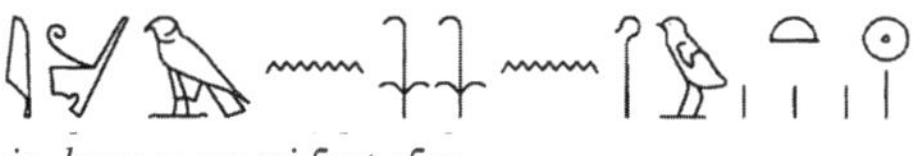

*jn ḥrw n nn nj ꜥwt rꜥw*

Horus says to this cattle of Re,

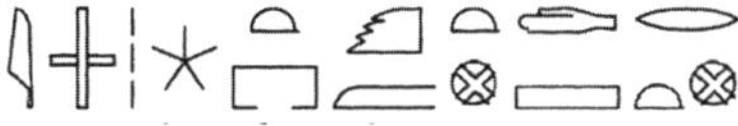

*jmyw dwꜣt kmt dšrt*

which are in the Duat, in Egypt and in the Desert:

*ꜣḫw n.ṯn ꜥwt rꜥw*

«Transfiguration to you, cattle of Re,

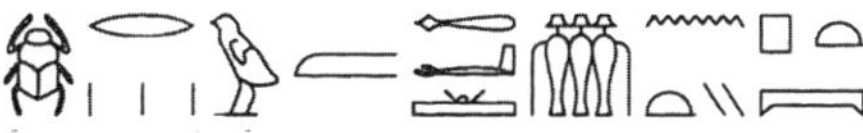

*ḫprw m ꜥꜣ ḫnty pt*

which came into being through the Great one who is in heaven!

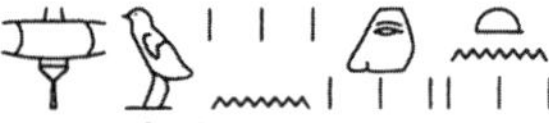

*ṯ3w n fnḏw.ṯn*

Breath for your noses,

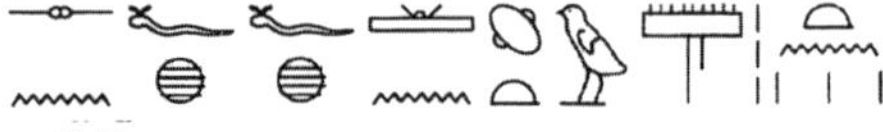

*snfḫfḫ n wtw.ṯn*

loosening for your mummy-wrappings!

*ntṯn rmyt 3ḫt.j*

Your are the tears of my Brilliant Eye

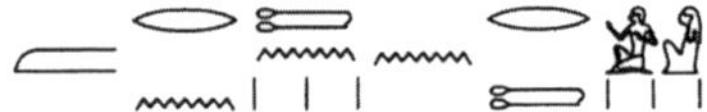

*m rn.ṯn nj rmṯw*

in your name of "human beings".

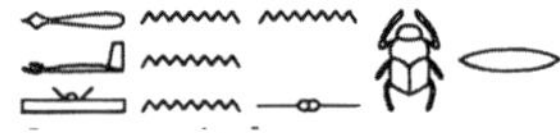

*ʿ3 mw n sḫpr*

Great is the water of him who created,

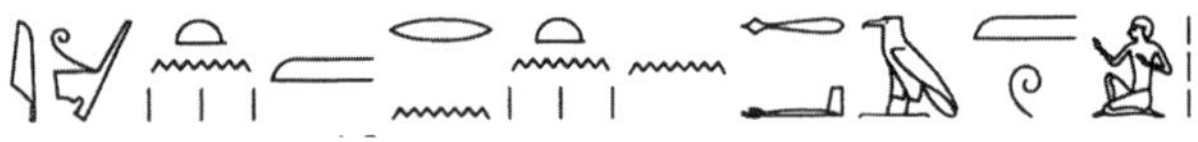

*jn.ṯn m rn.ṯn nj ʿ3mw*

you say in your name of 'Syrians'.

*ḫpr n.sn sḫmt nts nḏt b3w.sn*

For them Sakhmet came into existence, she protects their *Ba*-souls.

*ntṯn nn ḥwyn.j r.sn*

You are these against whom I struck,

From the tomb of Pharaoh Seti I, 1820.

From the tomb of Pharaoh Seti I, 2005.

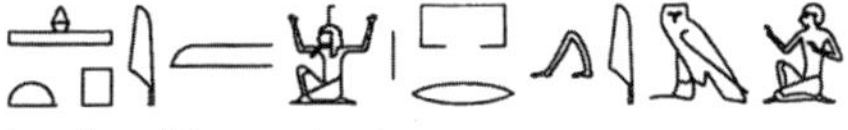

*ḥtp.j m ḥḥ pry jm.j*

I am content with the million who came forth from me,

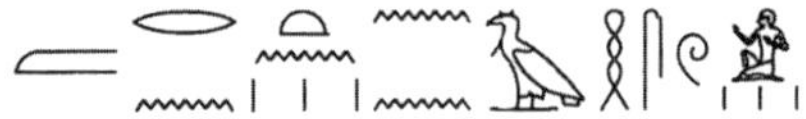

*m rn.ṯn nj nḥsyw*

in your name of 'Nubians'.

*ḫpr n.sn n ḥrw ntf nḏ b3w.sn*

They came into existence for Horus, and he protects their *Ba*-souls.

*ḥḥyn.j jrt.j ḫprn.ṯn*

I searched for my eye when you came into existence,

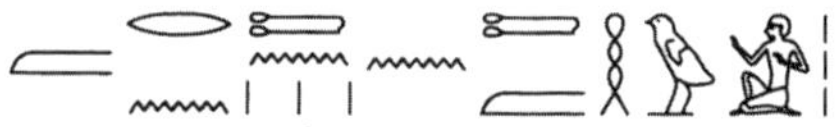

*m rn.ṯn nj ṯmḥw*

in your name of 'Libyans'.

*ḫpr n.sn sḫmt nt(s) nḏt b3w.sn*

For them Sakhmet came into existence, she protects their *Ba*-souls.»

From the tomb of Pharaoh Merenptah, one Syrian and one Nubian.

## 31ST SCENE

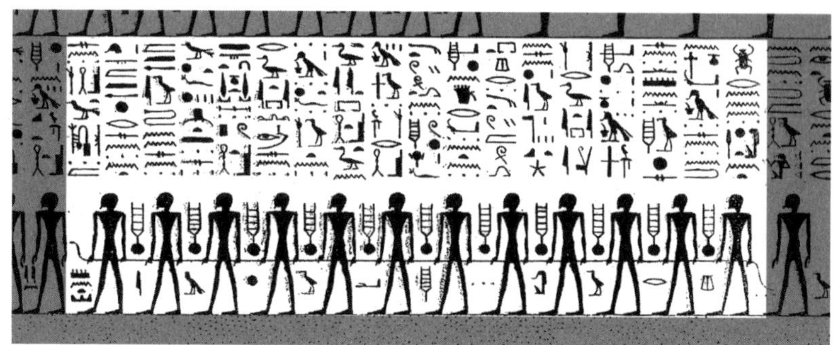

Twelve gods are carrying the serpent of time, adorned with hieroglyphs for "lifetime".

*ẖryw ꜥḥꜥw m jmnt*

"Those who carry the lifetime in the West".

*ntsn smnw ꜥḥꜥw sꜥḥꜥ hrww*

They are those who establish the lifetime and fix the days

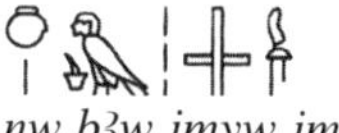

*nw bꜣw jmyw jmnt*

of the *Ba*-souls who are in the West,

*wḏw r ḥtmyt*

and (those who are) condemned to the Place of Destruction.

From the tomb of Pharoh Seti I.

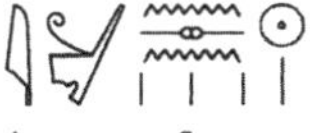

*jn n.sn rʿw*

Re says to them:

*j nṯrw ḫntyw dwꜣt*

«O gods who are in the Duat

*ḫryw mtwj m sṯꜣ ʿḥʿw*

who carry the double rope which measures lifetime –

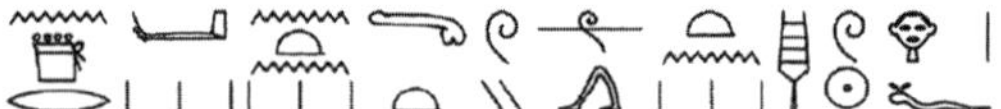

*nḏr n.ṯn mtwj sṯ3.ṯn ꜥḥꜥw ḥr.f*

may you grasp the double rope and measure the lifetime on it

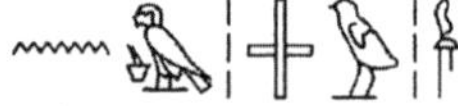

*n b3w jmyw jmnt*

for the *Ba*-souls who are in the West,

*wḏw r ḥtmyt*

and (for those who are) condemned to the Place of Destruction!

*ḥtm.ṯn b3w ḫftyw.j*

May you extinguish the *Ba*-souls of my enemies,

*wḏw.ṯn r ḥtmyt*

whom you have assigned to the Place of Destruction

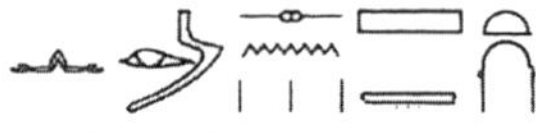

*n m33.sn št3yt*

so that they do not see the Shetit!

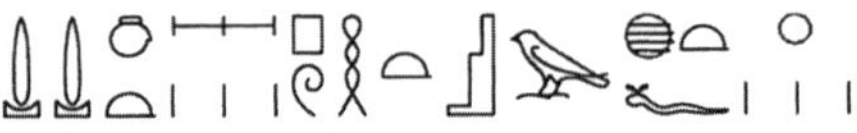

*ḏ3ḏ3t pw ḥtmw ḫftyw*

It is the council which destroys the enemies.»

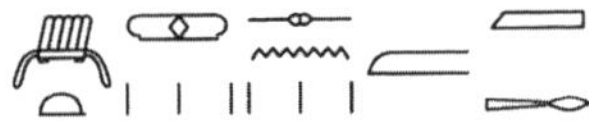

*ꜣwt.sn m mꜣꜥ-ḫrw*

Their oblations are justifications.

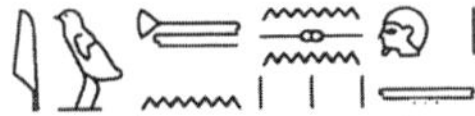

*jw wdnw n.sn tp tꜣ*

Whoever makes an offering to them on earth

*m mꜣꜥ-ḫrw ḫr.sn*

is one who is justified with them.

From the tomb of Pharaoh Seti II.

## 32ND SCENE

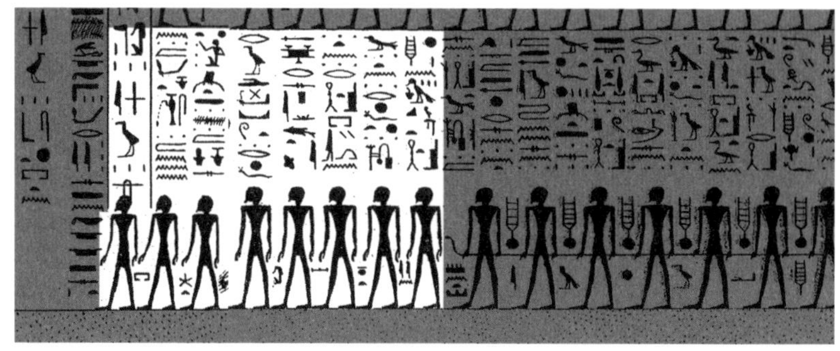

Eight (var. nine) gods without attributes:

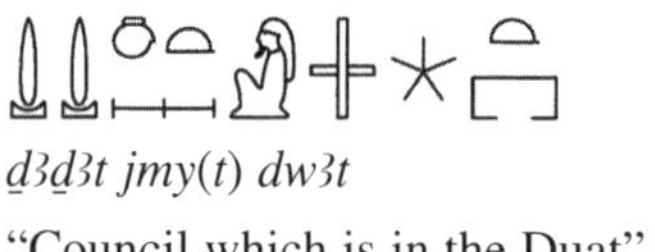

*ḏ3ḏ3t jmy(t) dw3t*

"Council which is in the Duat".

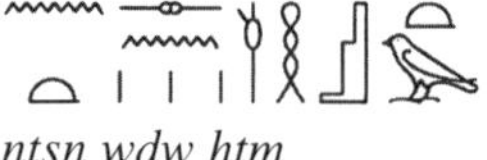

*ntsn wḏw ḫtm*

They are those who order destruction

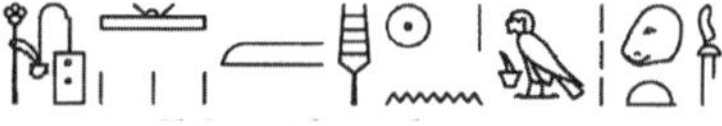

*zšw m ꜥḥꜥw n b3w ḫntyw jmnt*

and register lifetime for the *Ba*-souls who are in the West.

(Re speaks:)

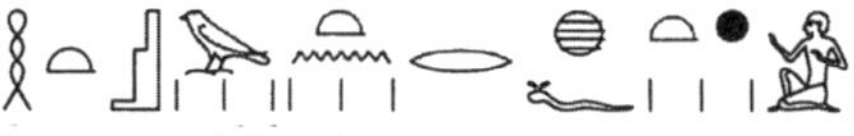

*ḥtmw.ṯn r ḫftyw.j*

«Your destruction is directed against my enemies,

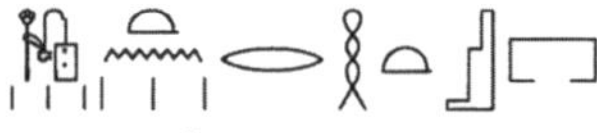

*zšw.ṯn r ḥtmyt*

whom you have assigned to the Place of Destruction!

From the tomb of Pharaoh Seti II.

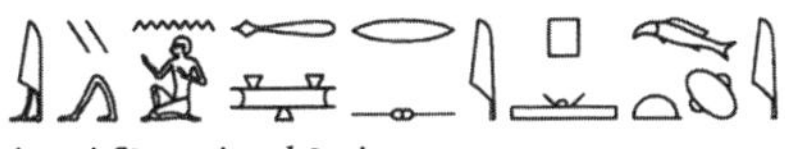

*jyn.j ꜥꜣ r sjpt ẖꜣt.j*

I have come hither to inspect my corpse,

*r wdy ḏwt r ḫftyw.j*

to inflict evil on my enemies.»

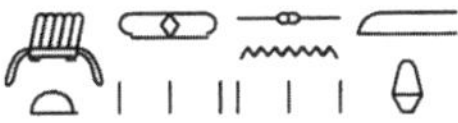

*ꜣwt.sn m tꜣ*

Their oblations are bread,

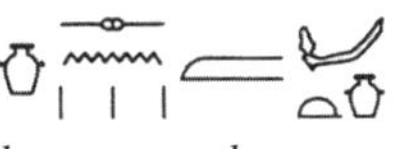

*ḥnqt.sn m ḏsrt*

their beer is Djeseret,

*qbḥw.sn m mw*

Their refreshment is water.

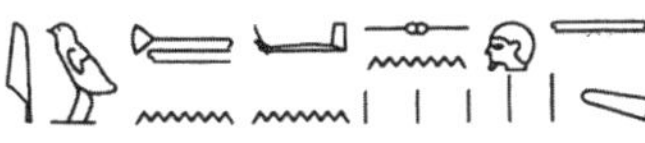

*jw wdnw n.sn tp tꜣ*

Whoever makes an offering to them on earth

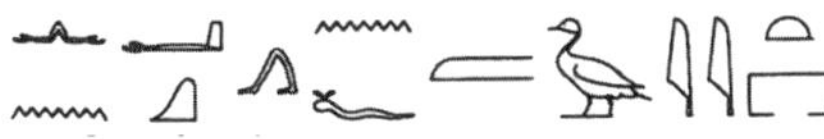

*nn ꜥqn.f m ḥtmyt*

he cannot enter the Place of Destruction!

## Fifth gate

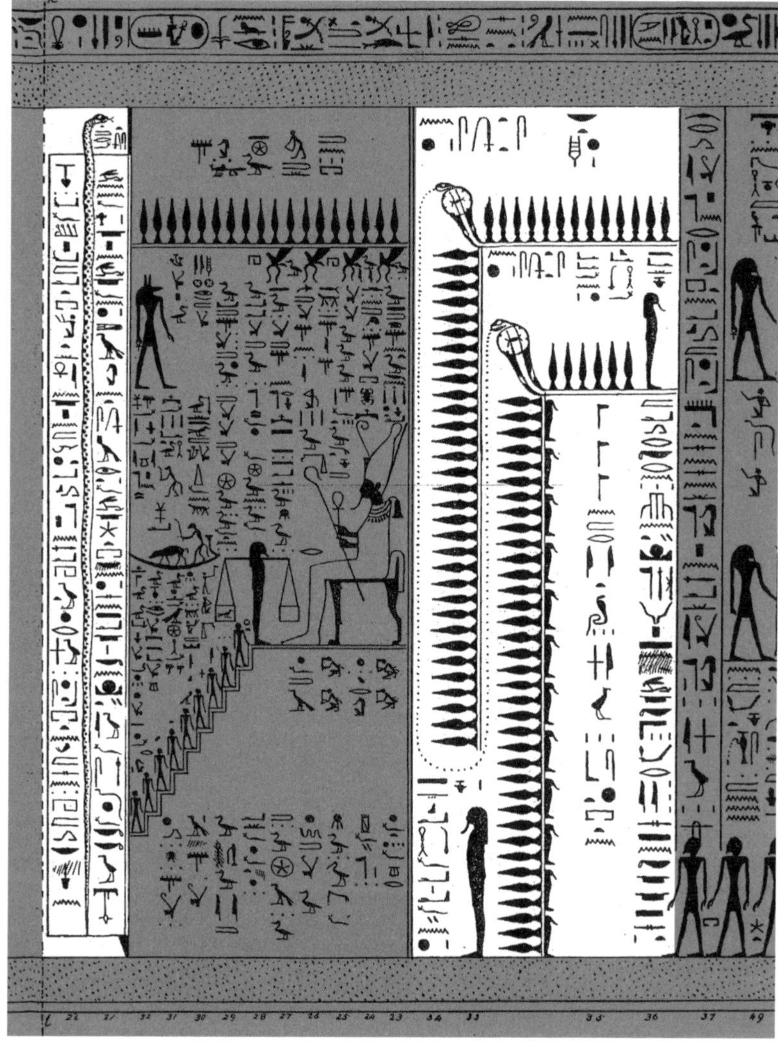

*spr jn nṯr pn r sbḫt tn*

Arrival of this god at this gate,

*ʿq m sbḫt tn*

entering into this gate.

*snsn nṯr pn ʿꜣ jn nṯrw jmyw.s*

Adoration of this great god by the deities who are in it.

Name of the gate:

*nbt ʿḥʿw*

"Mistress of Lifetime".

At the two Uraeus-serpents on the wall:

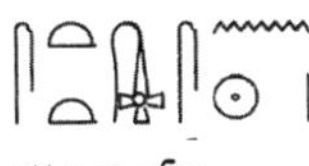

*stt.s n rʿw*

"She lights up for Re".

Upper guardian:

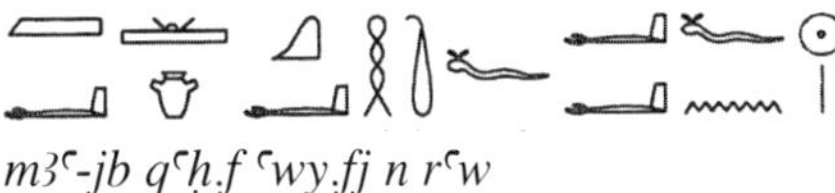

*mꜣʿ-jb qʿḥ.f ʿwy.fj n rʿw*

"He with right heart". He bends his arms for Re.

Lower guardian:

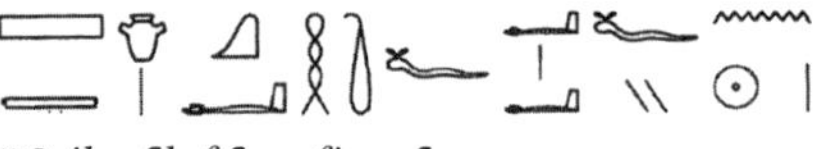

*št3-jb qꜥḥ.f ꜥwy.fj n rꜥw*

"He with mysterious heart". He bends his arms for Re.

Twelve mummies:

*nṯrw nṯryt jmyw sbḫt tn*

"The gods and goddesses who are in this gate".

Their legend:

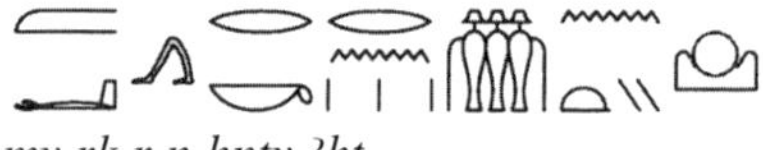

*my rk r.n ḫnty 3ḫt*

«Come to us, Foremost of the horizon,

*nṯr ꜥ3 wpy št3w*

Great god who has opened the mysteries!

*wnw n.k sbḫwt ḏsryt*

Open for you are the protected gates,

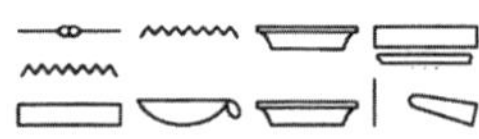

*znw n.k ꜥ3w št3w*

unlocked for you are the mysterious doors!»

## 33RD SCENE

The text of the Judgement Hall of Osiris is mainly cryptographic.

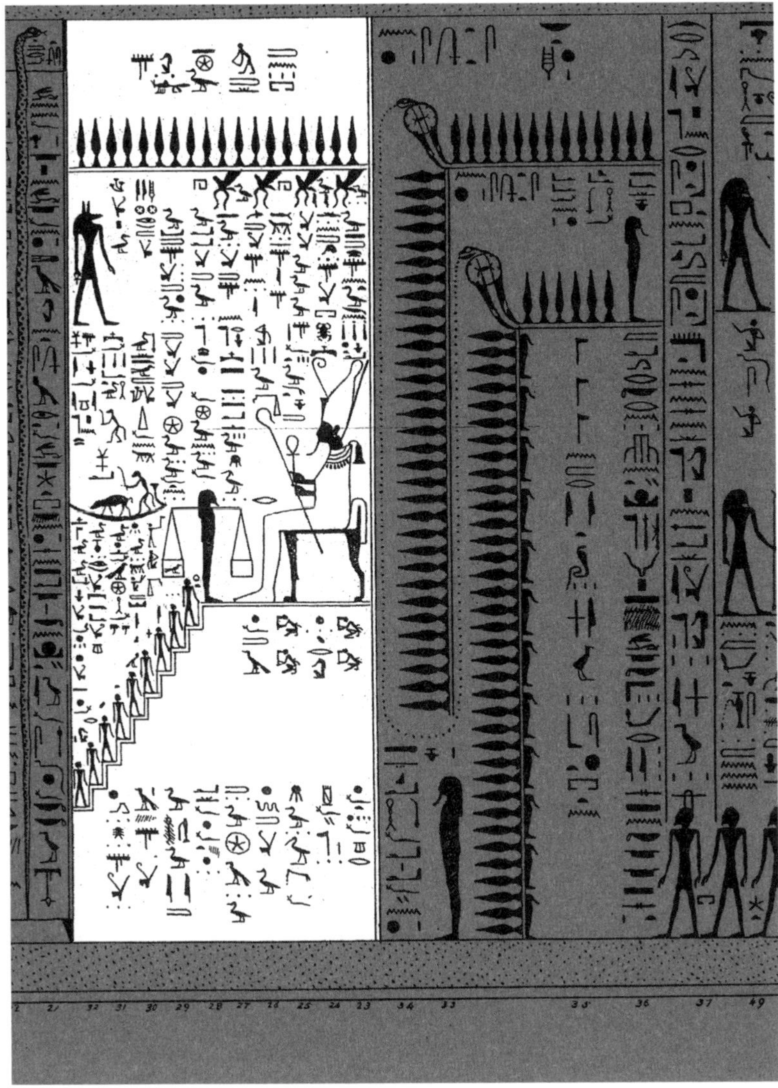

The Judgement Hall of Osiris.

From the tomb of Pharaoh Ramses V/VI,1836.

From the tomb of Pharaoh Ramses V/VI, 2005.

*mḏꜣt nt nḏ wsjr m dꜣtyw*

The Book of Protecting Osiris among those of the Netherworld.

Four heads of antelopes emerging from the ceiling:

*hmhmyw*

“The bellowing ones”.

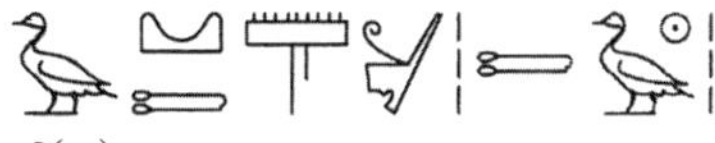

*zꜣ(w)t.sn mtyw*

What they guard are the dead;

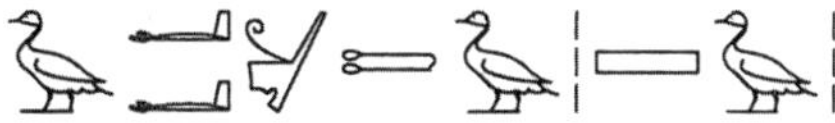

*wḏꜥ ntyw sjpw*

judging those who are damned.

*ntsn p(w) ṯny.sn*

It is they who are exalted,

*jn jmyw tꜣ swḏ.sn n ḥtmyt*

and those within the earth assign them to the place of destruction.

*nty(w) tpw.sn pryw m pt*

Those whose heads have emerged out of heaven,

*ḫꜥy.sn m wsṯn*

and they appear unhindered.

From the tomb of Pharaoh Horemheb.

Anubis:

*ꜥḥꜥw nj rmṯ(w)*

The lifetime of human beings

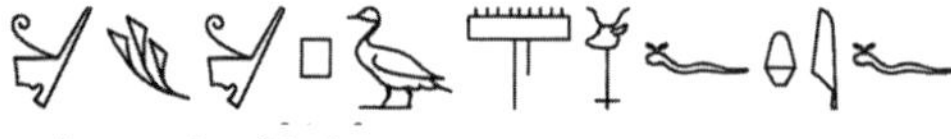

*n jnpw sꜥm.f jt.f*

belongs to Anubis, as he swallows his father.

The monkey outside:

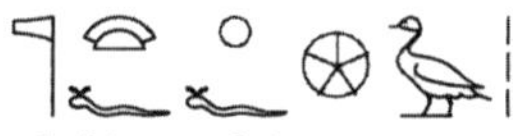

*nḫ.f jrt gwf dꜣtyw*

He protects the eye, the monkey of those of the Netherworld.

*ntyw gwf ṯnn(w).ṯn*

Those who are monkeys exalt you,

*dwꜣtyw m wsṯn*

dwellers of the Netherworld, unhindered.

The monkey with the pig:

*nṯr pn ḫꜥw*

When this god has appeared,

*dy.f nḫ ꜥm(w)*

he causes what was swallowed to be spat out.

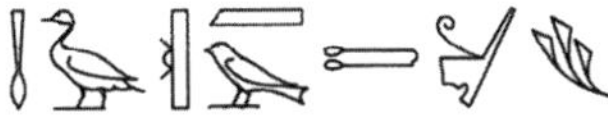

*mdw mꜣꜥtyw ṯny*

The words of the justified are exalted,

*wḏꜥ.f mdw ḏḥwty*

as he renders judgement, (namely) Thoth.

The blessed dead before Osiris:

*nṯr fꜣy mḫꜣt*

The god who carries the balance.

*ꜣḫw jmyw jmnt*

The blessed dead (*Akh*-spirits) who are in the West.

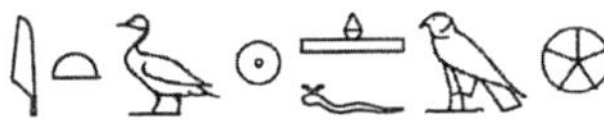

*jw rꜥw ḥtp.f m dwꜣt*

When Re has settled down in the Netherworld,

*wbꜣ.f kkw zmꜣw rnpw m ꜥnḫ*

he opens up the primeval darkness so that he is rejuvenated in life.

*ḥtp nṯr ꜥ3 m jtn.f*

The great god goes to rest in his sun disc,

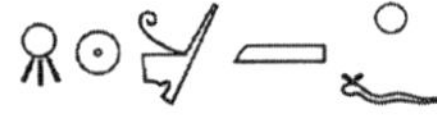

*wbn(w) m jrt.f*

and shines forth from his eye.

The carrier of the balance:

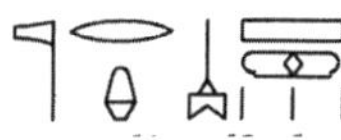

*nṯr rdj wḏꜥ šbw*

The god who causes the apportioning of offerings,

*šꜥw n 3ḫw*

and the portions to the blessed dead.

*f3y mdw m mḫ3t*

Who weighs the affairs with the scales,

*jsftyw mwwt tm(w) ḫpr*

so that the evildoers and the damned cease to exist.

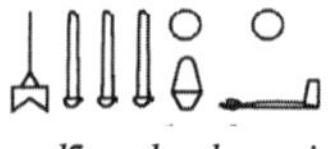

*wḏꜥ mdw ḫwy jrt*

Who judges and protects the eye.

Nine blessed dead on the steps before the enthroned Osisis:

*psḏt jmyt wsjr*

The Ennead who is in (the following of) Osiris.

The enemies beneath the staircase:

*ḫftyw wsjr*

Enemies of Osiris.

Osiris:

*ḫftyw.f ḫr rdwy.fj*

His enemies are beneath his feet,

*nṯrw 3ḫw m-b3ḥ.f*

(but) the gods and the blessed dead are in front of him.

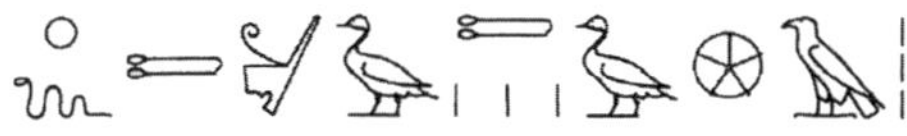

*jry.f ṯnwt m dw3tyw*

He makes a "census" among those of the Netherworld,

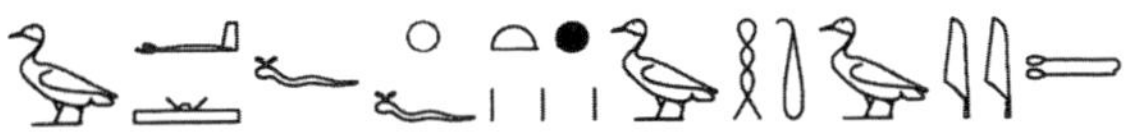

*wḏ.f ḫftyw n ḥtmyt*

he assigns the enemies to the place of destruction,

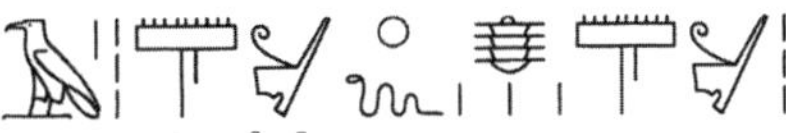

*b3w.sn jry.f šʿt.sn*

and their *Ba*-souls, he slaughters them.

The serpent upon the doorway:

*sty m jrt.f*

"Who burns with his eye".

*wnn.f ḥr ꜥꜣ pn*

He is upon this door,

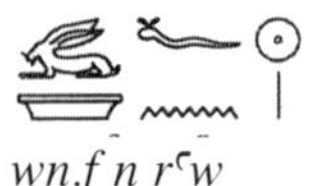

*wn.f n rꜥw*

he opens for Re.

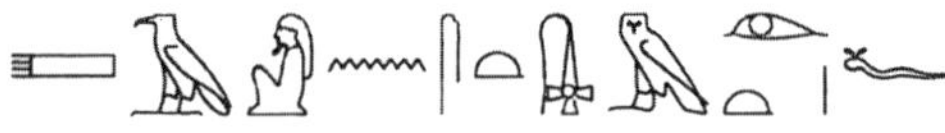

*sjꜣ n sty m jrt.f*

Sia (speaks) to him "who burns with his eye":

*wn sbꜣ.k n rꜥw*

«Open your gate for Re,

*zn ꜥꜣ.k n ꜣḫty*

unlock your door for Akhty!»

*jw.f sḥḏ.f kkw zmꜣw*

He illuminates the Primeval Darkness,

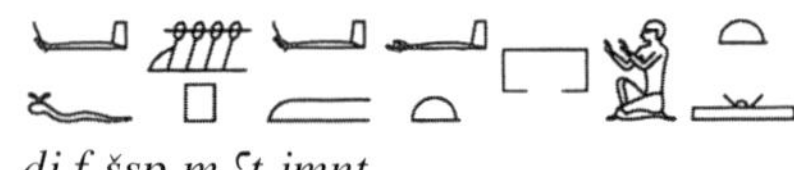

*dj.f šsp m ꜥt jmnt*

he throws light into the Hidden Region!

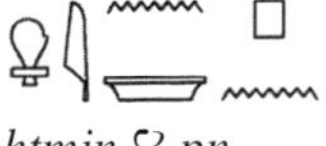

*ḫtmjn ꜥꜣ pn*

Then this door is closed,

*m-ḫt ꜥq nṯr pn ꜥꜣ*

after this great god has entered.

*hwtḫr jmyw sbḫt.tn*

Then those in this gate wail

*sḏm.sn hꜣꜣ ꜥꜣ pn*

when they hear this door being slammed.

From the sarcophagus of Djedher (probably late reign of Nectanebo II).

# SCHEMA OF

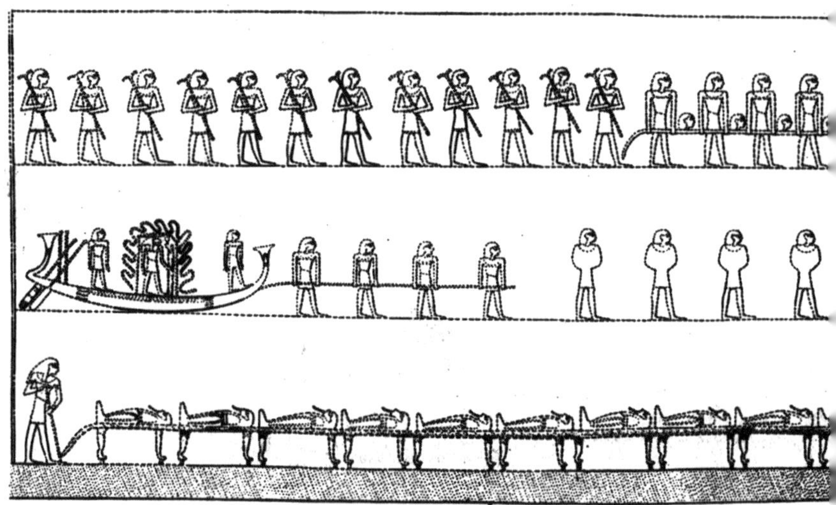

# THE SIXTH HOUR

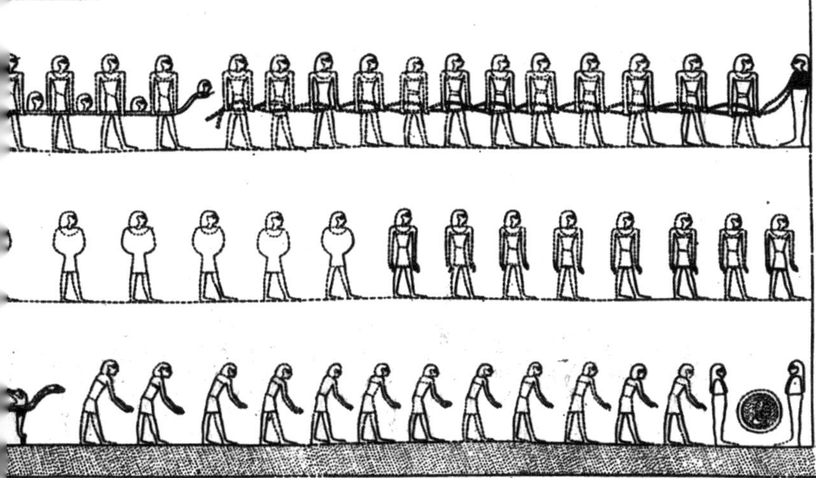

# DETAIL SIXTH HOUR FROM

# THE TOMB OF RAMSES III

## Upper Register, 34th Scene

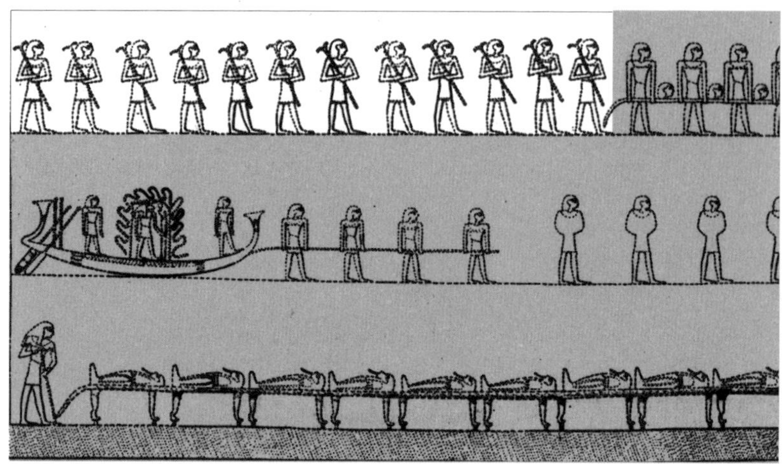

Twelve gods carrying forked sticks:

*ẖryw mtꜣw*

"Those carrying forked sticks".

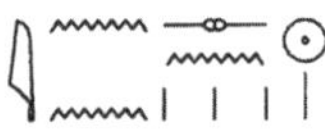

*jn n.sn rꜥw*

Re says to them:

*šzp n.ṯn mtꜣw.ṯn*

«Receive for you your forked sticks,

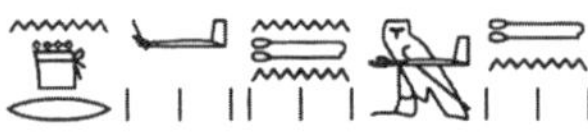

*nḏrw n.ṯn m ꜥ.ṯn*

which you have grasped with your hands!

From the tomb of Pharaoh Seti I.

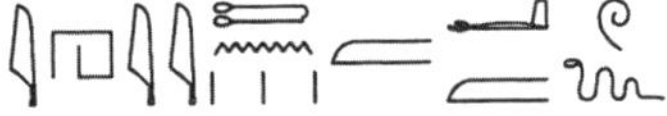

*jhy ṯn m ʿmw*

Lo! Your (forked sticks) are in the Devourer!

*jhy d3z(w).ṯn jm.f*

Lo! Your fetters are on him,

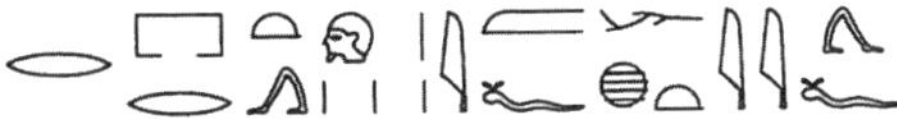

*r pryt tpw jm.f ẖty.f*

until the heads emerge out of him when he retreats!»

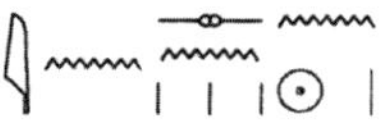

*jn.sn n rʿw*

They say to Re:

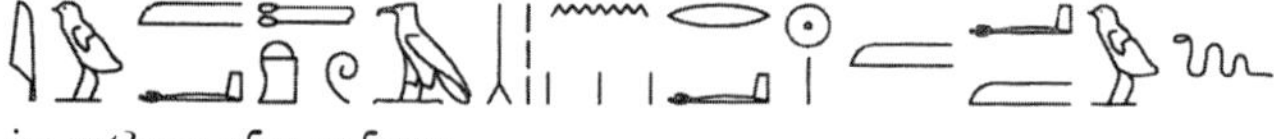

*jw mtȝw.n rʿw m ʿmw*

«Our forked sticks, Re, are (planted) into the Devourer,

*dȝz(w).n m ḥfȝw ḏw*

our strings are on the Evil Serpent.

*j rʿw mk tpw pry.sn*

O Re, behold heads emerge

*m qȝb pn (nj) ẖty*

out of this coil of the retreating one!»

*nṯrw pw jmyw wjȝ*

These are the gods who are in the barque,

*ẖsfyw ʿȝpp m nwt*

who ward off Apopis in heaven,

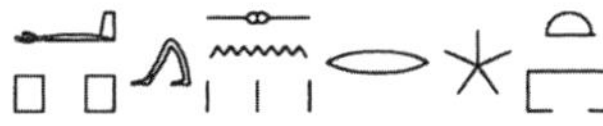

*ʿpp.sn r dwꜣt*

when they proceed to the Netherworld.

*ntsn ḫsfw ʿꜣpp ḥr rʿw m jmntt*

They are those who ward off Apopis from Re in the West,

*dwꜣtyw mꜣʿ(w) nṯr pn*

those of the Duat who guide this god.

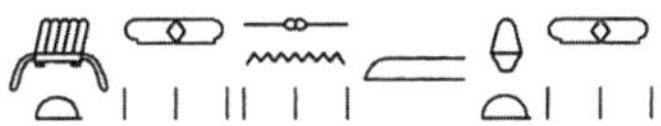

*ꜣwt.sn m tꜣ*

Their oblation is bread,

*ḥnqt.sn m ḏsrt*

their beer is Djeseret,

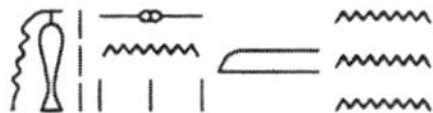

*qbḥw.sn m mw*

their refreshment is water.

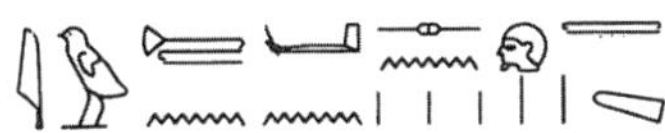

*jw wdnw n.sn tp tꜣ*

Whoever makes an offering to them on earth

*m ḫsf(w) sbj ḥr rʿw m jmntt*

is one who repels the rebel from Re in the West.

## 35TH SCENE

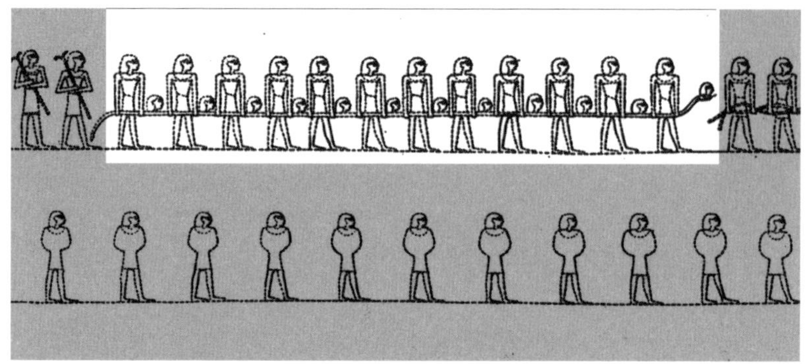

Twelve gods carrying the serpent «Devourer» mentioned before, with human heads emerging out of its coils:

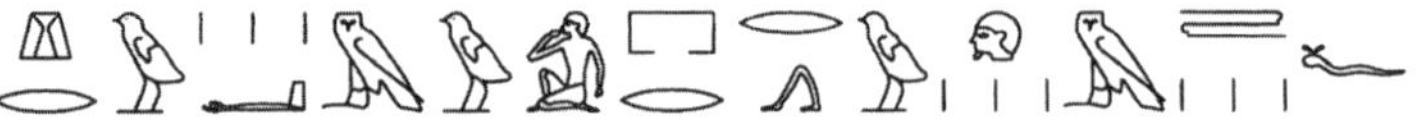

*ḫryw ʿmw prrw tpw m qꜣbw.f*

"Those who carry the Devourer, out of whose coils heads are emerging".

The text reads:

*wnw njk.sn ḏwy-ḥr*

Those who punish Evilface,

*sḫr.sn ḫftyw nw rʿw*

and overthrow the enemies of Re.

*ntsn nḏrw sbj*

It is they who seize the rebel,

From the tomb of Pharaoh Seti I.

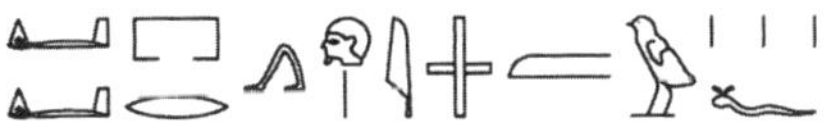

*ddw prj tp jmyw.f*

and let emerge the heads of those who are in him.

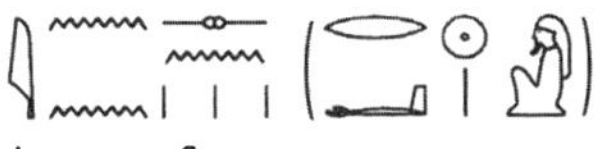

*jn n.sn rʿw*

Re says to them:

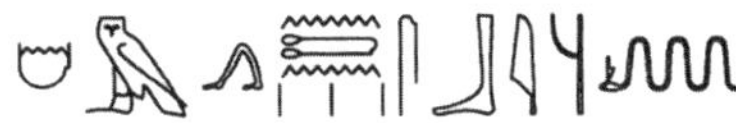

*ḥmw n.ṯn sbj*

«Drive back the rebel,

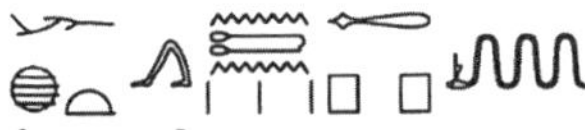

*ḫtw n.ṯn ʿ3pp*

repel Apopis for you,

*pry tpw jmyw.f sk.f*

that the heads which are in him may come out, so that he perishes.

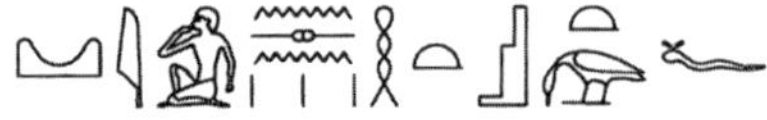

*ḏwy.j n.sn ḥtmw.f*

When I have called to them, he is destroyed.

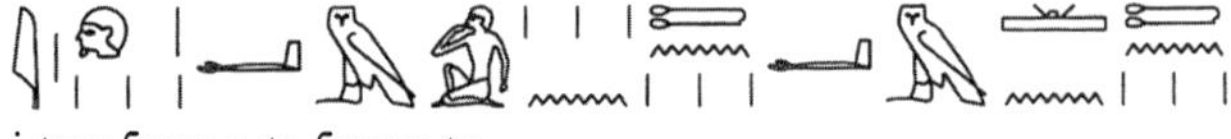

*j tpw ꜥmw n.ṯn ꜥmwn.ṯn*

O heads, swallow him who had swallowed you,

*wnm.ṯn pryn.ṯn jm.f*

so that you eat up him from whom you have come forth!»

*ḏwy rꜥw r.sn pry.sn*

When Re has called to them, they come forth.

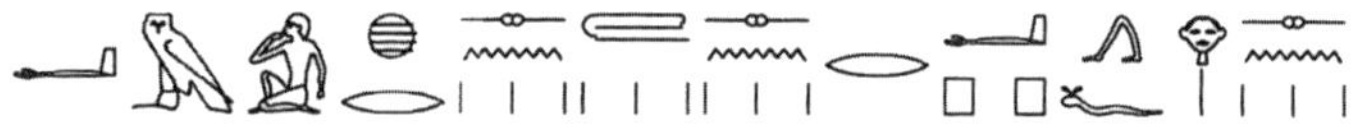

*ꜥmḫr.sn qꜣbw.sn r ꜥpp.f ḥr.sn*

Then they swallow their coils, till he has passed them,

*ꜥqḫr tpw m qꜣbw.sn m-ḫt*

and after that the heads enter their coils again.

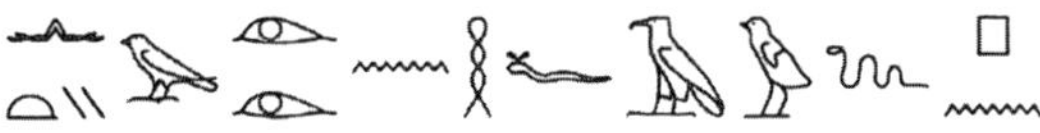

*jwty jrty nj ḥfꜣw pn*

This serpent is one without eyes,

*jwty fnḏ.f jwty msḏrwj.fj*

without nose and without ears;

*srq.f m hmhmt.f*

he breathes from his own cries,

*ʿnḫ.f m ḏwy.f ḏs.f*

and lives by his own call.

*ꜣwt.sn m ḥtpw tp tꜣ*

Their oblation is what is offered upon earth,

*ḫft rʿw prj.f m dwꜣt*

before Re when he comes out from the Netherworld,

*jw wdnw (n.)sn m ʿḥʿw ẖr jmꜣw*

Whoever makes an offering to them is one who is standing under trees.

## 36TH SCENE

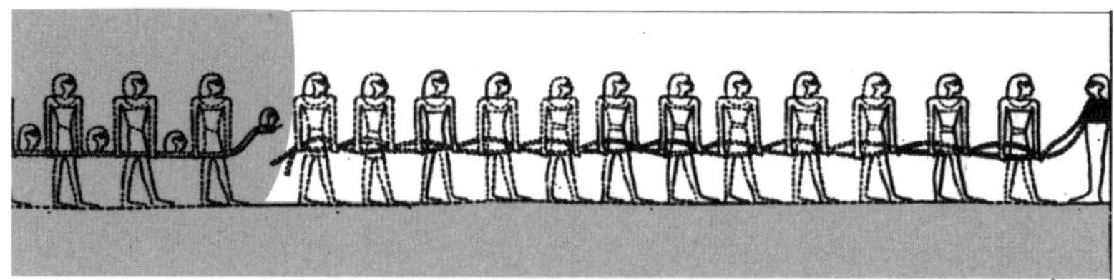

Twelve gods grasping the double-twisted rope of time which is fastened around the neck of a mummiform god; stars above each coil of the rope represent the hours.

The mummiform god:

*ʿqn*
"Aqen".

The gods at the rope:

*ẖryw mʿnnw(j) prrw wnwwt jm.f*
"Who carry the double-twisted (rope) out of which the hours emerge".

(Re says:)

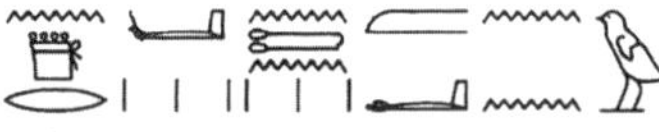

*nḏrw n.ṯn mʿnnw(j)*
«Grasp for yourself the double-twisted

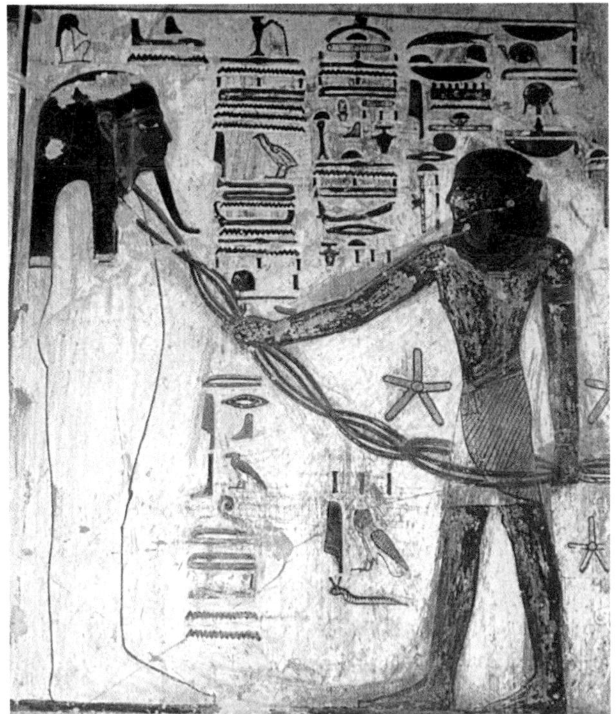

From the tomb of Pharaoh Seti I.

*šdjn.ṯn m r3 ˁqn*

which you have pulled out of the mouth of Aqen!

*pryt n*(*t*) *wnwwt.ṯn*

The going forth of your hours

*3ḫw.ṯn r.ṯn jm.sn*

(means) that you are turned into *Akh*-spirits through them,

*ḥtpw wnwwt r ẖryt.ṯn*

while the setting of the hours is for your provision,

*ʿq mʿnnw(j) m rꜣ ʿqn*

when the double-twisted enters (again) into the mouth of Aqen!»

*pry qꜣbw ḫpr wnwt*

When a coil (of the rope) appears, an hour comes into being;

*ḏwy rʿw ḥtp.s st.s*

when Re calls, it takes its seat,

*ʿm ẖr ʿqn mʿnnw(j)*

and then Aqen swallows the double-twisted (again).

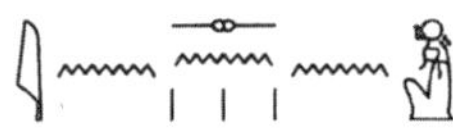

*jn.sn n rʿw*

They say to Re:

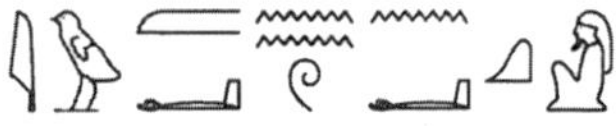

*jw mʿnnw(j) n ʿq(n)*

«The double-twisted belongs to Aqen,

*jw wnwwt n nṯr ʿꜣ*

and the hours belong to the great god.

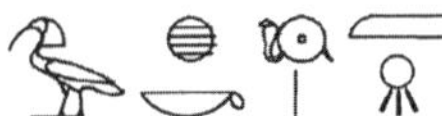

*3ḫ.k rˁw m j3ḫw*

You are glorious, Re, through the splendour of light,

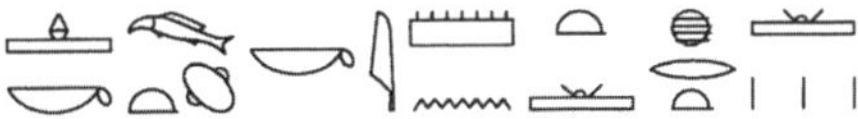

*ḥtp.k ẖ3t.k jmnt ḫrt*

you rest (in) your corpse whose nature is hidden!»

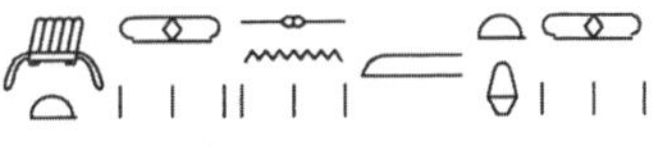

*3wt.sn m t3*

Their oblation is bread,

*ḥnqt.sn m ḏsrt*

their beer is Djeseret,

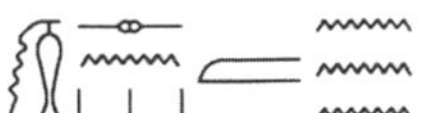

*qbḥw.sn m mw*

their refreshment is water.

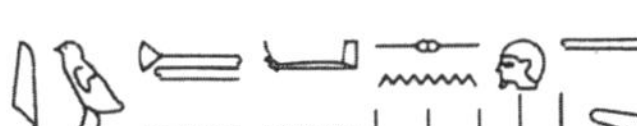

*jw wdnw n.sn tp t3*

Whoever makes an offering to them upon earth

*m jrj q3bw m mˁnnw(j)*

is one who belongs to a coil in the double-twisted.

From the tomb of Pharaoh Ramses III.

## MIDDLE REGISTER, 37TH SCENE

From the tomb of Seti I

The sun barque, represented as usual and carrying the gods *sjꜣ* (Sia, percipience) and *ḥkꜣ* (Heka, magic) as well as *jwf rꜥw* (flesh of Re). She is pulled by four *dwꜣtyw* (gods of the Netherworld). The text reads:

*sṯꜣ nṯr pn ꜥꜣ jn nṯrw dwꜣtyw*

This Great God is towed by the gods of the Netherworld.

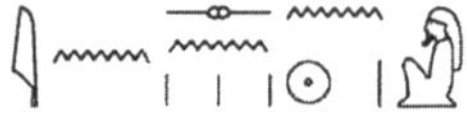

*jn.sn n rꜥw*

They say to Re:

*sṯꜣw n.k nṯr ꜥꜣ*

«The towing is (done) for you, great god.

*nb wnwt jry mḫrw tꜣ*

master of the hours, who cares for the Earth,

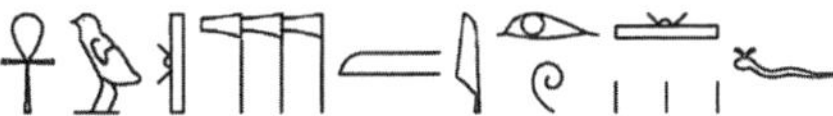

*ʿnḫw nṯrw m jrw.f*

through whose essence the gods live,

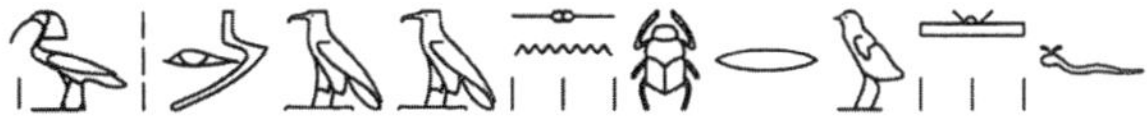

*ꜣḫw mꜣꜣw.sn ḫprw.f*

and the *Akh*-spirits when they look at his manifestations.»

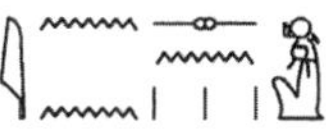

*jn n.sn rʿw*

Re says to them:

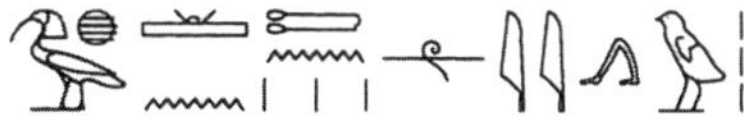

*ꜣḫw n.ṯn sṯꜣyw*

«The blessed state belongs to you who tow (me),

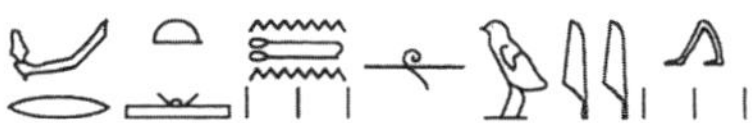

*ḏsrw n.ṯn sṯꜣyw*

protection (or seclusion) belongs to you who tow (me),

*nʿʿ.wj r ẖryt dwꜣt*

who let me glide to the depth of the Netherworld,

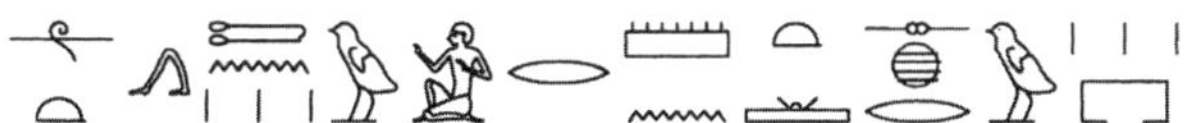

*sṯꜣ.ṯn.wj r mnt-sḫrw*

may you tow me to the place with lasting nature,

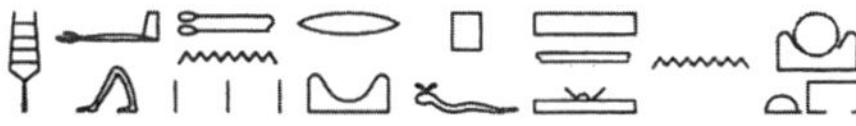

*ʿḥʿ.ṯn r ḏw pf štꜣ nj ꜣḫt*

may you pause at that mysterious mountain of the horizon!»

## 38TH SCENE

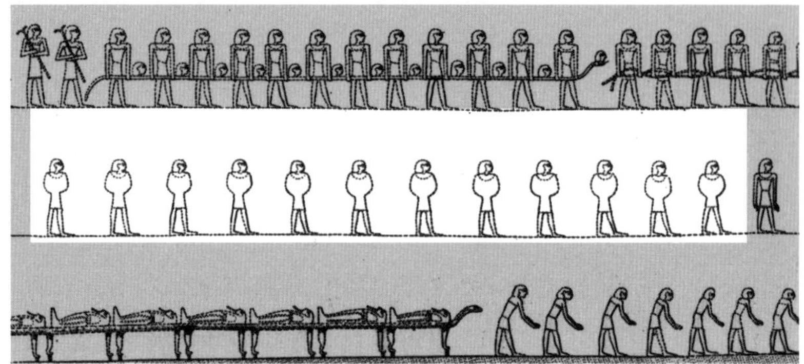

Twelve gods with hidden arms:

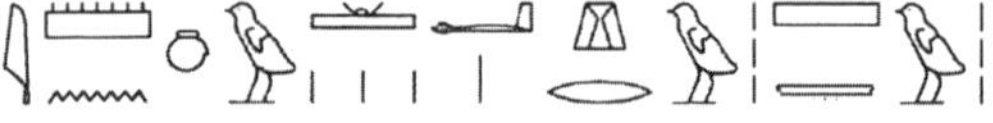

*jmnw-ꜥ ḫryw št3w*

"Those with hidden arm who carry the mystery".

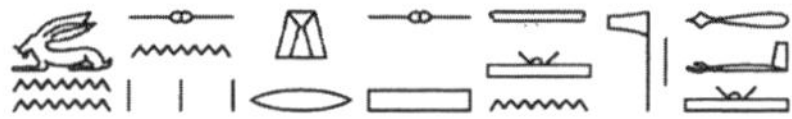

*wnn.sn ḫr sšt3w nj nṯr ꜥ3*

They carry the mystery of the great god (his corpse),

*jwty m33.sw jmyw dw3t*

which those in the Netherworld cannot see,

*m33.sw mtyw*

but which is seen by the dead

From the tomb of Pharaoh Seti I.

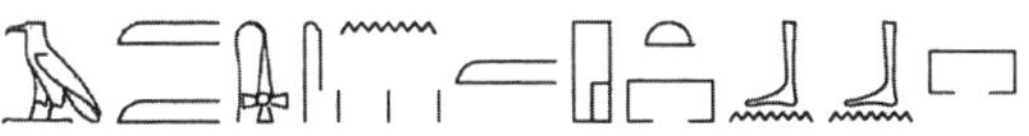

*3mm.sn m ḥwt bnbn*

when they are burnt in the Benben-house,

*r bw ẖr ẖ3t nṯr pn*

near the place where the corpse of this god is.

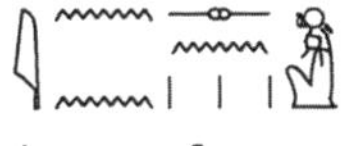

*jn n.sn rʿw*

Re says to them:

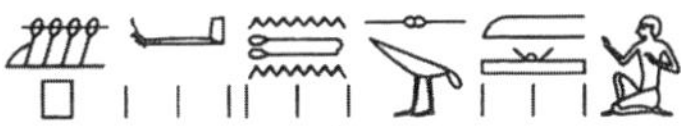

*šzpw n.ṯn sšmw.j*

«Receive for you my image,

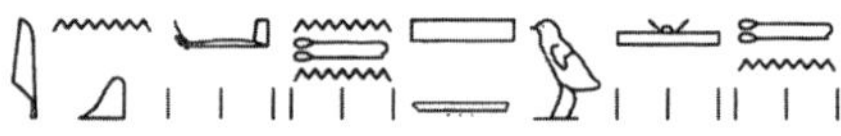

*jnqw n.ṯn šṯ3w.ṯn*

and embrace for you your mystery,

*ḥtp.ṯn m ḥwt-bnbn*

when you rest in the Benben-house,

*r bw ḫr ẖ3t.j jmyt.j*

near the place where my corpse is in which I am!

*sšṯ3w n jmyt.ṯn*

The mystery in which you are

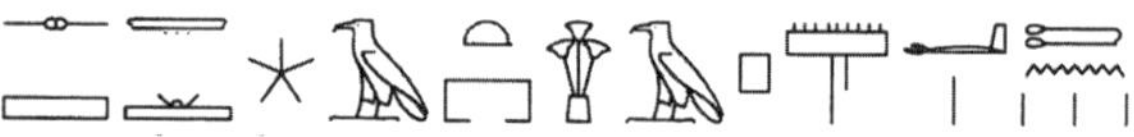

*sšṯ3w dw3t ḥ3pw ꜥ.ṯn*

is the mystery of the Duat which your arm conceals.»

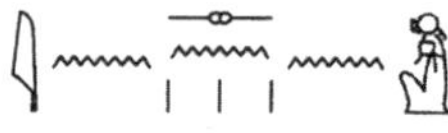

*jn.sn n rꜥw*

They say to Re:

*b3.k n pt ḫnty 3ḫt*

«Your *Ba*-soul belongs to heaven, Foremost of the horizon,

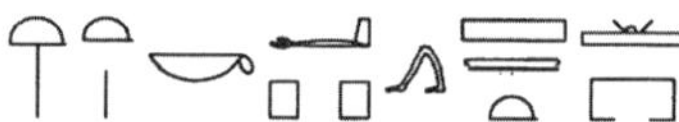

*šwt.k ꜥpp(tj) št3yt*

and it is your shadow which traverses the Shetit,

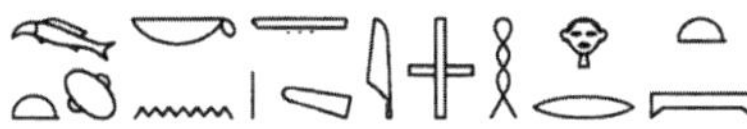

*ẖ3t.k n t3 jmj ḥrt*

while your corpse belongs to the Earth, you who are in heaven!

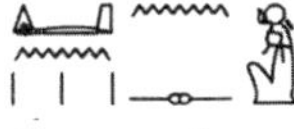

*dj.n n.s rʿw*

We restore Re to it (the heaven),

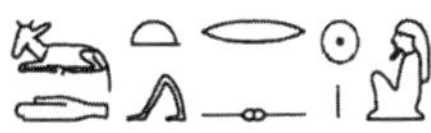

*jwd.tj r.s rʿw*

since you are separated from it, Re!

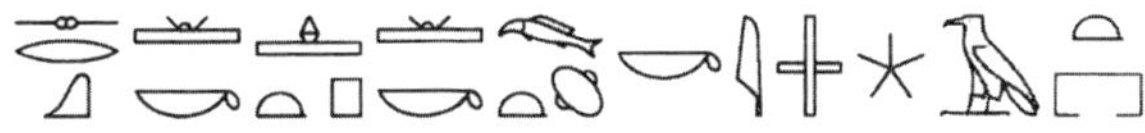

*srq.k ḥtp.k ẖ3t.k jmyt dw3t*

You breathe when you rest (in) your corpse which is in the Duat.»

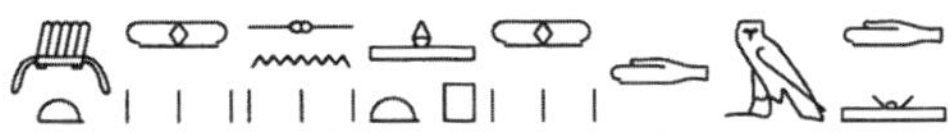

*3wt.sn ḥtp(w) dmḏ*

Their oblation is the complete offering

*ḥtpw b3w jm.f*

with which the *Ba*-souls are satisfied.

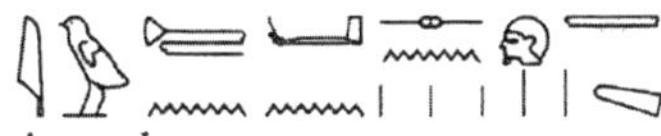

*jw wdnw n.sn tp t3*

Whoever makes an offering to them upon earth

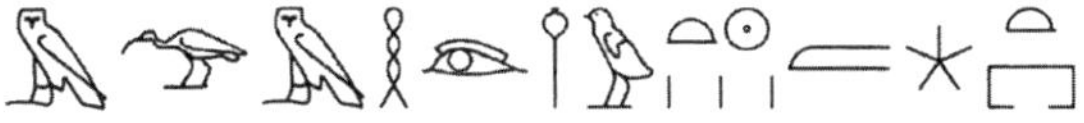

*m gmḥw ḥḏwt m dw3t*

is one who perceives light in the Duat.

## 39TH SCENE

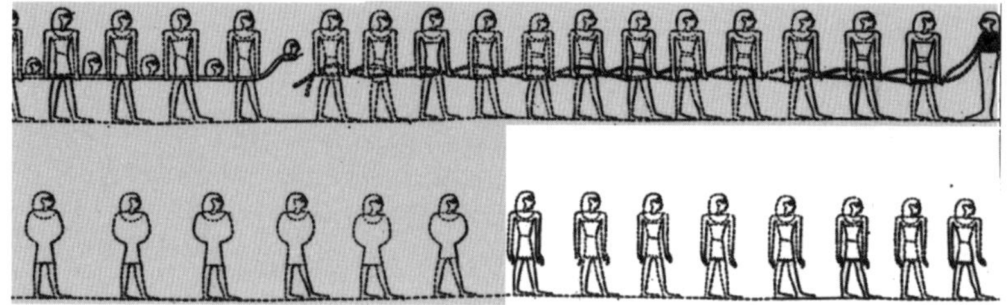

Eight gods, slightly bowing before the Sungod:

*nṯrw ḥwtyw*

"Gods belonging to the sanctuary".

*wnn.sn r-rwtj ḥwt-bnbn*

They are outside the sanctuary of the Benben-stone.

*m33.sn m33t rʿw*

They see what Re sees,

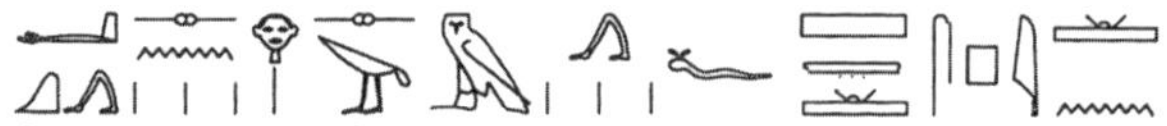

*ʿq.sn ḥr sšmw.f št3 sjpwn (rʿw)*

and they have access to his mysterious image which (Re) has revised.

*ntsn zbjw zjnw*

They are those who send out messengers.

From the tomb of Ramses III.

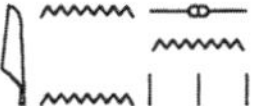

*jn n.sn (rʿw)*

(Re) says to them:

*ꜣwt.j m ꜣwt.ṯn*

«My oblation is your oblation.

*jw srqw.j m srqw.ṯn*

What I breathe is what you breathe.

*nttn jmyw štꜣw.j*

You are those who surround my mystery,

*wnn.wj m zꜣw štꜣw.j jmyw ḥwt-bnbn*

while I am protecting my mystery which is in the sanctuary of the Benben-stone.

*jhy n.ṯn ʿnḫ bꜣw.ṯn*

Hail to you, your *Ba*-souls shall live!»

*ꜣwt.sn ꜣwt ꜣḫty*

Their oblations are the oblations of Akhty (Re).

## Lower Register, 40th Scene

The register opens with the Sungod, leaning on a staff who is named:

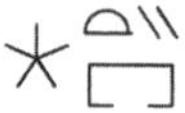

*dw3ty*
"Duati (Who belongs to the Netherworld)".

He inspects a long bier, shaped like a serpent named Nehep, with twelve mummies lying on it:

*jmyw-ḫt wsjr qddyw jmyw b3gy*
"Followers of Osiris, the sleeping ones who are in a state of weariness".

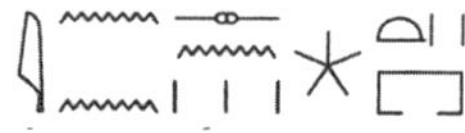
*jn n.sn dw3ty*
Duati says to them:

*j nṯrw ḫntyw dw3t*
«O gods in the Duat,

From the tomb of Pharaoh Seti I.

*jmyw-ḫt ḥq3-jmnt*

Followers of the Ruler of the West,

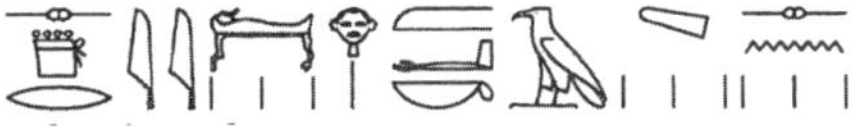

*ntyw m3ʿy ḥr gs.sn*

who are stretched out on their side,

*sḏry ḥr mk3(wt).sn*

lying on their biers –

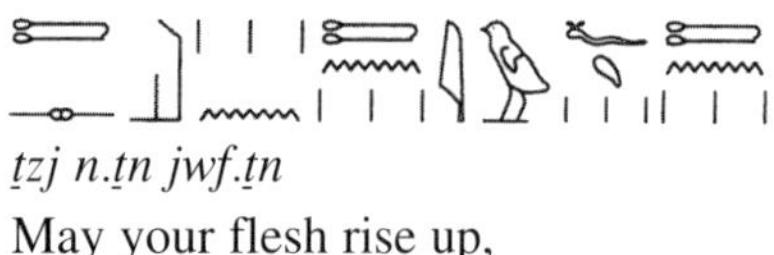

*ṯzj n.ṯn jwf.ṯn*

May your flesh rise up,

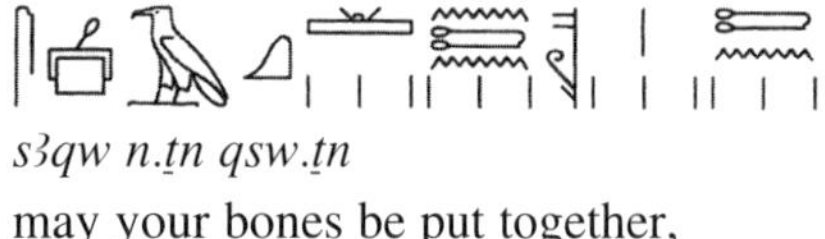

*s3qw n.ṯn qsw.ṯn*

may your bones be put together,

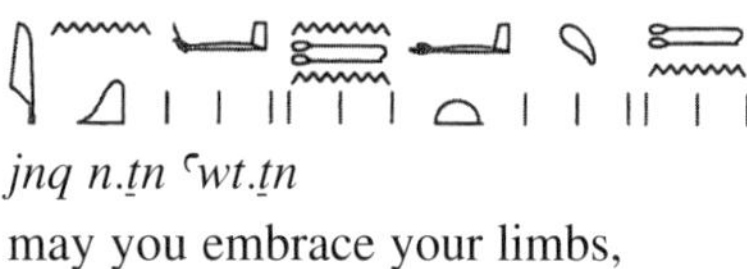

*jnq n.ṯn ʿwt.ṯn*

may you embrace your limbs,

*dmḏw n.ṯn jwf.ṯn*

may your flesh be united!

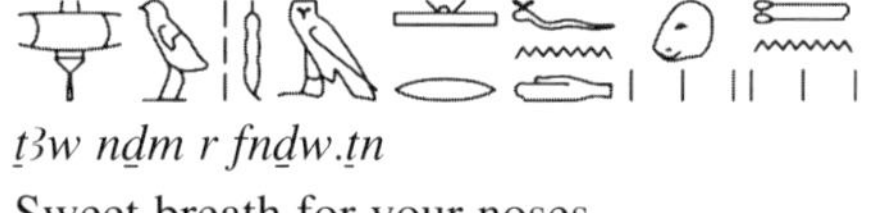

*ṯ3w nḏm r fnḏw.ṯn*

Sweet breath for your noses,

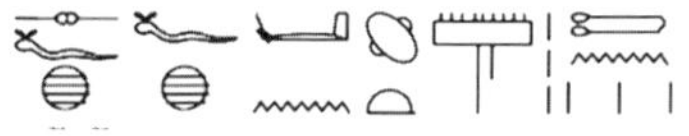

*sfḫfḫ n wtw.ṯn*

loosening for your mummy-wrappings,

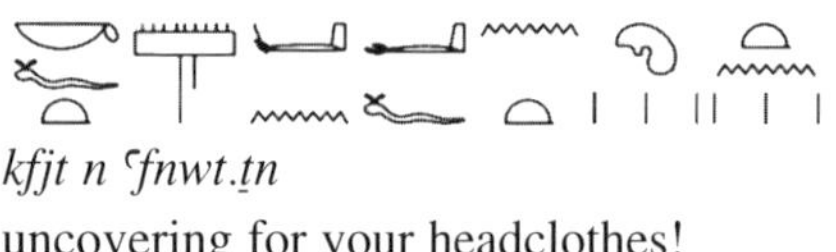

*kfjt n ʿfnwt.ṯn*

uncovering for your headclothes!

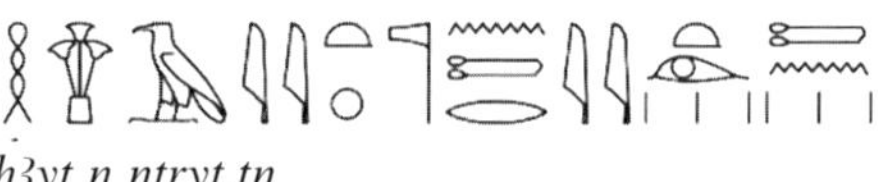

*ḥ3yt n nṯryt.ṯn*

Light be for your divine eyes,

From the tomb of Pharaoh Ramses III.

*m33.ṯn ḥḏwt jm.sn*

that you may see the light through them.

*ʿḥʿ n.ṯn m g3ḥw.ṯn*

Raise yourself from your weariness,

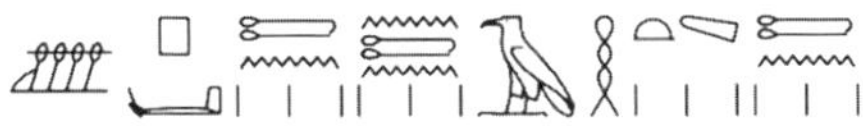

*šzp.ṯn n.ṯn 3ḥwt.ṯn*

that you receive your land

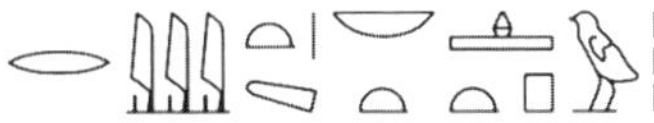

*r sḫt nbt-ḥtpw*

at the field of the Mistress of Offerings.

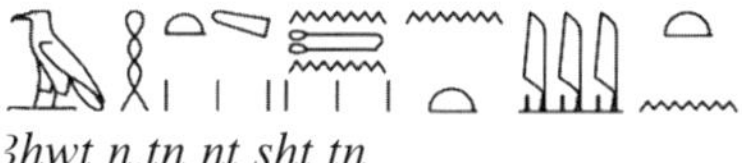

*ꜣḥwt n.ṯn nt sḫt ṯn*

Plots belongs to you from this field,

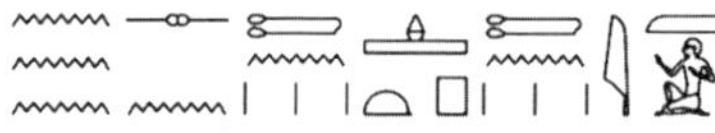

*mw.s n.ṯn ḥtp.ṯn jm.j*

its water belongs to you that you are content with me,

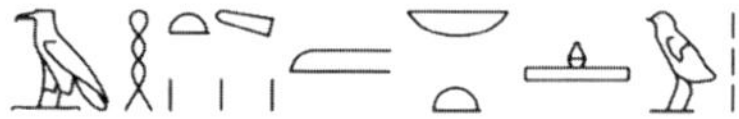

*ꜣḥwt m nbt-ḥtpw*

and with the plots of the Mistress of Offering.»

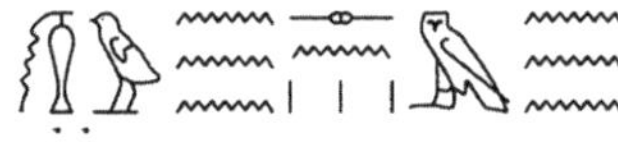

*qbḥw.sn m mw*

Their refreshment is water.

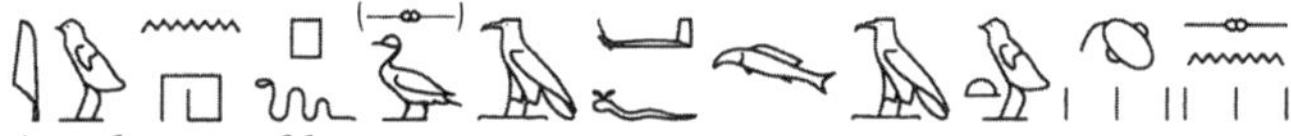

*jw nhp zꜣw.f ẖꜣwt.sn*

Nehep is guarding their corpses,

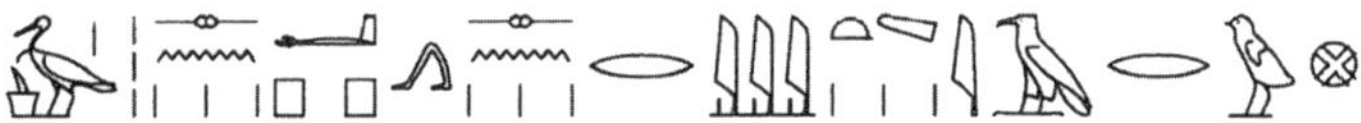

*bꜣw.sn ꜥpp.sn r sḫt-jꜣrw*

but their *Ba*-souls, they move to the Field of Rushes,

*r sḫm m qbḥw.sn*

to take hold of their refreshment.

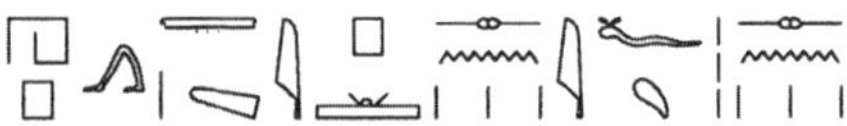

*hp tꜣ jp.sn jwf.sn*

When the Earth "springs" (trembles), they revise their flesh.

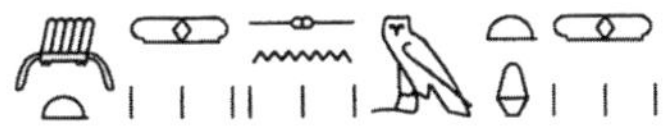

*ꜣwt.sn m tꜣ*

Their oblation is bread,

*ḥnqt.sn m ḏsrt*

their beer is Djeseret,

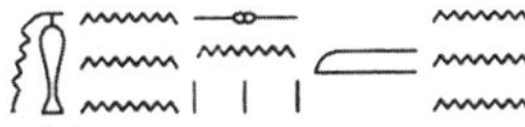

*qbḥw.sn m mw*

their refreshment is water.

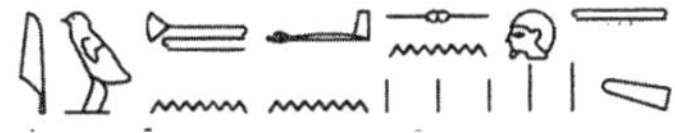

*jw wdnw n.sn tp tꜣ*

Whoever makes an offering to them on earth

*m sʿḥ ḥtpw ḥr mkꜣt.f*

is a mummy resting on his bier.

## 41st Scene

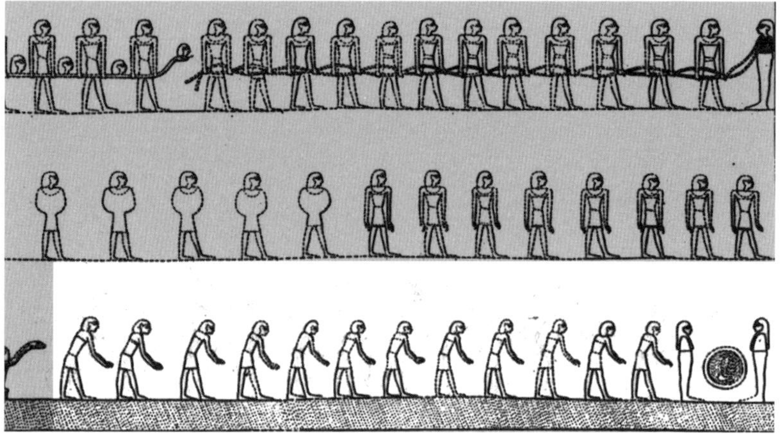

Twelve bowing gods in front of the Lake of Fire:

*nrṯw jmyw ḫ3st t3*

"Gods who are in the fiery pit of the Earth".

This circular pit, with a cobra in it, is flanked by two mummiform guardians:

*nbj-ḥr*

"He with burning face".

*stj-ḥr*

"He with fiery face".

*wnn.sn m dbnw nj ḫ3st tn*

They are around this fiery pit,

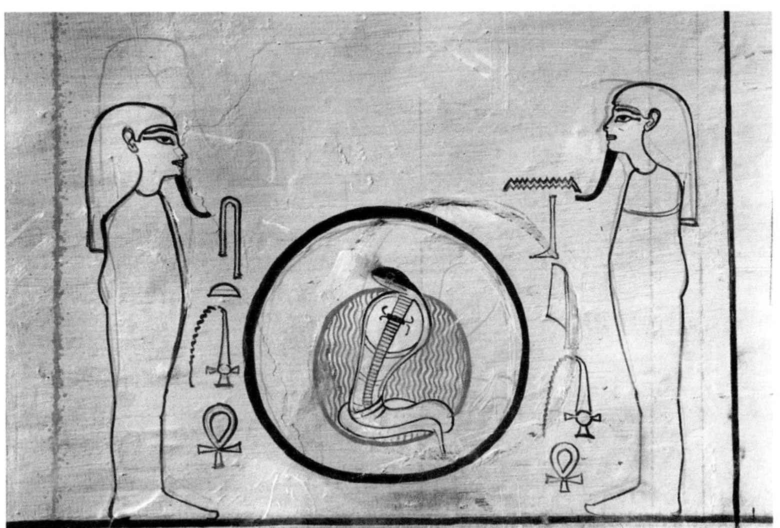

From the tomb of Pharaoh Horemheb.

*wnn jʿrt ʿnḫt m ẖ3st tn*

and a living cobra is in this fiery pit.

*wnn mw nj ẖ3st (tn) m sḏt*

The water of (this) pit is fire,

*jwty h3y nṯrw t3 b3w t3*

without the gods of the Earth and the Ba-souls of the Earth

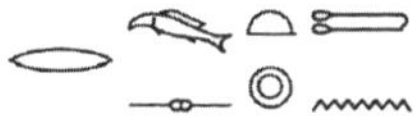

*r ẖ3st tn*

being able to approach this fiery pit,

*m-ʿ nsrt n(t) jʿrt tn*

because of the flame of this cobra;

*srq nṯr pn ʿ3 ḫnty dw3t*

but this great god at the head of the Duat breathes

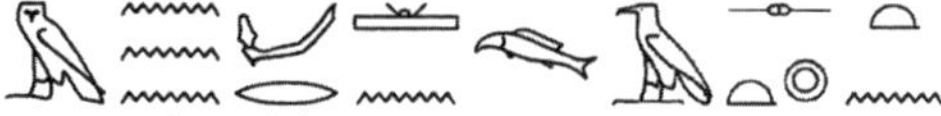

*m mw ḏsr nj ḫ3st tn*

by the unapproachable water of this fiery pit.

*jn n.sn rʿw*

Re says to them:

*jhy jrf nṯrw z3yw ḫ3st ḏsrt*

«Hail to you gods who guard the unapproachable pit,

*ddt mw n ḫnty jgrt*

which provides water for the Foremost of the Beyond –

*jw mw nj ḫ3st n wsjr*

The water of the fiery pit belongs to Osiris,

*qbḥw.ṯn n ḫnty dw3t*

and your refreshment to the Foremost of the Duat!

From the tomb of Pharaoh Ramses III.

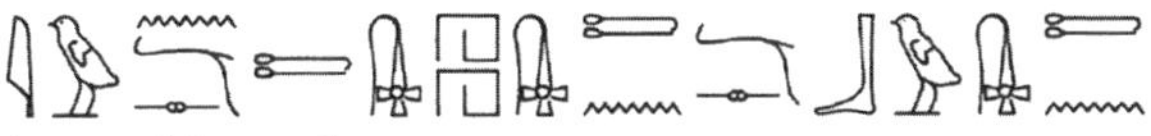

*jw nsrt hh.ṯn nsbw.ṯn*

(But) your blast of fire, your amber

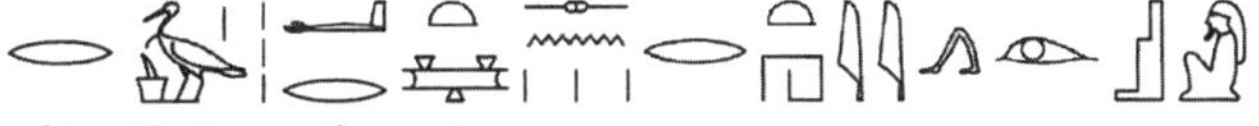

*r b3w jꜥrtj.sn r thy wsjr*

is against the *Ba*-souls who will approach to violate Osiris.

*n g3y kh3y ḫ3st nn kj.ṯ*

The power of the fiery pit is not in want; there is no other like you,

*jwtj sḫm nṯrw z33w.sj m mw.s*

over whose water the gods, who guard it, have no power.»

*3wt.sn m t3*

Their oblation is bread,

*ḥnqt.sn m ḏsrt*

their beer is Djeseret,

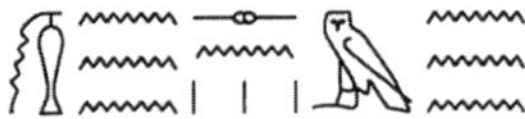

*qbḥw.sn m mw*

their refreshment is water.

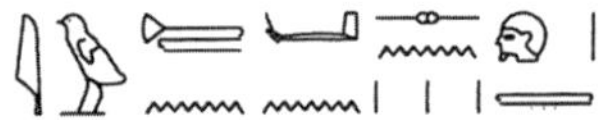

*jw wdnw n.sn tp t3*

Whoever makes an offering to them on earth

*m ḏsry m jmntt*

is unapproachable in the West.

## SIXTH GATE

*spr jn nṯr pn r sbḫt (tn)*
Arrival of this god at (this) gate,

*ʿq m sbḫt tn*
entering into this gate.

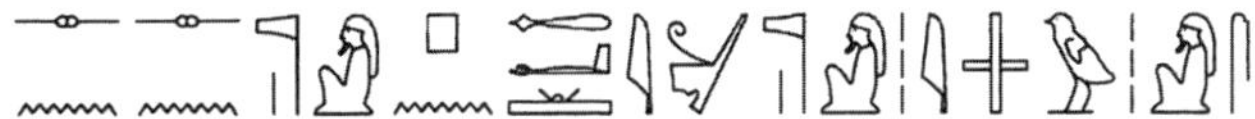

*snsn nṯr pn ʿ3 jn nṯrw jmyw.s*
Acclaming this Great God by the deities who are in it.

Name of the gate:

*ḥm(w)t nb.s*
"Artefact of its Lord".

At the two Uraeus-serpents on the wall:

*stt.s n rʿw*
"She lights up for Re".

Upper guardian:

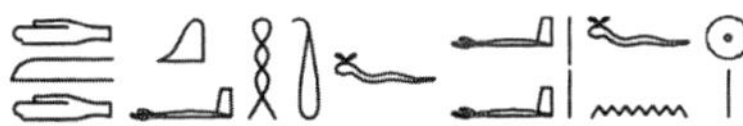

*dmḏ(w) qʿḥ.f ʿwy.fj n rʿw*
"Uniter". He bends his arms for Re.

Lower guardian:

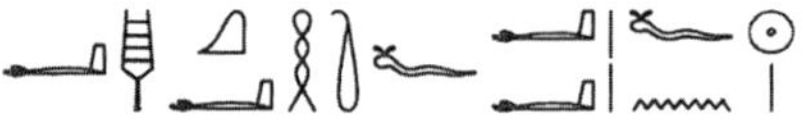

*ꜥḥꜥ(w) qꜥḥ.f ꜥwy.fj n rꜥw*

“Standing one”. He bends his arms for Re.

Nine mummies:

*psḏt* 6 (*nwt*) *m*

“Sixth Ennead in (…)”.

In front of the Ennead:

*my rk r.n ḫnty ꜣḫt*

«Come to us, Foremost of the Horizon,

*nṯr ꜥꜣ wpy štꜣw*

great god who has opened up the mysterious!

*wnw n.k sbḫwt ḏsrywt*

Open for you are the unapproachable gates,

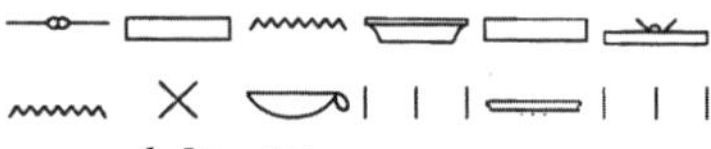

*znw n.k ꜥꜣw štꜣw*

unlocked for you are the mysterious doors!»

The serpent upon the doorway:

*jṯy m jrt.f*

"Who seizes with his eye".

*wnn.f ḥr ˁ3 pn*

He is upon this door,

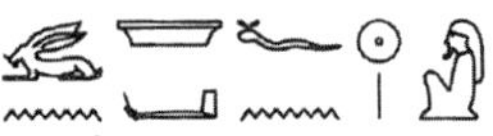

*wn.f n rˁw*

he opens for Re.

*sj3 n jṯy m jrt.f*

Sia (speaks) to him "who seizes with his eye"

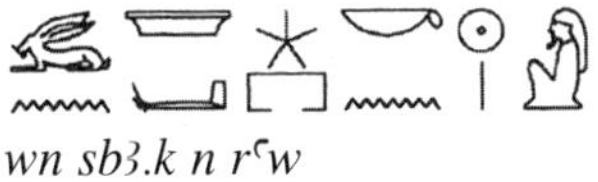

*wn sb3.k n rˁw*

«Open your gate for Re,

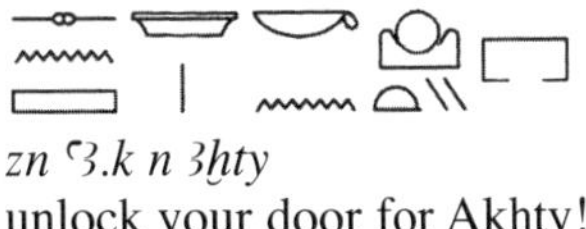

*zn ˁ3.k n 3ḫty*

unlock your door for Akhty!

*jw.f sḥḏ.f kkw zmꜣw*
He illuminates the Primeval Darkness,

*dj.f šsp m ꜥt-jmnt*
he throws light into the Hidden Region!»

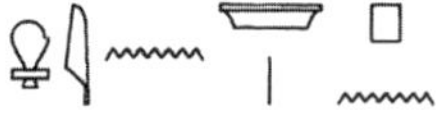

*ḫtmjn ꜥꜣ pn*
Then this door is closed,

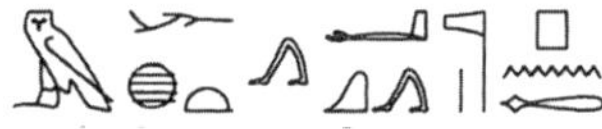

*m-ḫt ꜥq nṯr pn ꜥꜣ*
after this Great God has entered.

*hwtḫr bꜣw jmyw sbḫt.tn*
Then the *Ba*-souls in this gate wail

*sḏm.sn hꜣꜣ ꜥꜣ pn*
when they hear this door being slammed.

From the Sarcophagus of Djedher. The Gate is put in front of the third hour of the Amduat (probably late reign of Nectanebo II).

# SCHEMA OF

# THE SEVENTH HOUR

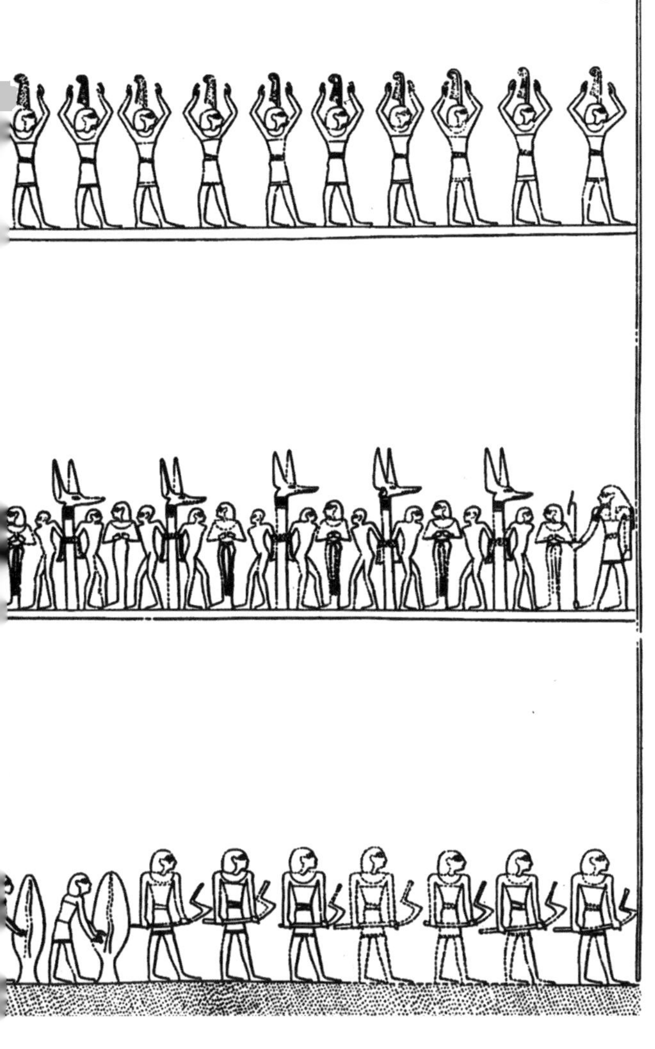

# PART OF THE

The lid of the alabaster sarcophagus of Seti I is only partially pre

# SEVENTH HOUR

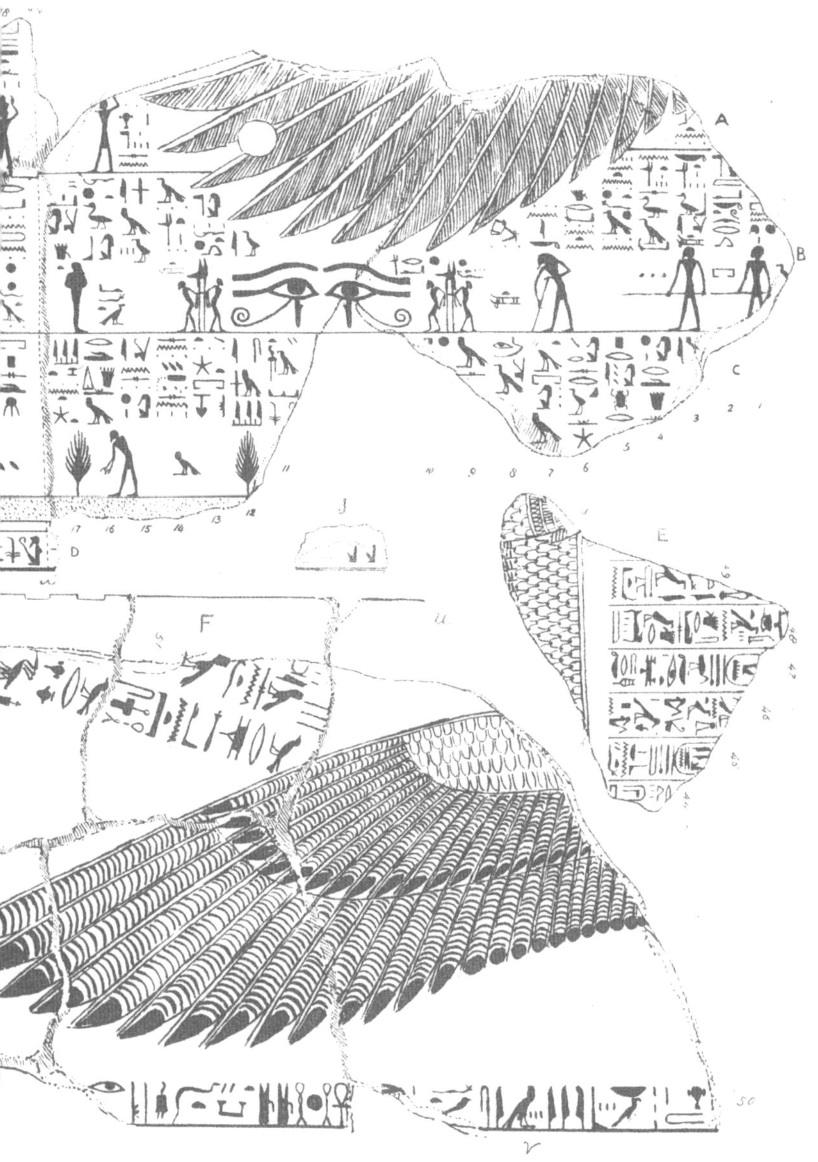

## Upper Register, 42nd Scene

Twelve gods carrying baskets with bread on their head:

*ḥtptyw ḫprw* (for: *ẖryw*) *ȝwt*
"Those who belong to offerings, who carry food offerings".

The text reads:

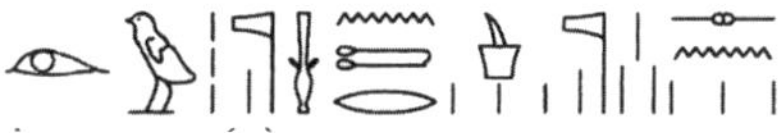

*jryw snṯr* (*n*) *nṯrw.sn*
Those who offered incense to their gods,

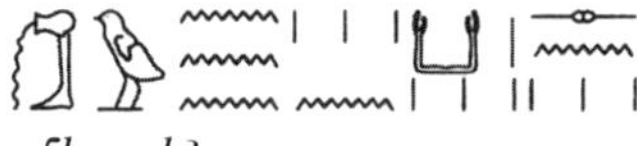

*wʿbwn kȝw.sn*
who purified their *Ka*-powers,

*tmw rq*(*w*) *ȝḫ ḥr srq.f*
who did not keep off an *Akh*-spirit from his breath,

From the tomb of Pharoh Ramses III.

*mtw ḥr qbḥw.f*

or a deceased from his refreshment.

*sn ḥtp.sn m ꜣwt.sn*

They are content with their food offerings,

*sprn.sn nṯrw.sn kꜣw.sn*

when they have reached their gods and their *Ka*-powers.

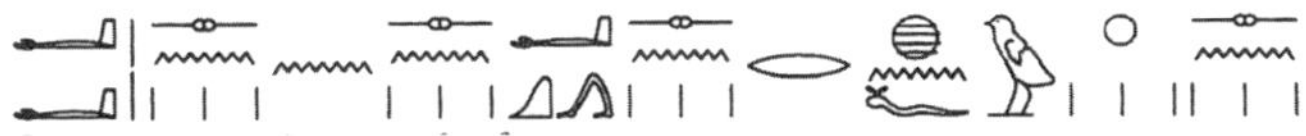

*ꜥwy.sn n.sn ꜥq.sn r ẖnfw.sn*

Their arms belong to them, when they have access to their cakes,

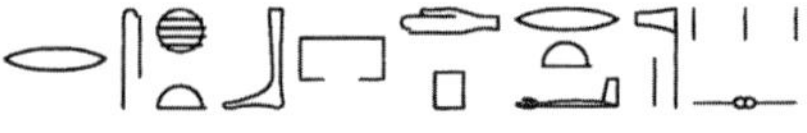

*r sbḫt drpt nṯrw.s*

at the gate which nourishes its gods.

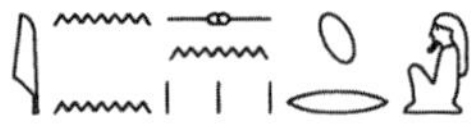

*jn n.sn wsjr*

Osiris says to them:

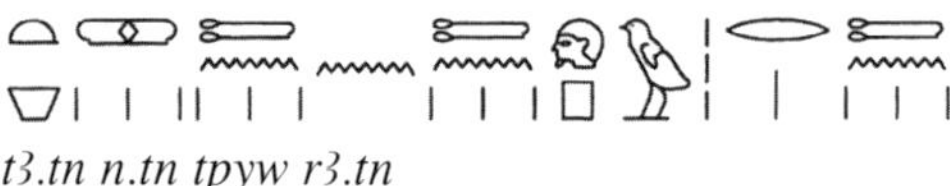

*tꜣ.ṯn n.ṯn tpyw rꜣ.ṯn*

«Your bread belongs to you in your mouth,

*ḥtptyw ḫprw ꜣwt*

you who belong to offerings, whose food offerings emerge!

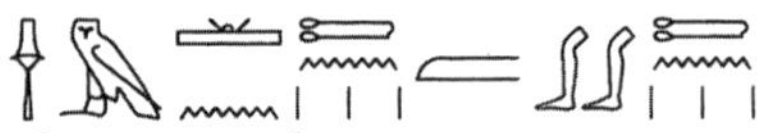

*sḫmn.ṯn m rdwy.ṯn*

You may have power over your feet,

*ḥtp.ṯn m jbw.ṯn*

and you are content in your hearts.

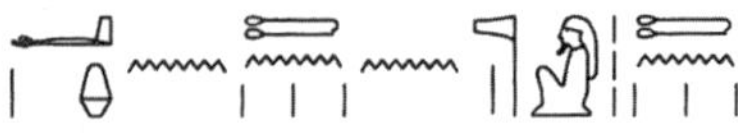

*ꜥ(w) n.ṯn nj nṯrw.ṯn*

The portions of your gods belong to you,

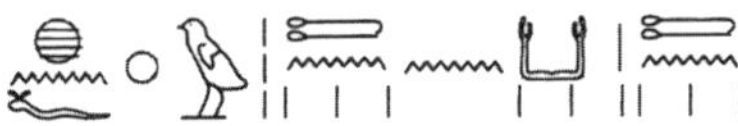

*ḫnfw.ṯn n k3w.ṯn*

your cakes belong to your *Ka*-powers!»

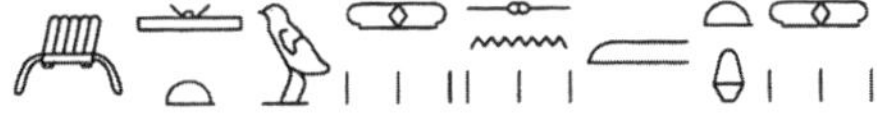

*3wt.sn m t3*

Their oblation is bread,

*ḥnqt.sn m ḏsrt*

their beer is Djeseret,

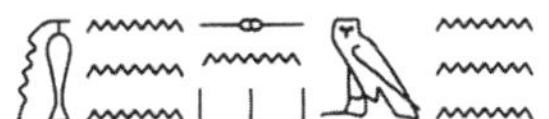

*qbḥw.sn m mw*

their refreshment is water.

*jw wdnw n.sn tp t3*

Whoever makes an offering to them on earth

*m nb ḥtpw m jmntt*

disposes of offerings in the West.

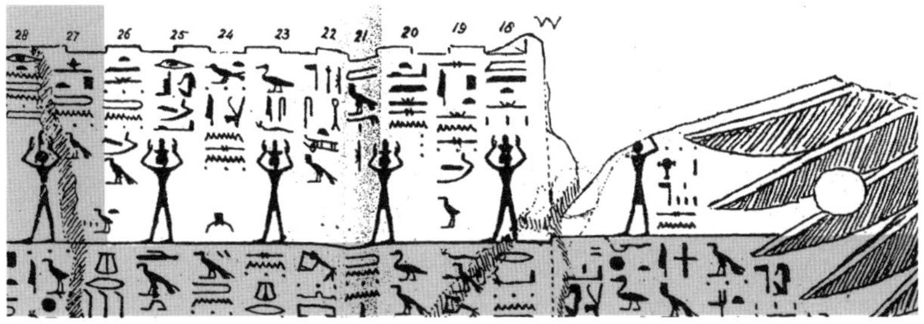

## 43RD SCENE

Twelve gods (or blessed deceased), each one carrying the sign of Maat on his head:

*mꜣꜥtyw ẖryw mꜣꜥt*

"Those belonging to Maat and carrying Maat".

The text reads:

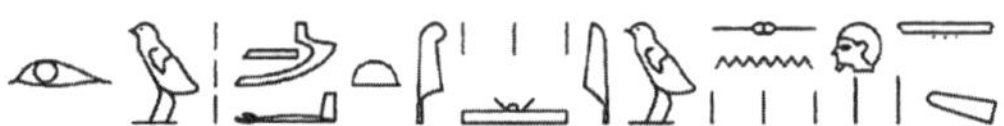

*jryw mꜣꜥt jw.sn tp tꜣ*

Who have practised Maat when they were (still) on earth,

*ꜥḥꜥw ḥr nṯr.sn*

who have fought for their god –

*njstw.sn r sḫnt tꜣ*

they are summoned to the resting place of the Earth,

From the tomb of Pharaoh Ramses III.

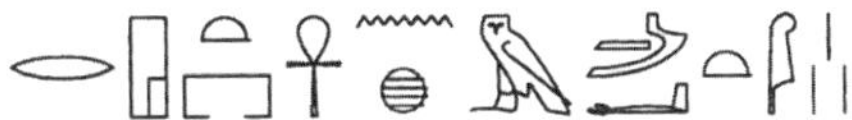

*r ḥwt ꜥnḫw m mꜣꜥt*

to the temple of Him who lives on Maat.

*sjptw n.sn mꜣꜥt.sn*

Their Maat is examined for them

*m-bꜣḥ nṯr ꜥꜣ sḥtm jsft*

in front of the Great God who destroys evil (jsft).

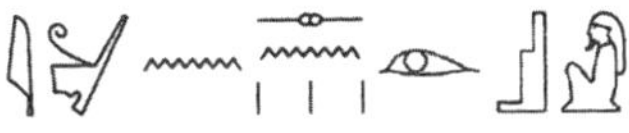

*jn n.sn wsjr*

Osiris says to them:

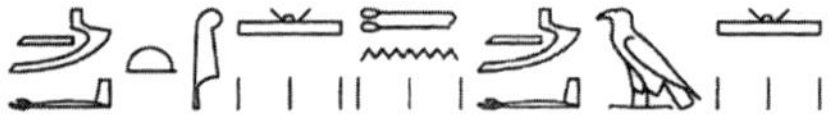

*m3ˁt (n.)ṯn m3ˁtyw*

«Maat belongs to you, who are truthful!

*ḥtp.ṯn m jrytn.ṯn*

You are satisfied with what you have done,

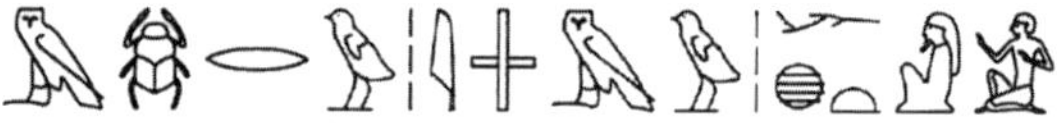

*m ḫprw jmyw-ḫt.j*

as those who have become my retinue,

*ḫntyw ḥwt ḏsrw b3.f*

who are in the temple of (the god) with protected (or secluded) *Ba*-soul.

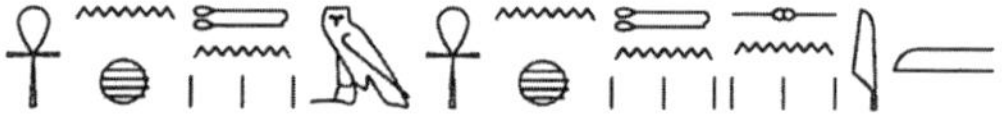

*ˁnḫ.ṯn m ˁnḫt.sn jm*

You live on what they live on,

*srq.ṯn m srq.sn jm*

you breathe on what they breathe on,

*sḫmn.ṯn m qbḥw ny š.ṯn*

you took hold of the refreshment of your lake.

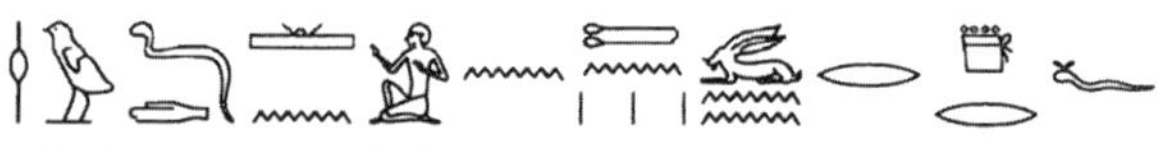

*wḏn.j n.ṯn wnn r-ḏr.f*

I have decreed for you a being until its end,

*ẖr m3ʿt jwty h3j jsft r.f*

carrying Maat, without evil being able to disturb it.»

*3wt.sn m m3ʿt*

Their oblation is Maat,

*ḥnqt.sn m jrp*

their beer is wine,

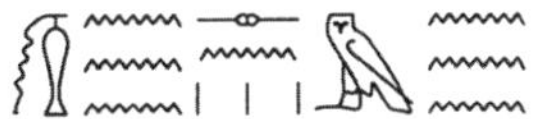

*qbḥw.sn m mw*

their refreshment is water.

*jw wdnw n.sn tp t3*

Whoever makes an offering to them on earth

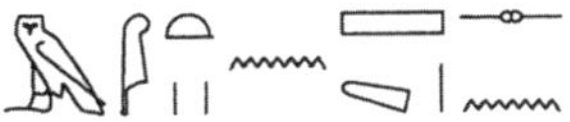

*m m3ʿty nj š.sn*

is a truthful one of their district.

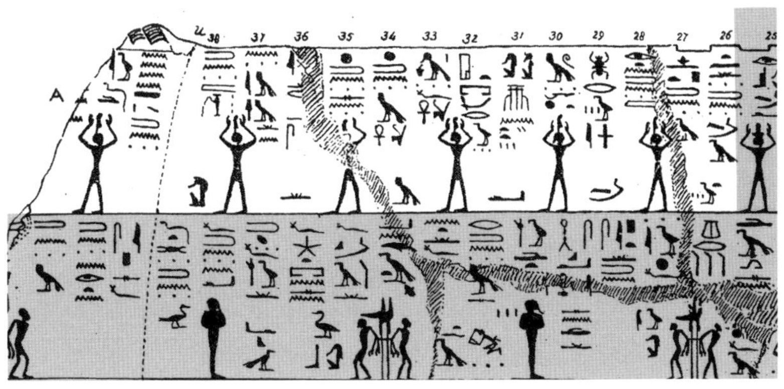

## Middle Register, 44th Scene

From the tomb of Ramses III.

The solar barque, and in it:

| | | | |
|---|---|---|---|
| *sjꜣ* | *mḥn* | *jwf-rꜥw* | *ḥkꜣ* |
| Sia (Percipience), | Mehen, | Flesh of Re, | Heka (Magic) |

Four towing gods or deceased:

*dwꜣtyw*

"(Gods) of the Netherworld".

*sṯꜣw nṯr pn ꜥꜣ jn nṯrw dwꜣtyw*

This great god is towed by the gods of the Netherworld.

*jn.sn sṯ3.sn rʿw*

They say when they tow Re:

*q3j jtn ḫnty mḥn*

«Elevated is the disc of him who disposes of Mehen,

*psḏ tp nj jmy k3r.f*

and shining is the head of him who is in his shrine.»

(Re says:)

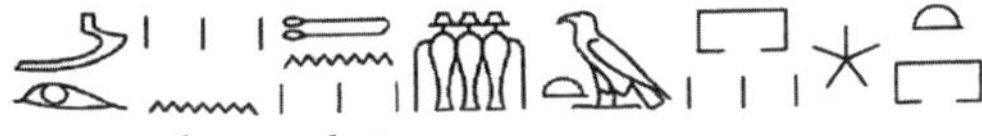

*m33n.ṯn ḫntyw dw3t*

«May you look, who are in the Netherworld,

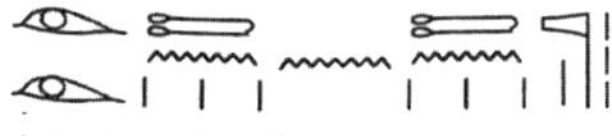

*jrty.ṯn n.ṯn nṯrw*

(for) your eyes belong to you, O gods!

*m.ṯn rʿw sḫmw m jgrt*

Behold, Re has power over the Jgeret (Beyond),

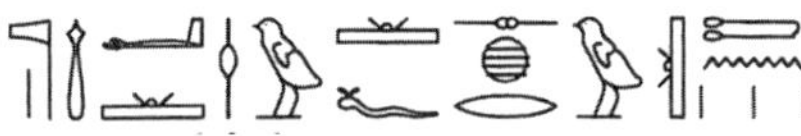

*nṯr ʿ3 wḏ.f sḫrw.ṯn*

The Great God cares for you.»

## 45TH SCENE

Seven poles (here only six are preserved) in the shape of the jackal-headed *wsr*-pole. To each one of them two enemies are bound, and to each group belongs a mummiform punishing demon. The whole scene is framed by two gods leaning on a staff.

At the beginning of the scene:

*jtmw*
Atum

First pole:

*ḫftyw rꜥw*
The enemies of Re,

*nḏrw*
Who seizes

Second pole:

*ḫftyw jtmw*
The enemies of Atum,

*ꜥftyw*
Who presses

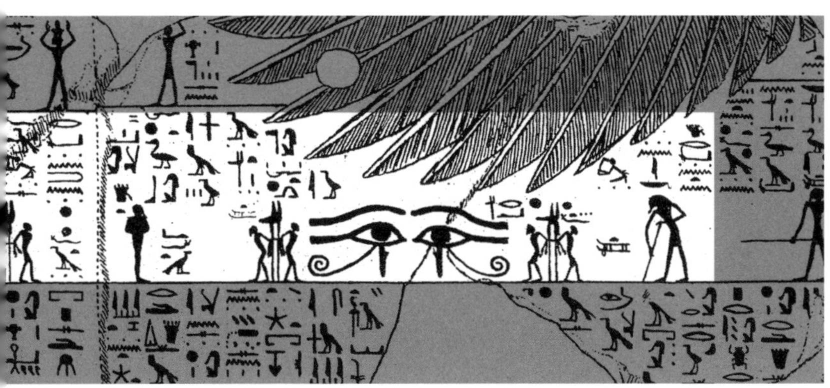

Third pole:

*ḫftyw ḫprj*
The enemies of Chepri,

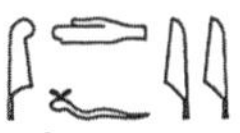
*jdy* (?)
Who is violent (?)

Fourth pole:

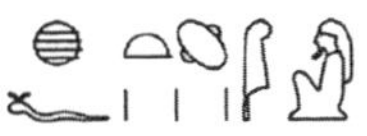
*ḫftyw šw*
The enemies of Shu,

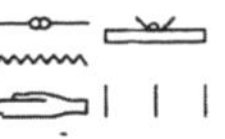
*snḏw*
Who is terrible

Fifth pole:

*ḫftyw gbb*
The enemies of Geb,

*ʿqꜣw*
Who is precise

Sixth pole:

*ḫftyw wsjr*

The enemies of Osiris,

*ˁ3gw*

Who squeezes

Seventh pole:

*ḫftyw ḥrw*

The enemies of Horus,

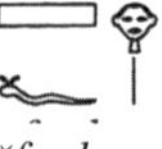

*šfw ḥr*

With authoritative face

At the end of the scene:

*nbw nṯrw*

"The Golden one of the gods".

The text belonging to this scene reads:

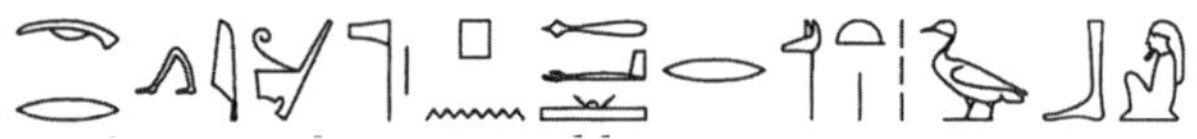

*spr jn nṯr pn ˁ3 r wsrwt gbb*

Arrival of this Great God at the poles of Geb

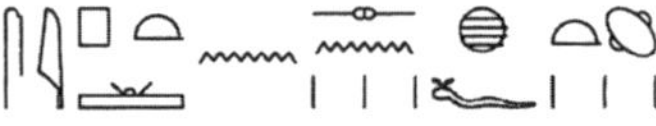

*sjpwt n.sn ḫftyw*

to which the enemies are condemned

*m-ḫt wḏˁ mdw m jmntt*

after the judgement pronounced in the West.

From the tomb of Pharaoh Ramses III.

*jn sj3 n nṯr pn*

Sia says to this god

*spr.f r wsrwt gbb*

when he arrives at the poles of Geb:

*hnn rʿw nṯr ʿ3*

«Give your consent, Re, great god,

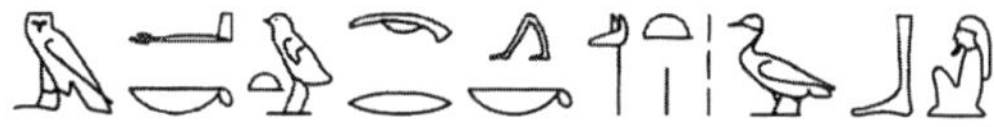

*mk.ṯw spr.k wsrwt gbb*

behold, you have reached the poles of Geb!»

*jn jtmw n wsrwt*

Atum says to the poles:

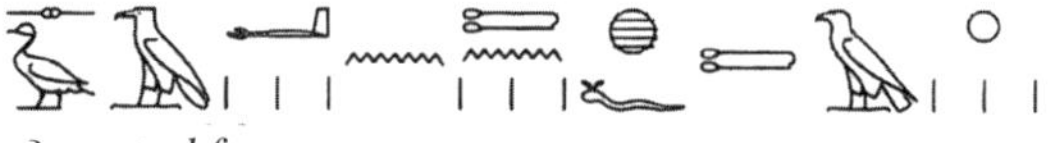

*z3w n.ṯn ḫftyw*

«Guard for yourselves the enemies,

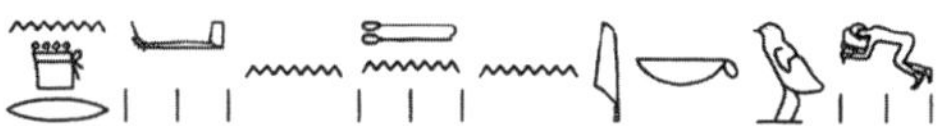

*nḏrw n.ṯn njkw*

seize for yourselves those to be punished,

*j nṯrw ḫtyw wsrwt*

O you gods behind the poles,

*jmyw-ḫt gbb rpꜥ(t)*

retinue of Geb, the prince!

From the tomb of Pharaoh Ramses V/VI.

*nḏrw n.ṯn ḫftyw*

Seize for yourselves the enemies

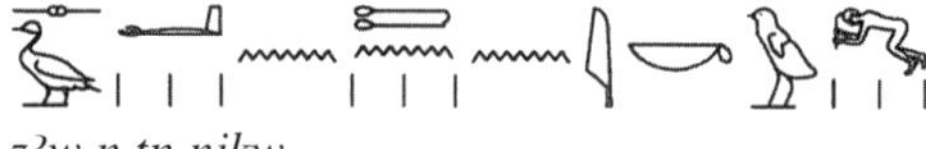

*z3w n.ṯn njkw*

guard for yourselves those to be punished,

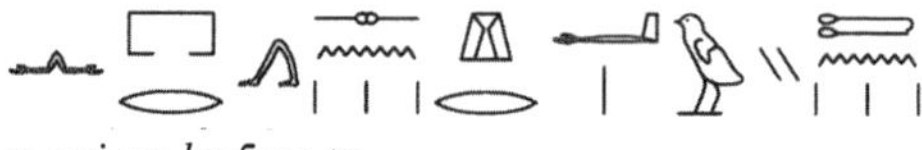

*n prj.sn ḫr ꜥwy.ṯn*

that they do not escape under your hands,

*nn d3.sn ḫr ḏbꜥw.ṯn*

nor get away under your fingers!

*j ḫftyw sjptw.ṯn (n) ḥsq*

O enemies, you are condemned to be beheaded,

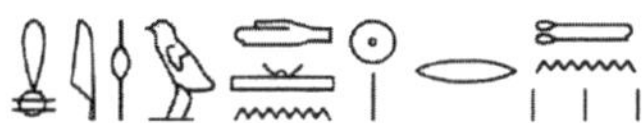

*mj wḏtn rꜥw r.ṯn*

as Re has decreed against you,

*m snṯ.f jgrt n ḫ3t.f*

when he established the Jgeret (Beyond) for his corpse,

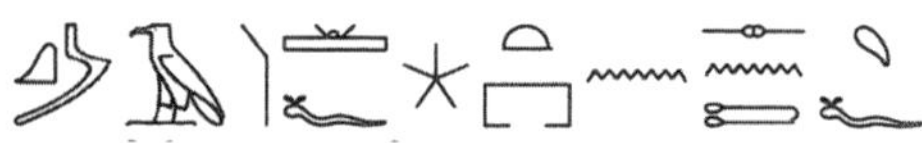

*qm3.f dw3t n snṯ.f*

and created the Netherworld for his limbs.

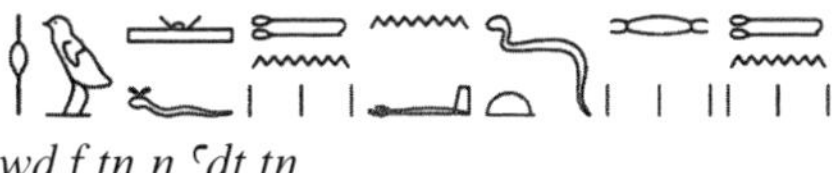

*wḏ.f.ṯn n ꜥḏt.ṯn*

He assigns you to your carnage,

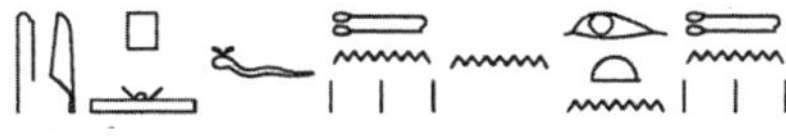

*sjp.f.ṯn n jrytn.ṯn*

he allots you to what you have done,

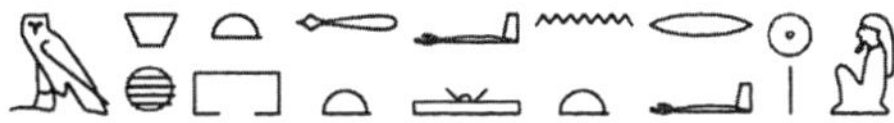

*m wsḫt ꜥꜣt nt rꜥw*

in the great hall of Re.

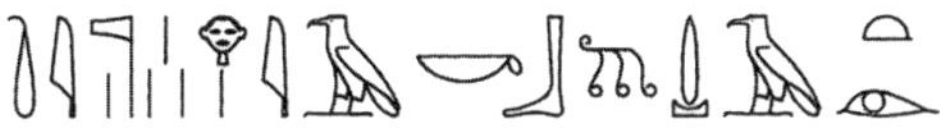

*ty nṯrw ḥr jꜣkb wḏꜣt*

While the gods bewail the *Udjat*-eye,

*dy.f nbw nṯrw m zꜣw.ṯn*

he appoints «the Golden one of the gods» as your guard.

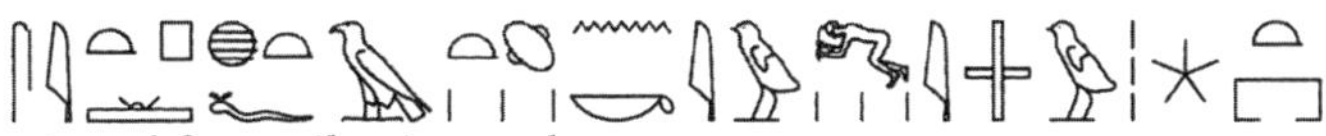

*sjptw ḫftyw njkw jmyw dwꜣt*

Condemned are the enemies and those to be punished who are in the Netherworld

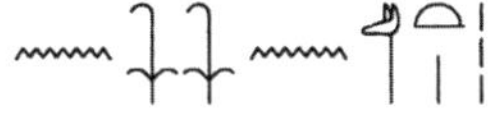

*n nn ny wsrwt*

to these poles.»

## LOWER REGISTER, 46TH SCENE

A god leaning on a staff:

*nb ꜣwt-jb*

"Master of joy".

followed by twelve gods without attributes, every one confronting a large ear of grain:

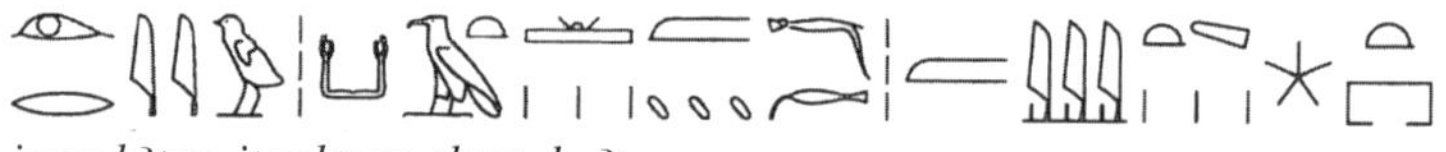

*jryw kꜣt m jt mḥy m sḫwt dwꜣt*

"Those who generate food from Lower Egyptian barley in the fields of the Netherworld".

To them belongs the text:

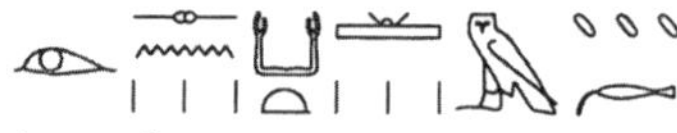

*jry.sn kꜣt m jt*

They generate food from barley,

From the tomb of Pharaoh Ramses III.

*zẖn.sn nprj ḥ(t)y*

they embrace (the grain god) Nepri-Heti.

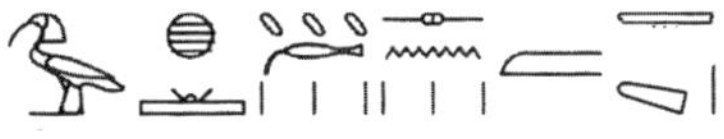

*ꜣḫ jt.sn m tꜣ*

More brilliant is their barley in the Earth

*r ꜣḫwt rꜥw prr.f*

than the brilliance of Re when he goes forth.

*ty.f ꜥp.f ḥr.sn*

But when he passes them,

*jn n.sn nb ꜣwt-jb*

the Master of joy says to them:

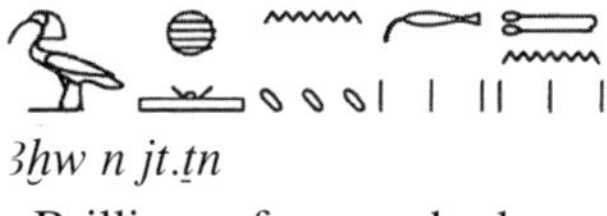

*ꜣḫw n jt.ṯn*

«Brilliance for your barley,

*rd n bdt.ṯn*

growth for your spelt!

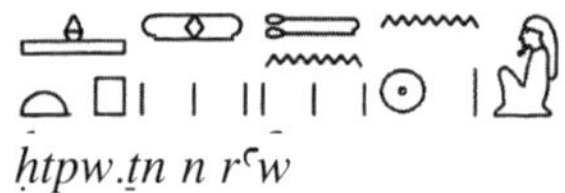

*ḥtpw.ṯn n rꜤw*

Your offerings belong to Re,

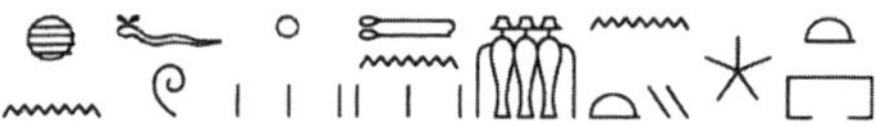

*ḫnfw.ṯn (n) ḫnty dwꜣt*

your cakes to the Foremost of the Netherworld.

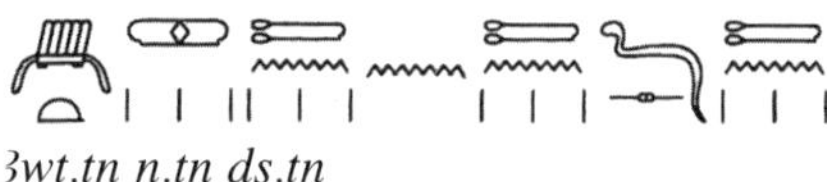

*ꜣwt.ṯn n.ṯn ḏs.ṯn*

Your oblations belong to yourself,

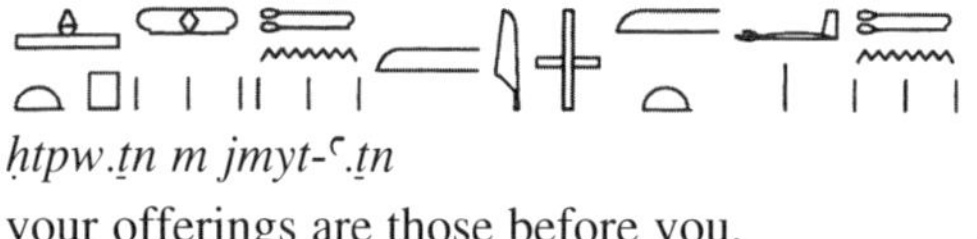

*ḥtpw.ṯn m jmyt-Ꜥ.ṯn*

your offerings are those before you,

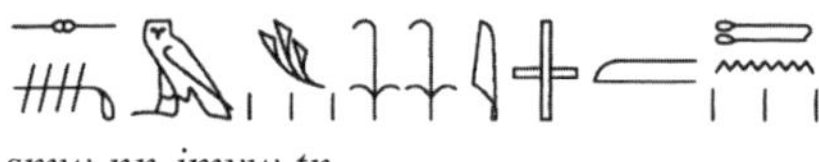

*smw nn jmyw.ṯn*

the greenery of these, among whom you are,

*n wsjr ḥtp.f jm.f*

belongs to Osiris that he is content with it.»

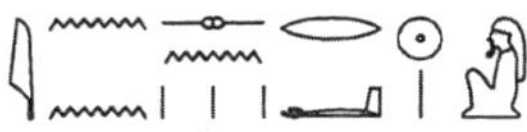

*jn n.sn rʿw*

Re says to them:

*rd nprj ḫpr wsjr*

«When Nepri grows, Osiris emerges,

*srqw dwꜣtyw m mꜣn.f*

upon whose sight those of the Netherworld breathe

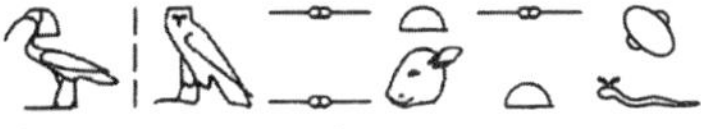

*ꜣḫw m ss(n)t stj.f*

and the *Akh*-spirits, when they smell his odour.

*ꜣḫw n.k wsjr*

Blessing for you, Osiris,

*bwꜣ n.k nprj-ḥ(t)y*

prosperity for you, Nepri-Heti,

*spd n.k ḫnty jmntyw*

success for you Khontamenti (Foremost of the Netherworld)!

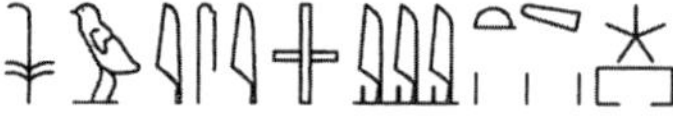

*sw(t) js jmy sḫwt dwꜣt*

It is he who is in the fields of the Netherworld,

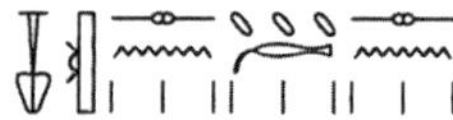

*zmꜣ.sn jt.sn*

when they unite with their barley.»

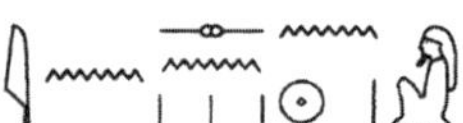

*jn.sn n rꜥw*

They say to Re:

*rd dy(w) m sḫwt nt dwꜣt*

«The grain rations are growing in the fields of the Netherworld,

*psḏ rꜥw ḥr ḥꜥwt wsjr*

when Re shines upon the limbs of Osiris.

*wbn.k ḫpr rnpyt*

When you arise, green plants come into being,

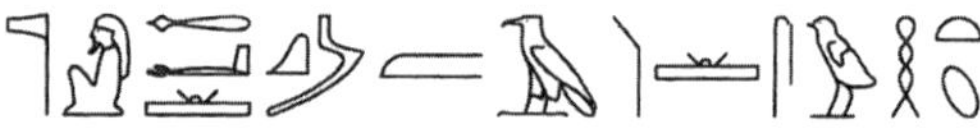

*nṯr ꜥꜣ qmꜣ swḥt*

Great God, who has created the egg!»

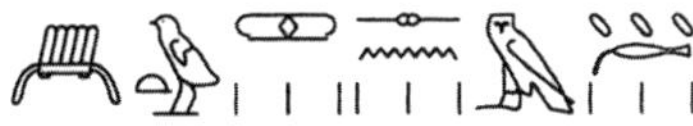

*ꜣwt.sn m jt*

Their oblation is barley,

*ḥnqt.sn m ḏsrt*

their beer is Djeseret,

*qbḥw.sn m mw*

their refreshment is water.

*jw wdnw n.sn tp tꜣ*

Whoever makes an offering to them on earth

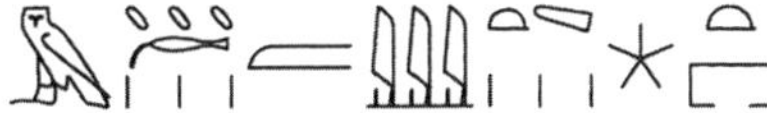

*m jt(y) m sḫwt dwꜣt*

disposes of barley in the fields of the Netherworld.

## 47TH SCENE

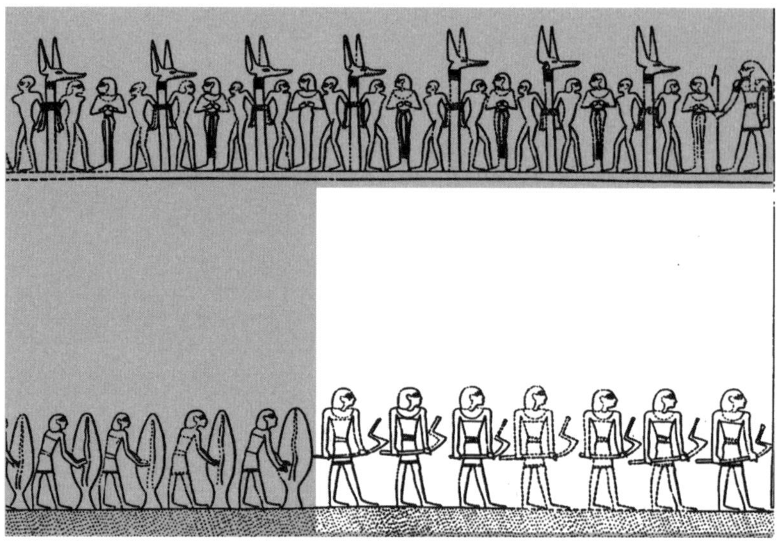

Seven gods carrying sickles with both hands:

*jryw ḫ3bw*
"Who belong to the sickles".

Some versions add an anonymous god leaning on a staff, as another form of the Sungod in the Netherworld.

The text reads:

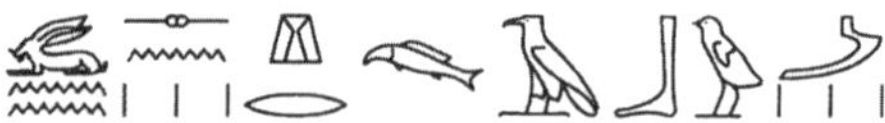

*wnn.sn ḫr ḫ3bw*
They carry sickles,

From the tomb of Pharaoh Ramses III.

*ꜣzḫ.sn jt m sḫwt.sn*

so that they mow the barley in their fields.

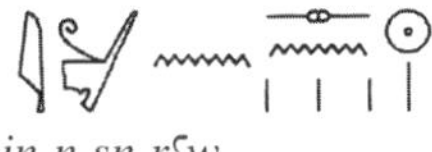

*jn n.sn rꜥw*

Re says to them:

*šzp n.ṯn ḫꜣbw.ṯn*

«May you receive your sickles,

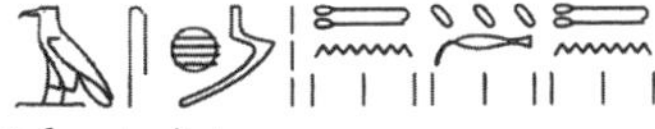

*ꜣzḫw.ṯn jt.ṯn*

may you mow your barley

*dy n.ṯn m tḥwt.ṯn*

and put it into your barns!

*sḥtp wsjr jw(.f) ḫnty qrrt št3t jrw*

Satisfy Osiris, since he is Foremost of the cavern with mysterious forms!

*jhy n.ṯn ḫ3byw*

Hail to you, mowers!»

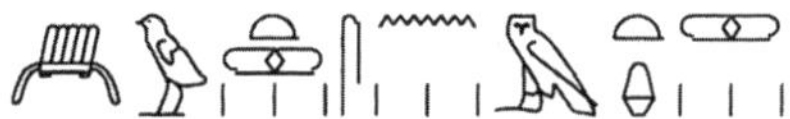

*3wt.sn m t3*

Their oblation is bread,

*ḥnqt.sn m ḏsrt*

their beer is Djeseret,

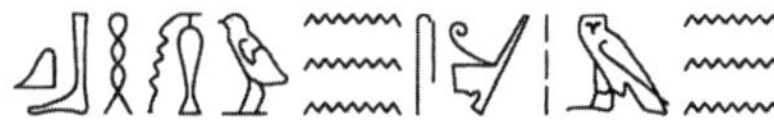

*qbḥw.sn m mw*

their refreshment is water.

*jw wdnw n.sn tp tꜣ*

Whoever makes an offering to them on earth

*m ẖryw ẖꜣbw m sḫwt dwꜣt*

will carry a sickle in the fields of the Netherworld.

## SEVENTH GATE

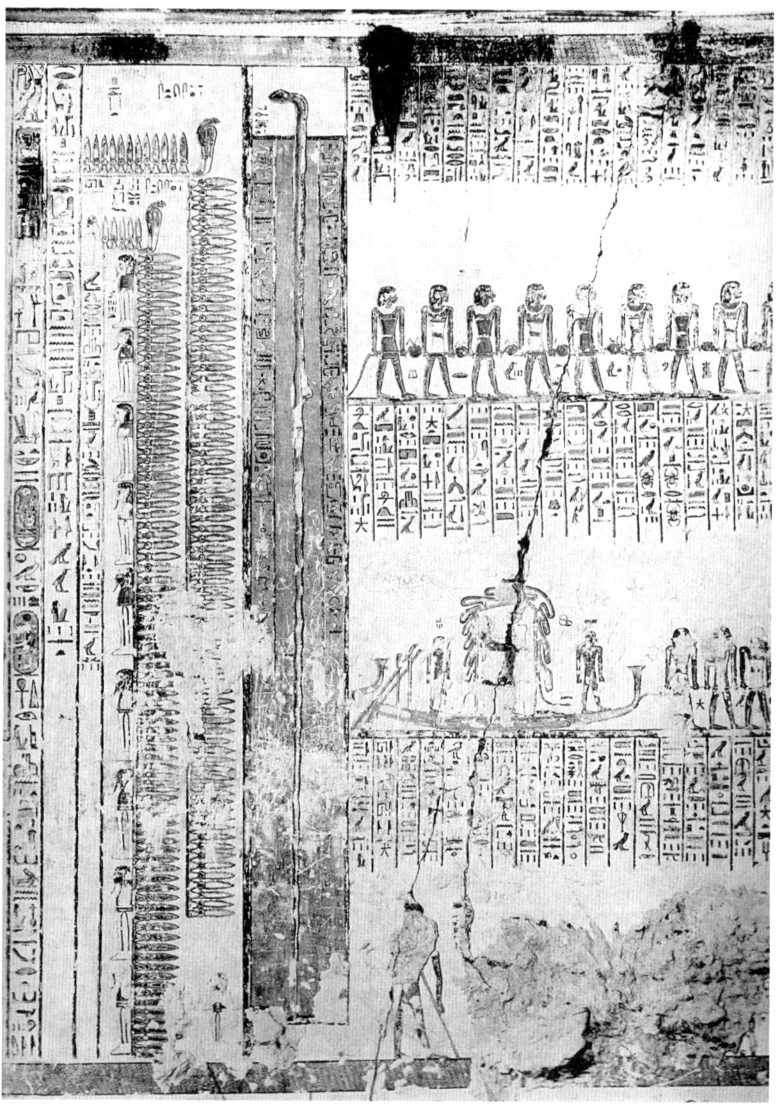

From the tomb of Pharaoh Ramses V/VI.

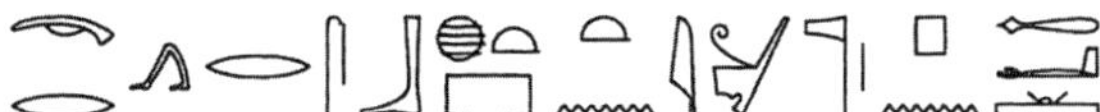

*spr r sbḫt tn jn nṯr pn ꜥ3*

Arriving at this gate by this great god,

*ꜥq m sbḫt tn*

entering into this gate,

*snsn nṯr pn ꜥ3 jn nṯrw jmyw.s*

praising this great god by the deities who are in it.

Name of the gate:

*psḏyt*

"Shining one".

Upper and lower Uraeus-serpents:

*stt.s n rꜥw*

"She lights up for Re".

Upper guardian:

*hqsw qꜥḥ.f ꜥwy.f(j) n rꜥw*

"The deficient one". He bends his arms for Re.

Lower guardian:

*špy qꜥḥ.f ꜥwy.f(j) n rꜥw*

"The blind one". He bends his arms for Re.

Nine mummies:

*psḏt 7nwt*

"The seventh Ennead".

In front of the Ennead:

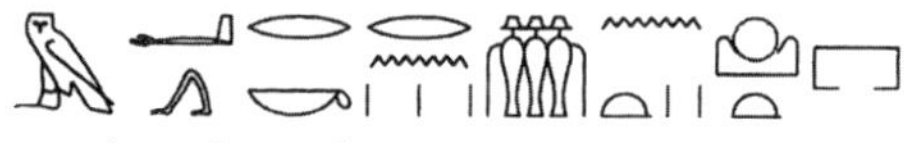

*my rk r.n ḫnty ꜣḫt*

«Do come to us, Foremost of the Horizon,

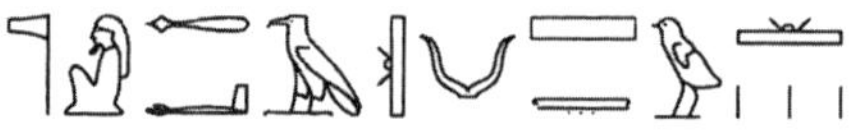

*nṯr ꜥꜣ wpj štꜣw*

Great god who has opened the Mysterious!

*wnw n.k sbḫwt ḏsryt*

Open are for you the unapproachable gates,

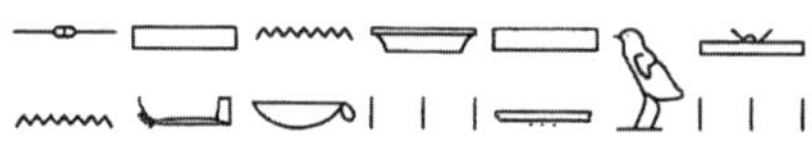

*znw n.k ꜥꜣw štꜣw*

unlocked are for you the mysterious doors!»

The serpent upon the doorway:

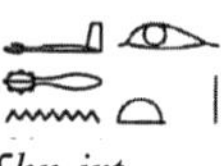

*ꜥḫn jrt*

"Whose eye is shut".

*wnn.f ḥr ꜥꜣ pn*

He is upon this door,

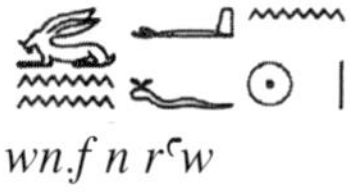

*wn.f n rꜥw*

he opens for Re.

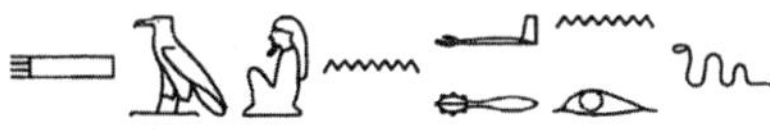

*sjꜣ n ꜥḫn-jrt*

Sia (speaks) to him “whose eye is shut”:

*wn sbꜣ.k n rꜥw*

«Open your gate for Re,

*zn ꜥꜣ.k n ꜣḫty*

unlock your door for Akhty!

*jw.f sḥḏ.f kkw zmꜣw*

He illuminates the Primeval Darkness,

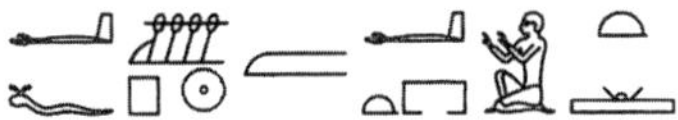

*dy.f šsp m ꜥt-jmnt*

he throws light into the Hidden Space!»

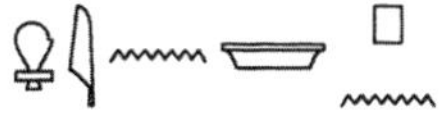

*ḫtmjn ꜥꜣ pn*

Then this door is shut,

*m-ḫt ꜥq nṯr pn ꜥꜣ*

after this great god has entered.

*hwtḫr ꜣḫw jmyw sbḫt.tn*

Then the *Akh*-spirits who are in this gate wail

*sḏm.sn hꜣꜣ ꜥꜣ pn*

when they hear this door being slammed.

# SCHEMA OF

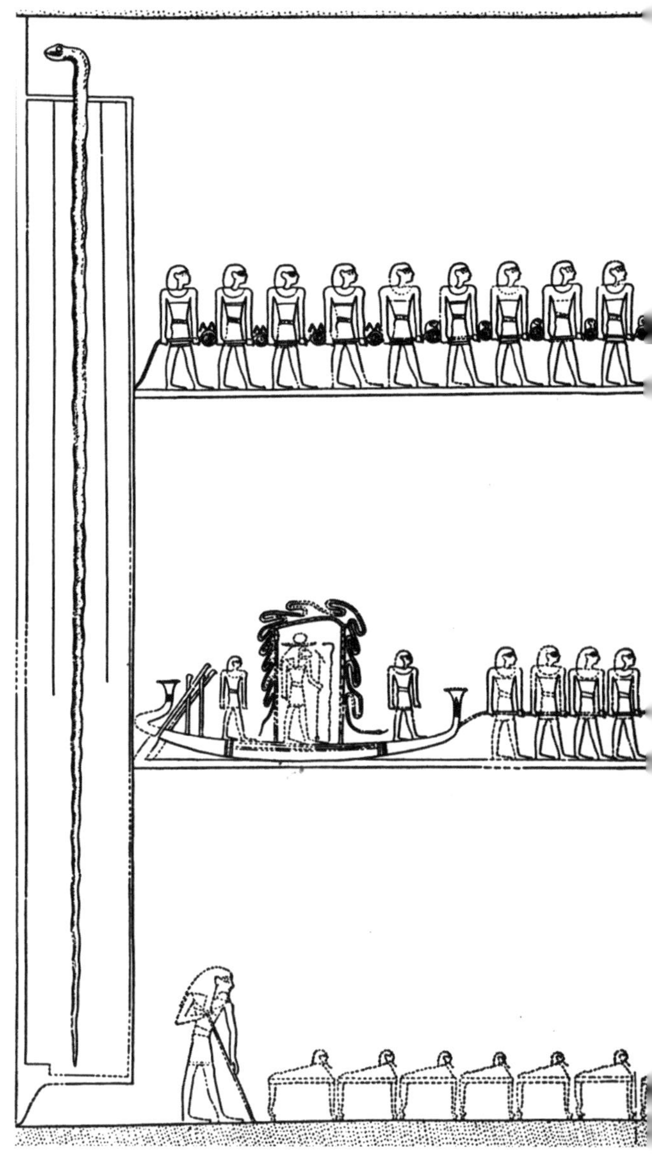

# THE EIGHTH HOUR

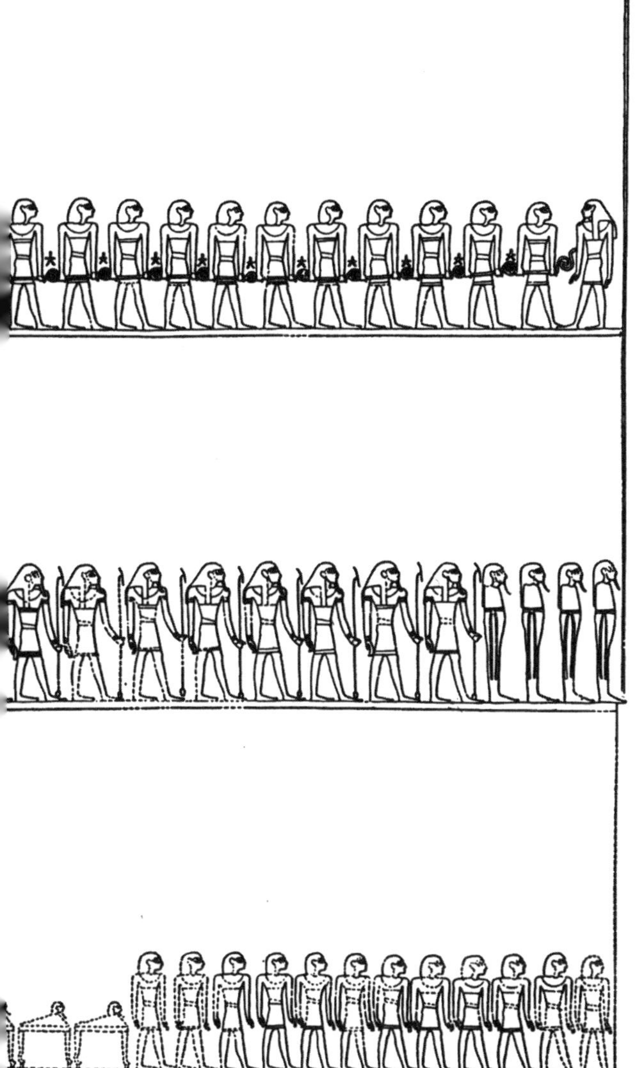

# PARTS FROM THE

The lid of the alabaster sarcophagus of Seti I is only partially

# EIGHTH HOUR

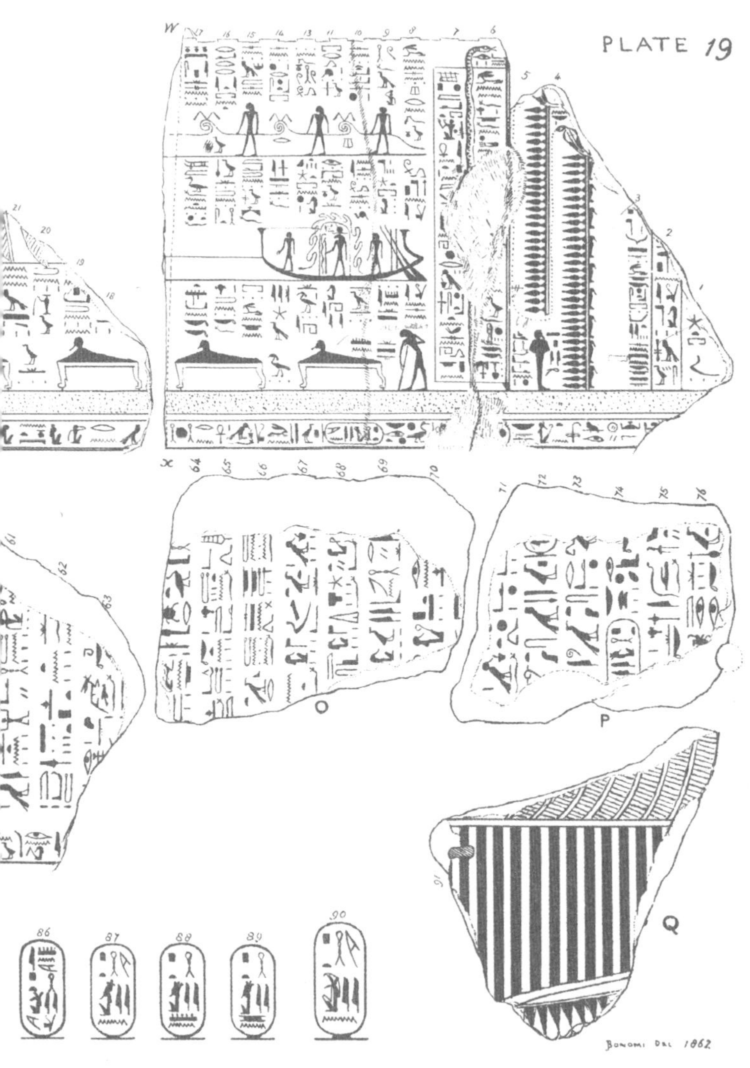

### Upper Register, 48th Scene

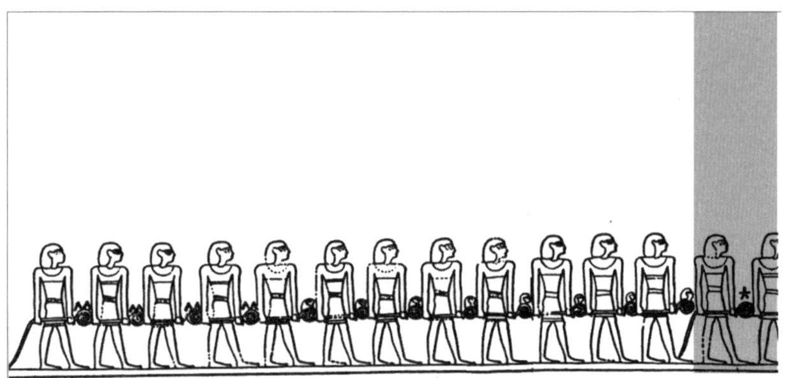

Twelve gods carrying a long rope from which emerge four human heads, four falcon heads, and four *dmḏ*, the sign for «unite»:

*ḫryw nwḥ msy sštȝw*

"Those who carry the rope which gives birth to mysteries".

The text reads:

*wnn.sn ḫr nwḥ fȝy.sn*

They carry the rope which they lift up.

*ḫʿʿ rʿw pry tpw jmyw nwḥ*

When Re appears, the heads emerge which are in the rope.

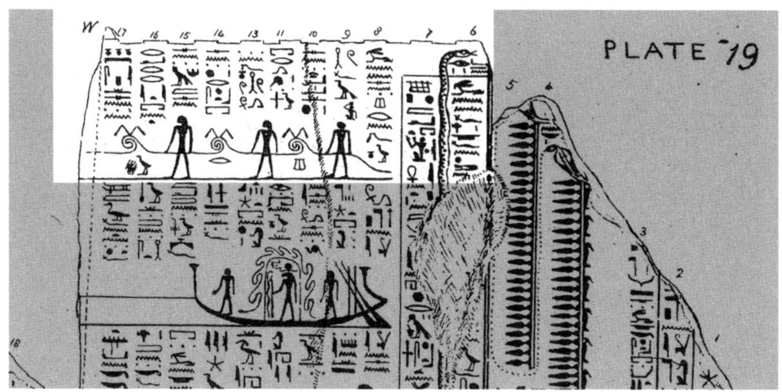


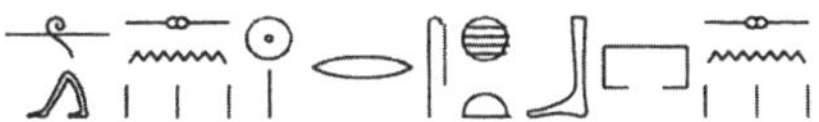

*sṯ3.sn rʿw r sbḫt.sn*

They tow Re to their gate

*ḥmm.sn r ʿrryt nt nww*

and (then) they turn back at the gateway of Nun.

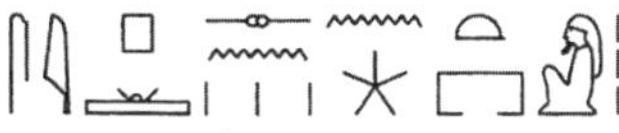

*sjpw.sn n dw3tyw*

They are ascribed to those of the Netherworld.

*pry wpwt ʿḳ3 nwḥ*

When the top of the heads emerge, the rope becomes straight.

(Re says:)

*ḥ3y sšt3w.j ḏs.j*

«My own mysteries shine,

*pry ḥrw m q3bw.sn*

when the faces emerge from their coils.

*ḥ3y msyw msyn.j*

The shapes which I have formed shine,

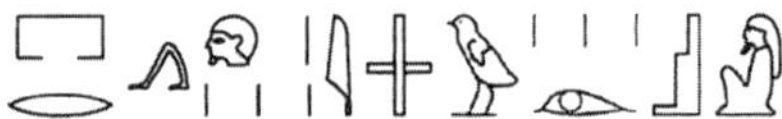

*prj tpw jmyw wsjr*

when the heads emerge among whom Osiris is.

*wnw sṯ3w ꜥq3 ꜥnnw*

Open, you who tow, when the serpent rope is straight!

*sṯ3w.ṯn n.j ẖryw nwḥ*

May you tow for me, carrier of the rope,

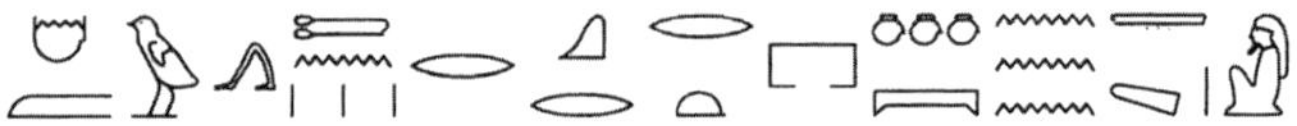

*ḥmw.ṯn r qrrt nww*

and may you turn back at the cavern of Nun!»

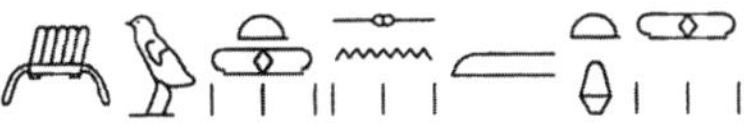

*ꜣwt.sn m tꜣ*

Their oblation is bread,

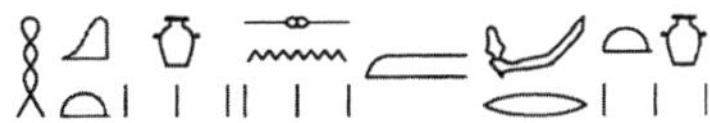

*ḥnqt.sn m ḏsrt*

their beer is Djeseret,

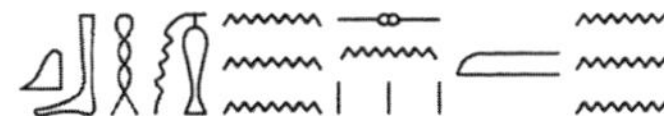

*qbḥw.sn m mw*

their refreshment is water.

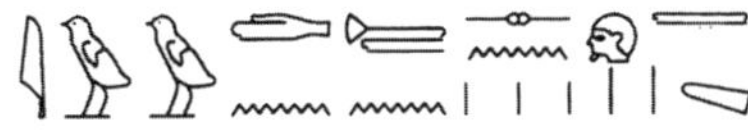

*jw wdnw n.sn tp tꜣ*

Whoever makes an offering to them on earth

*m ṯzw nwḥ m wjꜣ*

will tie the rope in the (solar) barque.

**49TH SCENE**

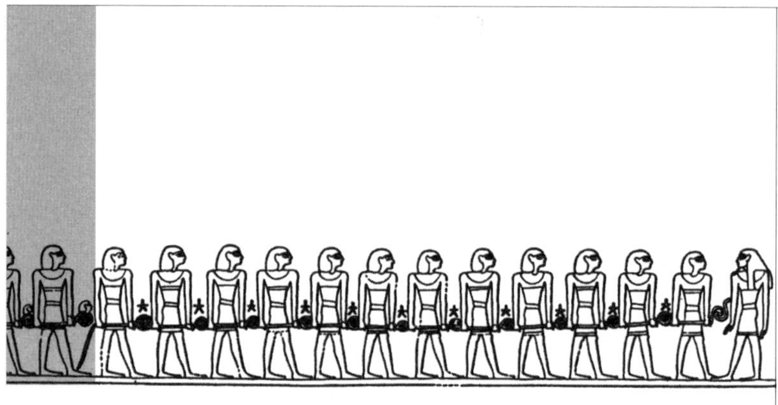

A god without attributes, called *jkky* Ikeki confronts twelve gods carrying another rope in the shape of a serpent; above each coil a star represents one of the hours:

*ẖryw ˁmw msy wnwt*

"Those who carry the (rope) Devourer, which gives birth to the hours".

The text reads:

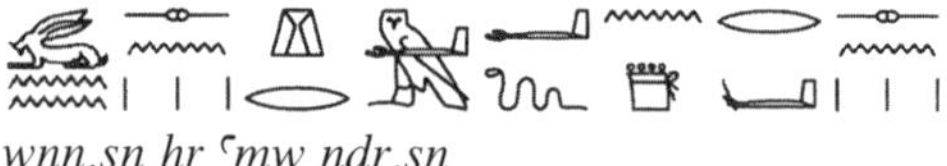

*wnn.sn ẖr ˁmw nḏr.sn*

They carry the Devourer whom they grasp

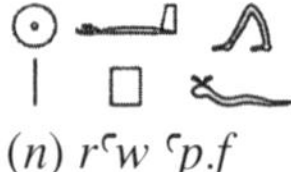

(*n*) *rˁw ˁp.f*

(for) Re when he passes by.

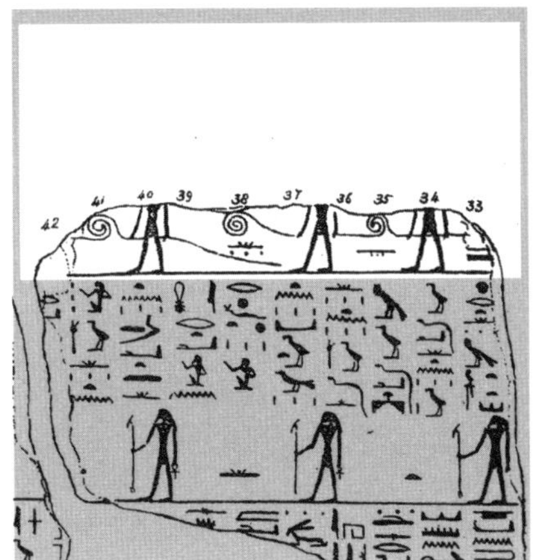

From the tomb of Ramses V/VI.

*sjꜣ n nn nj nṯrw*

Sia (says) to these gods:

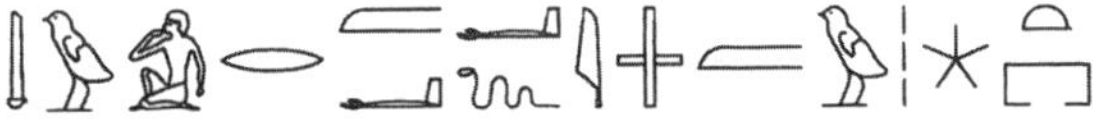

*mdw r ꜥmw jmyw dwꜣt*

«Speak to the Devourer, you who are in the Netherworld!

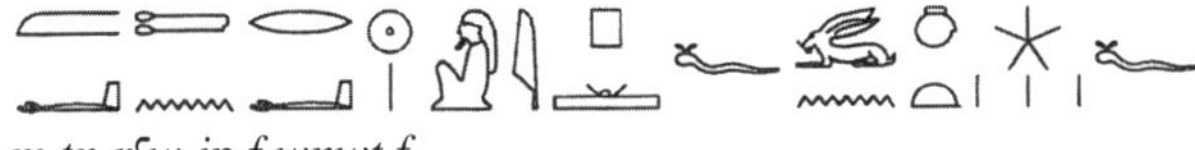

*m.ṯn rꜥw jp.f wnwt.f*

Look, Re counts his hours!»

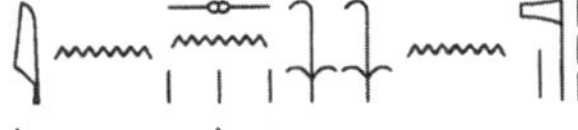

*jn.sn nn nj nṯrw*

They say, these gods:

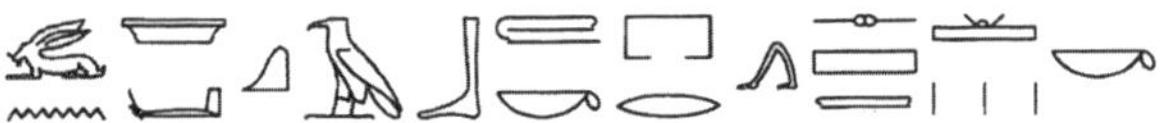

*wn qꜣb.k pry sštꜣw.k*

«Open your coil, that your mysteries (can) emerge! »

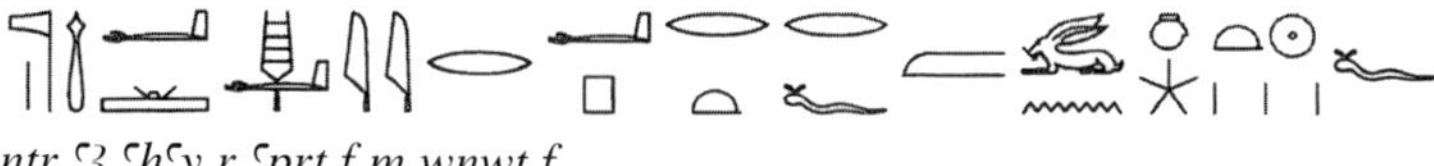

*nṯr ꜥ3 ꜥḥꜥy r ꜥprt.f m wnwt.f*

The great god is waiting till he is provided with his hour

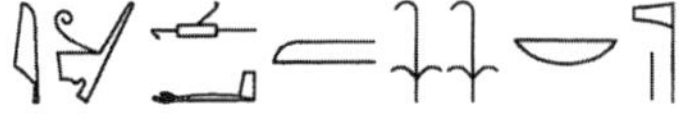

*jn wꜥ nb m nn (nj) nṯr(w)*

by every one of these gods.

*pry ḫr wnwt m q3b ḥtpḫr(.s) nst*

Then an hour emerges from a coil and takes (its) place.

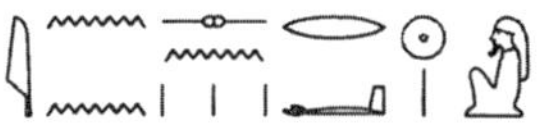

*jn n.sn rꜥw*

Re says to them:

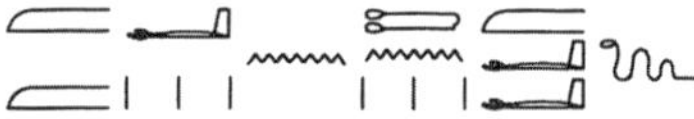

*jm n.ṯn ꜥmw*

«Take for you the Devourer,

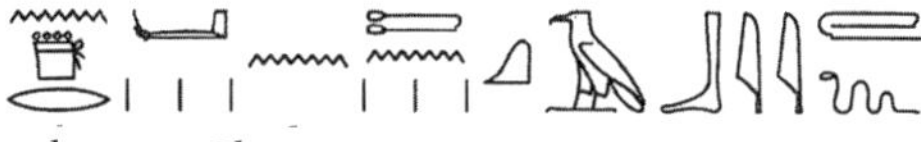

*nḏr n.ṯn q3by*

and grasp for you the coiled one!

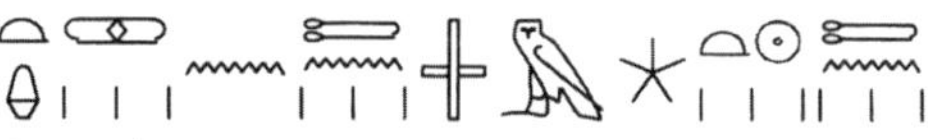

*t3 n.ṯn jmy wnwt.ṯn*

Bread belongs to you, which is in your hours,

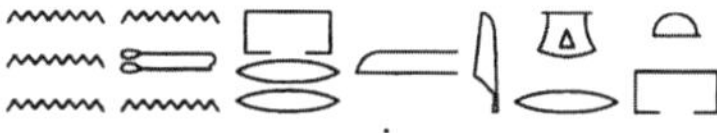

*mw n.ṯn prrw m jgrt*

water belongs to you which goes forth from the Igeret (Beyond).

*sḫm.ṯn m z3w.ṯn*

You have power over him whom you guard,

*nty jkky m z3w.sw*

whom also Ikeki is guarding.

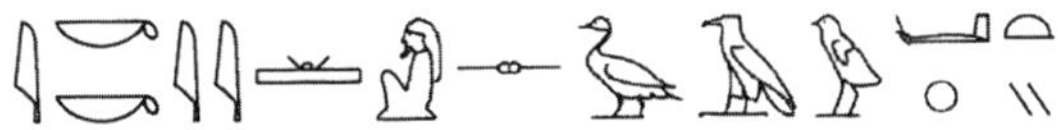

*jkky z3wty zp 2*

(since) Ikeki is the guardian of him who is to be guarded.»

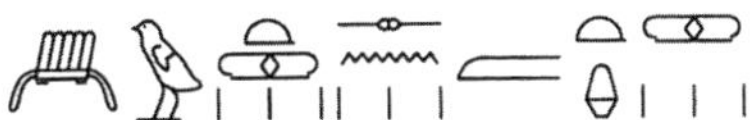

*3wt.sn m t3*

Their oblation is bread,

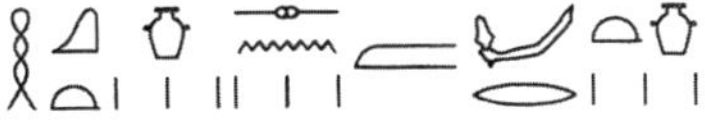

*ḥnqt.sn m ḏsrt*

their beer is Djeseret,

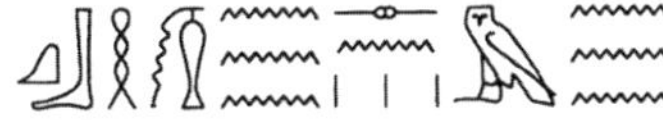

*qbḥw.sn m mw*

their refreshment is water.

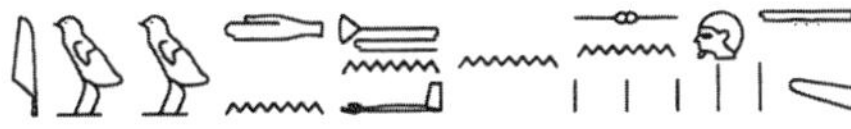

*jw wdnw n.sn tp t3*

Whoever makes an offering to them on earth

*m 3ḫ (nj) wnwt.f*

is an *Akh*-spirit of his hour.

## Middle Register, 50th Scene

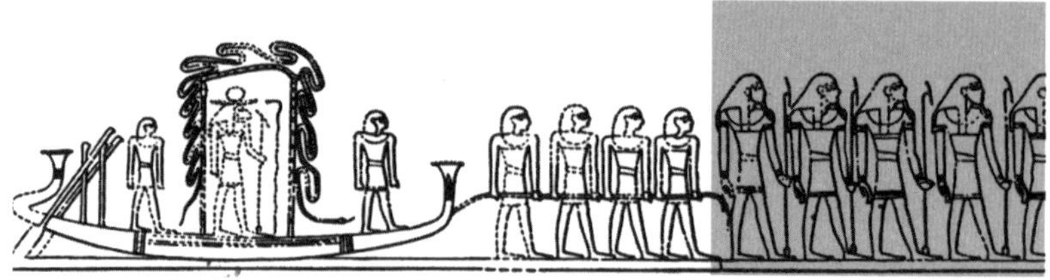

The solar barque with *ḥkȝw* (Magic), *jwf-rʿw* (Flesh of Re), *mḥn* (Mehen) and *sjȝ* (Sia, Percipience), towed by four *dwȝtyw* (gods of the Netherworld).

*sṯȝw nṯr pn ʿȝ jn nṯrw dwȝtyw*

This great god is towed by the gods of the Netherworld.

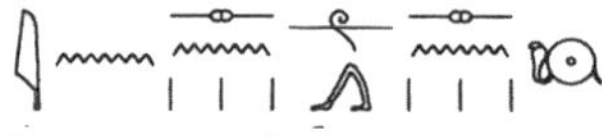

*jn.sn sṯȝ.sn rʿw*

They say when they tow Re:

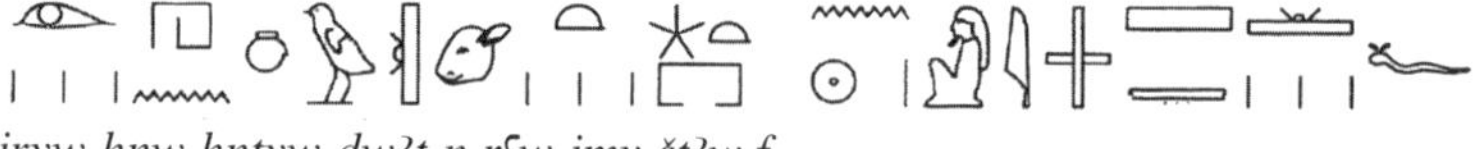

*jryw hnw ḫntyw dwȝt n rʿw jmy štȝw.f*

«Make jubilation, you in the Netherworld, for Re who is in his mystery

*m.ṯn.sw wḏʿ.f mdw.ṯn*

Look, he judges for you,

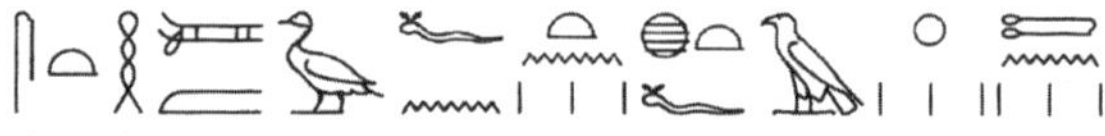

*sḥtm.f n.ṯn ḫftyw.ṯn*

he destroys for you your enemies!

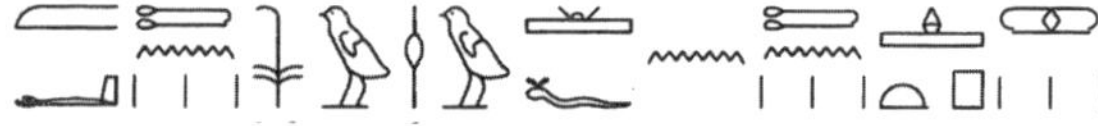

*m.ṯn.sw wḏ.f n.ṯn ḥtpw*

Look, he assigns to you offerings!

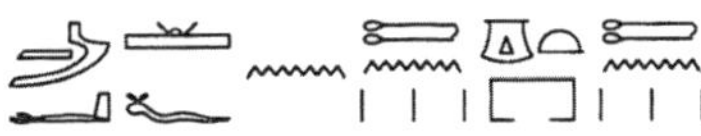
*mꜣꜥ.f n.ṯn nswt.ṯn*
He assigns to you your thrones!

*dy.ṯn n.f jꜣw m jrw.ṯn*
May you give him praise in your forms,

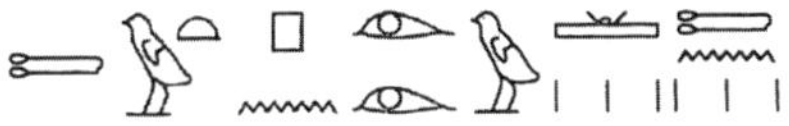
*ṯwt pn jry jrw.ṯn*
for it is he who created your forms!

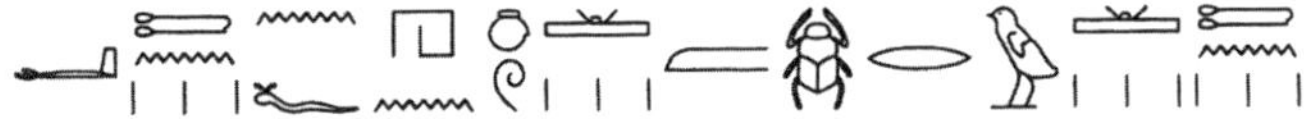
*dy.ṯn n.f hnw m ḫprw.ṯn*
May you give him jubilation in your manifestations,

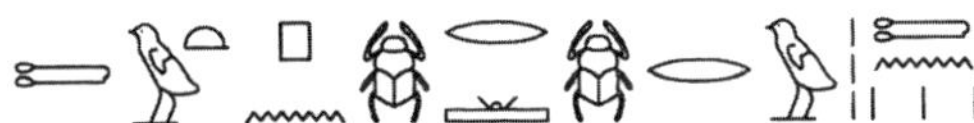
*ṯwt pn ḫpr ḫprw.ṯn*
for it is he who made your figures come into being!

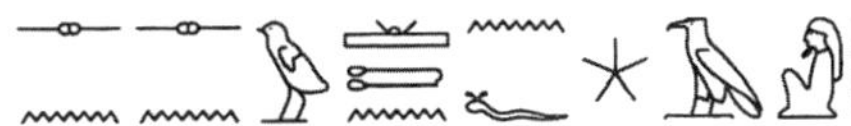
*snsn.ṯn n.f dwꜣtyw*
May you praise him, dwellers of the Netherworld!»

*ḏꜣḏꜣt pw imyt dwꜣt*
These are the magistrates who are in the Netherworld,

*wḏꜥt mdw ḥr ꜣḫty*
who judge on behalf of Akhty.

## 51st Scene

Twelve gods with *Ankh* and *Was* in their hands:

*nbw ḫrt m jmnt*
"Masters of provision in the West".

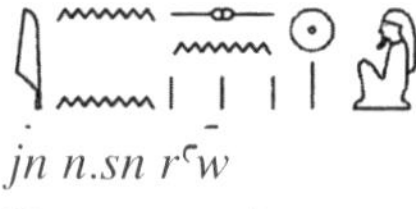

*jn n.sn rꜥw*
Re says to them:

*j ḏꜣḏꜣt jmyt dwꜣt*
«Oh you magistrates who are in the Netherworld,

*nbw ḫrt m jmntt*
masters of provision in the West -

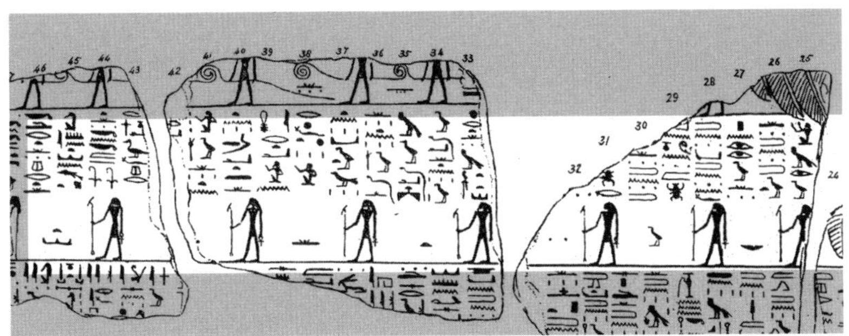

*wḏʿ.ṯn.wj m wḏʿw.ṯn*

May you judge (for) me by your verdicts,

*wḏ.ṯn ḏwt r ḫftyw.j*

may you command evil against my enemies,

*mj rdyt.j n.ṯn m3ʿt.j*

as I have given you my Maat!

*wḏw.ṯn r wḏʿw.ṯn*

You shall give orders in accordance with your judgement,

*jrywn.j mj nṯrw*

which I have done like (those of) the gods!»

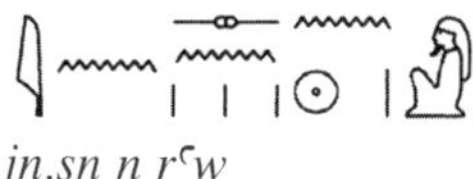

*jn.sn n rꜥw*

They say to Re:

*mꜣꜥ-ḫrw.k rꜥw drw ḫftyw.k*

«You triumph, Re, and you enemies are driven away,

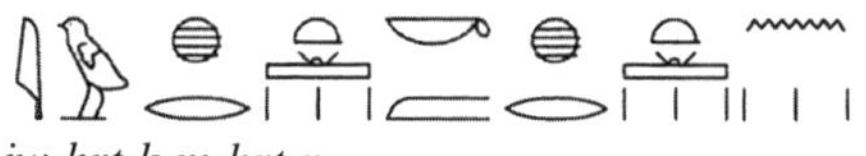

*jw ḫrt.k m ḫrt.n*

your affairs are our affairs!

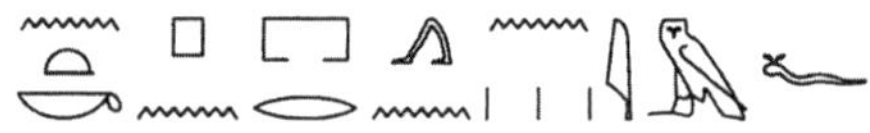

*ntk pn prywn.n jm.f*

You are it from whom we have come forth,

*qmꜣw.n r nḏ bꜣ.f*

who created us to assist his *Ba*-soul.

*ḫryt.k n.k m tꜣ(ṯ)nn*

Your share belongs to you in the depth of the Earth (Tatenen),

*jmnt n ẖꜣt.k ḏsrt*

and the West belongs to your holy corpse.

*ḫryt.k n.k m nwt*

Your share belongs to you in heaven (Nut),

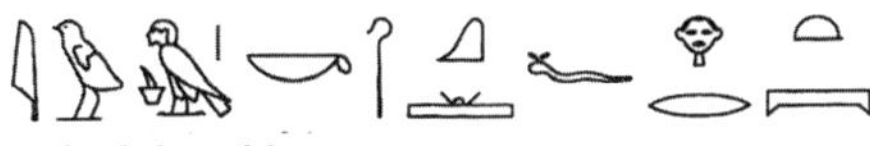

*jw b3.k ḥq3.f ḥrt*

while your *Ba*-soul rules (in) the sky.»

*3wt.sn m t3*

Their oblation is bread,

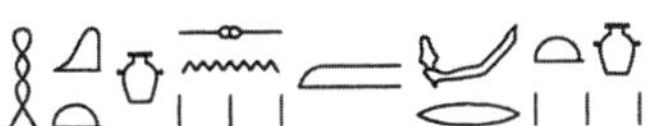

*ḥnqt.sn m ḏsrt*

their beer is Djeseret,

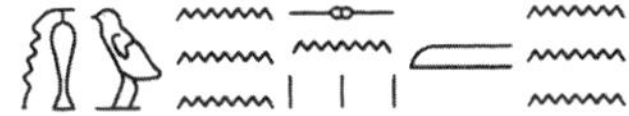

*qbḥw.sn m mw*

their refreshment is water.

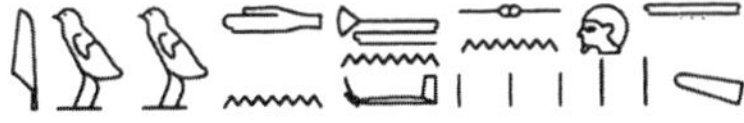

*jw wdnw n.sn tp t3*

Whoever makes an offering to them on earth

*m šmsw nbw ẖrt*

is a follower of the masters of provision.

**52ND SCENE**

Four upright mummies:

*ꜥḥꜣw ḥrw*

"Those with militant faces".

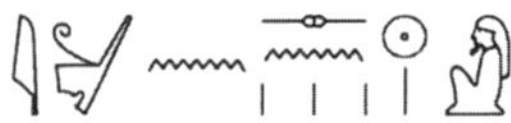

*jn n.sn rꜥw*

Re says to them:

*kfyt n ꜥfnwt.ṯn ꜥḥꜣw ḥrw*

«Uncovering for your headclothes, you with militant faces,

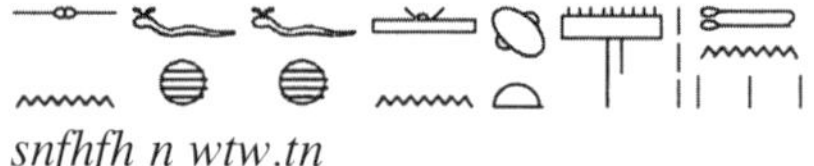

*snfḫfḫ n wtw.ṯn*

loosening for your mummy-wrappings!

*ḥḏwt.j n.ṯn nṯrw*

My light belongs to you, oh gods!»

*ꜣwt.sn m tꜣ*

Their oblation is bread,

*ḥnqt.sn m ḏsrt*

their beer is Djeseret,

*qbḥw.sn m mw*

their refreshment is water.

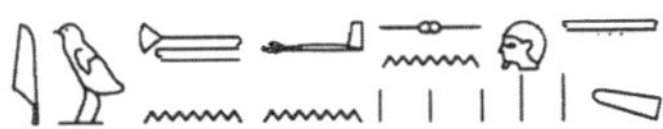

*jw wdnw n.sn tp tꜣ*

Whoever makes an offering to them upon earth

*m mꜣꜣw ḥḏwt m dwꜣt*

will see the light in the Netherworld.

## LOWER REGISTER, 53TH SCENE

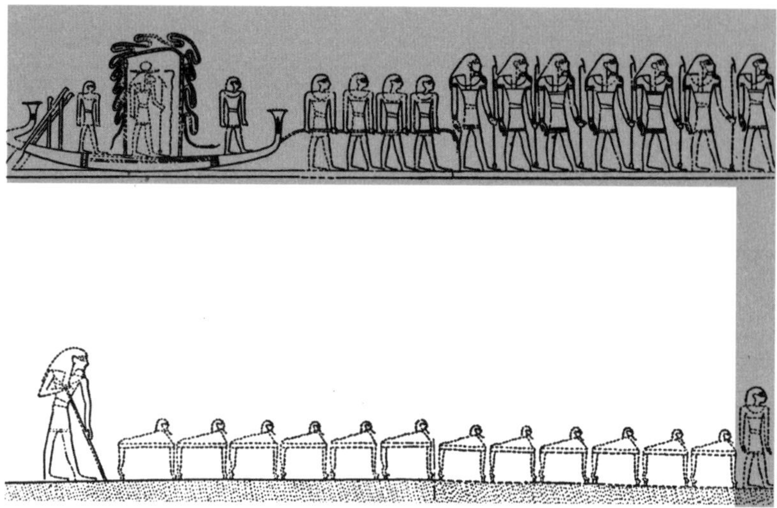

A single god, leaning on a staff, represents the Sungod:

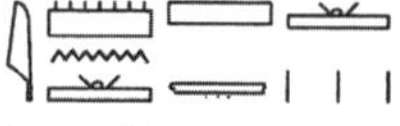

*jmnw št3w*
"He with hidden mysteries".

Before him, twelve mummies in sphinx-like position, heads raised, on biers:

*3ḫw* [...] *mnḫw 3ḫw jqrw*
"Excellent [and ... ] *Akh*-spirits, skilful *Akh*-spirits".

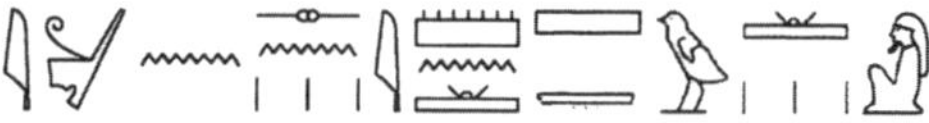

*jn n.sn jmnw št3w*
"He with hidden mysteries" says to them:

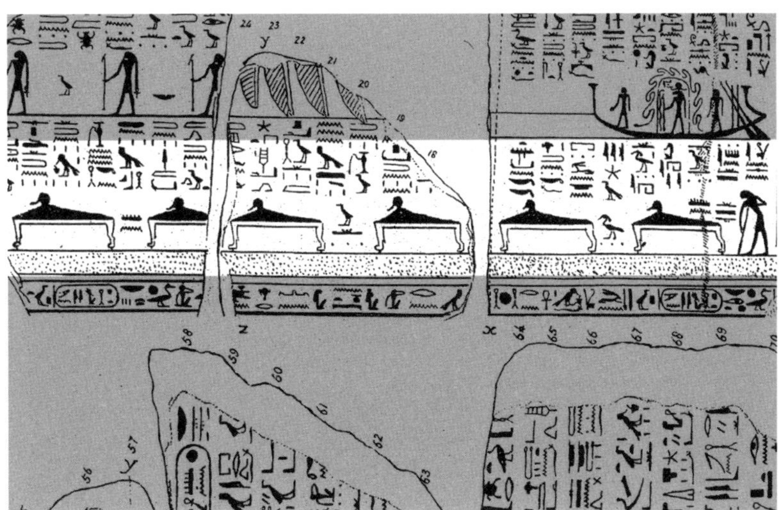

*jhy 3ḫw jhy dw3tyw*

«Hail to you, *Akh*-spirits, hail you of the Netherworld!

*wn n ḥrw.ṯn*

Opening for you faces,

*kfyt n kkw.ṯn*

uncovering for your darkness!

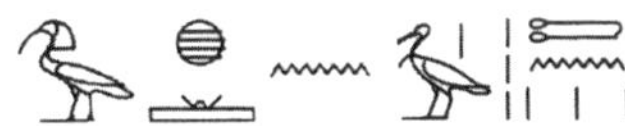

*3ḫ n b3w.ṯn*

Blessed state for your *Ba*-souls,

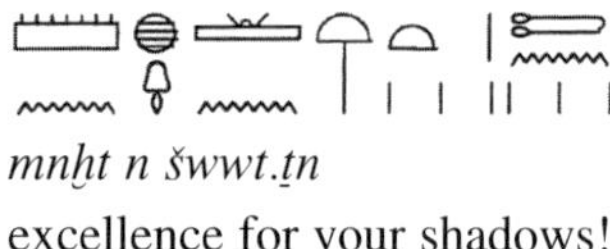

*mnḫt n šwwt.ṯn*

excellence for your shadows!

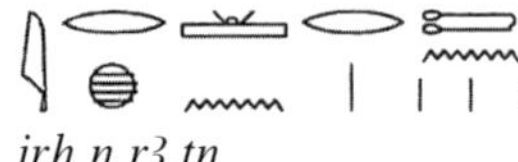

*jrḫ n r3.ṯn*

Knowledge for your mouth (or: spell),

*w3š n jbw.ṯn*

strength for your hearts (or: wishes)!

*ṯzjt n mk3wt.ṯn*

Raising for your biers,

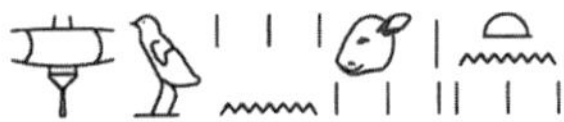

*ṯ3w n fnḏw.ṯn*

breath for your noses!

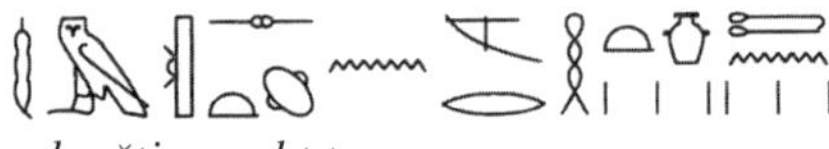

*nḏm štj n mrḥt.ṯn*

Sweet odour for your oil,

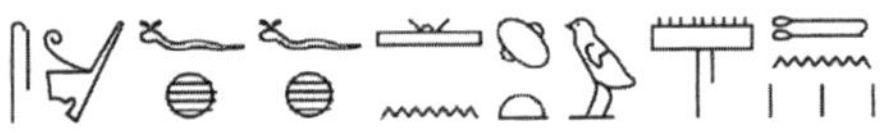

*snfḫfḫ n wtw.ṯn*

loosening for your mummy-wrappings!

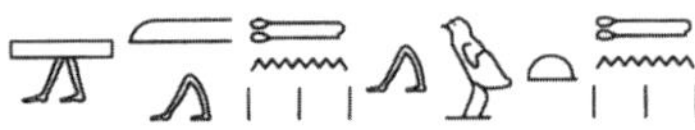

*šm.ṯn jwt.ṯn*

May you go and come (back),

*sḫm.ṯn m qbḥw*

may you dispose of cool water.

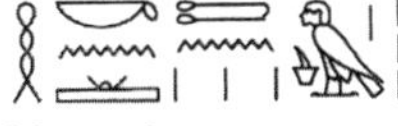

*ḥkn.ṯn b3w*

May you rejoice, oh *Ba*-souls,

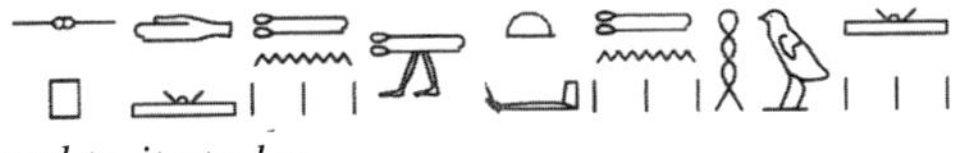

*spd.ṯn jṯy.ṯn ḥw*

may you be effective that you take food,

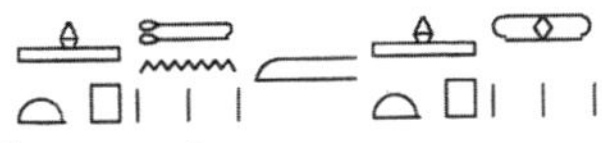

*ḥtp.ṯn m ḥtpw*

that you are content with the offerings.

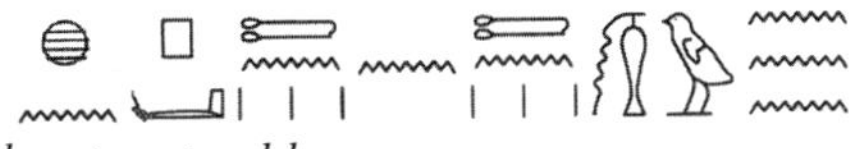

*ẖnp.ṯn n.ṯn qbḥw*

May you pour for you cool water

*m šw qꜥḥw m dw3t*

from the sinuous waters in the Netherworld.

*ꜥḥꜥ.ṯn ẖr wnwnyt*

May you stand under the leafy roof

*sṯzjt 3ḫ nj 3ḫty*

which raises the *Akh*-spirit of Akhty.

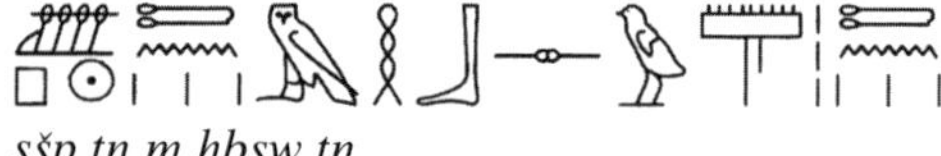

*sšp.ṯn m ḥbsw.ṯn*

May you shine by your clothes,

*ḥḏ.ṯn m j3ḫw rꜥw*

may you be bright by the splendour of Re.

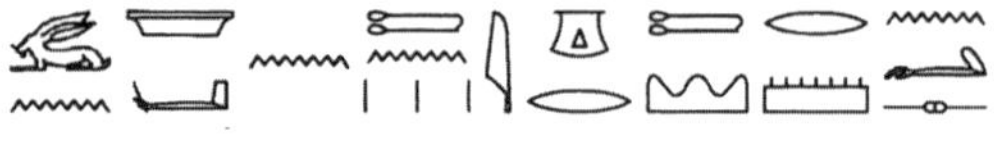

*wn n.ṯn jgrt rmn.s*

The realm of the dead (Igeret) opens up for you,

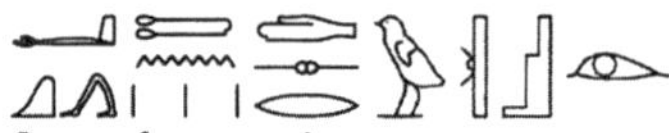

*ꜥq.ṯn ḏsrw wsjr*

that you may enter the seclusion of Osiris.

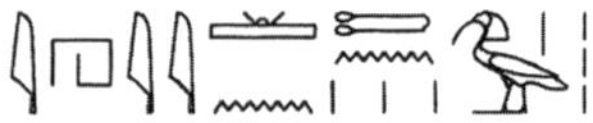

*jhy n.ṯn 3ḫw*

Hail to you, *Akh*-spirits!»

*wnn.sn ḥr mk(3)wt.sn*

They are on their biers,

*sḏry ḥr 3ṯwt.sn*

lying on their beds.

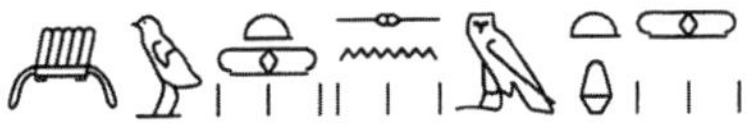

*ꜣwt.sn m tꜣ*

Their oblation is bread,

*ḥnqt.sn m ḏsrt*

their beer is Djeseret,

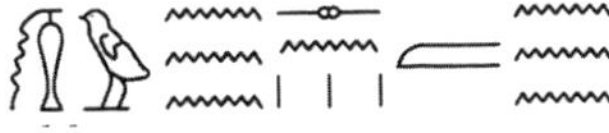

*qbḥw.sn m mw*

their refreshment is water.

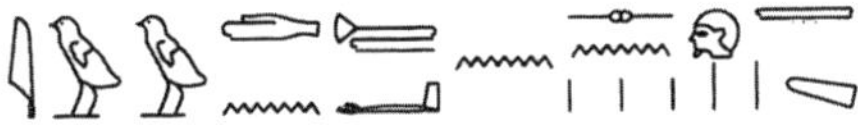

*jw wdnw n.sn tp tꜣ*

Whoever makes an offering to them on earth

*m ꜣḫ jqr sḫm šwt(.f?)*

is an excellent *Akh*-spirit who disposes of (his?) shadow.

### 54TH SCENE

Twelve gods without attributes:

*ḏ3ḏ3t nt wḏʿyw*

"The council of judges".

*ntsn wḏʿw r sbḫt tn sḏmw ḫrt jmyw*

It is they who judge at this gate, who examine those who are in (it).

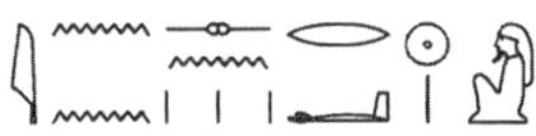

*jn n.sn rʿw*

Re says to them:

*jhy jrf nṯrw*

«Hail to you, oh gods,

*ḏȝḏȝt nt wḏʿyw*

council of judges,

*wḏʿw mtyw nḏw bȝw*

who judge the dead and protect the *Ba*-souls!

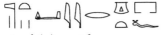

*nṯry dy(w) r nst.f*

The divine is placed on his throne,

*mȝʿt.ṯn n.ṯn nṯrw*

and your Maat belongs to you, oh gods!»

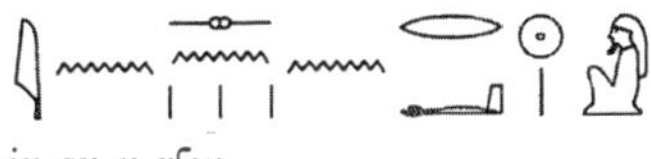

*jn.sn n rʿw*

They say to Re:

*jhy jrf ȝḫty*

«Hail to you, Akhty,

*nṯr ʿȝ nb psḏt*

Great god and Lord of the Ennead!

*jw.n jry.n wḏꜥw mtyw*

We judge the dead,

*jw.n nḏ.n ꜣḫw ḫpr.sn*

we protect the *Akh*-spirits when they transform,

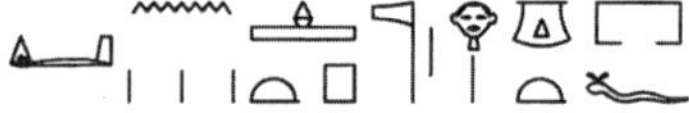

*dy.n ḥtp nṯr ḥr nst.f*

we cause the god to rest upon his throne.»

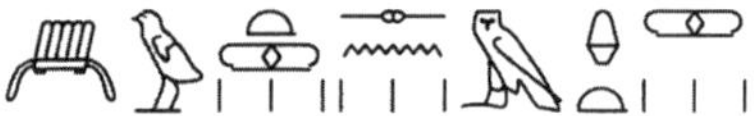

*ꜣwt.sn m tꜣ*

Their oblation is bread,

*ḥnqt.sn m ḏsrt*

their beer is Djeseret,

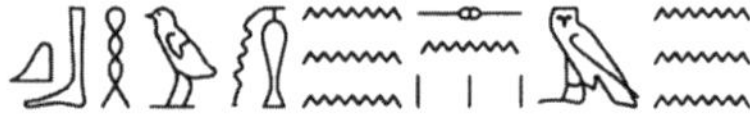

*qbḥw.sn m mw*

their refreshment is water.

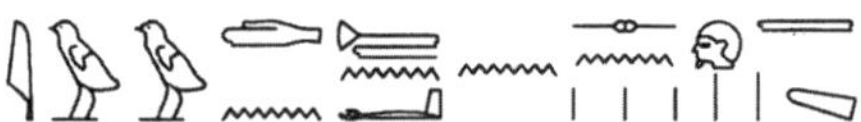

*jw wdnw n.sn tp tꜣ*

Whoever makes an offering to them upon earth

*m wḏꜥy m ḏꜣḏꜣt*

is one who judges in the council.

## Eighth Gate

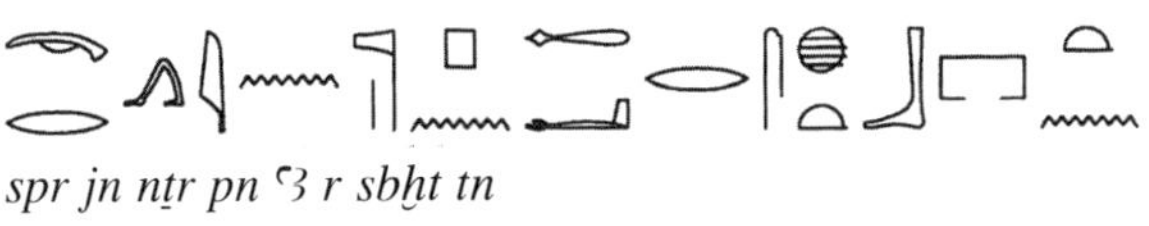

*spr jn nṯr pn ꜥꜣ r sbḫt tn*

Arrival of this great god at this gate,

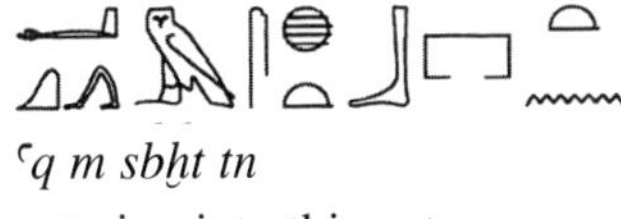

*ꜥq m sbḫt tn*

entering into this gate,

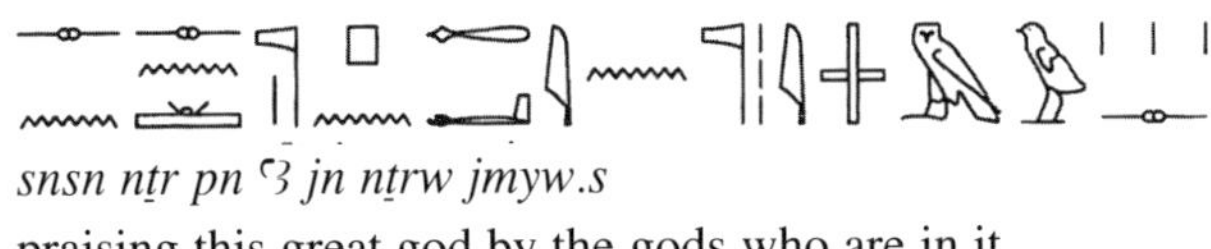

*snsn nṯr pn ꜥꜣ jn nṯrw jmyw.s*

praising this great god by the gods who are in it.

Name of the gate:

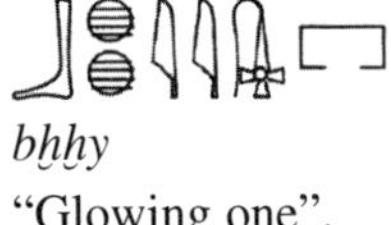

*bḫḫy*

“Glowing one”.

Upper and lower Uraeus-serpents:

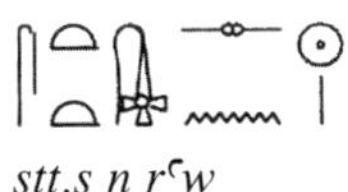

*stt.s n rꜥw*

“She lights up for Re”.

Upper guardian:

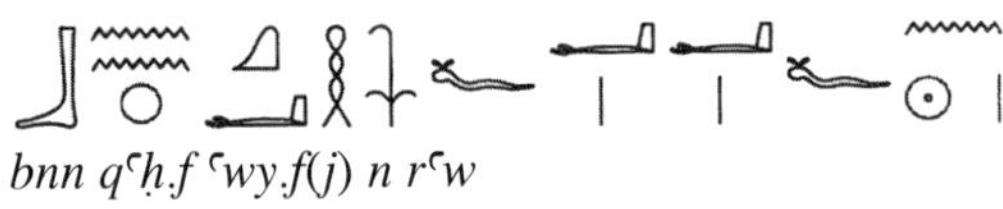

*bnn qꜥḥ.f ꜥwy.f(j) n rꜥw*

“The round one”. He bends his arms for Re.

From the tomb of Pharaoh Ramses V/VI.

Lower guardian:

*ḥptyw qꜥḥ.f ꜥwy.f(j) n rꜥw*

“He who embraces”. He bends his arms for Re.

Nine mummies:

*psḏt 8nwt*

“The eighth Ennead”.

In front of the Ennead:

*my rk r.n ḫnty ꜣḫt*

«Come to us, Foremost of the horizon,

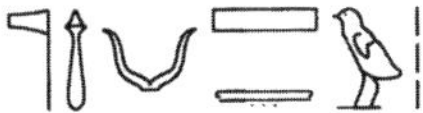

*nṯr ꜥꜣ wpj štꜣw*

great god who has opened the Mysterious!

*wnw n.k sbḫwt ḏsryt*

Open for you are the protected gates,

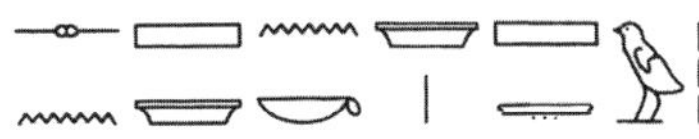

*znw n.k ꜥꜣ(w) štꜣw*

unlocked for you are the mysterious doors!»

Serpent on the door

*sty-ḥr*

“He with a flaming face”.

*wnn.f ḥr ꜥꜣ pn*

He is upon this door,

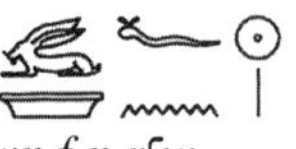

*wn.f n rꜥw*

he opens for Re.

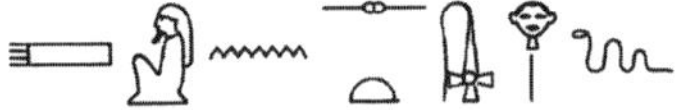

*sjꜣ n sty-ḥr*

Sia (says) to him "with a flaming face":

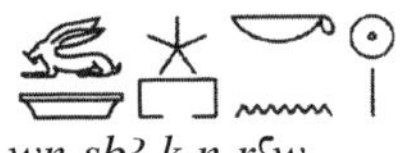

*wn sbꜣ.k n rꜥw*

«Open your gate for Re,

*zn ꜥꜣ.k n ꜣḫty*

unlock your door for Akhty!

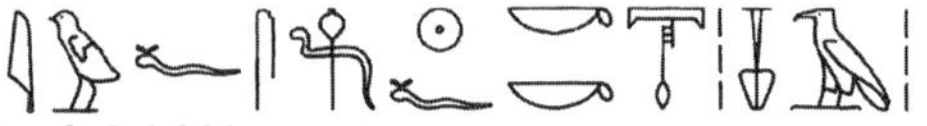

*jw.f sḥḏ.f kkw zmꜣw*

He illuminates the Primeval Darkness,

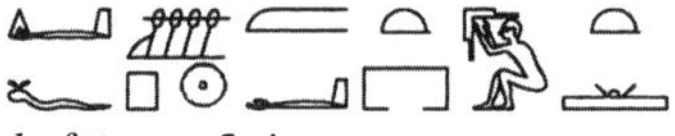

*dy.f šsp m ꜥt jmnt*

he throws light into the Hidden Space!»

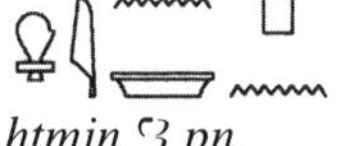

*ḫtmjn ꜥꜣ pn*

Then this door is shut,

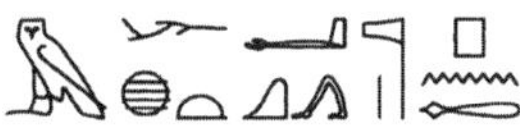

*m-ḫt ꜥq nṯr pn ꜥꜣ*

after this great god has entered.

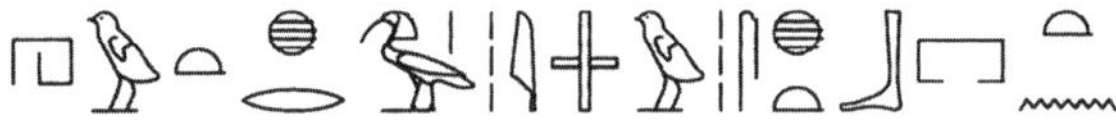

*hwtḫr ꜣḫw jmyw sbḫt tn*

Then the *Akh*-spirits who are in this gate wail

*sḏm.sn hꜣꜣ ꜥꜣ pn*

when they hear this door being slammed.

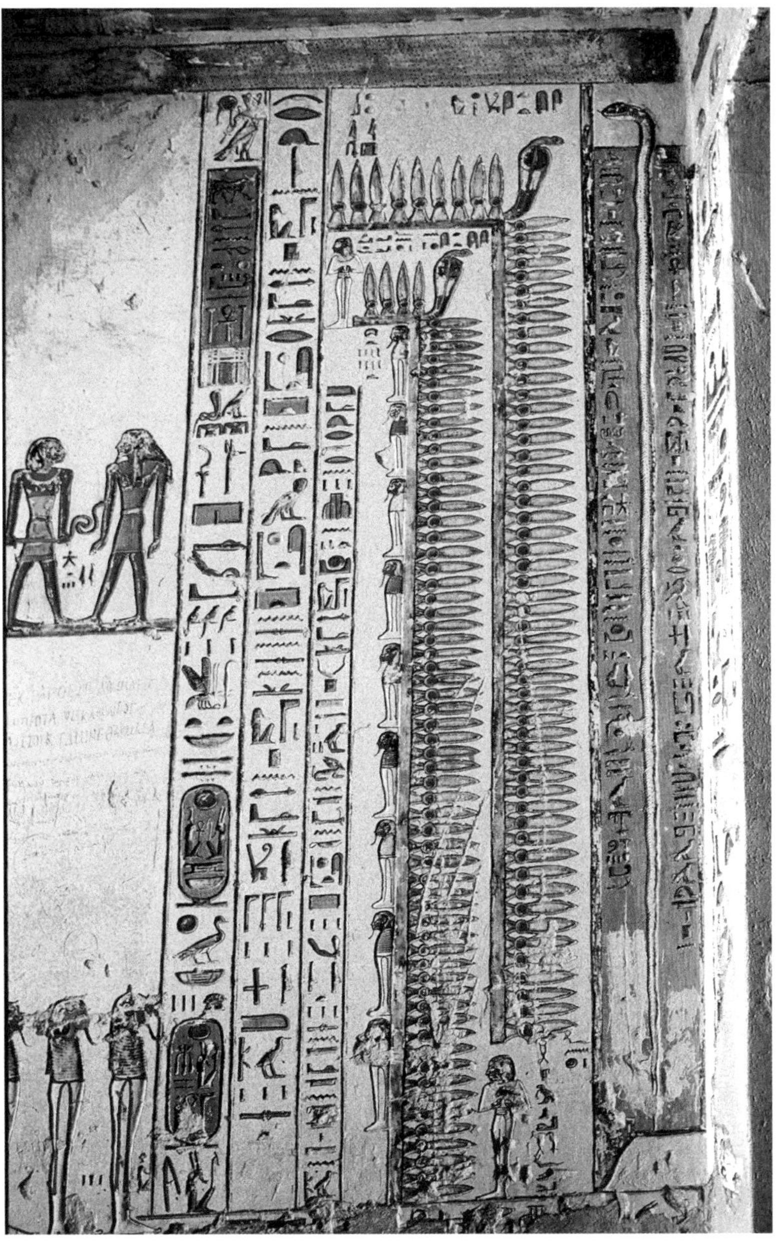

From the tomb of Pharaoh Ramses V/VI.

# NINTH

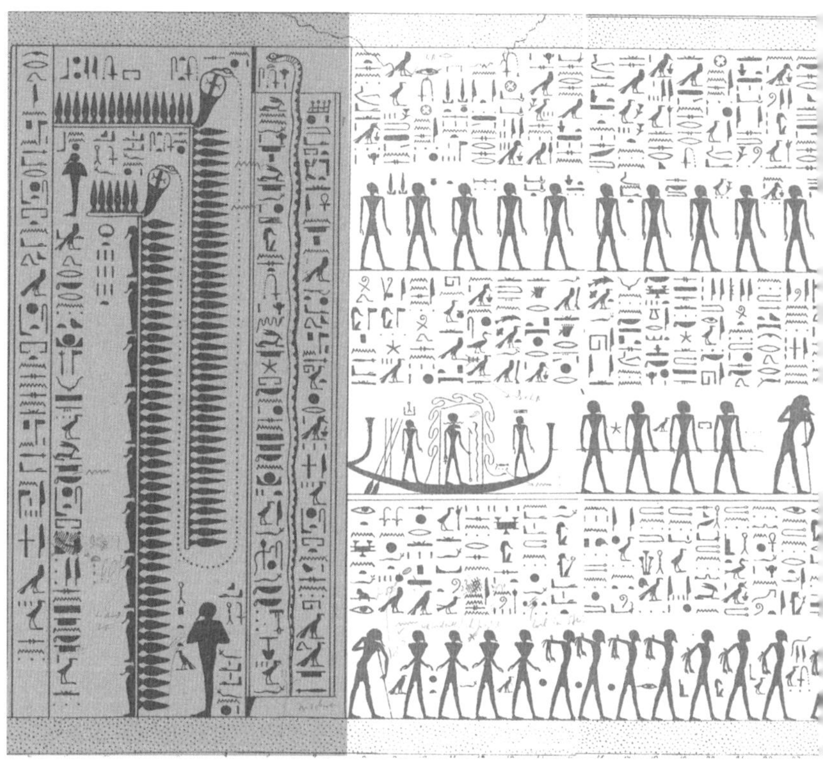

# HOUR

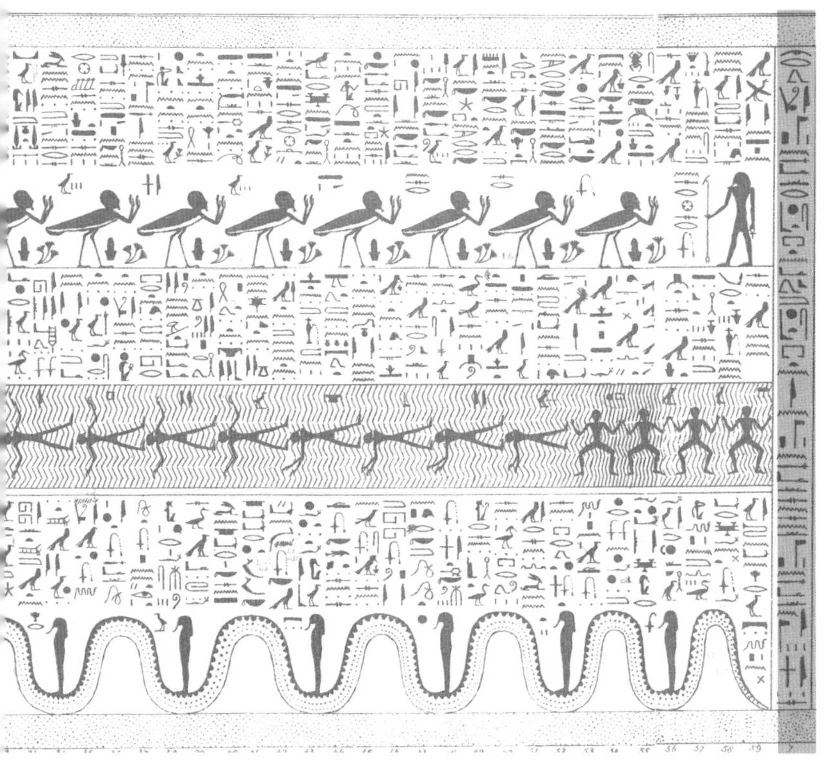

# PART OF THE

From the tomb of Queen Tawseret.

# NINTH HOUR

## Upper Register, 55th Scene

Twelve gods without attributes:

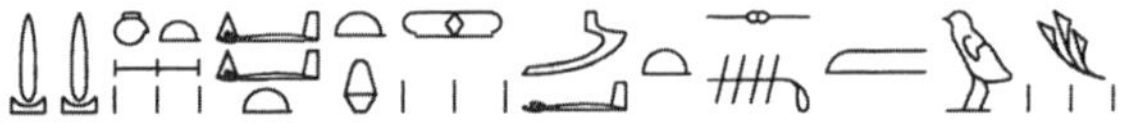

*ḏ3ḏ3t ddwt t3 m3ʿwt smw*

"Council which provides bread and bestowes vegetables

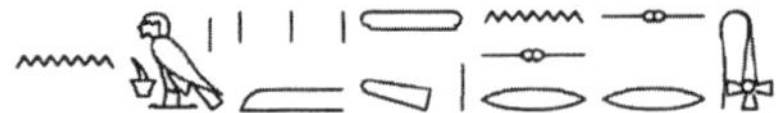

*n b3w m jw nsrsr*

for the *Ba*-souls in the Island of Fire".

*ntsn m3ʿw b3w ḥr smw m jw nsrsr*

It is they who conduct the *Ba*-souls to vegetables in the Island of Fire.

From the tomb of Pharaoh Ramses V/VI.

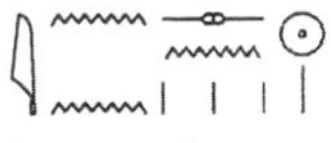

*jn n.sn rꜥw*

Re says to them:

*j ḏꜣḏꜣt nt nṯrw šnyt jw nsrsr*

«Oh council of gods which surrounds the Island of Fire,

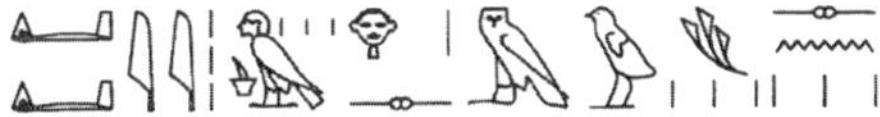

*ddy(t) bꜣw ḥr smw.sn*

which puts the *Ba*-souls to their vegetables,

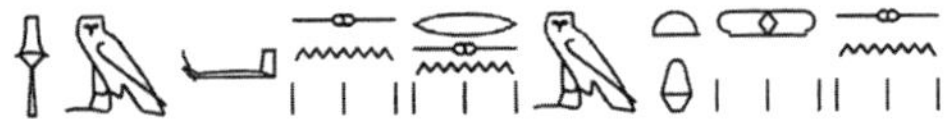

*sḫm.sn r.sn m t3.sn*

so that they dispose of their bread!

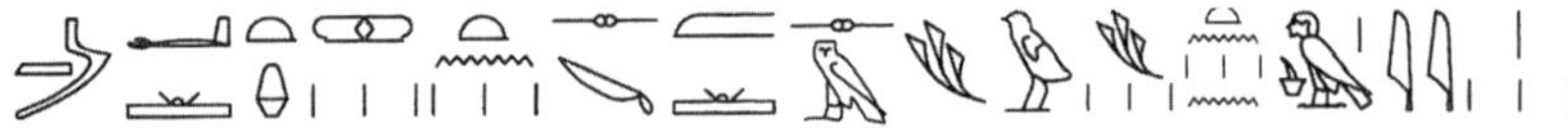

*m3ꜥ t3.ṯn sšm smw.ṯn n b3yw*

Offer your bread, bring your vegetables for the Ba-souls,

*wḏn.j srq m jw nsrsr*

which I have commanded to breathe in the Island of Fire!»

*jn.sn n rꜥw*

They say to Re:

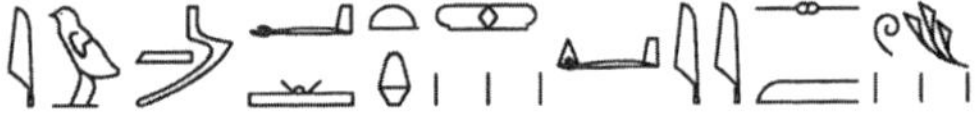

*jw m3ꜥw t3 dyw smw*

«Offered is the bread, given are the vegetables

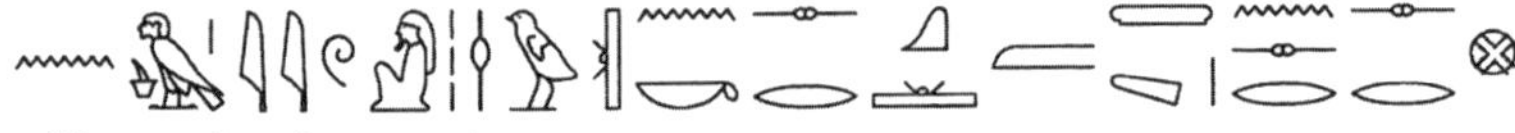

*n b3yw wḏwn.k srq m jw nsrsr*

to the *Ba*-souls which you have commanded to breathe in the Isle of Fire.

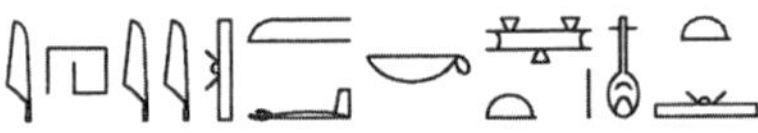

*jhy mk w3t nfrtj*

Hail (to you)! Look, the path is perfect!

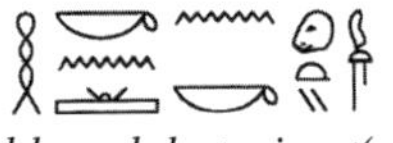

*ḥkn n.k ḫnty-jmnt(yw)*

Khontamenti praises you,

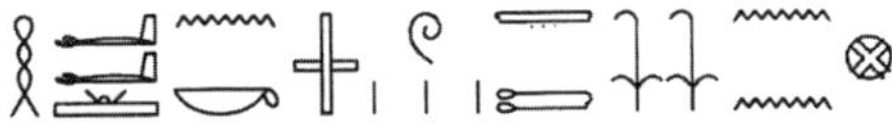

*ḥꜥꜥ n.k jmyw tꜣṯnn*

and those in Tatenen jubilate for you!»

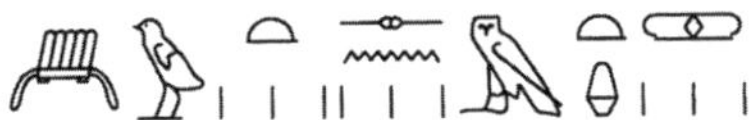

*ꜣwt.sn m tꜣ*

Their oblation is bread,

*ḥnqt.sn m ḏsrt*

their beer is Djeseret,

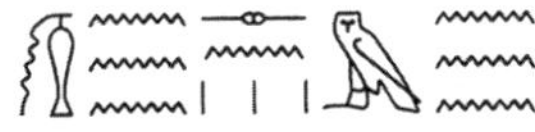

*qbḥw.sn m mw*

their refreshment is water.

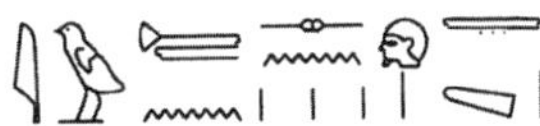

*jw wdnw n.sn tp tꜣ*

Whoever makes an offering to them upon earth

*m wḏy m ḏꜣḏꜣt*

is one who commands in the council.

## 56TH SCENE

Nine human-headed *Ba*-souls, adoring with human hands the Sungod (who has no name), leaning on a staff at the end of the register:

*bꜣyw jmyw jw nsrsr*

"*Ba*-souls which are in the Island of Fire".

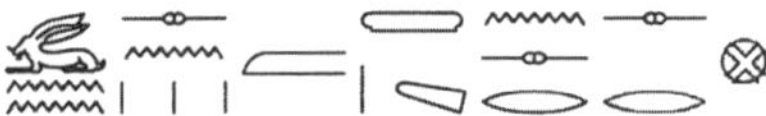

*wnn.sn m jw nsrsr*

They are in the Isle of Fire,

*šzp.sn tꜣ.sn sḫm.sn m jw pn*

they receive their bread, they dispose of this island,

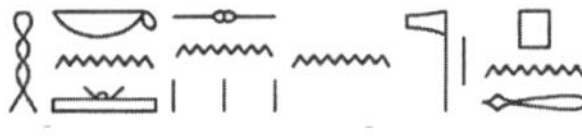

*ḥkn.sn n nṯr pn ꜥꜣ*

they praise this great god.

Both pictures here are from the tomb of Queen Tawseret.

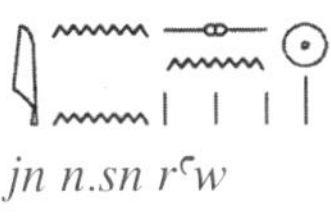

*jn n.sn rʿw*

Re says to them:

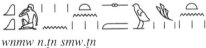

*wnmw n.ṯn smw.ṯn*

«Eat for you your vegetables,

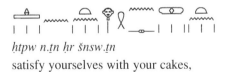

*ḥtpw n.ṯn ḥr šnsw.ṯn*

satisfy yourselves with your cakes,

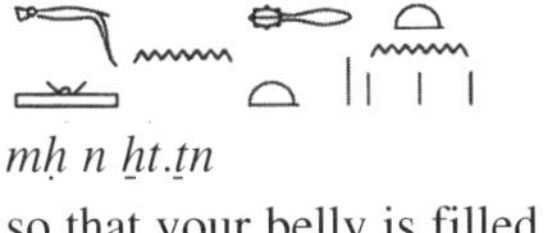

*mḥ n ẖt.ṯn*

so that your belly is filled,

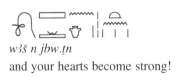

*wꜣš n jbw.ṯn*

and your hearts become strong!

*smw.ṯn n jw (n)srsr*

Your vegetables belong to the Island of Fire,

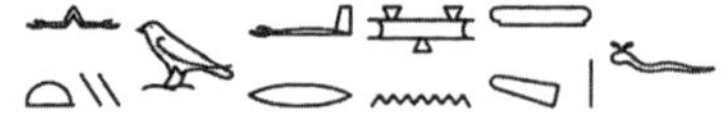

*jwtj (j)ʿr n jw.f*

which island nobody can approach.

*ḥkn.ṯn n.j w3š.ṯn n.j*

May you praise me and may you venerate me,

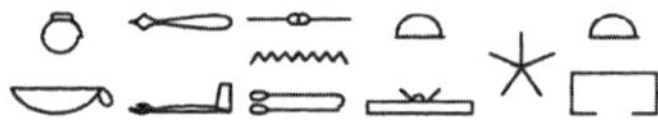

*jnk ʿ3 snṯ dw3t*

(for) I am the great one who has established the Netherworld.»

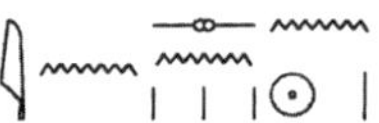

*jn.sn n rʿw*

They say to Re:

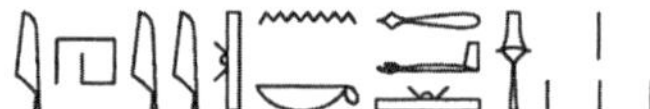

*jhy n.k ʿ3 sḫmw*

«Hail to you, Great of power!

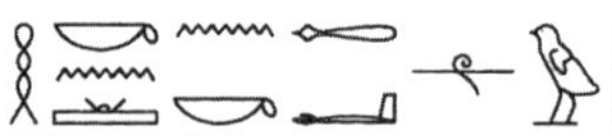

*ḥknw n.k ʿ3 st3w*

Praise to you with great orbit!

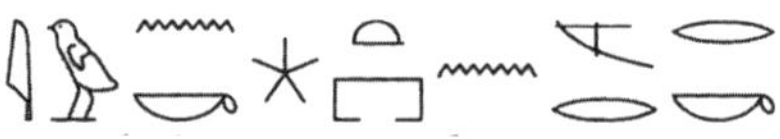

*jw n.k dw3t n mrrw.k*

To you belongs the Netherworld, according to your will,

*jmntn.k r ntyw m qr(r)wt.sn*

which you have hidden for those who are in their caverns.

*jw n.k ḥrt n mrrw.k*

To you belongs the sky, according to your will,

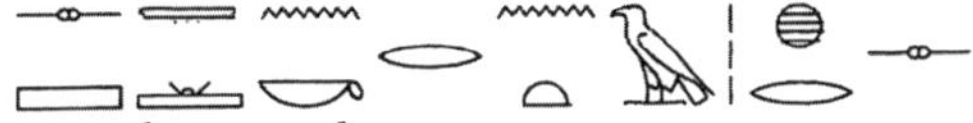

*sštȝn.k r ntyw ẖr.s*

which you made secret for those who are at it.

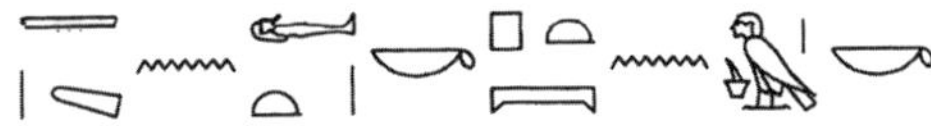

*tȝ n ẖȝt.k pt n bȝ.k*

The earth belongs to your body, heaven to your *Ba*-soul,

*ḥtp.k rʿw m sḫprtn.k*

so that you are content, Re, with what you have brought into being»

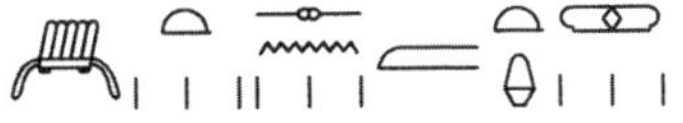

*ȝwt.sn m tȝ*

Their oblation is bread,

*smw.sn m rnpyt*

their vegetables are fresh plants,

*qbḥw.sn m mw*

their refreshment is water.

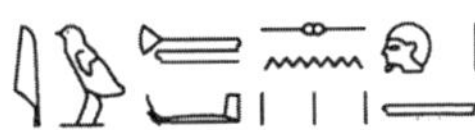

*jw wdnw (n).sn tp tȝ*

Whoever makes an offering to them upon earth,

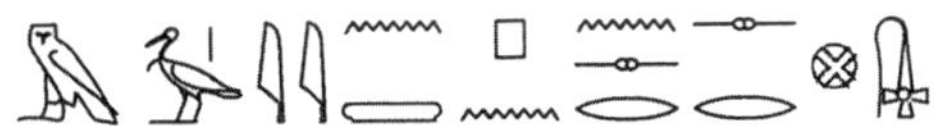

*m bȝy nj jw pn nsrsr*

is a *Ba*-soul of this Isle of Fire.

## Middle Register, 57th Scene

The solar barque with *ḥk3w* (Magic), *jwf-rˁw* (Flesh of Re), *mḥn* (Mehen) and *sj3* (Sia, Percipience), towed by four *dw3tyw* (gods of the Netherworld).

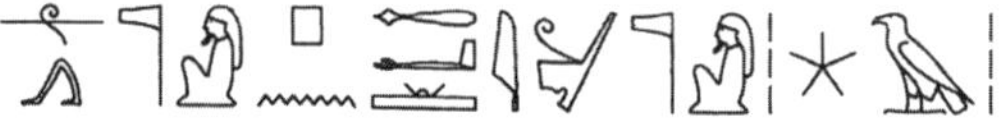

*st̠3w nt̠r pn ˁ3 jn nt̠rw dw3tyw*

This great god is towed by the gods of the Netherworld.

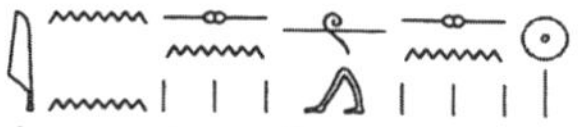

*jn.sn st̠3.sn rˁw*

They say when they tow Re:

*hnw m pt n b3 nj rˁw*

«Jubilation in heaven for the *Ba*-soul of Re,

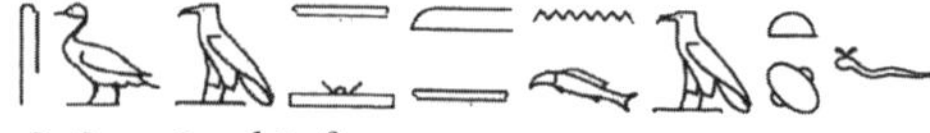

*z3-t3 m t3 n ẖ3t.f*

praise in the earth for his corpse!

*wḥm ḏr pt ḫr b3.f*

Again in heaven for his *Ba*-soul,

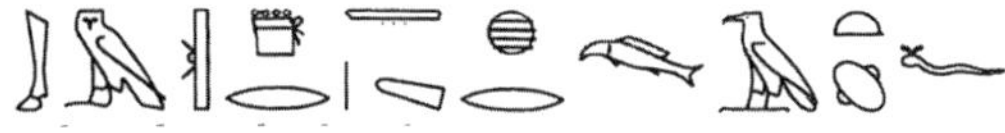

*wḥm ḏr t3 ḫr ḫ3t.f*

again in the earth to his corpse!

*jhy wpj.n n.k št3t*

Hail, we open for you the Shetit,

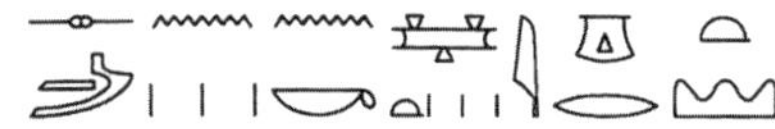

*sm3ʿ.n n.k w3wt jgrt*

we prepare for you the ways of the Igeret!

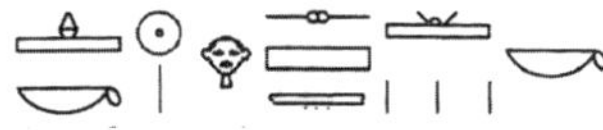

*ḥtp.k rʿw ḥr sšt3w.k*

May you rest, Re, upon your mystery,

*dw3.ṯw št3yw m jrw.k*

that the mysterious (dead) may adore you in your form.

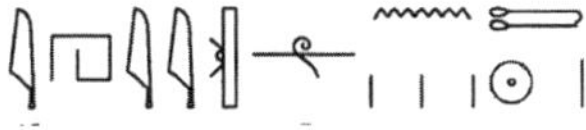

*jhy sṯ3.n.ṯw rʿw*

Hail, we tow you, Re,

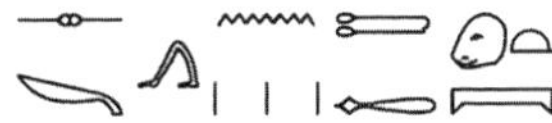

*sšm.n.ṯw ʿ3 ḫnty pt*

we conduct you, Great one, Foremost of Heaven!»

## 58TH SCENE

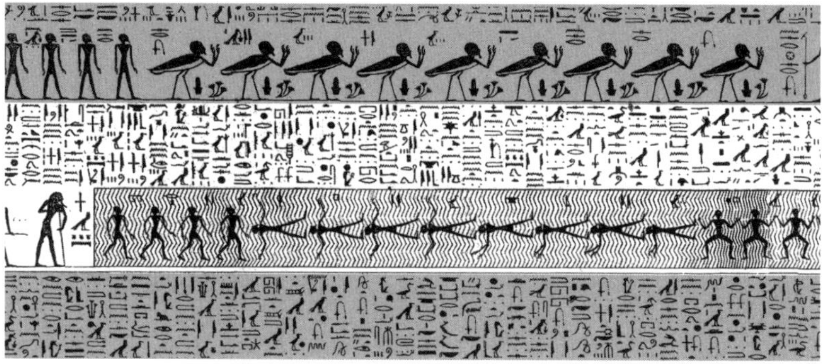

A god leaning on a staff: *jmy-nww* "Who is in the Nun". Before him, a huge rectangle filled with water, with four groups of four swimming bodies:

*hrpyw*
Those who are immersed

*jgyw*
Those who have capsized

*nbyw*
Those who swim

*pg3w*
Those who are spread out.

The text reads:

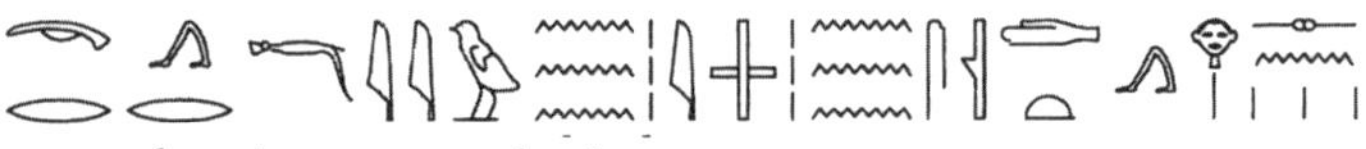

*spr r mḥyw jmyw mw sqdwt ḥr.sn*
Arriving at those who float, who are in the water, passing by them.

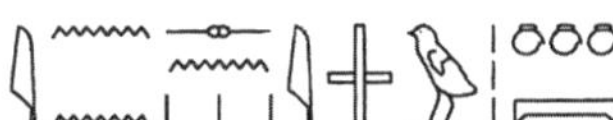

*jn n.sn jmyw nww*
"Who is in the Nun" says to them:

From the tomb of Queen Tawseret.

*j mḥyw jmyw mw*

«Oh you who float, who are in the water,

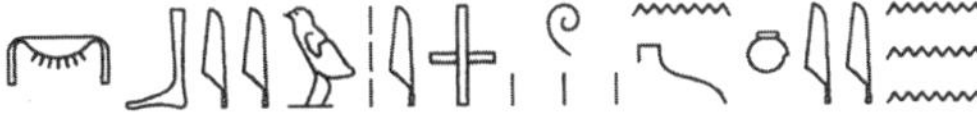

*nbyw jmyw nwy*

those who swim, who are in the flood,

*m3w rʿw ntj ʿp.f*

look (on) Re who passes by

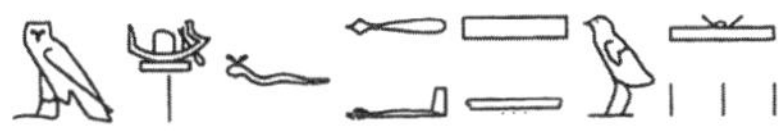

*m wj3.f ʿ3 št3w*

in his barque, with great mysteries!

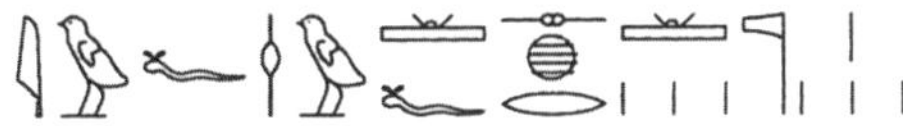

*jw.f wḏ.f sḫrw nṯrw*

He cares for the gods

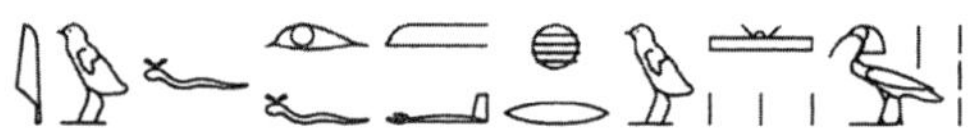

*jw.f jrj.f mḫrw ꜣḫw*

and he provides for the *Akh*-spirits.

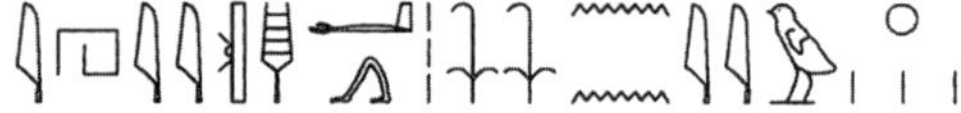

*jhy ꜥḥꜥw nnyw*

Hail, stand up, you weary ones -

*m.ṯn rꜥw wḏ.f sḫrw.ṯn*

look, Re, he cares for you!»

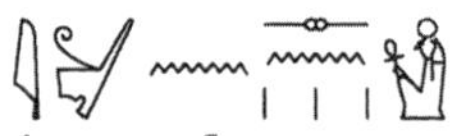

*jn n.sn rꜥw*

Re says to them:

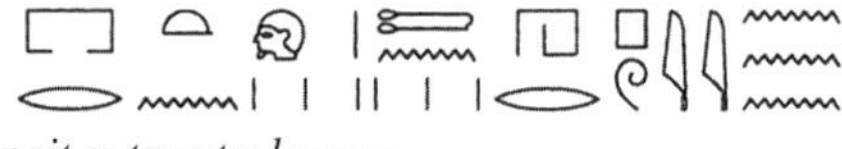

*prjt n tpw.ṯn hrpyw*

«Emerging for your heads, you who are immersed!

*ḫnjt n ꜥwj.ṯn jgyw*

Rowing for your arms, you who have capsized!

*pḥr n ḥpwt.ṯn nbyw*

Speed for your movement, you who swim!

*ṯꜣw n fnḏw.ṯn pg(ꜣ)yw*

Breath for your noses, you who are spread out!

*sḫm n.ṯn m mw.ṯn*

May you have power over your water,

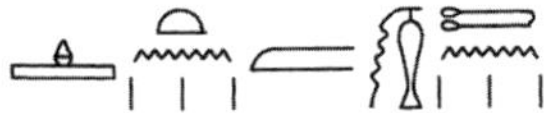

*ḥtp.ṯn m qbḥw.ṯn*

may you be content with your refreshment!

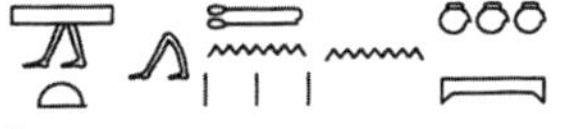

*šmt.ṯn n nww*

Your going belongs to the Nun,

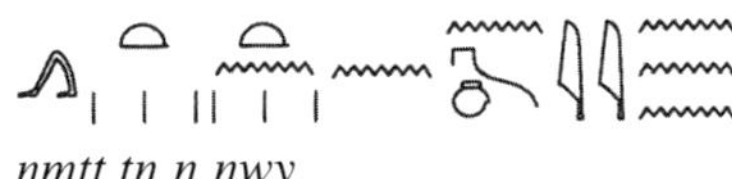

*nmtt.ṯn n nwy*

your steps belong to the flood.

*b3w.ṯn tpyw t3 ḥtp.sn*

Your *Ba*-souls which are upon earth, they are satisfied

*m srqw.sn jwty js swt ḥtmw.sn*

with what they breathe, without their being destroyed.»

*3wt.sn m ḥtpw n(w) t3*

Their oblation are the offerings of the earth.

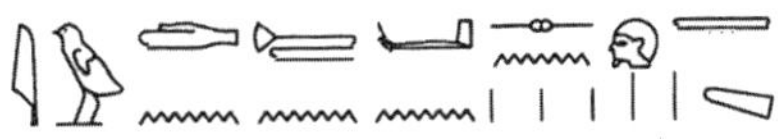

*jw wdnw n.sn tp t3*

Whoever makes an offering to them upon earth,

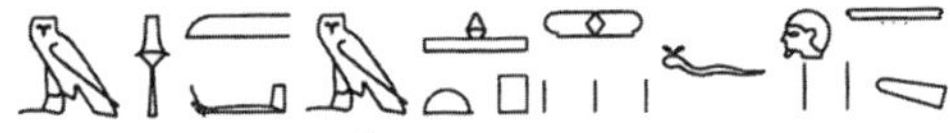

*m sḫmw m ḥtpw.f tp t3*

will dispose of his offering upon earth.

## LOWER REGISTER, 59TH SCENE

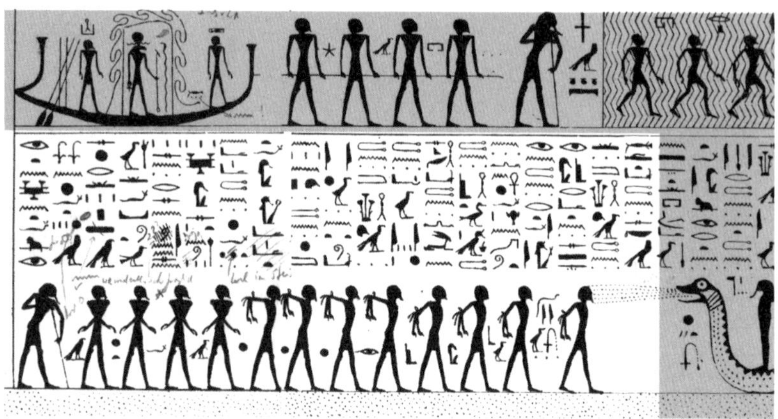

The falcon-headed god Horus, leaning on a staff. Before him, three groups of four enemies each, bound in different fashion:

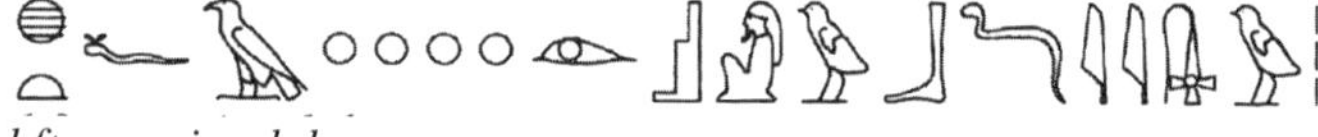

*ḫftyw wsjr wbdyw*

"Enemies of Osiris, to be burned".

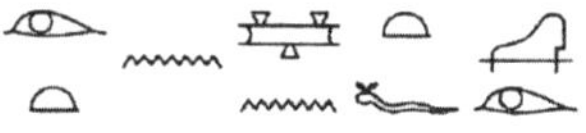

*jrjtn ḥrw n jt.f wsjr*

What Horus has done for his father Osiris.

*nn nj ḫftyw m sḫr pn*

These enemies are like this:

*ḥrw wḏ.f ḏwt.sn r.sn*

Horus assigns their evil against them.

From the tomb of Ramses V/VI.

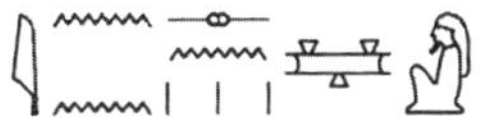

*jn n.sn ḥrw*

Horus says to them:

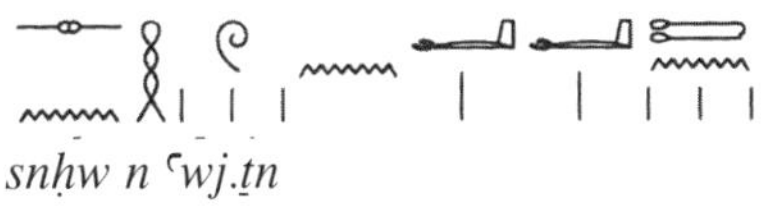

*snḥw n ˁwj.ṯn*

«Fetters are at your arms,

*ḫftyw (nw) jt.j*

enemies of my father!

*ˁwj.ṯn n tpw.ṯn ḫmyw*

Your arms are at your heads, subversive ones!

*nṯṯ.ṯn m ḥꜣw.ṯn ḏwyw*

Your are fettered from behind, evildoers,

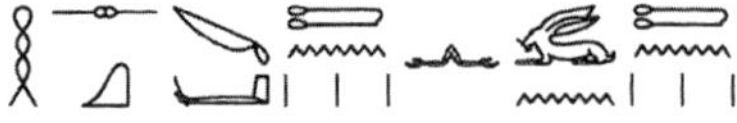

*ḥsq.ṯn n wn.ṯn*

that you are beheaded and cease to exist!

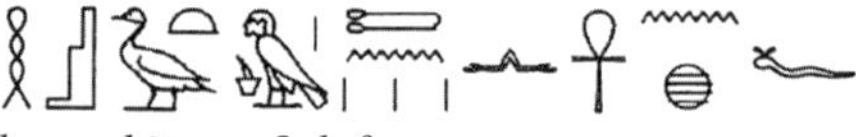

*ḥtmw bꜣ.ṯn n ꜥnḫ.f*

Your *Ba*-soul is destroyed and does not live,

*ḥr nw jrywn.ṯn r jt.j wsjr*

because of what you have done against my father Osiris.

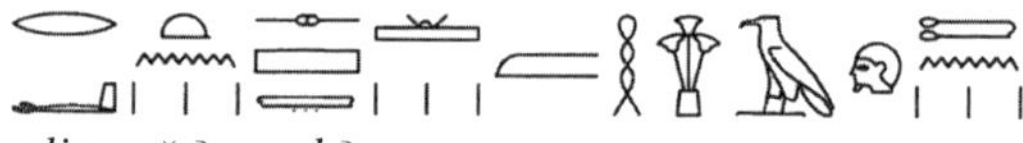

*rdj.ṯn sštꜣw m ḥꜣ.ṯn*

You have cast the mystery behind you

*šdj.ṯn sšmw nj štꜣt*

and you have removed the image of the Shetit!

*mꜣꜥ-ḫrw jt.j wsjr r.ṯn mꜣꜥ-ḫrw.j r.ṯn*

My father Osiris is justified against you, and I am justified against you.

*ntṯn sḥꜣyw jmnt*

You have uncovered what should be hidden,

*m ḥtp ꜥꜣꜥ.wj m dwꜣt*

when he who has engendered me rested in the Netherworld.

*jhy tm.ṯn tmyw*

Hail, you do not exist, you who are not!»

From the tomb of Queen Tawseret.

## 60TH SCENE

A giant, multi-coiled serpent, spitting fire from its mouth against the enemies of the 59th scene:

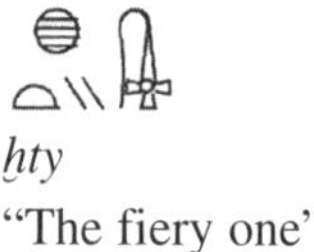

*ẖty*
"The fiery one".

Seven mummies standing in the coils of the serpent:

*nṯrw ḥryw ẖty*
"Gods who are upon the fiery one".

The text reads:

*jn ḥrw (n) ẖty*
Horus says to "The fiery one":

From the tomb of Queen Tawseret.

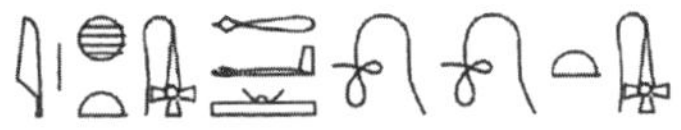

*j ḫty ꜥ3 w3w3t*

«Oh fiery one, with great flame,

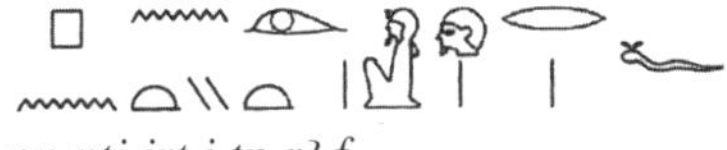

*pn ntj jrt.j tp r3.f*

you, upon whose mouth my eye is,

*msw.j z3w q3bw.f*

whose coils my children are guarding -

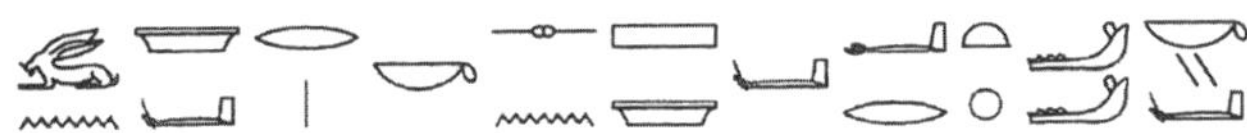

*wn r3.k zn ꜥrtj.kj*

Open your mouth and unlock your jaws,

*nsr.k m ḫftyw jt.j*

that you put flames into the enemies of my father!

*wbd.k ẖ3wt.sn snws(.k) b3w.sn*

May you burn their corpses and cook their *Ba*-souls

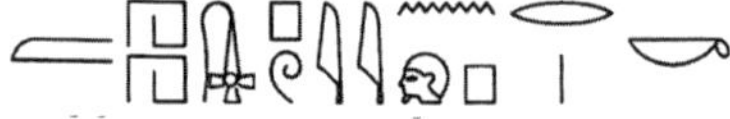

*m hh pwy nj tp-r3.k*

by that fiery blaze which is in your mouth,

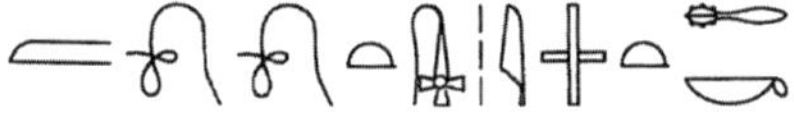

*m w3w3t jmjt ẖt.k*

by the flame which is in your body!

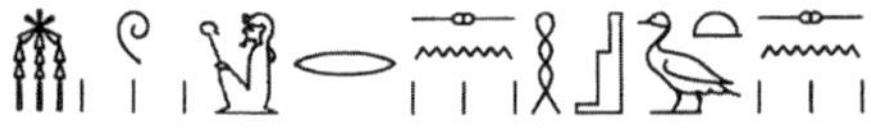

*msw.j r.sn ḥtmw.sn*

My children are against them, so that they are destroyed.

*3ḫw pryw jm.j r.sn n wnn.sn*

The *Akh*-spirits who came forth from me are against them so that they do not exist.

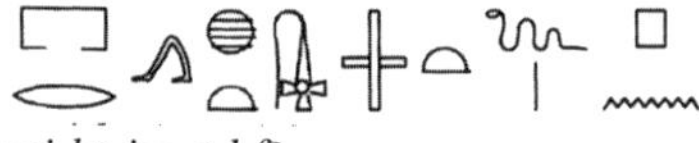

*prj ẖt jmyt ḥf3w pn*

Then the flame goes forth which is in this serpent,

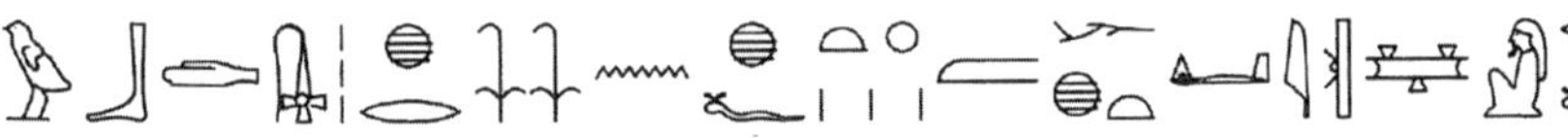

*wbdḥr nn nj ḫftyw m-ḫt ḏwj ḥrw r.f*

then these enemies are burned, after Horus has called to him.»

*jw rḫw ḥkꜣ ḥfꜣw pn*

Whoever knows the enchanting of this serpent

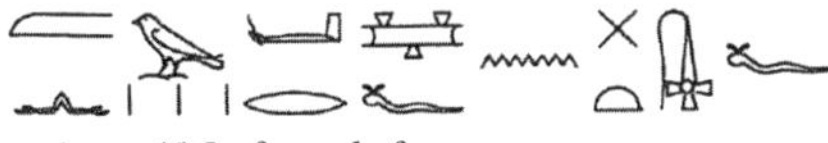

*m jwty (j)ʿr.f n sḏt.f*

will not come near to its flame.

*jw wdnw n ḥryw ḥfꜣw pn*

Whoever makes an offering to those upon this serpent,

*m jwty bꜣ.f m s(ḏ)t*

his *Ba*-soul will not be in the fire.

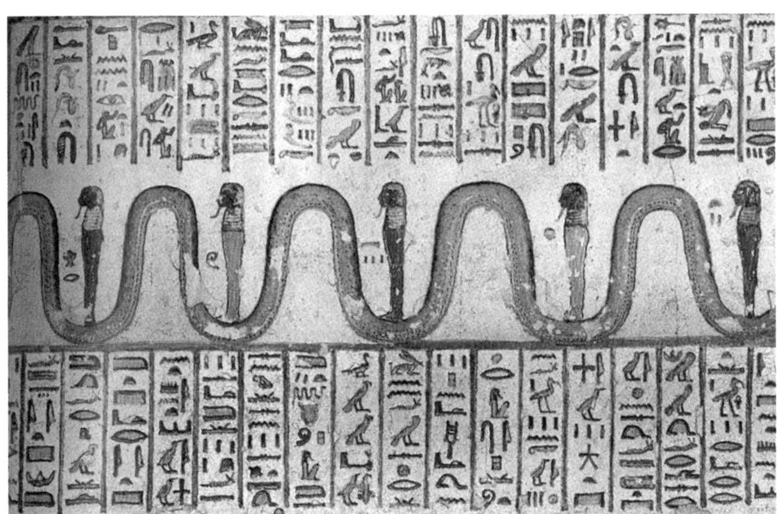

From the tomb of Pharaoh Ramses V/VI.

## Ninth Gate

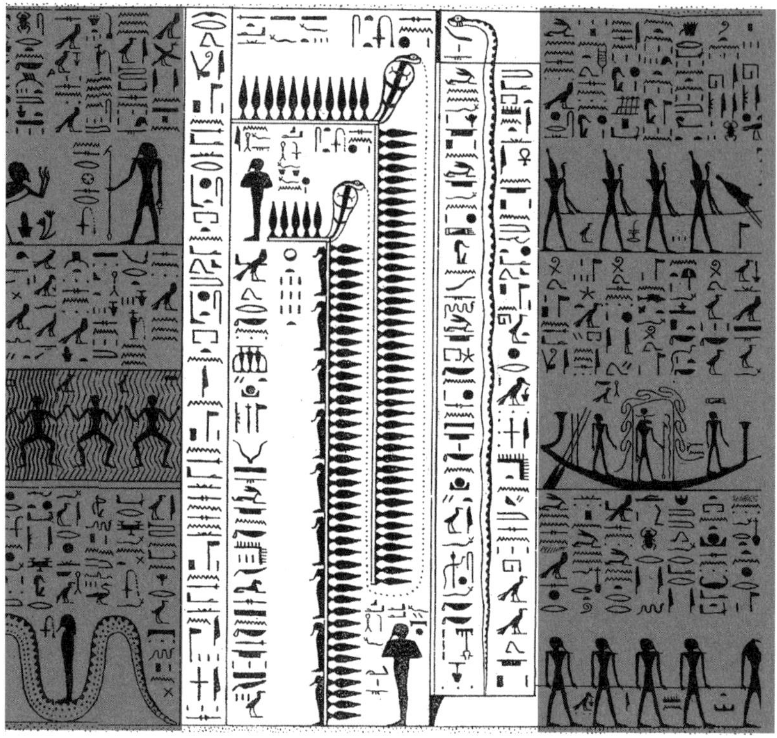

*spr jn nṯr pn ꜥꜣ r sbḫt tn*

Arrival of this great god at this gate,

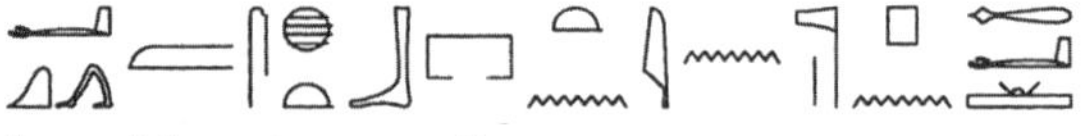

*ꜥq m sbḫt tn jn nṯr pn ꜥꜣ*

entering of this great god into this gate,

*snsn nṯr pn ꜥꜣ jn nṯrw jmyw.s*

praising this great god by the gods who are in it.

Name of the gate:

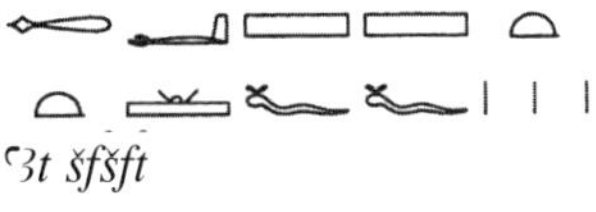

*ˁ3t šfšft*

"With great authority".

Upper and lower Uraeus-serpents:

*stt.s n rˁw*

"She lights up for Re".

Upper guardian:

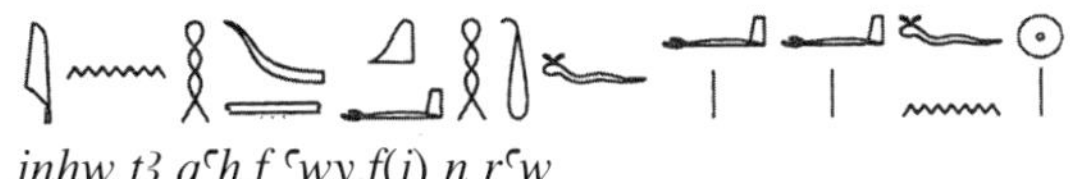

*jnḥw t3 qˁḥ.f ˁwy.f(j) n rˁw*

"Who encloses the Earth". He bends his arms for Re.

Lower guardian::

*rmnw t3 qˁḥ.f ˁwy.fj n rˁw*

"Who carries the Earth". He bends his arms for Re.

Nine mummies:

ⲫ|||
|||⌓
⌓|||

*psḏt* 9 *nwt*

"The ninth Ennead".

In front of the Ennead:

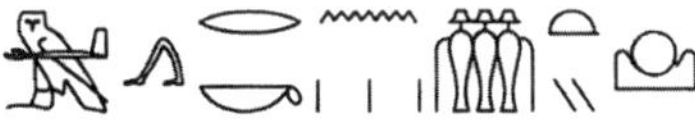

*my rk (r.)n ḫnty 3ḫt*

«Come to us, Foremost of the horizon,

*nṯr ꜥꜣ wpj štꜣw*
great god who has opened up the Mysterious!

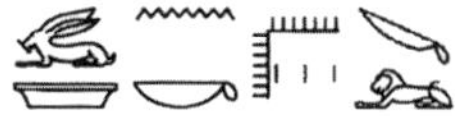

*wnw n.k sbḫwt ḏsryt*
Open for you are the unapproachable gates,

*znw n.k ꜥꜣw štꜣw*
unlocked for you are the mysterious doors!»

The serpent upon the doorway:

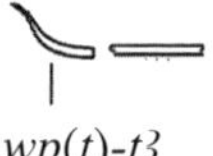

*wp(t)-tꜣ*
"Horn of the Earth".

*wnn.f ḥr ꜥꜣ pn*
He is upon this door,

*wn.f n rꜥw*
he opens for Re.

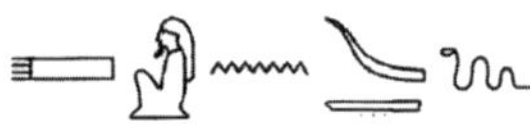

*sjꜣ n wp(t)-tꜣ*
Sia (says) to "Horn of the Earth":

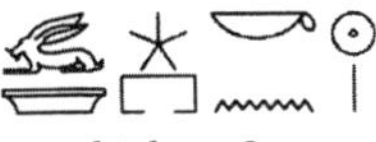

*wn sbꜣ.k n rꜥw*

«Open your gate for Re,

*zn ꜥꜣ.k n ꜣḫty*

unlock your door for Akhty!

*jw.f sḥḏ.f kkw zmꜣw*

He illuminates the primeval darkness,

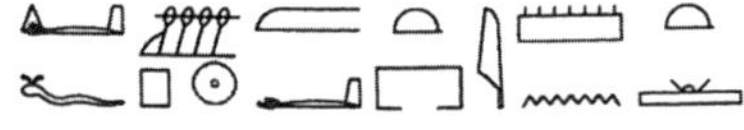

*dy.f sšp m ꜥt-jmnt*

he throws light into the Hidden Space!»

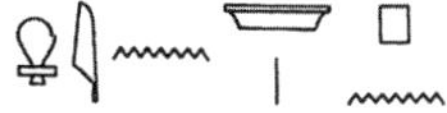

*ḫtmjn ꜥꜣ pn*

Then this door is shut,

*m-ḫt ꜥq nṯr pn*

after this god has entered.

*hwtḫr ꜣḫw jmyw sbḫt.tn*

Then the *Akh*-spirits who are in this gate wail

*sḏm.sn hꜣꜣ ꜥꜣ pn*

when they hear this door being slammed.

# TENTH

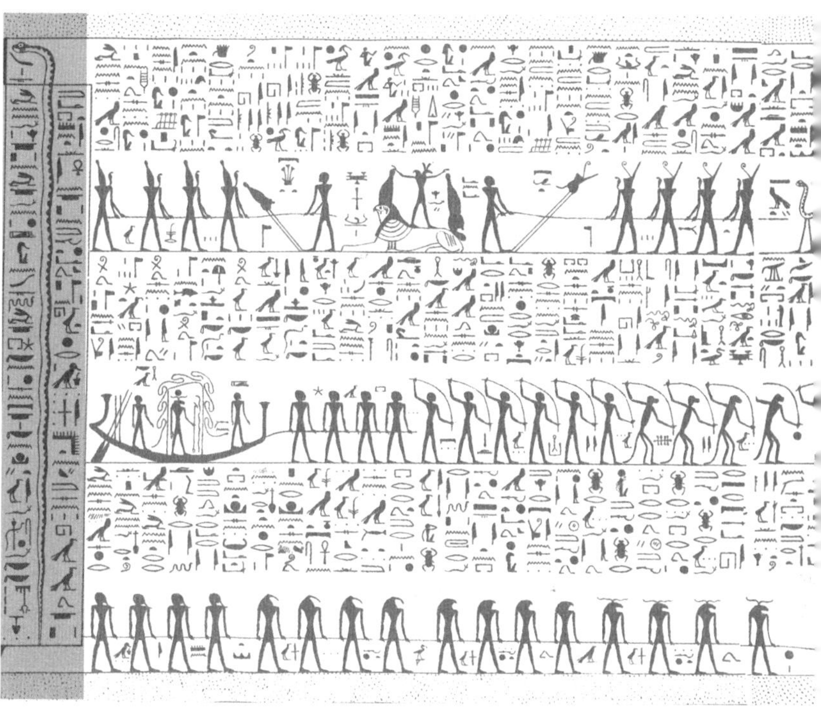

# HOUR

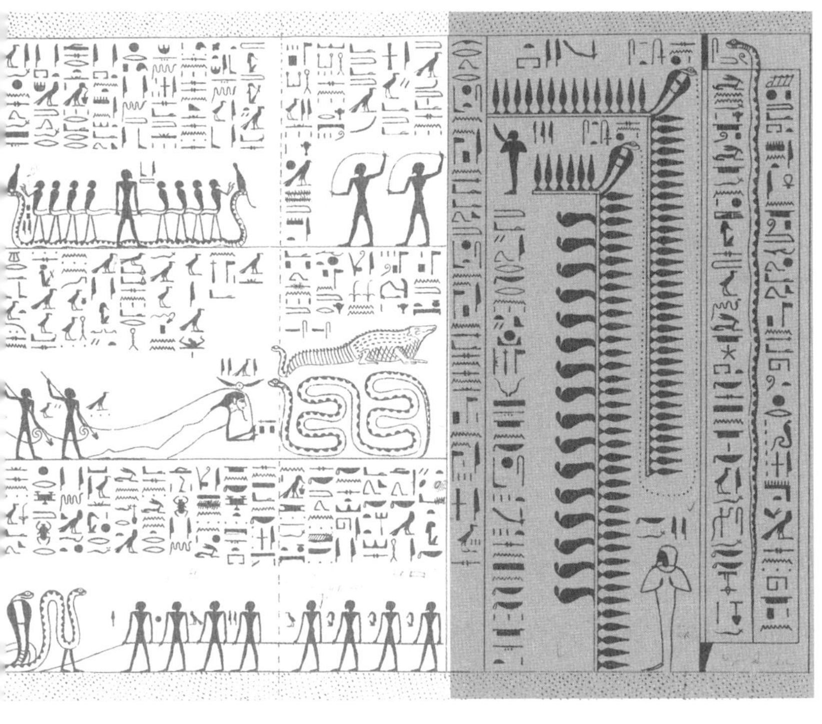

## Upper Register, 61st Scene

In the centre of the scene, a double-headed sphinx is shown; both his heads (a falcon and a human) wear the White Crown. His name is *ḥrw jmy wjꜣ* (Horus who is in the boat). Beside the human head we read *ꜥn(ꜥ)* (The reverse). On the back of this complex creature stands *ḥr(wj).fj* (His double faces), the heads of Horus and Seth on one neck. In front of the sphinx, four *nṯrw rsyw* (southern gods) , with the White Crown and an Uraeus as heads grasp a rope, together with the normal-headed *ḥrj-ḥꜣtt* (He over the front-rope). Behind, *ḥry-pḥtt* (He over the hind-rope) and four *nṯrw mḥtyw* (northern gods), with the Red Crown and Uraeus as heads, grasp another rope.

The text reads:

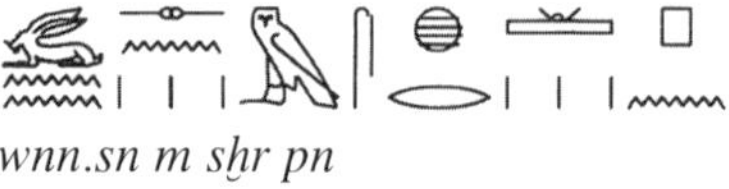

*wnn.sn m sḫr pn*
They are like this:

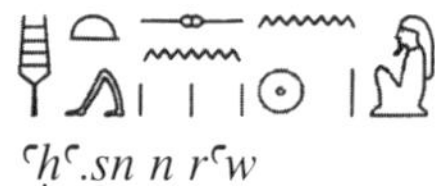

*ꜥḥꜥ.sn n rꜥw*
They stand up for Re.

From the tomb of Queen Tawseret.

(At the southern gods:)

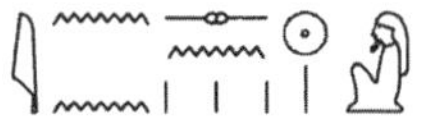

*jn n.sn rꜥw*

Re says to them:

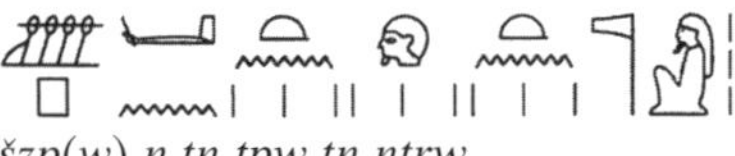

*šzp(w) n.ṯn tpw.ṯn nṯrw*

«Receive your heads, oh gods,

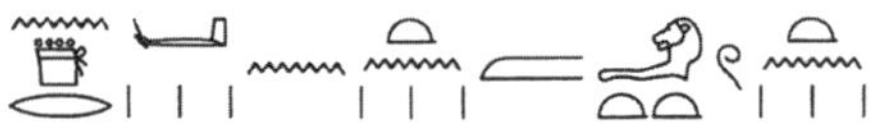

*nḏrw n.ṯn m ḥꜣtt.ṯn*

and grasp your front rope!

*jhy ḫprw nṯrw*

Hail, forms of the gods,

*jhy 3ḫw nṯrw*

and hail, Akh-spirits of the gods!

*ḫprn.ṯn nṯrw 3ḫn.ṯn nṯrw*

You have transformed, O gods, you have become an Akh, O gods

*n ḫprw.j m št3yt*

by my appearance in the Shetit,

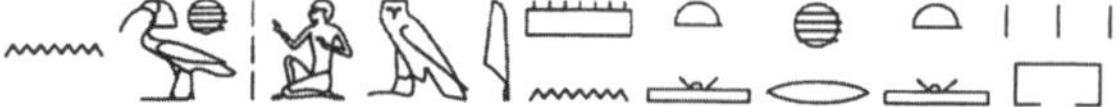

*n 3ḫw.j m jmnt ḫrt*

by my magic power in (the place) "With Hidden Character"!»

From the tomb of Pharaoh Ramses V/VI.

(At the sphinx:)

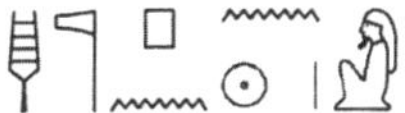

*ʿḥʿ nṯr pn n rʿw*

This god rises for Re.

*ʿqḫr ḥrwj.fj m nṯr pn*

Then "His Double Faces" enters (back) into this god,

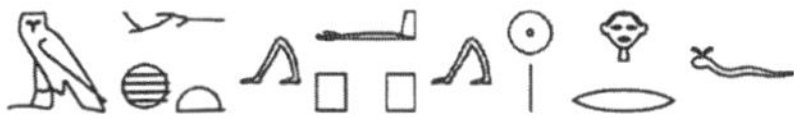

*m-ḫt ʿpp rʿw ḥr.f*

after Re has passed by him.

From the tomb of Queen Tawseret.

(At the northern gods:)

*jn n.sn rʿw*

Re says to them:

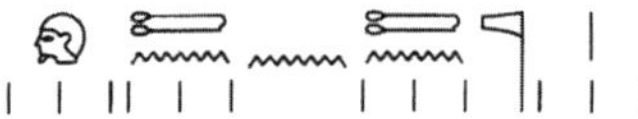

*tpw.ṯn n.ṯn nṯrw*

«Your heads belong to you, oh gods!

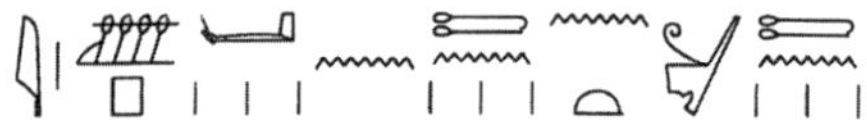

*j šzpw n.ṯn nt.ṯn*

Oh receive your Red Crown(s)

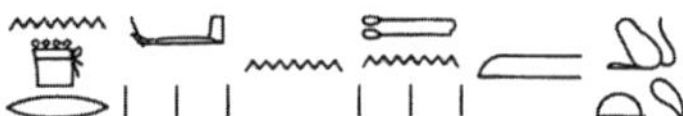

*nḏrw n.ṯn m pḥt*

and grasp for you the back rope

*nt wjꜣ nj ḫprw jm.j*

of the boat of Him who has emanated from me -

*ṯwt js ḥrw sṯnw ḥr*

you really are Horus with crowned head!»

From the tomb of Queen Tawseret.

### 62ND SCENE

From the tomb of Pharaoh Ramses V/VII.

A six-headed serpent on twelve human legs, called *šmty* (Who walks). He is held in his midst by a god without attributes, *wpw* (The divider).

*wnn.f m sḫr pn*
He is like this:

*jw.f ḫnz.f št3yt*
He traverses the Shetit.

*ḥmm.f r q3(w)-dm(w)t*
and turns back at the (gate) "With high knives",

From the tomb of Queen Tawseret.

(*r*) *ʿryt nt jmnt*

at the gateway of the West.

*jw jmyw.s ʿmw tpw.sn*

Those who are in it, their heads are swallowed up,

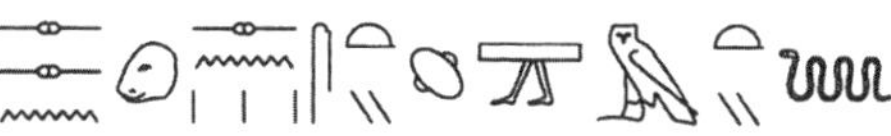

*ssn.sn stj šmty*

when they smell the stench of Him who walks.

*wpw m z3w.sw*

The divider is the one who guards him.

## 63RD SCENE

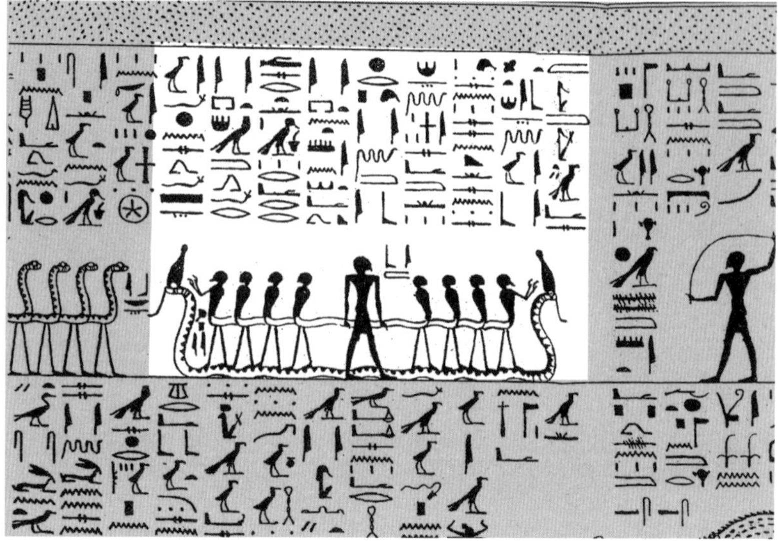

A double serpent: The outer one with two heads, each with the White Crown; the inner one with eight human heads, a pair of human arms raised in praise at each end, and walking on 16 human legs. She is called *tpy* (With (human) heads) and held in the middle by a god without attributes: *jbṯ* (The catcher). The outer serpent is the *bjꜣ(y)-tꜣ* (Marvel of the Earth).

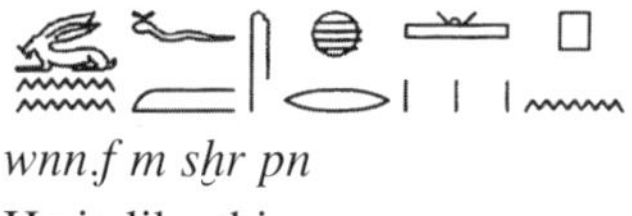

*wnn.f m sḫr pn*

He is like this:

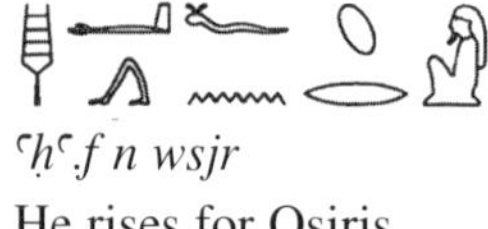

*ꜥḥꜥ.f n wsjr*

He rises for Osiris,

From the tomb of Queen Tawseret.

*sjptw n.f b3w njkw jmyw dw3t*

and the Ba-souls of the punished ones who are in the Netherworld are assigned to him.

*jw.f ḫnz.f št3yt*

He traverses the Shetit

*ḥmm.f r ḏsrt-b3w*

and turns back at the (gate) with protected Ba-souls,

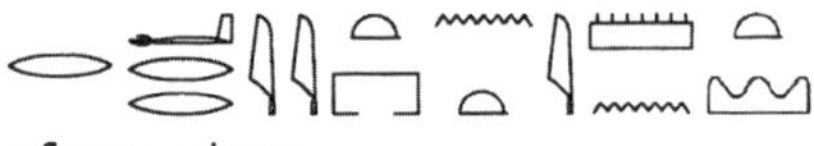

*r ˁrryt nt jmnt*

at the gateway of the West.

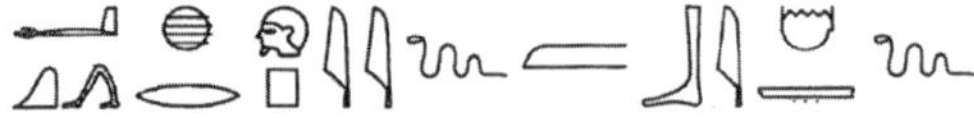

*ˁq ḫr tpy m bjȝ(y)-tȝ*

Then He with heads enters into Marvel of the Earth.

*jw jmyw.s ˁmw tpw.sn*

Those who are in it (the West) swallow their heads,

*ssn.sn stj bjȝ(y)-tȝ*

when they smell the stench of Marvel of the Earth.

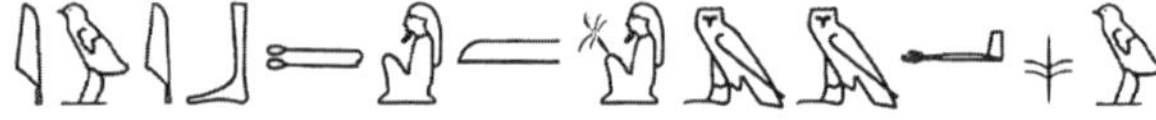

*jw jbṯ m zȝw.sw*

The catcher is the one who guards him.

From the tomb of Pharaoh Ramses V/VI.

## 64TH SCENE

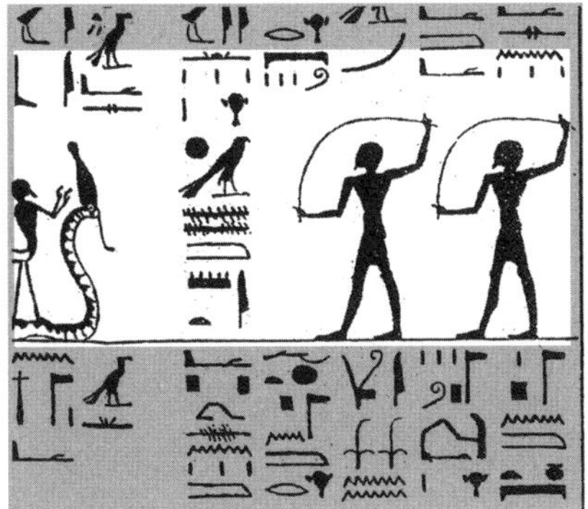

From the tomb of Pharaoh Ramses V/VI.

Two anonymous gods, each holding a net with both hands

*nṯrw pw ḥk3yw*
Those are the gods who work charms

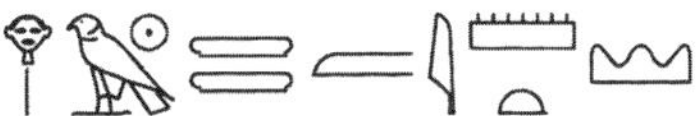

*ḥr rʿw-ḥrw-3ḫty m jmnt*
on behalf of Re-Horakhty in the West.

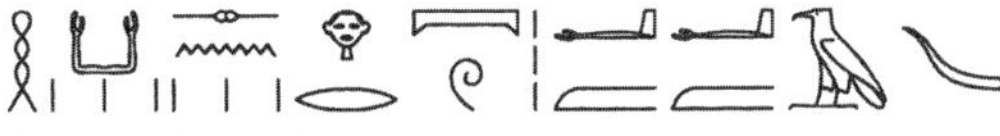

*ḥk3w.sn ḥryw ʿm3w*
Their magic is what is upon the nets

*jmyw ʿm3w m ʿwj.sn*
and what is in the net in their hands.

## Middle Register, 65th Scene

The solar barque with *ḥkꜣw* (Magic), *jwf-rꜥw* (Flesh of Re), *mḥn* (Mehen) and *sjꜣ* (Sia, Percipience), towed by four *dwꜣtyw* (gods of the Netherworld).

*sṯꜣw nṯr pn ꜥꜣ jn nṯrw dwꜣtyw*

This great god is towed by the gods of the Netherworld.

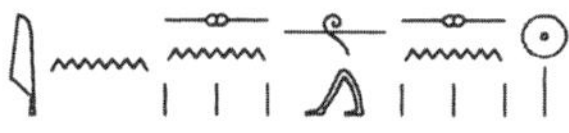

*jn.sn sṯꜣ.sn rꜥw*

They say when they tow Re:

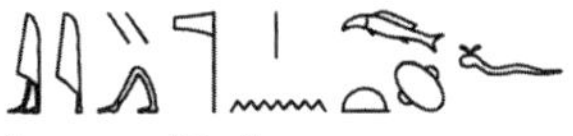

*jy nṯr n ḫ3t.f*

«The god has come to his corpse,

*sṯ3w nṯr n šwt.f*

the god has been towed to his shadow.

*ḥtp.k ḏt.k sṯ3w.k*

You rest (in) your body, and you are towed,

*wḏ3w m št3w.f*

(you) who are whole in his mystery!

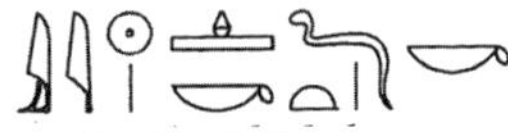

*jy rʿw ḥtp.k ḏt.k*

Re has come that you rest (in) your body.

*nḏ.ṯw ḥryw ʿm3w.sn*

Those who are over their nets protect you.»

## 66TH SCENE

Fourteen deities, each holding a net with both hands. The first three are the *ḥryw mdw* (Who command [magic] words), one with human head, the second with a double serpent head, the third with a bird's head. The next group of three, all human-headed, are called *ḥkꜣyw* (Who work charms), followed by four monkeys *zꜣyw rʿw* (Who protect Re), and four goddesses *zꜣywt rʿw* (Who protect Re).

*wnn.sn m sẖr pn*
They are like this:

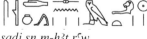

*sqdj.sn m-ḥꜣt rʿw*
They navigate in front of Re,

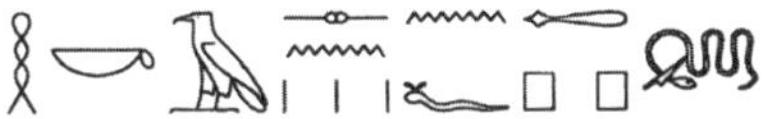

*ḥkꜣ.sn n.f ꜥꜣpp*

they enchant Apopis on behalf of him,

*ḥmm.sn r ꜥr(r)yt nt ꜣḫty*

they turn back at the gateway of Akhty.

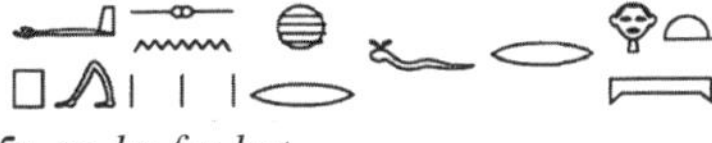

*ꜥp.sn ḫr.f r ḥrt*

They proceed with him to the sky,

*ḫpr.sn n.f m jtrtj*

they manifest themselves for him on both sides,

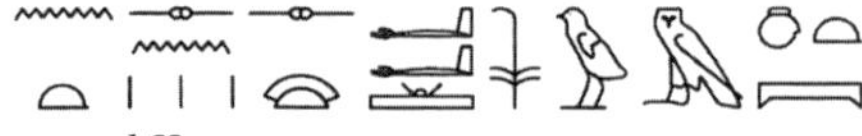

*ntsn sḫ<sup>ꜥꜥ</sup>.sw m nwt*

they cause him to appear in heaven (Nut).

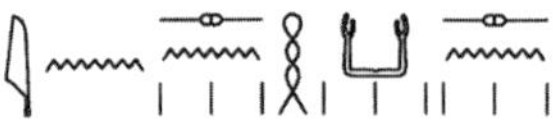

*jn.sn ḥkꜣ.sn*

They say, when they enchant:

*jḥy sbj wꜣyw ꜥꜣpp*

«You rebel! Bound is Apopis

*dy ḏwt.f*

to whom his evil is done!

*ḥtmw ḥr.k ꜥꜣpp*

Destroyed is your face, Apopis,

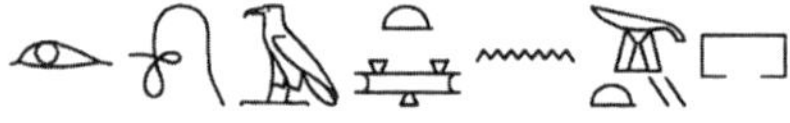

*jry wꜣt n nmtj*

make (your) way to the slaughterer!

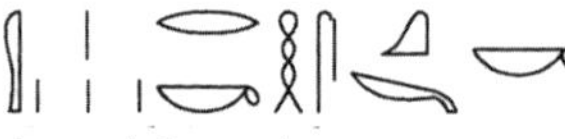

*dsw r.k ḥsqw.k*

Knives are against you, so that you are cut to pieces,

*jꜣy r.k ḥtmw.k*

the old one is against you, so that you are destroyed!

*ꜥbbwtyw dj.sn jm.k*

They who bear spears stab you,

*ḥkꜣ.n.ṯw m jmjt ꜥ.n*

and we enchant you with what is in our hand.

*jhy drt(w) ḥtmtj sswnt(w) ssy*

Hail, driven away is the destroyed one, punished is the captive.»

From the tomb of Pharaoh Ramses V/VI.

## 67TH SCENE

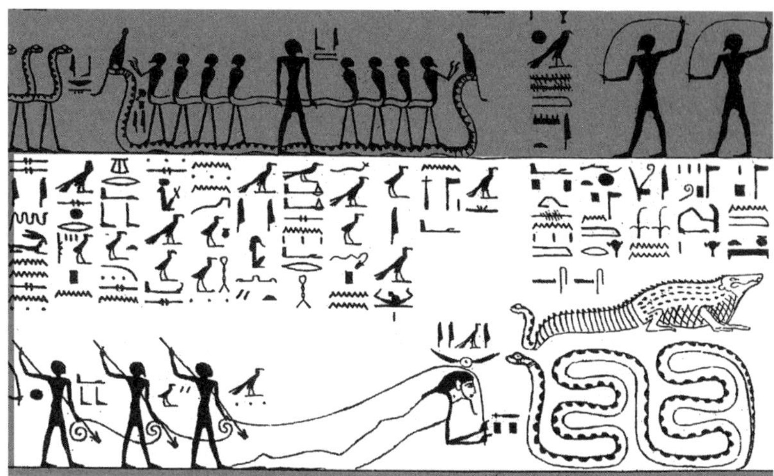

Three gods armed with spears: *ʿbbwtyw* (Those who bear spears). They grasp a rope which is held by the half-lying god *j3y* (The old one). Facing this group is the multi-coiled serpent *ʿ3pp* (Apopis), with the crocodile *šsšs* above him.

*wnn.sn m sḫr pn ḥr ʿbbwt.sn*

They are like this, carrying their spears.

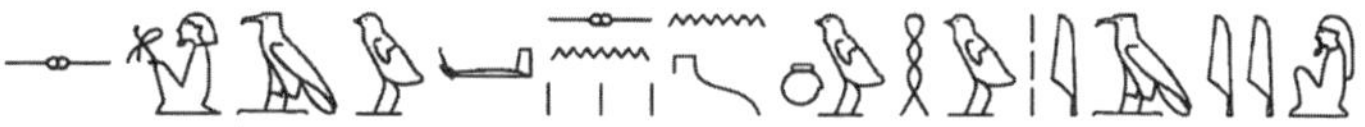

*z3w.sn nwḥw j3y*

They guard the rope of The old one

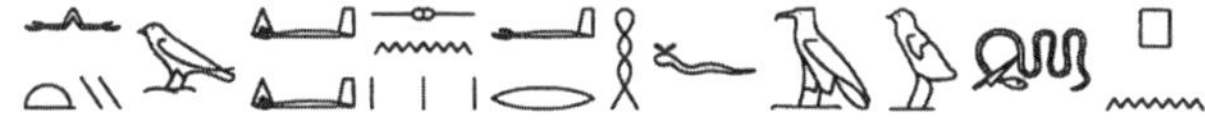

*jwty dd.sn (j)ʿr ḥf3w pn*

and they prevent this serpent from approaching

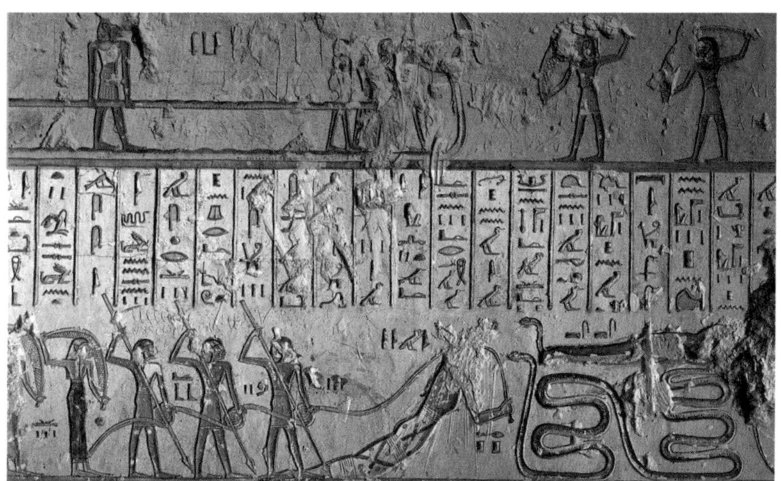

From the tomb of Pharaoh Ramses V/VI.

*n wj3 nj nṯr ꜥ3*

the barque of the great god.

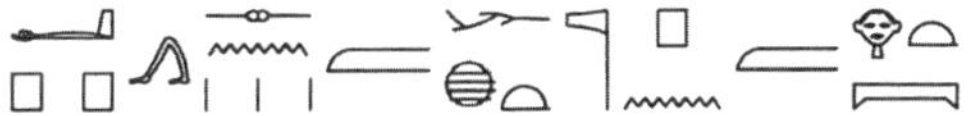

*ꜥpp.sn m-ḫt nṯr pn m ḥrt*

They proceed after this god in the sky.

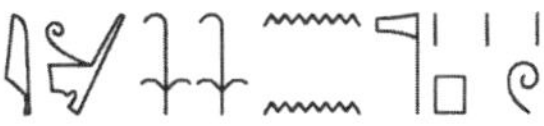

*jn nn nj nṯrw pw*

These are the gods

*ꜥḥ3w ḥr nṯr pn m nwt*

who fight on behalf of this god in heaven (Nut).

## Lower Register, 68th Scene

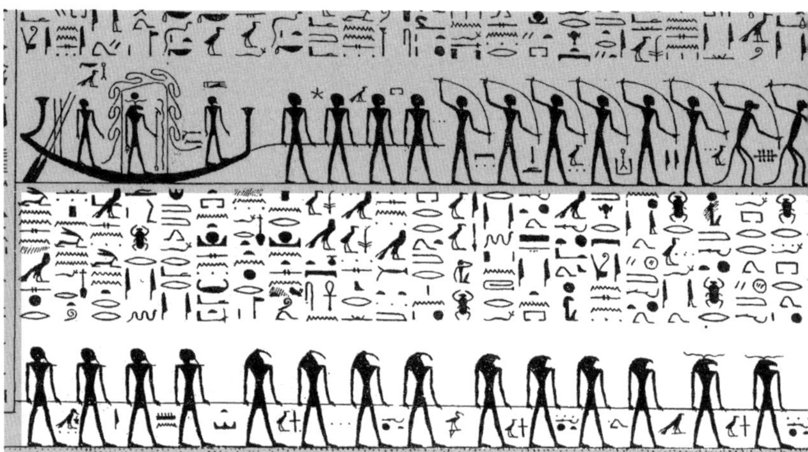

All figures are connected by a rope, grasping it with both hands. The first group of four are the *b3w-jmnt* (*Ba*-souls of the West) without attributes; four gods with heads of an ibis follow, the *jmyw-ḫt ḏḥwtj* (retinue of Thot), after them four falcon-headed the *jmyw-ḫt ḥrw* (retinue of Horus), and four ram-headed *jmyw-ḫt rʿw* (retinue of Re). Then the rope is bound around the human legs of a double serpent, a manifestation of *ḫpry* (Khepri), the rejuvenated Sungod, carrying a falcon with the Double Crown: *ḥrw dw3ty* (Horus of the Netherworld). Behind this complex image, the rope continues and is grasped by eight gods shown facing front: *sḫmyw* (The powerful ones).

*wnn.sn m sḫr pn*

They are like this:

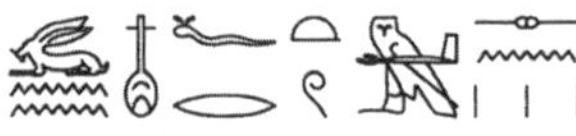

*wnn nfrt m ʿ.sn*

The tow-rope is in their hand,

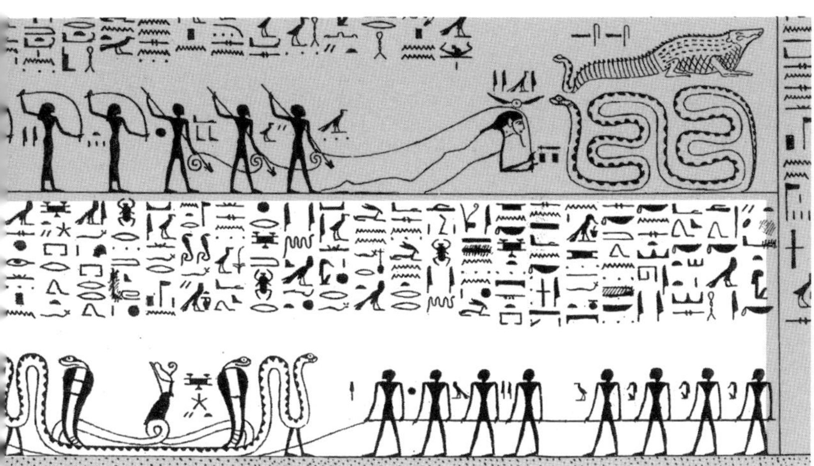

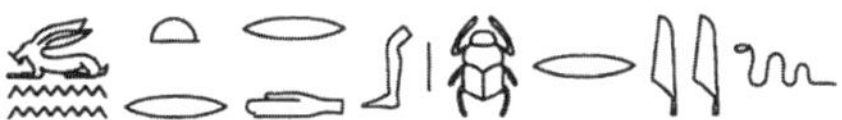

*wnnt r rd ḫpry*

which is (fastened) at the foot of Khepri.

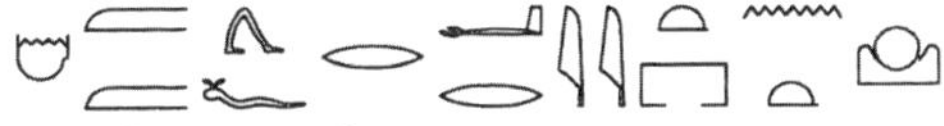

*ḥmm.f r ꜥryt nt ꜣḫt*

When he turns back at the gateway of the horizon,

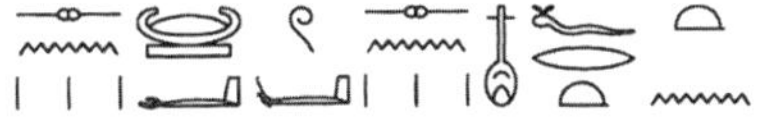

*sn wḥꜥ.sn nfrt tn*

they loosen this rope

*ḫr nṯr pn r ꜣḫt*

from this god on the horizon.

*ntsn sṯ3w.sw m nwt*

It is they who drag him in heaven (Nut).

*ʿnḫ.sn m rsyw*

They live on the south wind,

*srq.sn m mḥttyw*

they breathe on the north wind,

*m prrt m r3 nj rʿw*

on that which goes forth from the mouth of Re.

*jw ḫrw ḫprj pn pḫr.f ḫt št3yt*

The voice of this Khepri serpent goes round through the Shetit

*m-ḫt ʿq rʿw m ḥrt*

after Re has entered the sky.

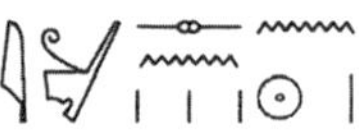

*jn.sn n rʿw*

They say to Re:

*jy jy m-ḫt ḫprw.f*

«(He) comes, who comes behind his manifestation,

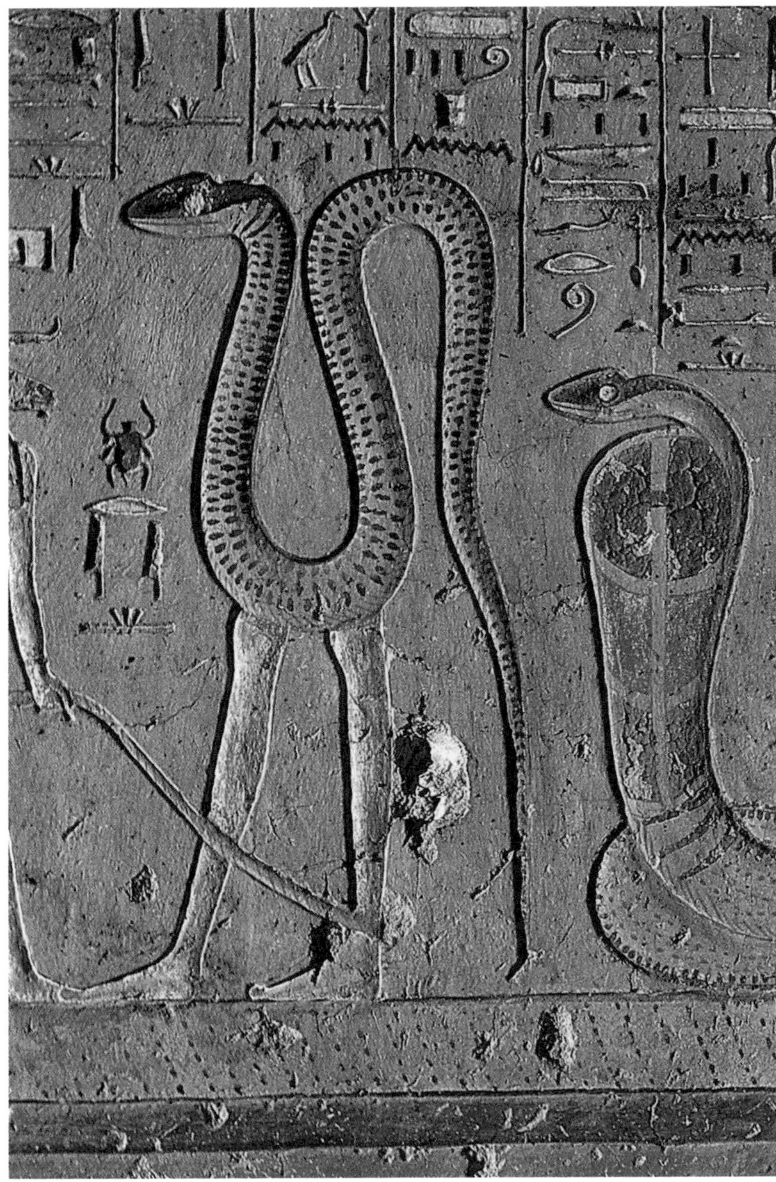

From the tomb of Queen Tawseret.

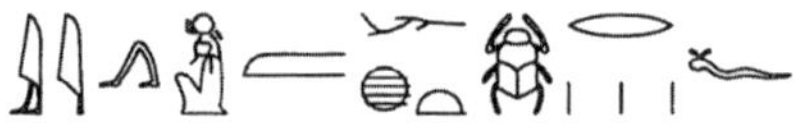

*jy rʿw m-ḫt ḫprw.f*

Re comes behind his manifestation!

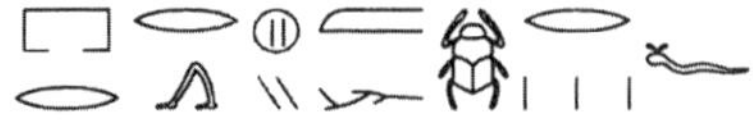

*prr prrw m-ḫt ḫprw.f*

(He) emerges who emerges behind his manifestation,

*pr(r) rʿw m-ḫt ḫprw.f*

Re emerges behind his manifestation!

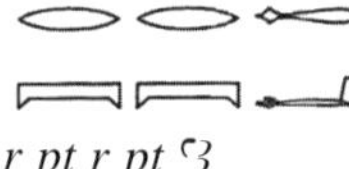

*r pt r pt ʿ3*

To heaven, to heaven, Great one!

*jhy wḏ.n.ṯw ḥr nst.k*

Hail, we place you on your throne

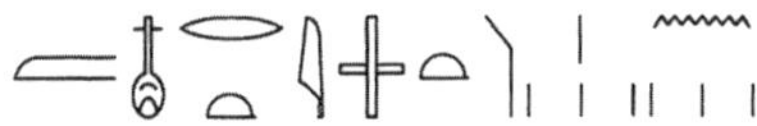

*m nfrt jmjt ḏbʿw.n*

by means of the tow-rope which is in our fingers,

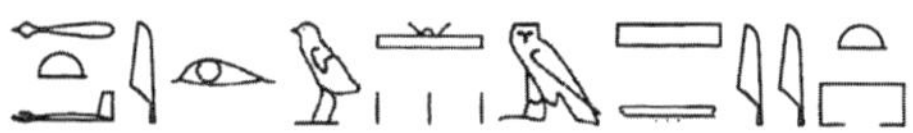

*ʿ3t jrw m št3yt*

with an important function in the Shetit!»

(The Khepri serpent:)

*wnn.f m sḫr pn*

He is like this:

From the tomb of Queen Tawseret.

*ḥrw dw3ty prj.f jm.f tp*

Horus of the Netherworld emerges first out of him,

*prr ḫprw m q3b(w)*

and (then) the forms emerge out of the coil(s).

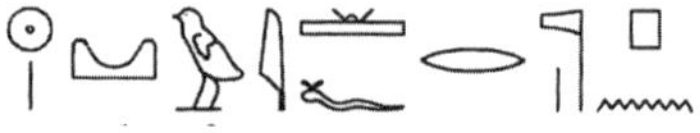

*rʿw ḏwj.f r nṯr pn*

Re calls to this god,

*nṯrtj.fj ḫnm.sn.sw*

and his two divine ones unite with him.

*ʿqḫr ḥrw m ḫpry*

Then Horus enters (back) into the Khepri serpent,

*m-ḫt ḏwj rʿw r.f*

after Re has called to him.

(At the powerful ones:)

*wnn nfrt m ʿ.sn*

In their hand is the tow-rope.

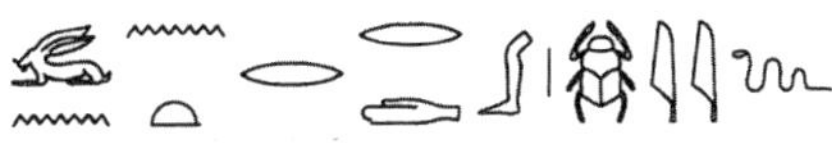

*wnnt r rd (nj) ḫpry*

which is (fastened) at the foot of Khepri.

*jn.sn n rꜥw*

They say to Re:

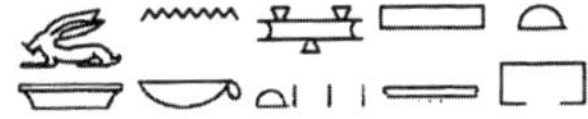

*wnw n.k wꜣwt štꜣyt*

«Opened for you are the paths of the Shetit,

*znw n.k ꜥꜣw jmyw tꜣ*

opened for you are the doors which are in the Earth,

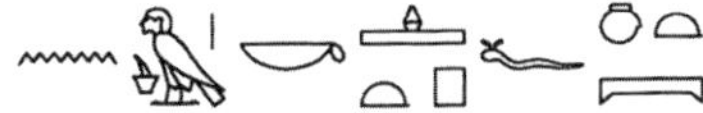

*n bꜣ.k ḥtp.f nwt*

for your Ba-soul that she rests in heaven (Nut)!

*sšm.n.ṯw m šw knzt*

We guide you in the districts of Kenset (East).

*jhy ꜥq.k jꜣbtt*

Hail, you are entering the East,

*sqdj.k m jḥtj mwt.k*

you sail between the thighs of your mother!»

## Tenth Gate

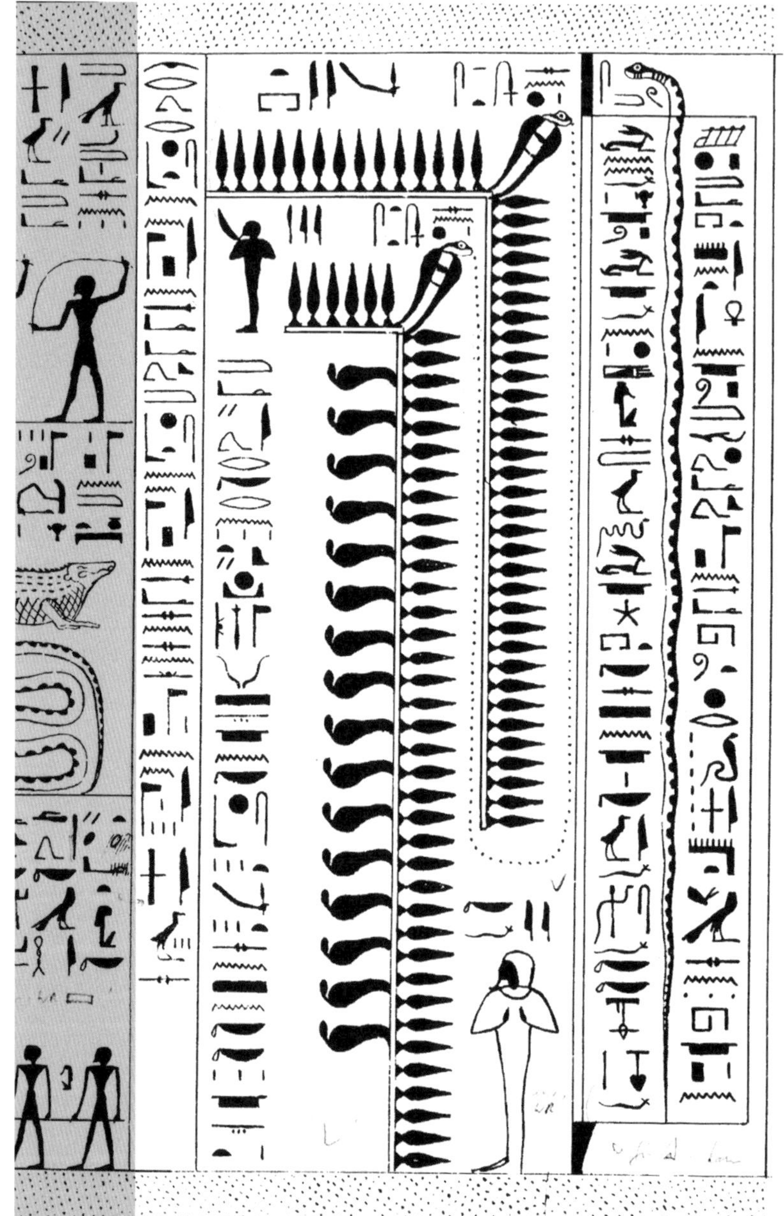

*spr r sbḫt tn jn nṯr pn ꜥ3*
Arriving at this gate by this great god,

*ꜥq m sbḫt tn jn nṯr pn ꜥ3*
entering into this gate by this great god,

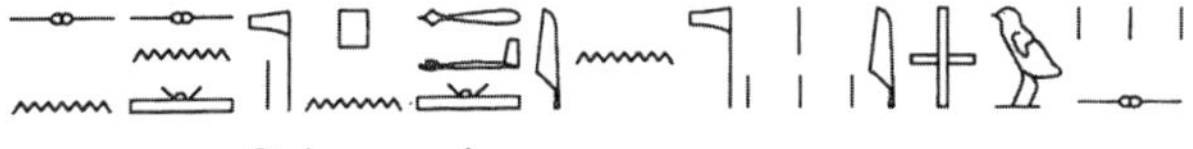

*snsn nṯr pn ꜥ3 jn nṯrw jmyw.s*
praising this great god by the gods who are in it.

Name of the gate:

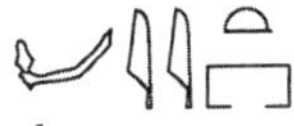

*ḏsryt*
"Holy (secluded?) one".

Upper and lower Uraeus-serpents:

*stt.s n rꜥw*
"She lights up for Re".

Upper guardian:

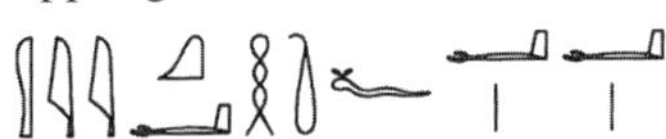

*nmy qꜥḥ.f ꜥwj(.f) (n rꜥw)*
"The roaring one". He bends (his) arms (for Re).

Lower guardian:

*kfy*
"Who uncovers".

24 Uraeus-serpents:

*my rk r.n ḫnty ꜣḫt*

«Come to us, Foremost of the horizon,

*nṯr ꜥꜣ wpj štꜣw*

Great god who has opened the Mysterious!

*wnw n.k sbḫwt ḏsryt*

Open for you are the unapproachable gates,

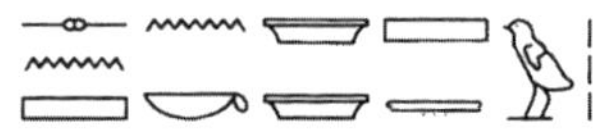

*znw n.k ꜥꜣw štꜣw*

unlocked for you are the mysterious doors!»

Serpent on the door:

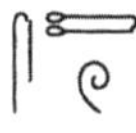

*sty*

"The burning one".

*wnn.f ḥr ꜥꜣ pn*

He is upon this door,

*wn.f n rꜥw*

he opens for Re.

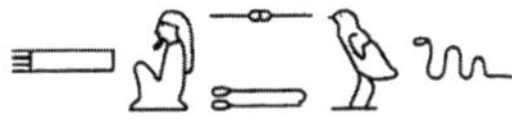

*sjꜣ (n) sṯw*

Sia (says to) "the burning one":

*wn sbꜣ.k n rꜥw*

«Open your gate for Re,

*zn ꜥꜣ.k n ꜣḫty*

unlock your door for Akhty!

*jw.f sḥḏ.f kkw zmꜣw*

He illuminates the primeval darkness,

*dy.f šsp m ꜥt-jmnt*

he throws light into the Hidden Space!»

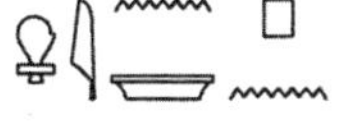

*ḫtmjn ꜥꜣ pw*

Then this door is shut,

*m-ḫt ꜥq nṯr pn ꜥꜣ*

after this great god has entered.

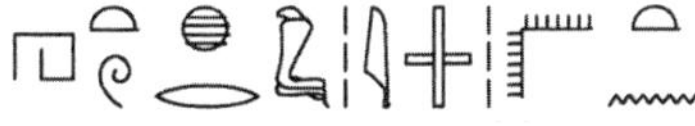

*hwtḫr jꜥrwt jmyw(t) sbḫt.tn*

Then the Uraeus serpents who are in this gate wail

*sḏm.sn hꜣꜣ ꜥꜣ pn*

when they hear this door being slammed.

# ELEVENTH

# Hour

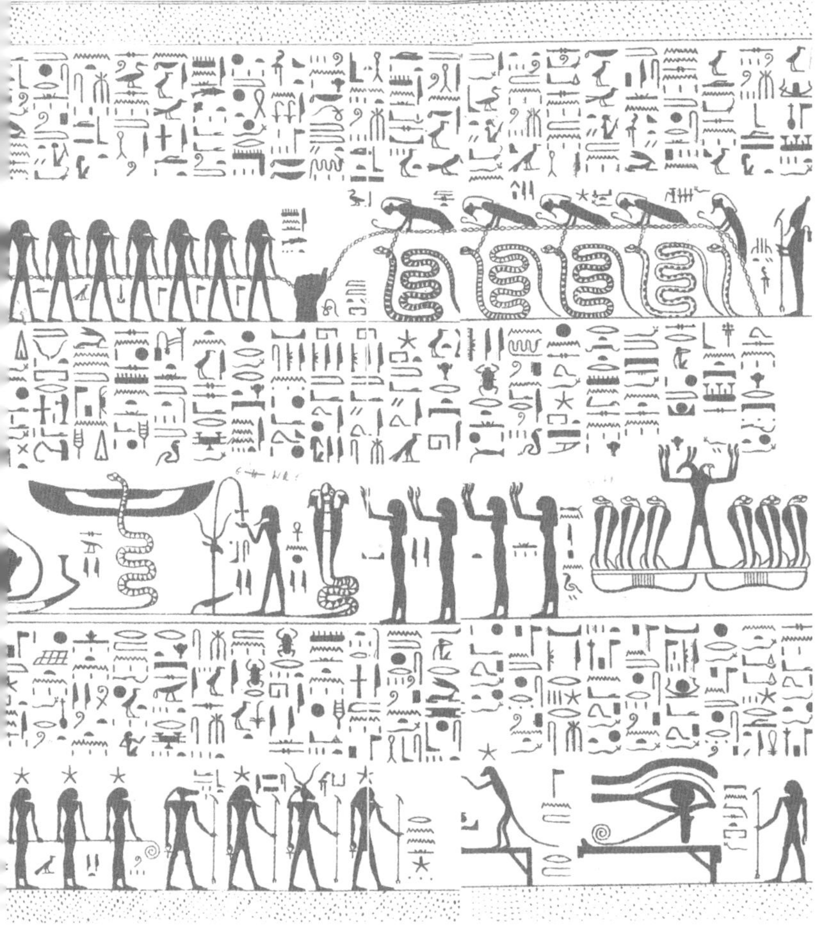

# Parts of the Eleventh Hour

# From The Tomb of Ramses V/VI

## Upper Register, 69th Scene

A first group of four gods, a rope in the one hand and a knife in the other: *jntjw* (The Fetterers). The next group is also armed with rope and knife, but each of the four gods has four serpent heads: *ḥntjw* (The Slaughterers).

Then Apopis as serpent follows, tied around his neck by a rope: *ꜥ3pp ḫrw.f pḫr.f m dw3t* (Apopis. His voice goes round in the Netherworld). The rope is tied by *srqt* (Selkis, the scorpion-goddess). Behind her, four gods grasp the rope: *sdfyw* (Those who enchain). Changing the direction, twelve more gods at the rope are called *nṯrw ḏ3dyw* (Gods who cut off throats). An enormous fist belongs to the *jmnw ḫ3t* (He with hidden body).

Of the four serpents chained to the rope, the first is *w3mmtj* (Wamemti), the others are the *msw bdšt* (The children of the faint one); all are confederates of Apopis and therefore kept in check by Geb and the four sons of Horus above them, Amset, Hapi, Duamutef and Qebehsenuef A figure of Osiris Khontamenti (*ḫntj jmntyw*), with the White Crown and *Was*-sceptre, closes the register.

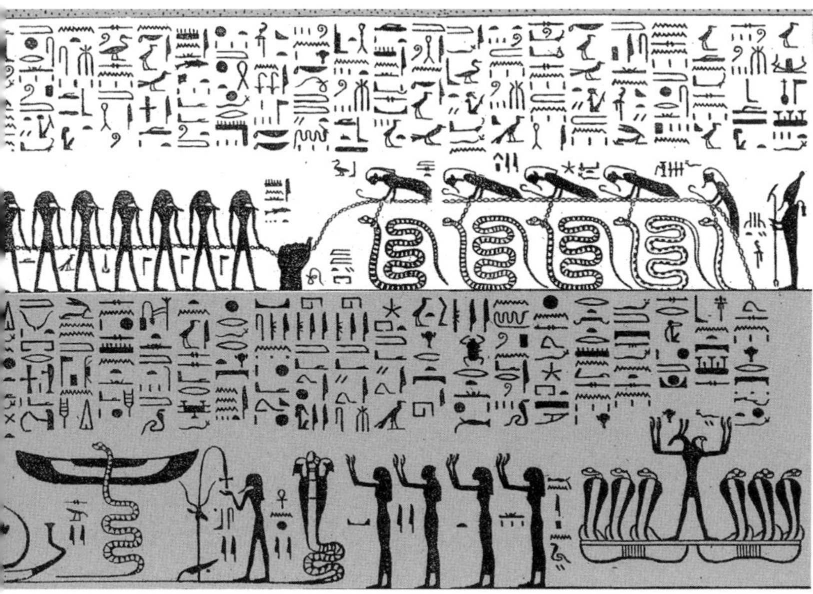

The text reads:

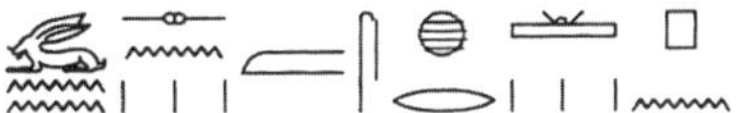

*wnn.sn m sẖr pn*

They are like this:

*ꜥḥꜥ.sn n rꜥw*

They raise themselves for Re

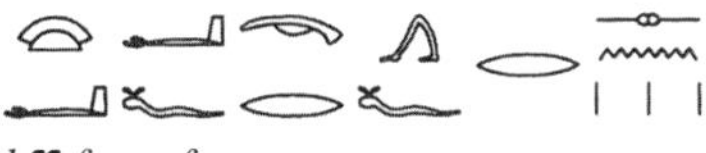

*ḫꜥꜥ.f spr.f r.sn*

when he appears and approaches them.

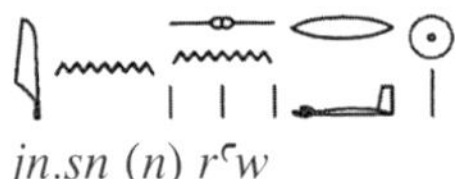

*jn.sn (n) rʿw*

They say to Re:

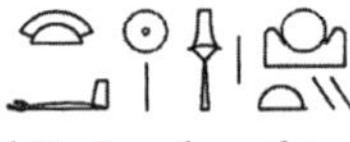

*ḫʿj rʿw sḫm ꜣḫty*

«Shine forth, Re, be powerful, Akhty!

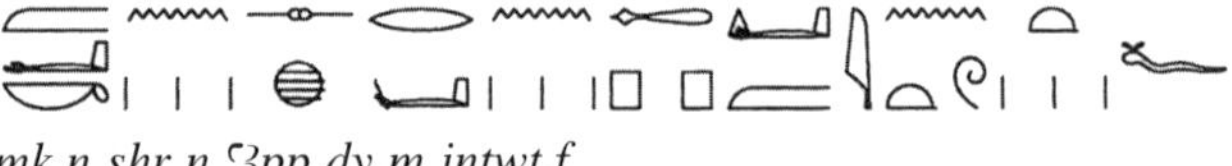

*mk.n sḫr.n ʿꜣpp dy m jnṯwt.f*

Behold we have overthrown Apopis, who is put into his fetters.

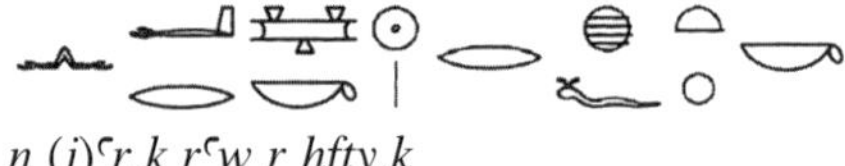

*n (j)ʿr.k rʿw r ḫfty.k*

You do not approach, Re, your enemy,

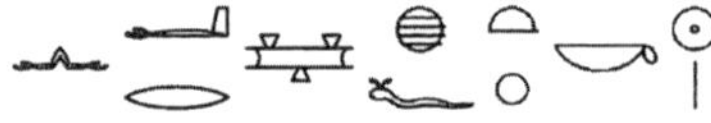

*n (j)ʿr ḫfty.k rʿw*

and your enemy does not approach (you), Re!

*ḫpr ḏsrw.k jmy mḥn*

Your safety is established, you who are in Mehen,

*ʿꜣpp ḥsbw m snf.f*

while Apopis is smashed in his blood.»

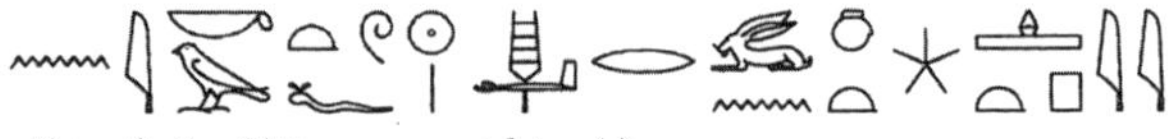

*njktw.f rʿw ʿḥʿw r wnwt ḥtpy(t)*

He is punished, while Re stops at the hour of rest.

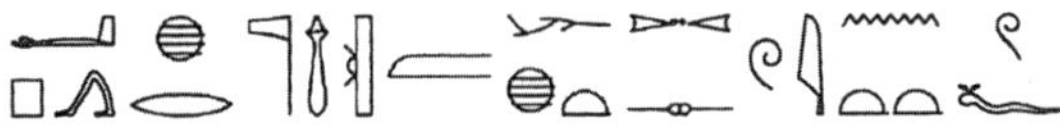

*ꜥpḫr nṯr ꜥ3 m-ḫt ṯzw jnṯwt.f*

Then the great god passes on, after his fetters have been bound.

(At Apopis:)

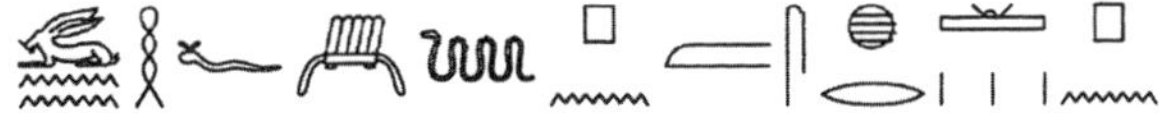

*wnn ḥf3w pn m sḫr pn*

This serpent is like this:

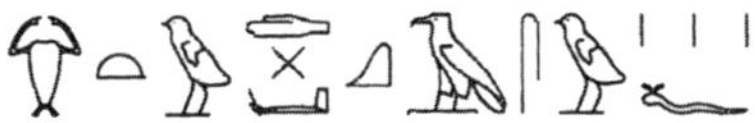

*(jn )srqt wdj q3sw.f*

It is Selkis who puts on his fetters.

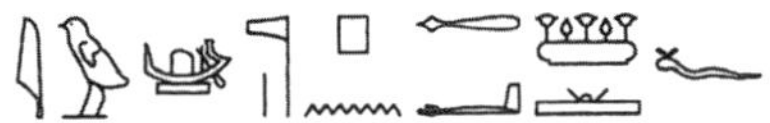

*jw wj3 nṯr pn ꜥ3 š3j.f*

When the boat of this great god runs aground

*r h3w pn (nj) ꜥ3pp*

in the neighbourhood of Apopis here.

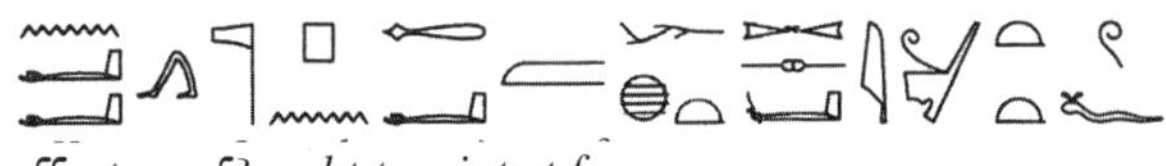

*nꜥꜥ nṯr pn ꜥ3 m-ḫt ṯzw jnṯwt.f*

This great god proceeds after his fetters have been bound.

(The gods at the rope:)

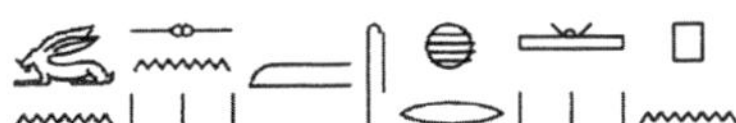

*wnn.sn m sḫr pn*

They are like this:

From the tomb of Pharaoh Ramses V/VI.

*nḏrj.sn sdfw ḏwy pw*

they grasp the chain of that evil one.

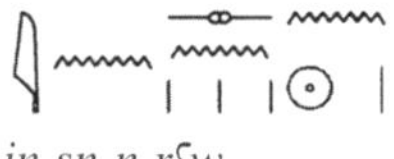

*jn.sn n rˁw*

They say to Re:

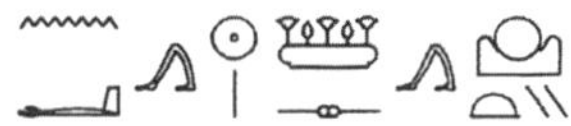

*nˁj rˁw šȝs ȝḫty*

«Proceed, o Re, go ahead, Akhty!

*mk zfw dy(w) m nḥȝ-ḥr*

Behold, knives are planted in the Terrible of face,

*ˁȝpp m ˁbwt.f*

Apopis is in his bonds!»

(Geb and the sons of Horus:)

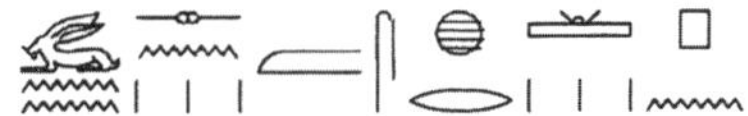

*wnn.sn m sẖr pn*

They are like this,

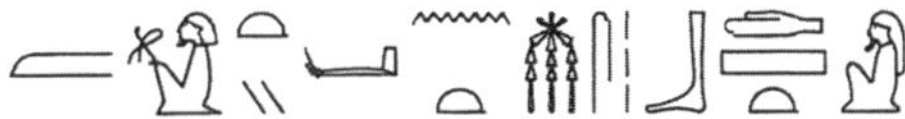

*m zꜣwt nt msw bdšt*

guarding the children of the faint one.

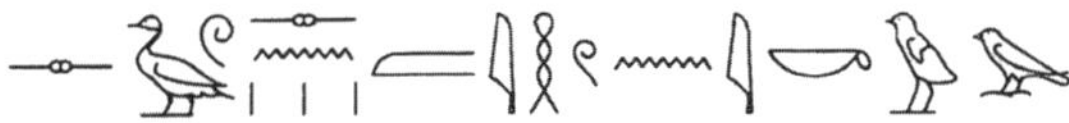

*zꜣw.sn m jḥ njkw*

They guard (them) with the punishing rope,

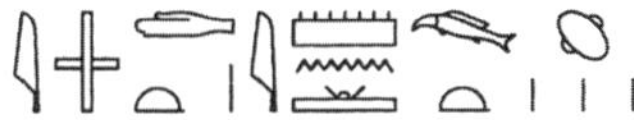

*jmj ḏrt jmnw-ḫꜣt*

which is in the hand of Him with hidden body.

*ddtw mtw m šnwt.f* *r sbḫt ḫnty-jmntyw*

Ropes are fastened around him at the gate of Khontamenty.

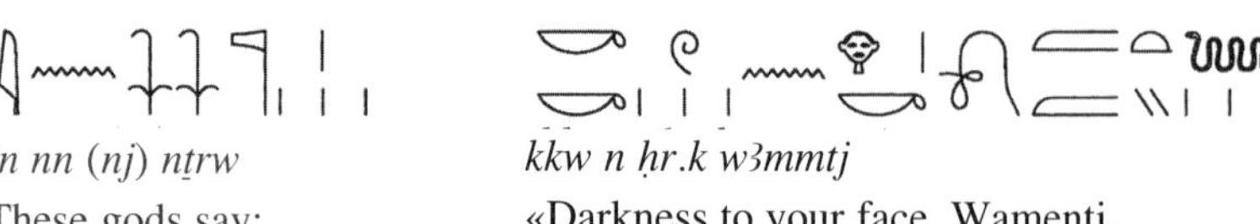

*jn nn (nj) nṯrw*
These gods say:

*kkw n ḥr.k w3mmtj*
«Darkness to your face, Wamenti,

*ḥtm(w) n.ṯn msw bdšt*
destruction for you, children of the faint one!

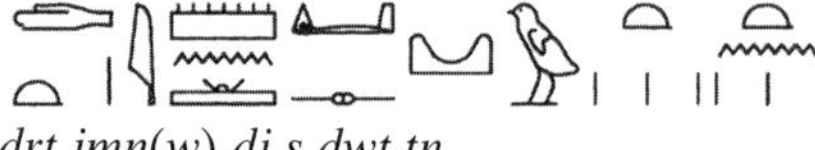

*ḏrt jmn(w) dj.s ḏwt.ṯn*
The hand of the Hidden one causes your evil

*m jḥ njkw jm.f*
by means of the rope by which he is punished.

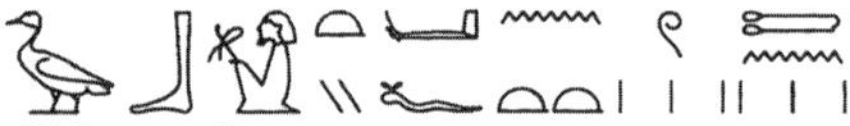

*Gbb z3w.f nṯṯw.ṯn*
Geb, he guards your fetters,

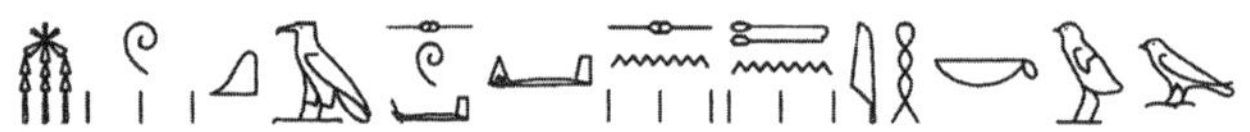

*msw q3sw dj.sn.ṯn (n) jḥw*
and the children of the chains deliver you to weakness.

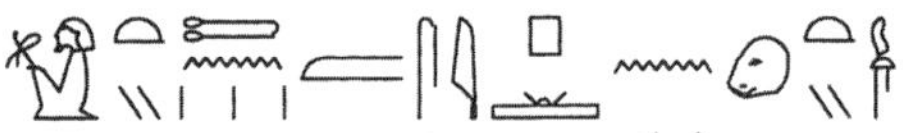

*z3w.ṯn m sjp(w) nj ḫnty jmntj(w)*
Beware you before condemnation by Khontamenti!»

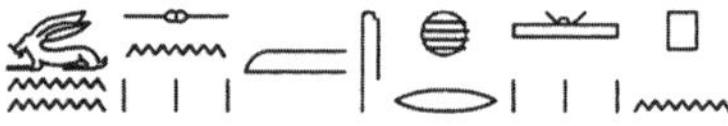

*wnn.sn m sḫr pn*
They are like this:

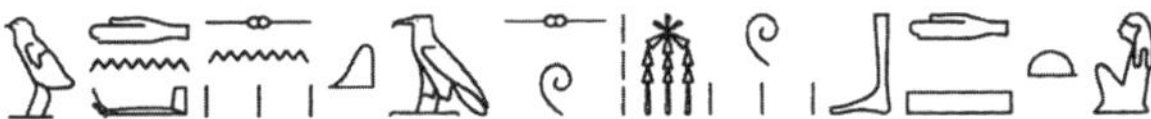

*wdn.sn q3sw msw bdšt*

They weigh down the rope/chains (for) the children of the faint one,

*jw wj3 (nj) nṯr ˁ3 š3j.f*

when the boat of the great god runs aground

*r h3w pn (nj) ˁ3pp*

at this neighbourhood of Apopis.

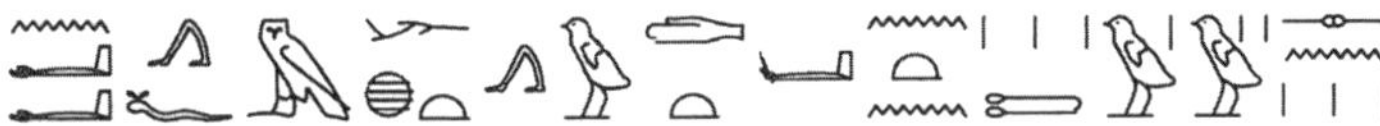

*nˁˁ.f m-ḫt wdjtw nṯṯw.sn*

He proceeds after their chains have been fettered.

From the tomb of Pharaoh Ramses V/VI.

## Middle Register, 70th Scene

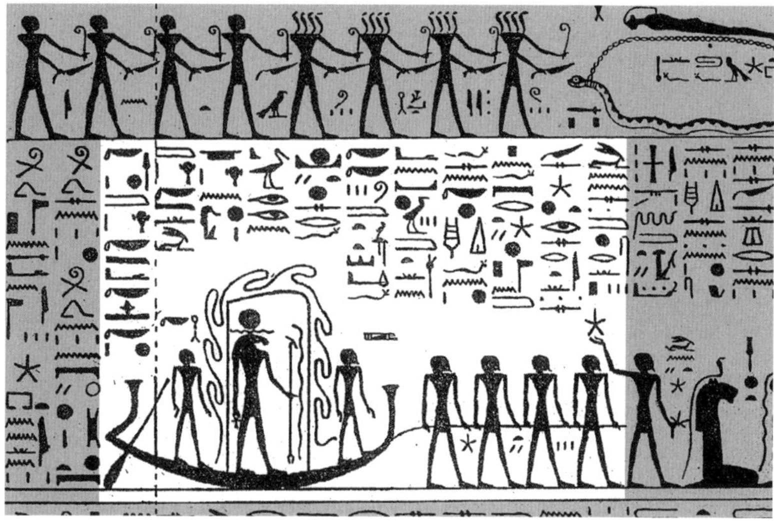

(Solar barque and towing gods)

*sṯ3w nṯr pn ꜥ3 jn nṯrw dw3t(yw)*

This great god is towed by the gods of the Netherworld.

*jn.sn sṯ3.sn rꜥw*

They say when they tow Re:

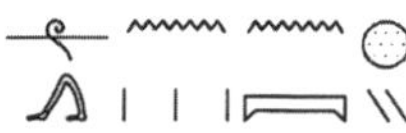

*sṯ3.n n pt sṯ3.n n pt*

«We tow towards heaven, we tow towards heaven,

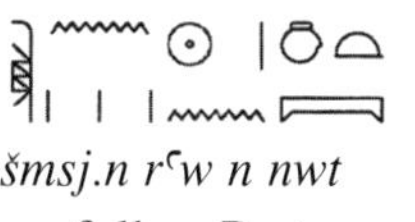

*šmsj.n rʿw n nwt*

we follow Re towards Nut!

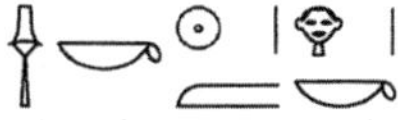

*sḫm.k rʿw m ḥr.k*

You are powerful, Re, by your face,

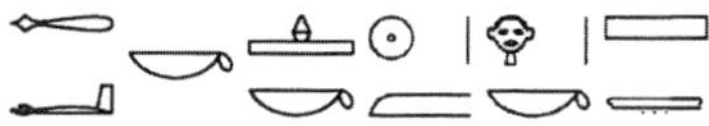

*ʿȝ.k ḥtp.k rʿw m ḥr.k štȝ*

you are great, when you rest, Re, in your mysterious face!

*wnw ḥr nj rʿw*

Open is the face of Re,

*bȝqw jrtj nj ȝḫty*

brilliant are the eyes of Akhty,

*ḫsr.f kkw m jmntt*

that he chases away the darkness in the West,

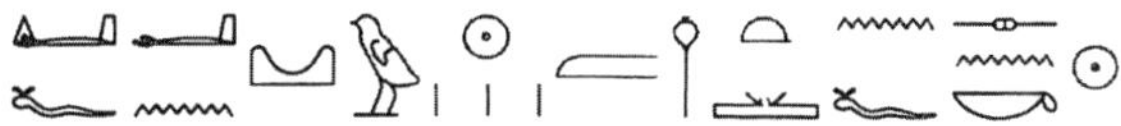

*dj.f ʿnḏw m ḥḏt n.f snkw*

that he spreads splendour through (the eye) which illuminates for him the obscurity.»

### 71ST SCENE

A single god carrying in each hand a star, his hind arm is raised: *wnwtj* (Who belongs to the hour).

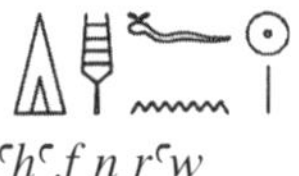

*ʿḥʿ.f n rʿw*

He attends on Re,

*ḥtp.f pt r wnwtj*

when he goes to rest in heaven at the hour-god.

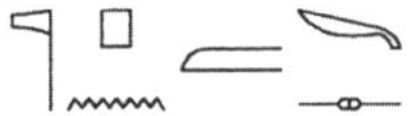

*nṯr pn m sšmw.s(w)*

This god is it who guides him,

*wnwt jrj.s jryt.s*

while the hour does her duty.

## 72ND SCENE

Four kneeling mummiform gods, all with an Uraeus upon the head: *sḫmt* Sakhmet (head of a lioness) - *ꜥbš* Who drowns (head of Ptah) - *srqw* Who breathes (human head with divine beard) - *ḥrw* Horus (falcon's head)

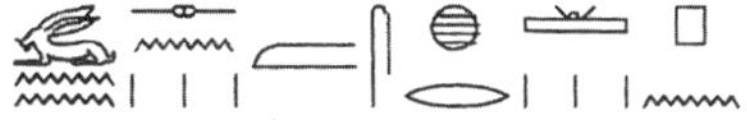

*wnn.sn m sḫr pn*

They are like this:

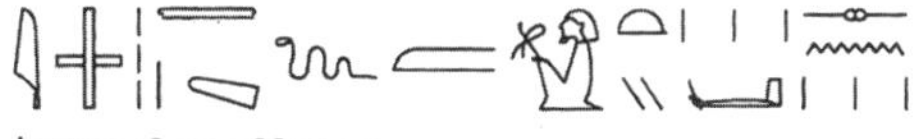

*jmyw tꜣ m zꜣꜣw.sn*

Those in the Earth (serpents) are watching them.

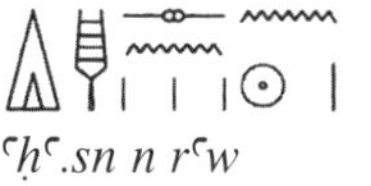

*ꜥḥꜥ.sn n rꜥw*

They attend on Re,

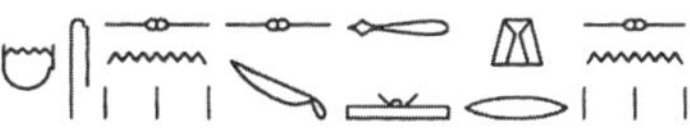

*ḥmzj.sn sšmw ꜥꜣ ẖr.sn*

and they sit down, while the great image is among them.

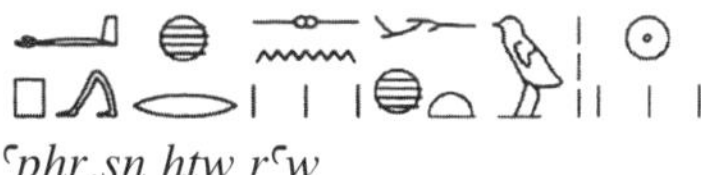

*ꜥpḫr.sn ḫtw rꜥw*

Then they proceed behind Re,

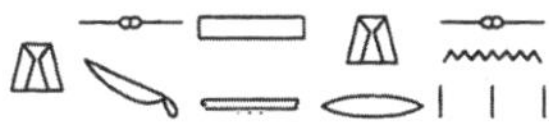

*ẖr sšmw štꜣ ẖr.sn*

carrying the mysterious image which is among them.

### 73RD SCENE

Three gods grasping a rope with one hand and carrying a star with the raised other hand: *sbꜣyw* Star-gods. The rope is towing a boat in which an Uraeus-serpent carries the face of the sungod, shown in frontal view: *ḥr pw nj rꜥw* This is the face of Re (Variant: *nj jtn* of the disc).

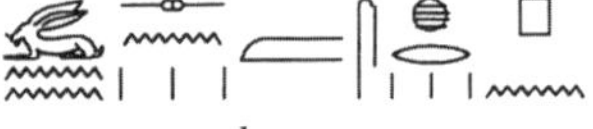

*wnn.sn m sḫr pn*

They are like this:

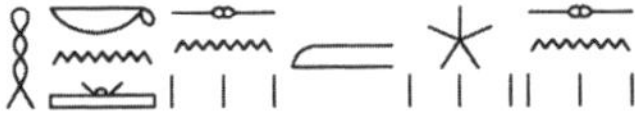

*ḥkn.sn m sbꜣw.sn*

They praise with their stars,

*nḏrj.sn ḥꜣt (nt) wjꜣ pn*

they grasp the front rope of this barque,

Incomplete 73rd scene from the tomb of Pharaoh Ramses V/VI.

*sn ʿqw m nwt*

when they have entered heaven (Nut).

*ḥr pw nj rʿw*

This is the face of Re,

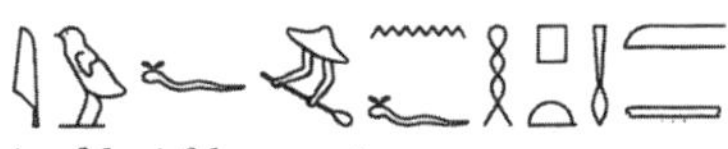

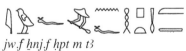

*jw.f ẖnj.f ḥpt m tꜣ*

when he sails along in the Earth.

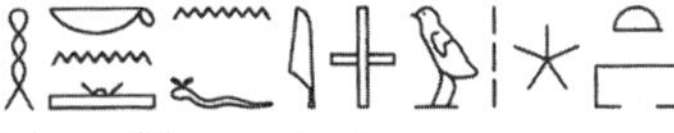

*ḥkn n.f jmyw dwꜣt*

Those who are in the Netherworld are praising it.

From the Corridor to the Osireion, in Abydos.

From the tomb of Queen Tawseret.

## 74TH SCENE

From the tomb of Pharaoh Ramses V/VI

A winged serpent: *sšmyt* “She who conducts”, with the text

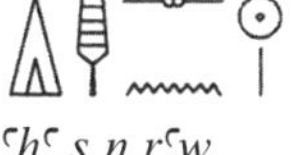

*ꜥḥꜥ.s n rꜥw*

She attends on Re.

*nts sšm(t) nṯr pn ꜥꜣ*

It is she who conducts this great god

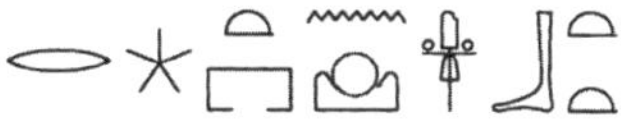

*r sbꜣ nj ꜣḫt jꜣbtt*

to the gate of the eastern horizon.

### 75TH SCENE

From the Osireion in Abydos.

A torch, a bull's head and a knife are combined with a pole. A god lifts up both hands to the torch: *bsy* (The flaming one), with the text

*ʿḥʿ.f n rʿw*

He attends on Re.

*dd.f sḏt m wpt*

When he puts fire into the (bull's) horn,

*prj ds jmj ʿ ʿḥ3w*

the knife emerges which is in the hand of the fighter

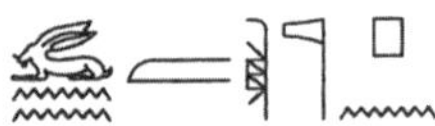

*wnn m šms(w) (nj) nṯr pn*

who is in the retinue of this god.

## 76TH SCENE

From the Osireion in Abydos.

An Uraeus-serpent whose head is flanked by two human heads: *ʿnḫy* (The living one), with the text

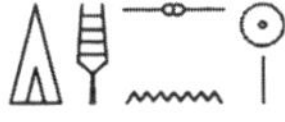

*ʿḥʿ.s n rʿw*

She attends on Re.

*smntw ʿḥʿw zštw m rnpwt m jʿrt tn*

The lifetime is established and noted down in years in this Uraeus serpent.

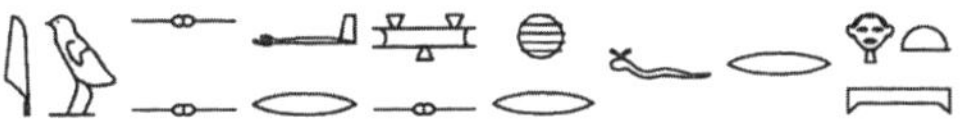

*jw.s s(j)ʿr.s ḫr.f r ḥrt*

She approaches him (Re) up to the sky.

### 77TH SCENE

From the Osireion in Abydos.

Four goddesses, their arms raised in adoration: *ḏwywt* (Those who call), with the text

*jn.sn ḏwj.sn rꜥw m ꜥp(w) rꜥw*

They say when calling Re, when Re passes by:

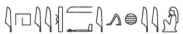

*jhy my ẖy*

«Hail, do come, oh child!

*jhy my msw dwꜣt*

Hail, do come, whom the Netherworld has (re)born!

*my ꜣṯw ḥrt*

Come, who sets foot (into) the sky!

*jhy ḫprt(j) rꜥw*

Hail, you are transformed, oh Re!»

## 78TH SCENE

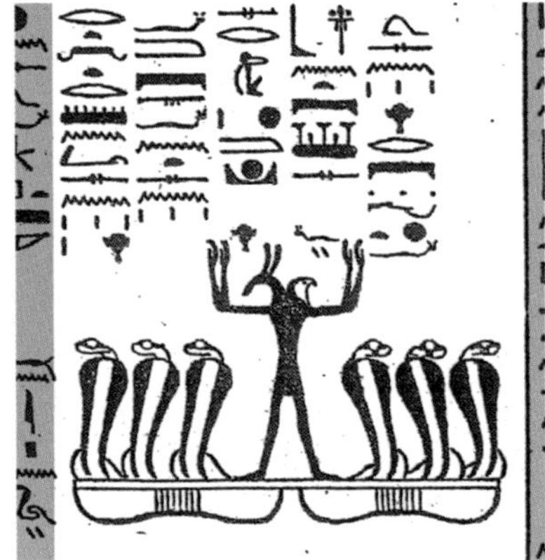
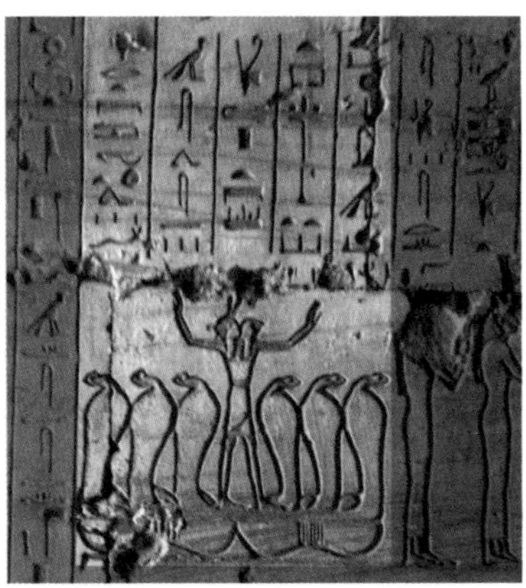

From the Osireion in Abydos.

A double bow with three Uraeus-serpents on each side. Between them a god with the double head of Horus and Seth raises four arms in adoration: *ḥrwj.fj* (His-two-Faces)

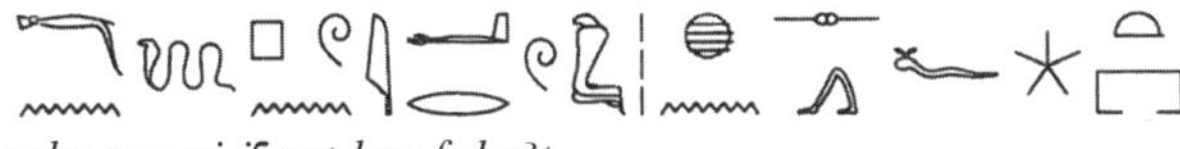

*mḥn pw nj jʿrwt ḫnz.f dw3t*

This is the Mehen of Uraeus-serpents, he traverses the Netherworld.

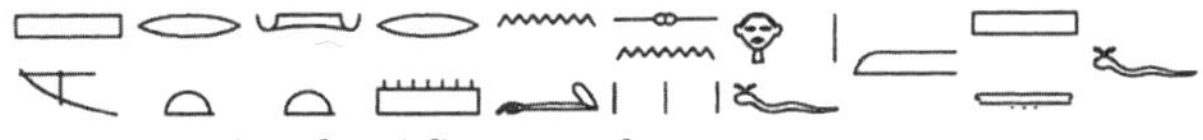

*šmrwt rmnj.sn ḥrwj.fj m št3w.f*

The bows, they carry "His-two-Faces" as his (Re's) mystery.

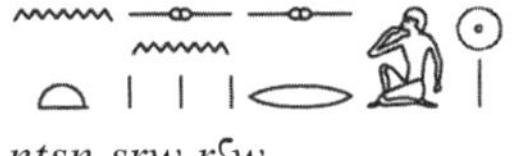

*ntsn srw rʿw*

It is they who announce Re

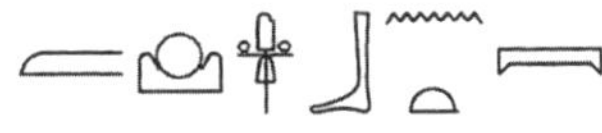

*m 3ḫt j3b(tt) nt pt*

in the eastern horizon of heaven.

*š3s.sn ḥrt m-ḫt.f*

They travel (in) the sky after him.

From the tomb of Pharaoh Ramses V/VI.

## Lower Register, 79th Scene

Twelve gods with oars in their hands: *nṯrw jḫmw sk* "Gods who know no decay".

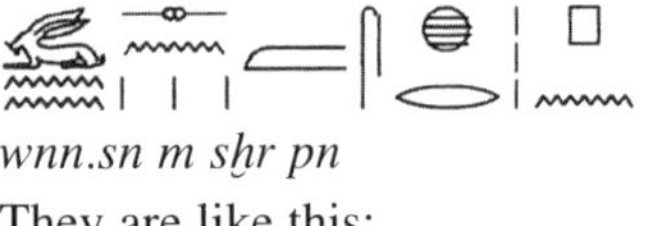

*wnn.sn m sḫr pn*

They are like this:

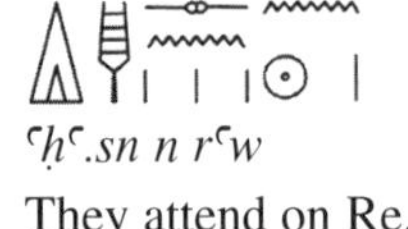

*ꜥḥꜥ.sn n rꜥw*

They attend on Re.

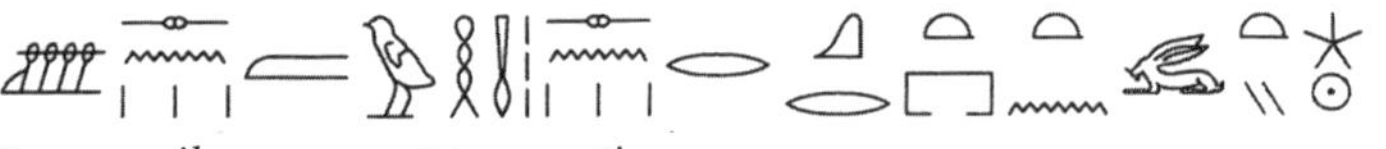

*šzp.sn mjḫw.sn r qrrt tn wnwtj*

They receive their oars at this cavern of the hour

*ḫpr.sn r.sn r mswt rꜥw m nwt*

They transform for the (re)birth of Re in heaven (Nut).

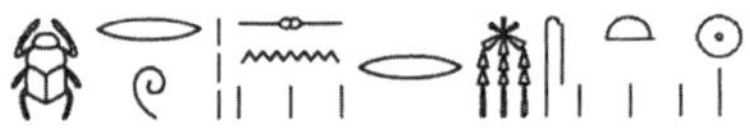

*ḫprw.sn r mswt rꜥw*

They transform at the (re)birth of Re,

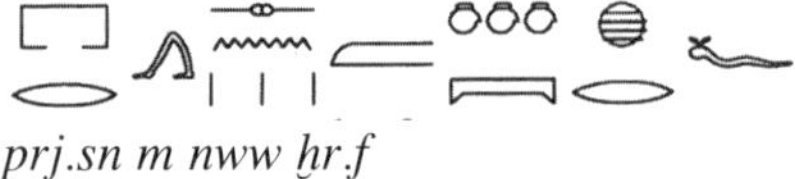

*prj.sn m nww ḫr.f*

and they emerge with him from Nun.

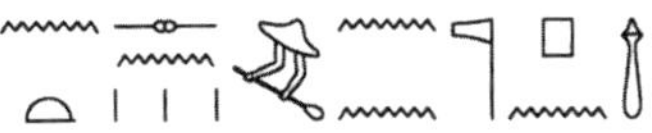

*ntsn ḫnnw nṯr pn ꜥ3*

It is they who row this great god.

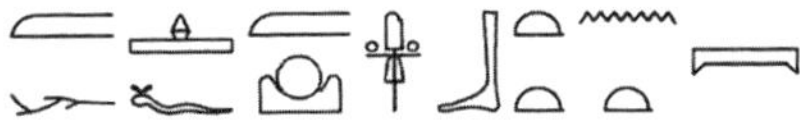

*m-ḫt ḥtp.f m 3ḫt j3btt nt pt*

after he rests in the eastern horizon of heaven.

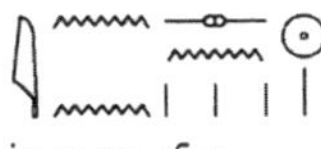

*jn n.sn rꜥw*

Re says to them:

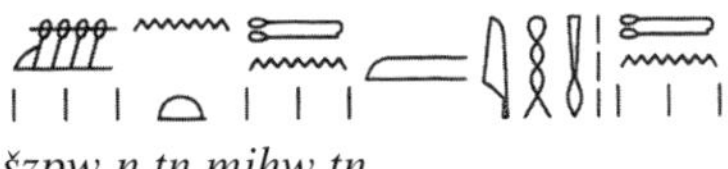

*šzpw n.ṯn mjḥw.ṯn*

«Receive for you your oars

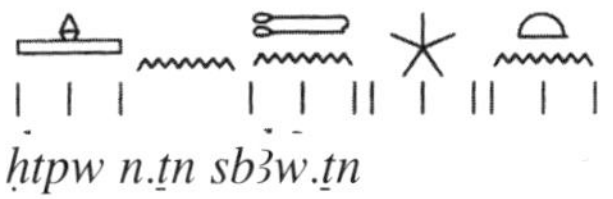

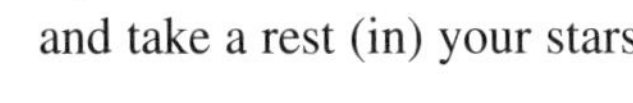

*ḥtpw n.ṯn sb3w.ṯn*

and take a rest (in) your stars!

*ḫprw.ṯn swt ḫprw.j*

your transformation is verily my transformation,

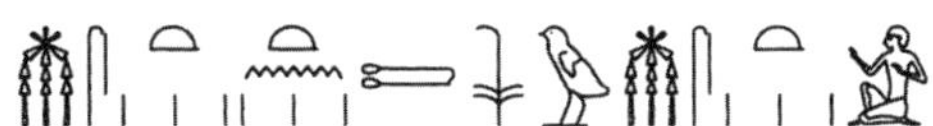

*mswt.ṯn swt mswt.j*

your (re)birth is verily my (re)birth!

*ḫnyt.j n nk* (read: *sk*)*.ṯn*

My oarsmen, you shall not decay,

*nṯrw jḫmw sk*

oh you gods, who know no decay!»

### 80TH SCENE

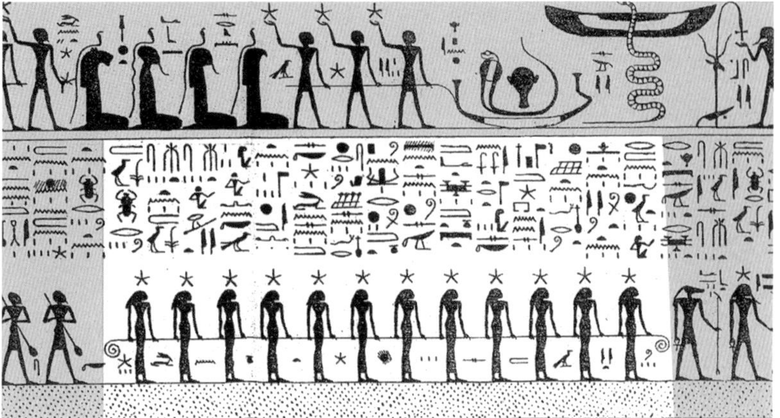

Twelve goddesses, all with a star above their head: They grasp a rope with their hands and are identified as *wnwwt stꜣywt* (The hour(-goddesse)s who tow).

*wnn.sn m sḫr pn*

They are like this:

*šzp.sn nfrt n(t) wjꜣ*

They receive the tow rope of the barque,

*r stꜣ rꜥw m nwt*

to tow Re in heaven (Nut).

From the tomb of Pharaoh Ramses V/VI.

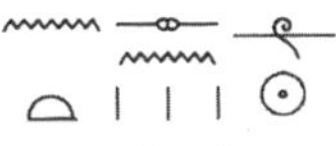

*ntsn sṯ3w rꜥw*

They are those who tow Re

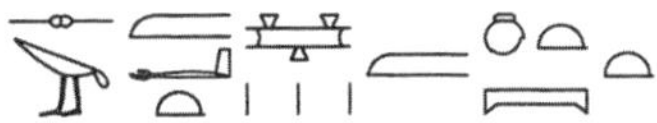

*sšmw (m) mṯnw m nwt*

and who guide (him) on the ways in heaven (Nut).

*jn nn (nj) nṯrwt*

It is these goddesses,

*sšmw nṯr pn ꜥ3 m dw3t*

who guide this great god (also) in the Netherworld.

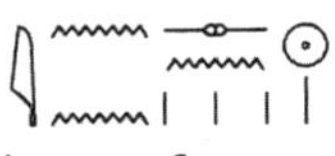
*jn n.sn rꜥw*
Re says to them:

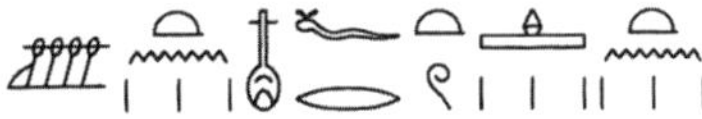
*šzp.ṯn nfrt ḥtp.ṯn*
«May you receive the tow rope, that you may be satisfied!

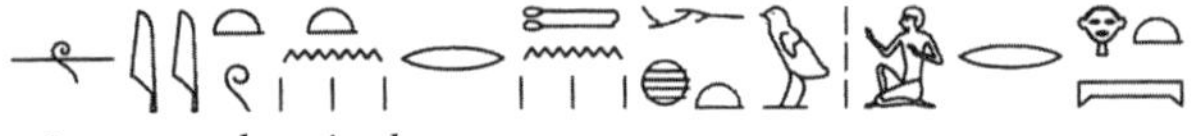
*stꜣy.ṯn r.ṯn ḫtw.j r ḥrt*
May you tow my retinue to the sky,

*sšm.ṯn.wj r wꜣwt.ṯn*
may you guide me to your paths!

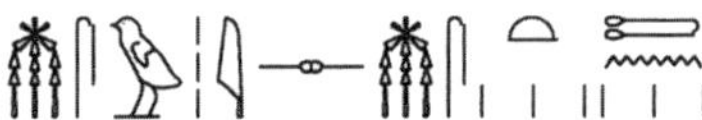
*mswt.j swt mswt.ṯn*
My (re)birth is verily your (re)birth,

*ḫprw(.j) swt ḫprw.ṯn*
my transformation is verily your transformation!

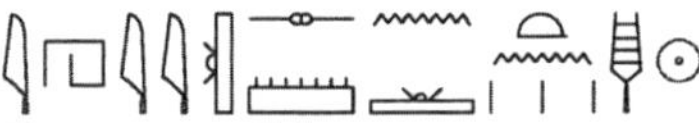
*jhy smn.ṯn ꜥḥꜥw*
Hail, you establish the lifetime,

*dj.ṯn rnpwt r jmjt.ṯn*
you offer years as much as you have!

## 81ST SCENE

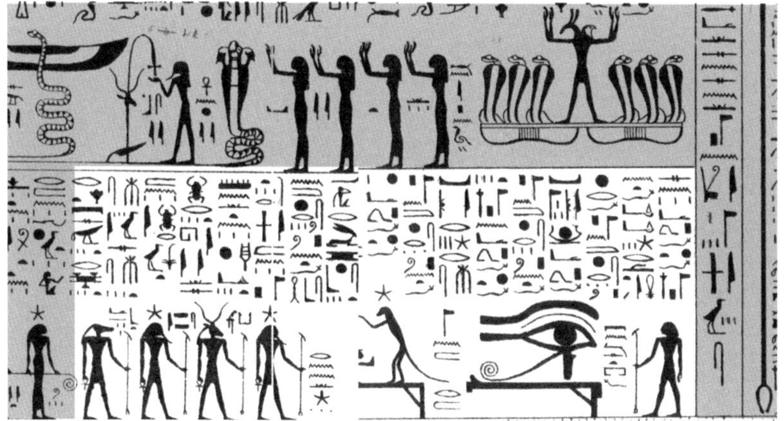

Seven deities with individual texts. The first four all carry a *Was*-sceptre.

The first is crocodile-headed and called *bꜥntj* (He with a neck?), with the short text

*nṯr pn m sḫr pn*
This god is like this.

*ntf sbḥw r wn sbḫwt (n) rꜥw*
It is he who cries that the gates do open (for) Re.

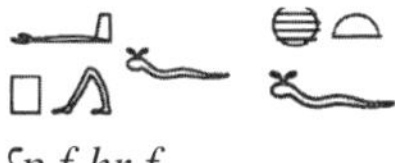

*ꜥp.f ḫr.f*
He passes with him.

The next is human-headed, with a star above his head: *zšš(j)* (The rattling one).

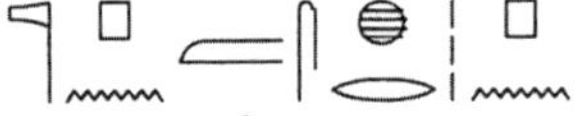

*nṯr pn m sḫr pn*

This god is like this.

*ntf ḏwjw r sbꜣw r mswt nṯr pn ꜥꜣ*

It is he who calls to the stars at the (re)birth of this great god.

*ꜥp.f ḫft* (read: *ḫr.f*)

He passes with him.

The next is bull-headed: *kꜣ jmntt* "Bull of the West":

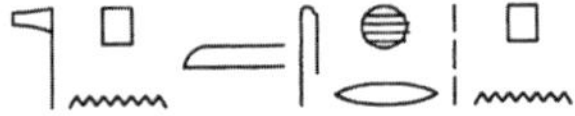

*nṯr pn m sḫr pn*

This god is like this.

*ntf ḏwjw nṯrw wjꜣ-rꜥw*

It is he who calls (to) the gods of the solar barque.

*ꜥp.f ḫr.f*

He passes with him.

The fourth is again human-headed, with a star above his head: *rnn sbꜣw* "Who nurses the stars".

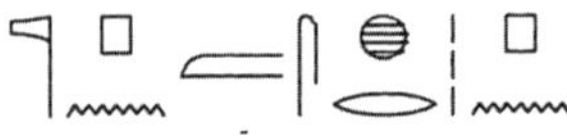

*nṯr pn m sḫr pn*

This god is like this.

*ntf ddw sb3w r dmjw.sn*

It is he who puts the stars at their places.

*ʿp.f ḫr nṯr pn ʿ3*

He passes with this great god.

A monkey upon a standard follows, in opposite direction: *nntj* (He from the nethersky).

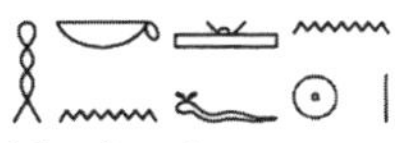

*ḥkn.f n rʿw*

He praises for Re,

*jrj.f hnw n 3ḫty*

he makes jubilation for Akhty.

From the tomb of Ramses V/VI.

The next group shows an *Udjat*-eye on a standard: *nṯrt* (The divine eye).

*jrt pw nt rꜥw*
This is the eye of Re.

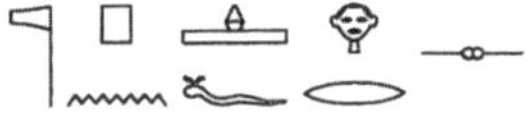

*nṯr pn ḥtp.f ḥr.s*
This god is satisfied with it

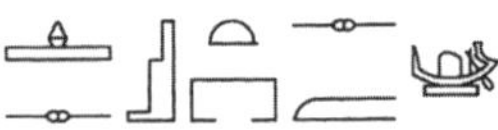

*ḥtp.s st.s m wjꜣ*
when it takes its place in the barque.

The last god is standing in opposite direction and holding a *Was*-sceptre: *ḥrj nst.f* (Who is upon his throne).

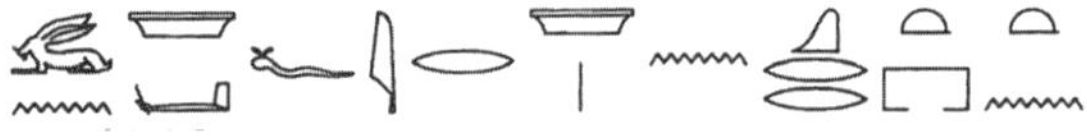

*wn.f jrj ꜥꜣ nj qrrt.tn*
He opens, the doorkeeper of this cavern.

*mn.f m st.f*
He remains at his place,

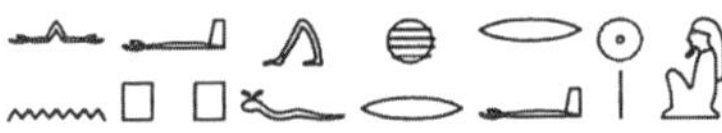

*nn ꜥpp.f ẖr rꜥw*
he will not pass on with Re.

From the tomb of Ramses V/VI.

## Eleventh Gate

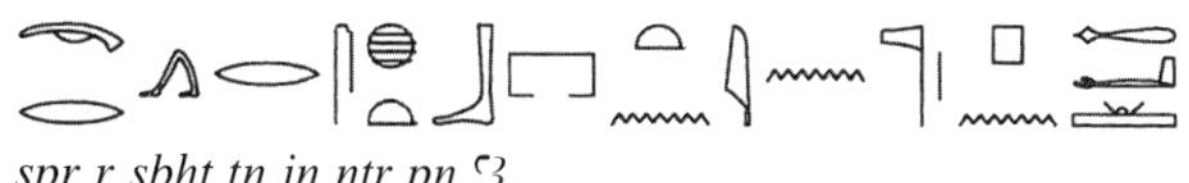

*spr r sbḫt tn jn nṯr pn ꜥꜣ*

Arriving at this gate by this great god,

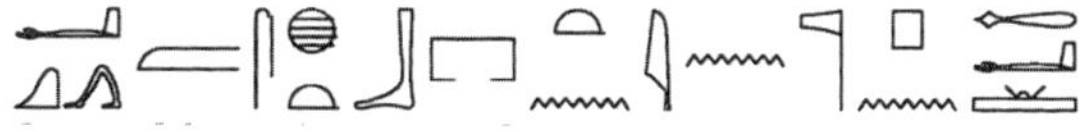

*ꜥq m sbḫt tn jn nṯr pn ꜥꜣ*

entering into this gate by this great god,

*snsn nṯr pn ꜥꜣ jn nṯrw jmyw.s*

praising this great god by the gods who are in it.

Name of the gate:

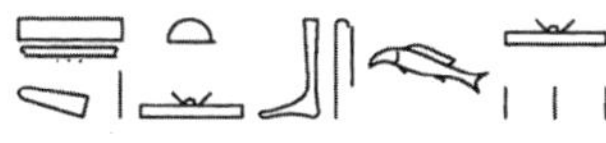

*štꜣt bzw*

"With mysterious initiation".

Upper and lower Uraeus-serpents:

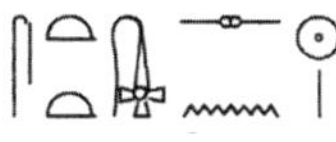

*stt.s n rꜥw*

"She lights up for Re".

Upper guardian:

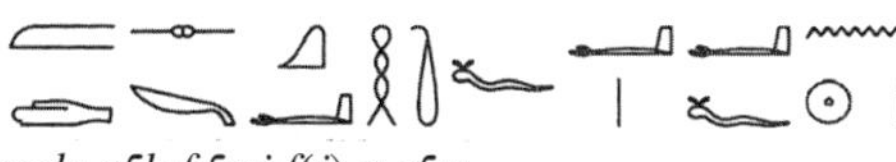

*mds qꜥḥ.f ꜥwj.f(j) n rꜥw*

"The Violent (one?)". He bends his arms for Re.

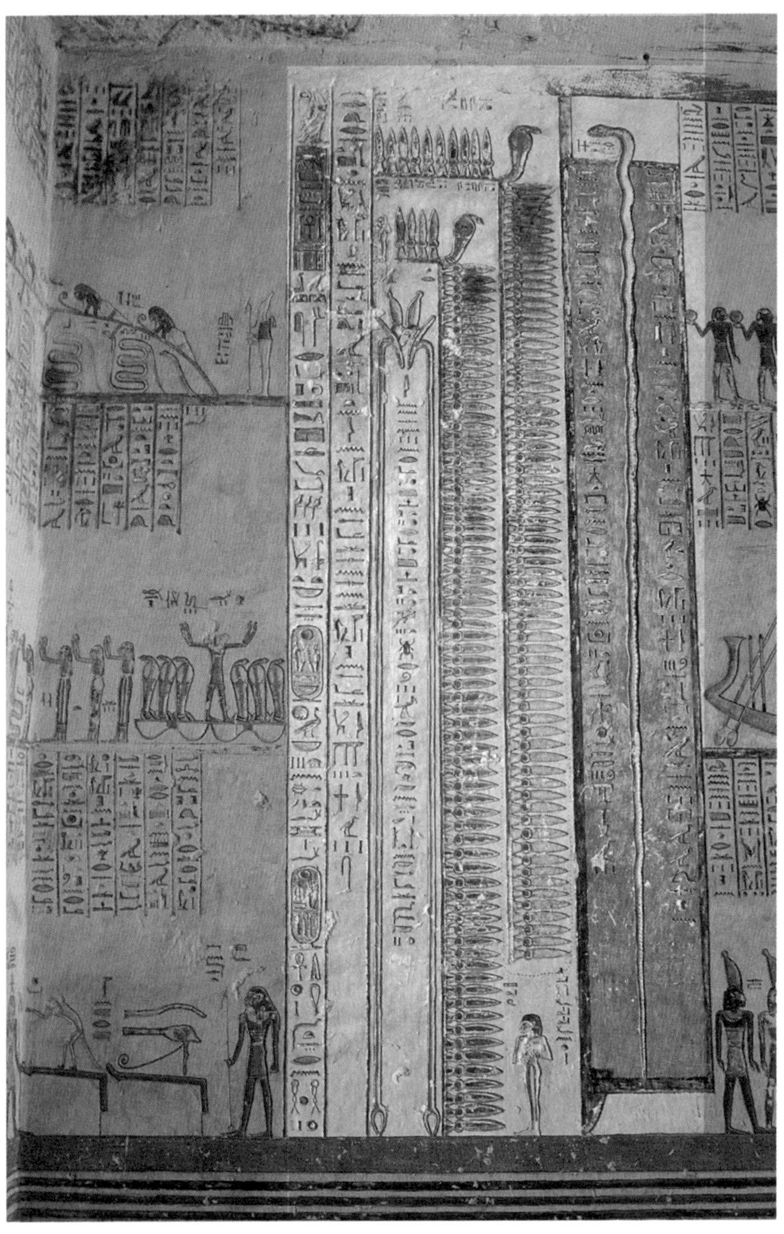

From the tomb of Ramses V/VI.

Lower guardian:

*šʿw qʿḥ.f ʿwj.f(j) n rʿw*

"He who cuts down". He bends his arms for Re.

*Was*-sceptre with falcon's head:

*ḥrw*

Horus

*Was*-sceptre with human head:

*wsjr*

Osiris

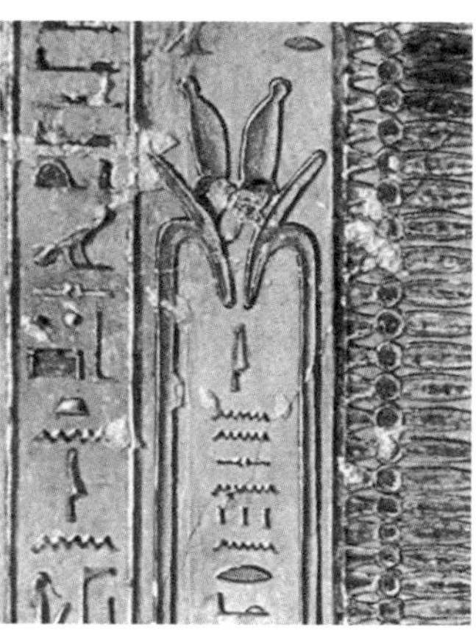

Between the sceptres:

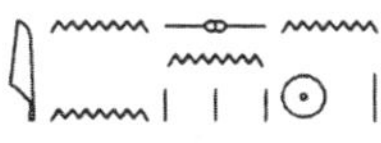

*jn.sn n rʿw*

They say to Re:

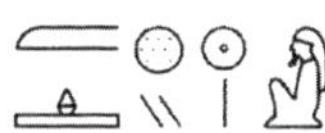

*m ḥtp zp 2 rʿw*

«In peace, in peace, o Re!

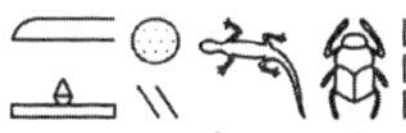

*m ḥtp zp 2 ʿšȝw ḫprw*

In peace, in peace, you who are rich in forms!

*b3.k n pt ẖ3t.k n t3*

Your *Ba*-soul belongs to heaven, your corpse to the earth,

*wḏn.k ꜥ3w ḏs.k*

you who decreed (your) greatness yourself!»

The serpent upon the doorway

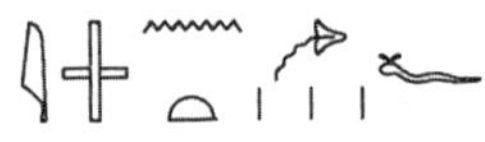

*jmj nt.f*

"Who is in his poison".

*wnn.f ḥr ꜥ3 pn*

He is upon this door,

*wn.f n rꜥw*

he opens for Re.

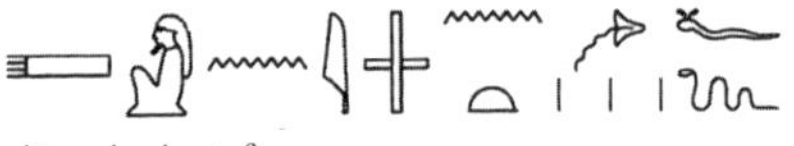

*sj3 n jmj nt.f*

Sia says to "who is in his poison":

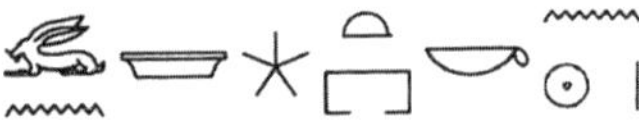

*wn sb3.k n rꜥw*

«Open your gate for Re,

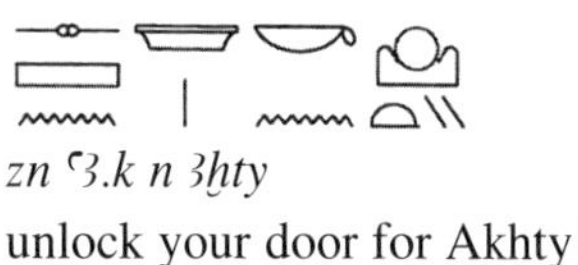

*zn ꜥꜣ.k n ꜣḫty*

unlock your door for Akhty!

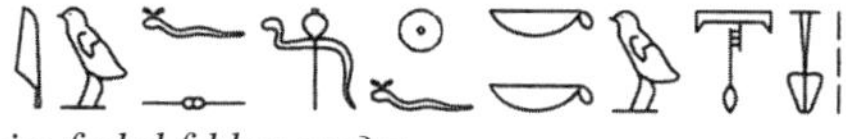

*jw.f sḥḏ.f kkw zmꜣw*

He illuminates the primeval darkness,

*dj.f šsp m ꜥt-jmnt*

he throws light into the Hidden Space!»

*ḫtmjn ꜥꜣ pn*

Then this door is shut,

*m-ḫt ꜥq nṯr pn ꜥꜣ*

after this great god has entered.

*hwtḫr nṯrw jmyw sbḫt.tn*

Then the gods who are in this gatc wail

*sḏm.sn hꜣꜣ ꜥꜣ pn*

when they hear this door being slammed.

# TWELFTH

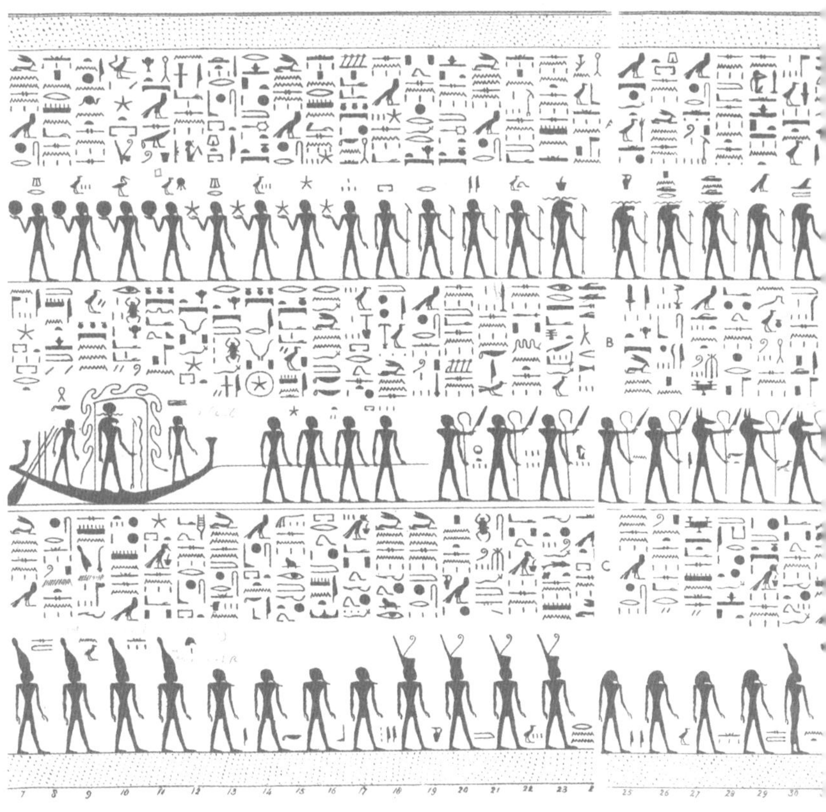

# Hour

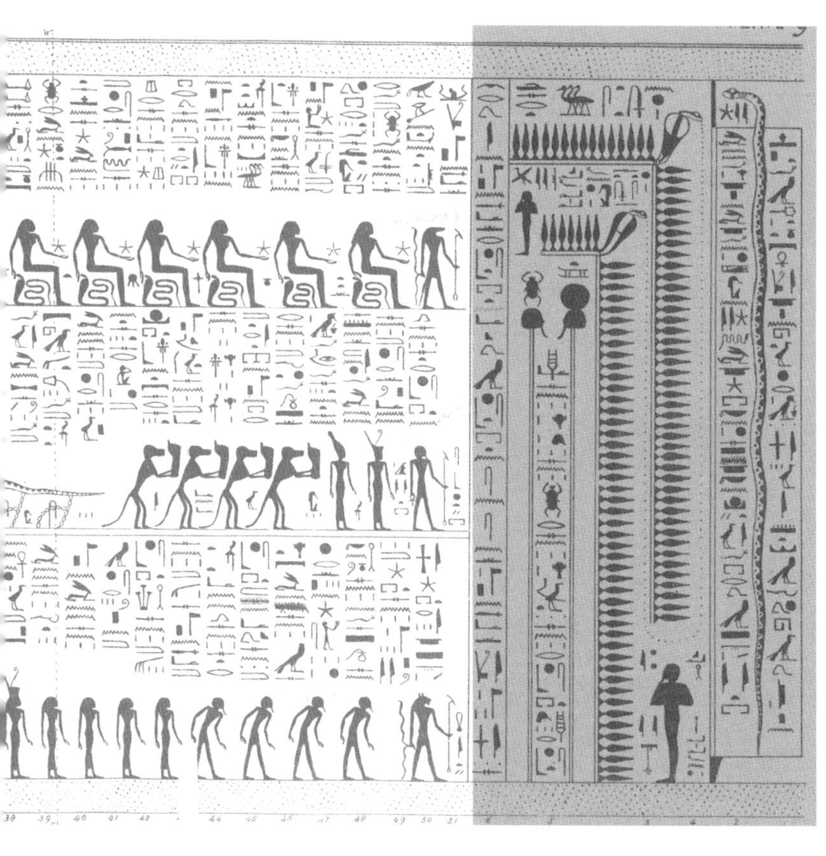

## Upper Register, 82nd Scene

Four gods carrying a disc with one hand: *ḫryw (j)ꜣḫw* (Those who carry radiance).

*wnn.sn m sḫr pn*

They are like this:

*rmnj.sn jtn nj rʿw*

They carry the sun disc of Re.

*ntsn zmꜣw dwꜣt n ḥrt*

It is they who unite the Netherworld with the sky

*m sšmw pn jmj ʿ.sn*

by means of this image which is in their hand,

*z3w mdwt r sbẖt jg(r)t*

and who guard matters at the gate of the realm of the dead (*jgrt*)

*r ḥtp rʿw m ẖt nwt*

till Re goes to rest in the womb of Nut.

### Upper Register, 83rd Scene

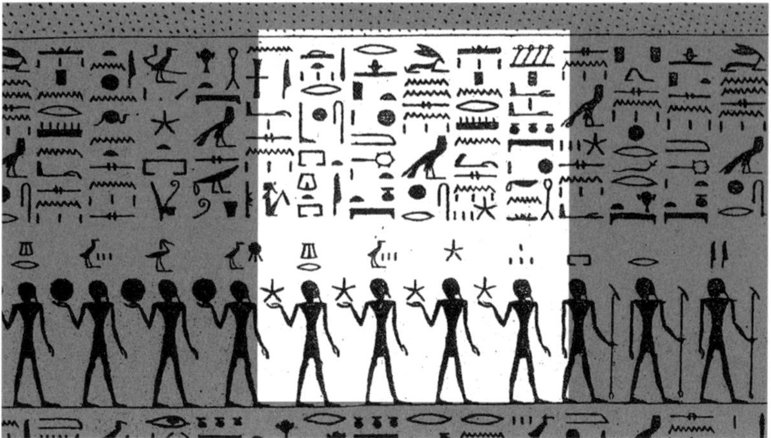

Four gods carrying a star with one hand: *ẖryw sb3w* (Those who carry stars).

*wnn.sn m sẖr pn*

They are like this:

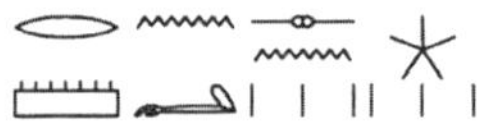

*rmnj.sn sb3w*

They carry stars.

*šzp ꜥwj nww rꜥw*

When the arms of Nun receive Re,

*ḥkn.sn m sb3w.sn*

they make jubilation with their stars.

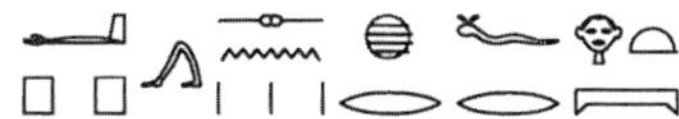

*ʿpp.sn ẖr.f r ḥrt*

They go with him to the sky,

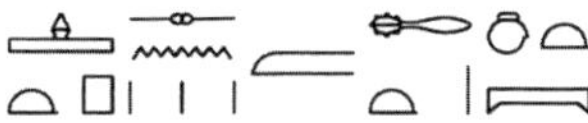

*ḥtp.sn m ẖt nwt*

they rest in the womb of Nut.

**84TH SCENE**

Four gods, all carrying a *Was*-sceptre (called *Djam* in the text) in one hand: *pryw* (Those who come forth).

*wnn.sn m sḫr pn*
They are like this:

*ḏꜥmw.sn m ꜥ.sn*
Their *Djam*-sceptres are in their hand.

*ntsn smnw ḥnbw n nṯr pn m ḥrt*
It is they who establish portions for this god in the sky,

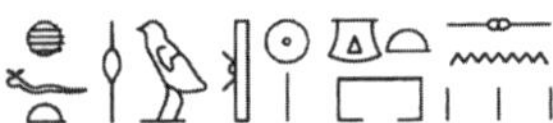

*ḫft wḏ rꜥw nst.sn*
when Re assigns their seat.

### 85TH SCENE

Four ram-headed gods, all carrying a *Was*-sceptre in one hand: *b3* (ram) - *ẖnmw* (Khnum) - *pnḏr* (?) - *dnd*(*n*) (Who travels about).

*wnn.sn m sḫr pn*

They are like this:

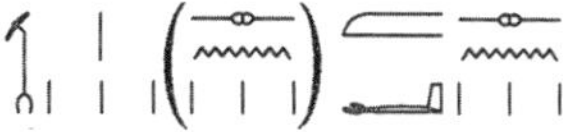

*ḏʿmw.sn m ʿ.sn*

Their *Djam*-sceptres are in their hand.

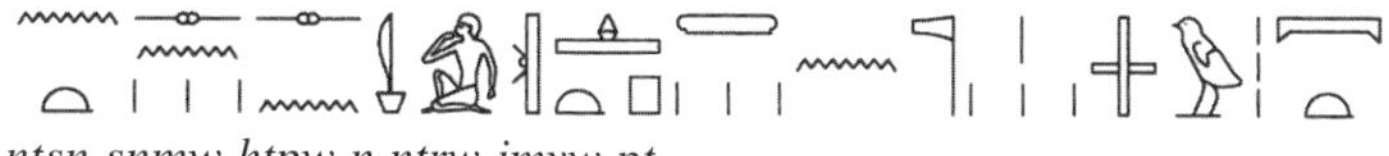

*ntsn snmw ḥtpw n nṯrw jmyw pt*

It is they who nourish the gods who are in heaven with offerings,

*n wddt nwy n sprt rʿw r nww*

before the flood streams forth, before Re approaches Nun.

## 86TH SCENE

Four falcon-headed gods, all carrying a *Was*-sceptre in one hand: *ḥrw* (Horus) - *šnbtj* (Divine falcon) - *spdw* (Sopdu) - *jmj dptj.f(j)* (Who is in his two boats).

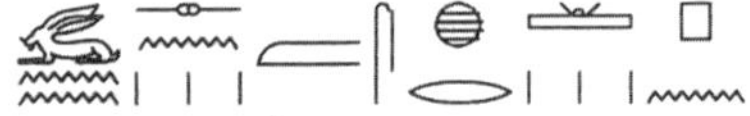

*wnn.sn m sẖr pn*

They are like this:

*ḏꜥmw(.sn) m ꜥ.sn*

Their *Djam*-sceptres are in their hand.

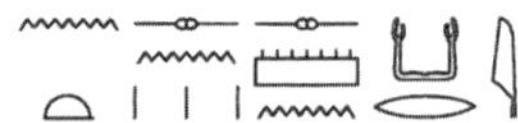

*ntsn smnw kꜣr*

It is they who established the shine,

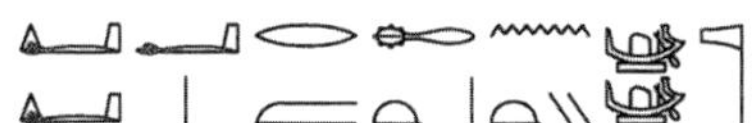

*ddw ͑ r mẖt ntj (m) dprj nṯr*

who give a hand to the crew which is in the two boats of the god.

*m-ẖt prjt mr3 zm3w*

after coming forth from the mouth of the uniter.

*dd.sn ḥpwt m nwt*

They cause the navigation in heaven (Nut),

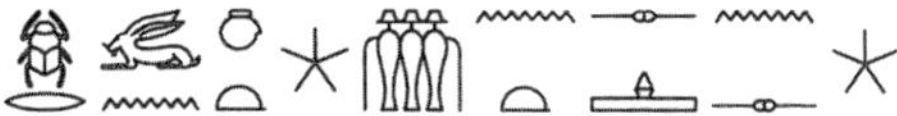

*ḫpr wnwt ḫnt(j) sḥtpn.s*

when the hour before (the hour) Sehetepenes emerges.

## 87TH SCENE

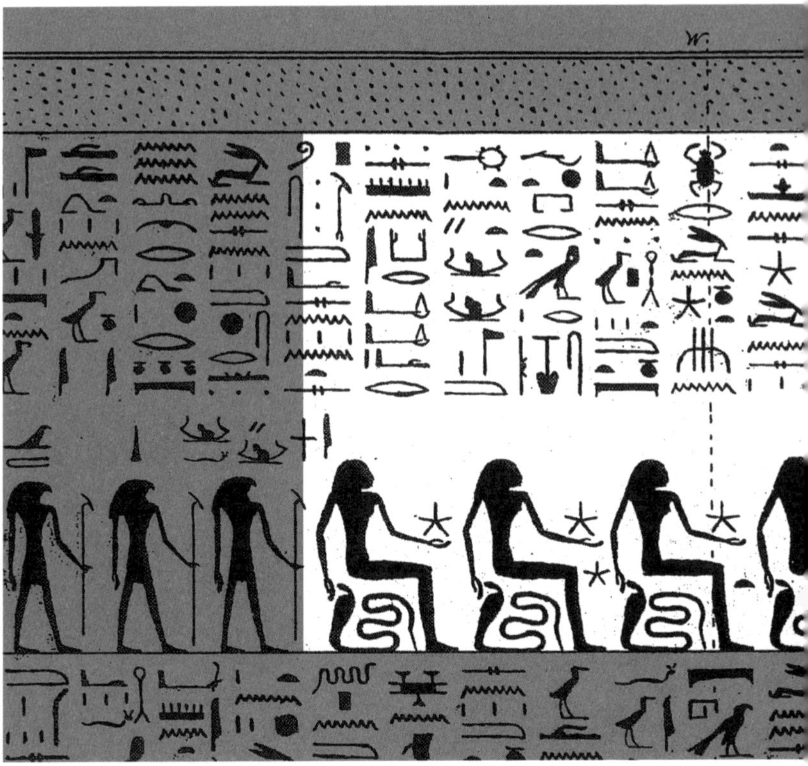

Eight goddesses enthroned on Uraeus-serpents, each holding a star in the outstretched forehand: *dwꜣwt nḏwt* (The matutinal who greet).
They are followed by a single crocodile-headed god, holding a *Was*-sceptre and a serpent: *sbq rꜣ* (He with a wise mouth).

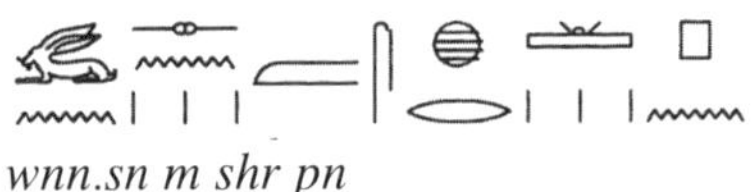

*wnn.sn m sḫr pn*
They are like this:

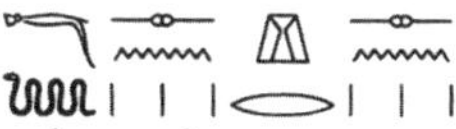

*mḥn.sn ẖr.sn*

Their Mehen-serpent is under them,

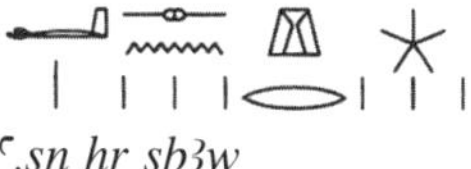

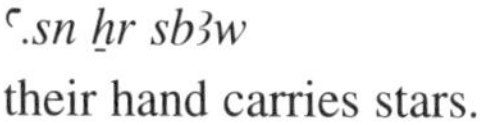

*ʿ.sn ẖr sbꜣw*

their hand carries stars.

*prj.sn m jtrtj nj nṯr pn ʿ3*

They emerge on both sides of this great god,

*4 n j3btt 4 n jmntt*

four to the East, four to the West.

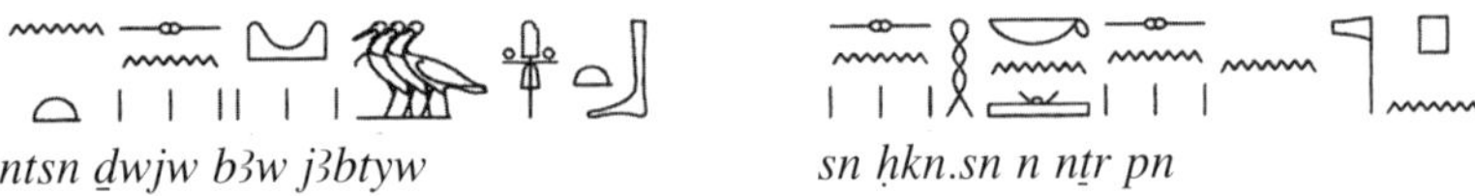

*ntsn ḏwjw b3w j3btyw*

It is they who call the eastern *Ba*-souls.

*sn ḥkn.sn n nṯr pn*

They praise this god,

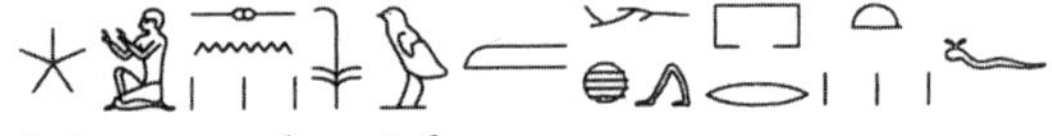

*dw3.sn.sw m-ḫt prjt.f*

and they adore him, after he has gone forth -

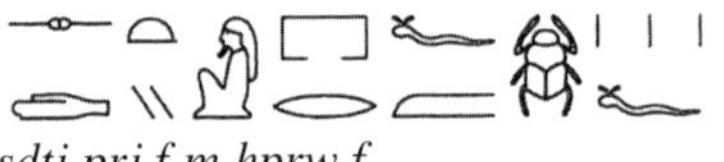

*sḏtj prj.f m ḫprw.f*

the child, when he has gone forth in his manifestations.

*ntsn sšmw ḫnjt nt jzt*

It is they who conduct the rowing of the crew

*m wj3 nj nṯr pn ʿ3*

in the barque of this great god.

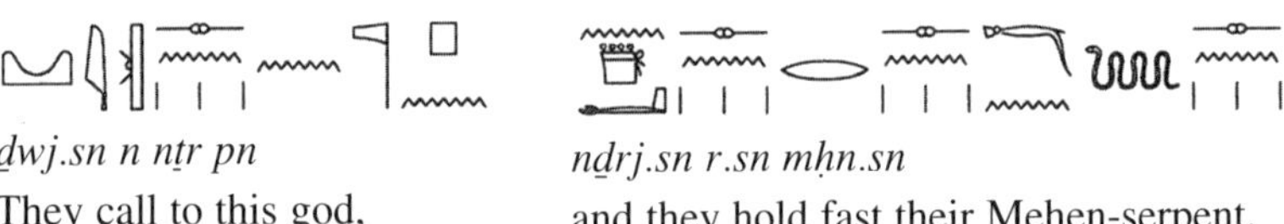

*ḏwj.sn n nṯr pn*

They call to this god,

*nḏrj.sn r.sn mḥn.sn*

and they hold fast their Mehen-serpent.

(The god *sbq-r3*:)

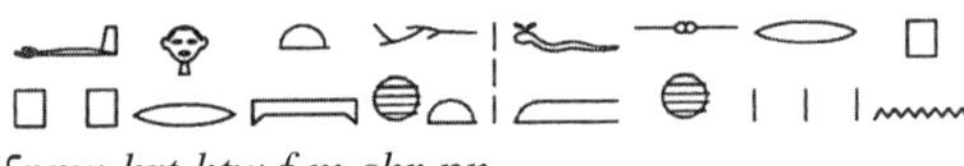

*ʿppw ḥrt ḫtw.f m sḫr pn*

Who traverses the sky after him is like this:

*jw nmtt.f r nmtt.sn*

His strides correspond with their strides.

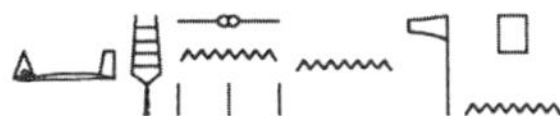

*ꜥḥꜥ.sn n nṯr pn*

They attend on this god,

*ꜥn.sw nṯr pn r sbḫt tn*

when this god turns himself at this gate.

*prr ꜥḥꜥ.f r ꜥrryt nt jmnt*

(He) goes forth and stops at the gateway of the West.

From the tomb of Ramses V/VI.

### Middle Register, 88th Scene

The solar barque with *ḥk3w* (Magic), *jwf rʿw* (Flesh of Re), *mḥn* (Mehen), *sj3* (Percipience), *dw3tyw* (gods of the Netherworld).

*jn nṯrw dw3tyw*
The gods of the Netherworld say (to Re):

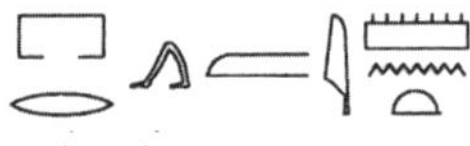

*prj m jmnt*
«Go forth from the West,

*ḥtp m jdbwj nww*
take a rest on both banks of Nun,

*jrj ḫprw ḥr ʿwj nww*
transform yourself on the arms of Nun!»

*n ꜥq nṯr pn ḥrt*
This god has not (yet) entered the sky,

*wpp.f dwꜣt r ḥrt*
when he opens the Netherworld against the sky

*m ḫprw.f jmj nww*
by his image which is in Nun.

*jr wpt dwꜣt r nwt*
What concerns the opening of the Netherworld against heaven (Nut) -

*ꜥwj pw nj jmn rn.f*
it is the arms of (the god) Imenrenef (With hidden name).

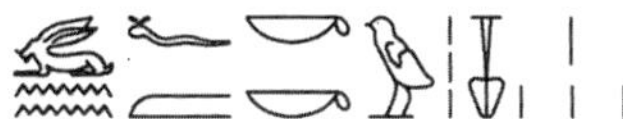

*wnn.f m kkw zmꜣw*
He (himself) is in the Primeval Darkness,

*prj.st rꜥw m jḫḫw*
(but) when they come forth, Re is in the twilight.

**89TH SCENE**

Nine gods, four of them jackal-headed, all armed with a knife and a *Heqa*-sceptre: *psḏt njkt ꜥ3pp* (The ennead which punishes Apopis).
In front of them, the serpent *ꜥ3pp* (Apopis) is fettered to five staffs which are defined as *msw ḥrw* (children of Horus) (who are four in number, the fifth is probably Geb).

*wnn.sn m sḫr pn*
They are like this:

*mdw.sn m ꜥ.sn*
Their staffs are in their hand,

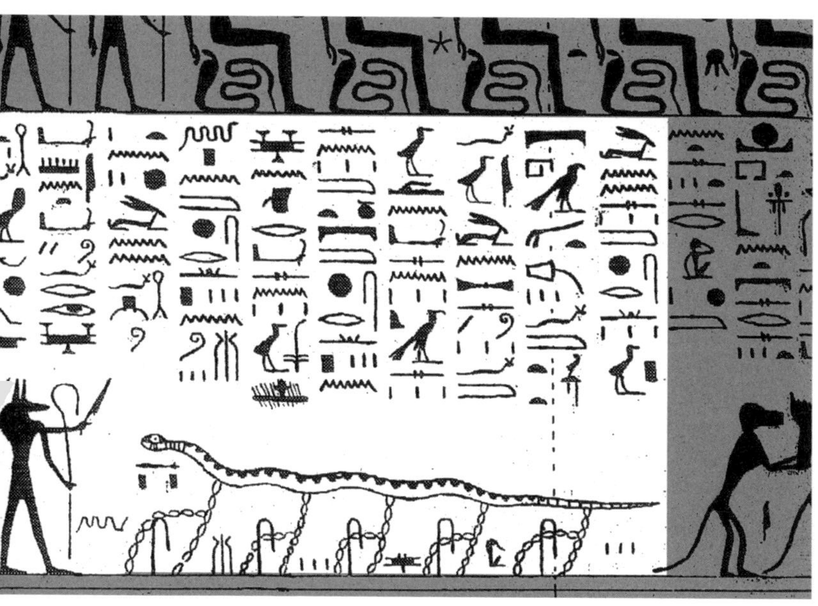

*šzp.sn nmwt.sn njk.sn ꜥ3pp*

and they receive their knives, so that they punish Apopis.

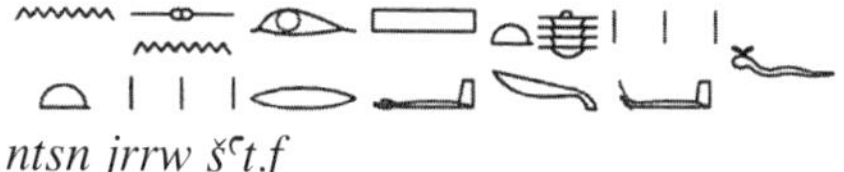

*ntsn jrrw šꜥt.f*

It is they who execute his slaughter,

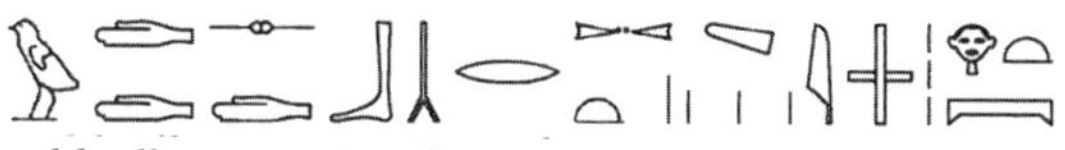

*wdd sḏbw r ṯzw jmy ḥrt*

and cause (his) damage at the sandbank which is in the sky

*wnn ḫ3w sbjw pn m ḏrwt nt msw ḥrw*

The ropes of this rebel are in the hand of the children of Horus.

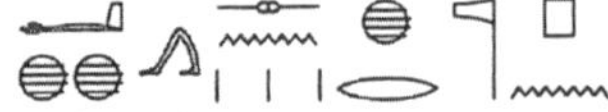

*ʿḫḫ.sn ḫr nṯr pn*

They raise themselves to this god,

*nwḥw.sn m ḏbʿw.sn*

while their ropes are in their fingers.

*jp nṯr pn ḥʿw.f m-ḫt wn jmnw ʿwj.f(j)*

This god inspects his limbs, after the Hidden one has opened his arms,

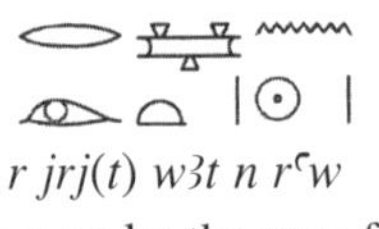

*r jrj(t) w3t n rʿw*

to make the way for Re.

From the tomb of Pharaoh Ramses V/VI.

(At Apopis:)

*wnn ḥf3w pn m sḫr pn*

This serpent is like this:

*msw ḥrw nḏrj.sn sw*

The children of Horus grasp him,

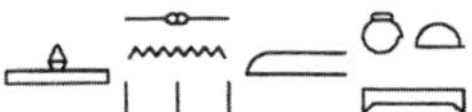

*ḥtp.sn m nwt*

when they take a rest in heaven (Nut).

(The children of Horus:)

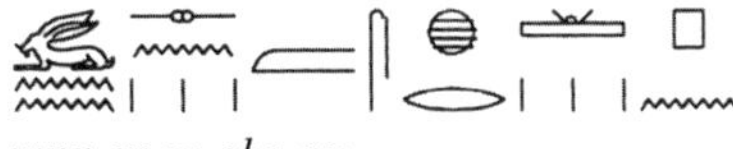

*wnn.sn m sḫr pn*

They are like this:

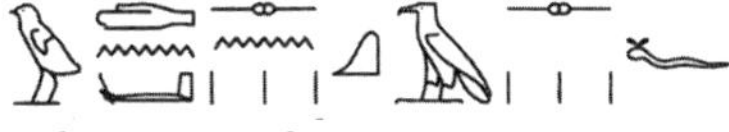

*wdn.sn q3sw.f*

They put on his fetters.

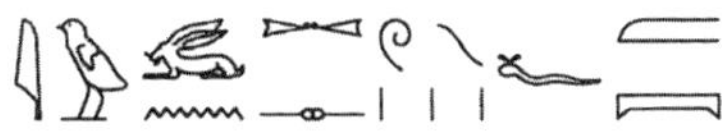

*jw wn ṯzw.f m pt*

His sandbank is in heaven,

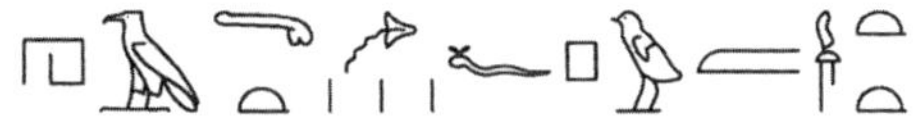

*h33 mtwt.f pw m jmntt*

but his venom descends in the West.

**90TH SCENE**

Four baboons, each holding a human fist. Their name *jꜥnꜥw* (baboons) is written between them.

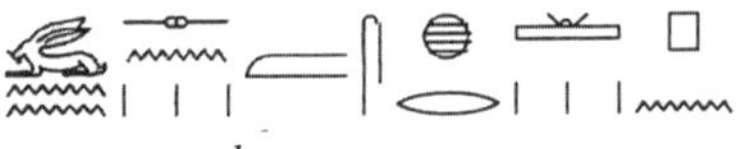

*wnn.sn m sẖr pn*
They are like this:

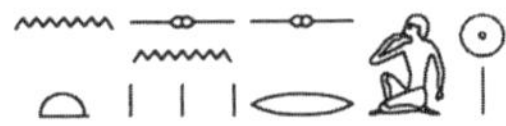

*ntsn srw rꜥw*
It is they who proclaim Re

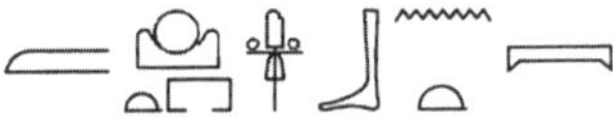

*m ꜣḫt jꜣb(tt) nt pt*
in the eastern horizon of heaven.

*sr.sn nṯr pn qmꜣw.sn m ꜥ.sn*
They announce this god who created them with their hand,

From the tomb of Tawseret.

*2 ḥr jꜣbtt 2 ḥr jmntt*

two on the left, two on the right,

*m jtrtj n(j) nṯr pn*

on both sides of this god.

*prr.sn m-ḫt.f*

They go forth behind him,

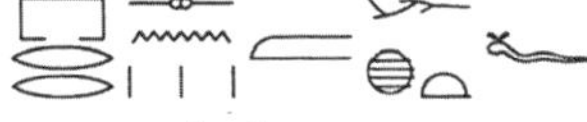

*wꜣš bꜣ.f mꜣꜣ.f.sn*

and his *Ba*-soul becomes strong when he sees them.

*ntsn smnw jtn.f*

It is they who establish his sun disk.

**91ST SCENE**

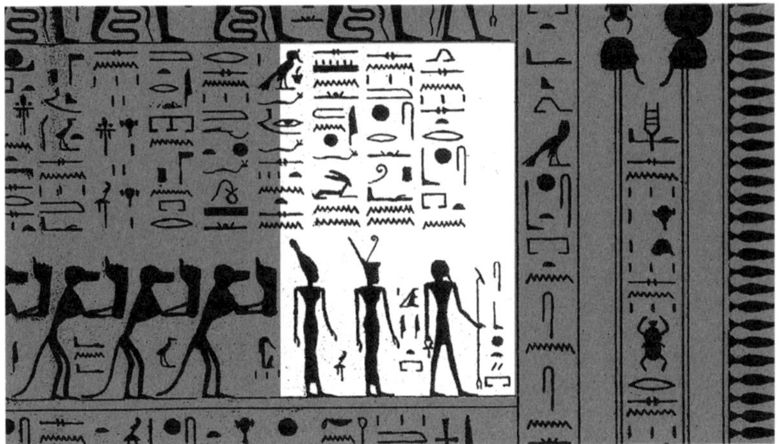

Three deities: *jmntt* (Goddess of the West (with White Crown)) - *z3yt* (She of Sais (with Red Crown)) - *sbḫtj* (He of the gate (holding a *Was*-sceptre)).

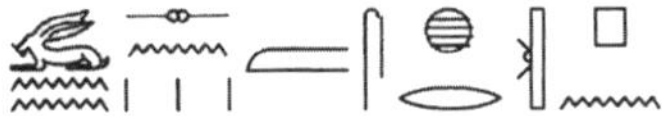

*wnn.sn m sḫr pn*
They are like this:

*ʿnn.sn.st r sbḫt tn nt dw3tj*
They turn back at this gate of the god of the Netherworld,

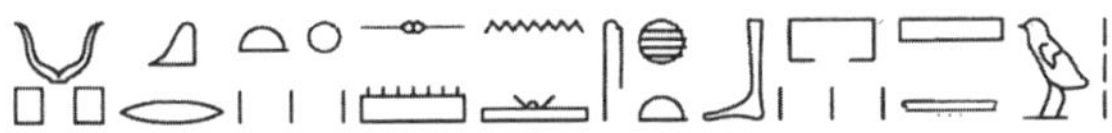

*wppw qr(r)wt smnw sbḫwt št3w(t)*
who opens the caverns and establishes the hidden gates.

*b3w.sn ʿpp.sn m-ḫtw.f*
Their *Ba*-souls, they follow behind him (Re).

From the tomb of Pharaoh Ramses V/VI.

### Lower Register, 92nd Scene

Four gods with the White Crown: *sṯnw tp* They with crowned head.

*wnn.sn m sḫr pn*

They are like this:

*ntsn smnw ḥḏt n nṯrw ḫtyw rꜥw*

It is they who establish the White Crown for the gods who are in the retinue of Re.

*mn.sn m dwꜣt*

They stay in the Netherworld,

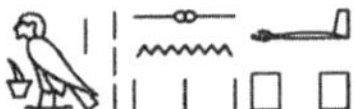

*bꜣw.sn ꜥppw*

while their *Ba*-souls have proceeded,

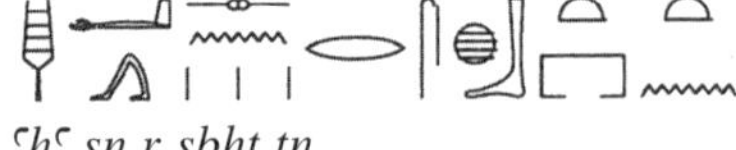

*ꜥḥꜥ.sn r sbḫt tn*

they stop at this gate.

## 93RD SCENE

Four gods without attributes: *j3kbyw* (Those who mourn)

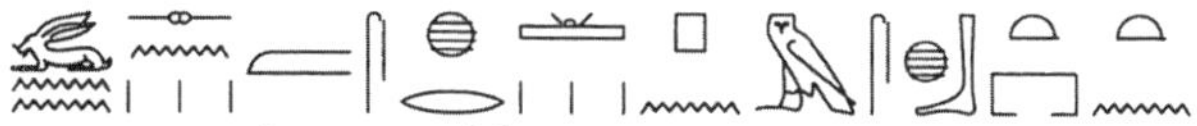

*wnn.sn m sḫr pn m sbḫt tn*

They are like this in this gate:

*j3kb.sn wsjr m-ḫt prj rꜥw m jmnt*

They bewail Osiris after Re has left the West.

*b3w.sn ꜥppw ḫtw.f*

Their *Ba*-souls go forth behind him,

*wnn.sn ḫt wsjr*

while they (themselves) are behind Osiris.

**94TH SCENE**

Four gods with the Red Crown: *ẖnmw* (The Khnum-gods)

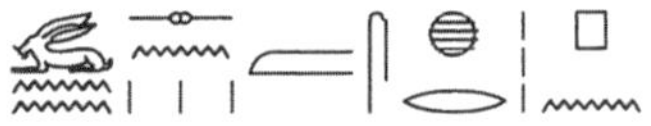

*wnn.sn m sḫr pn*

They are like this:

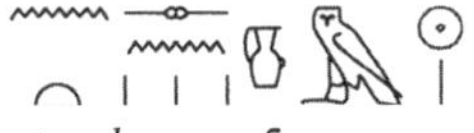

*ntsn ẖnmw rˁw*

It is they who join Re

*sḫprw msw(t).f m tꜣ*

who let his (re)birth happen in the Earth.

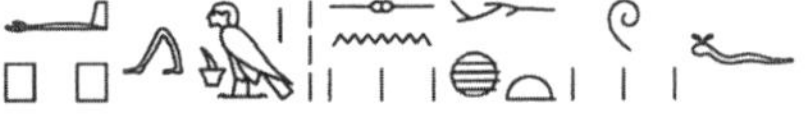

*ˁpp bꜣw.sn ḫtw.f*

Their *Ba*-souls proceed behind him,

*ẖꜣ(w)t.sn mnw m st.sn*

(but) their corpses remain in their place.

From the tomb of Pharaoh Ramses V/VI.

### 95TH SCENE

Four gods without attributes: *rnnyw* (Those who nurse).

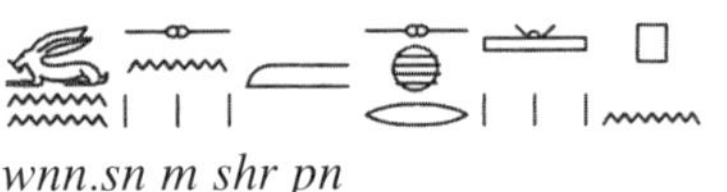

*wnn.sn m sḫr pn*
They are like this:

*ntsn rnnw rʿw*
It is they who nurse Re

*sʿ3 rnw ḫprw.f nb(w)*
and who make great the names of all his forms.

*b3w.sn ʿpp.sn ḫtw.f*
Their Ba-souls proceed behind him,

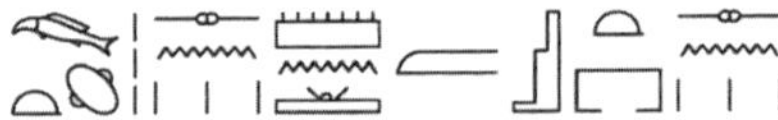

*ẖ3wt.sn mnw m st.sn*
(but) their corpses remain in their place.

From the tomb of Pharaoh Ramses V/VI.

## 96TH SCENE

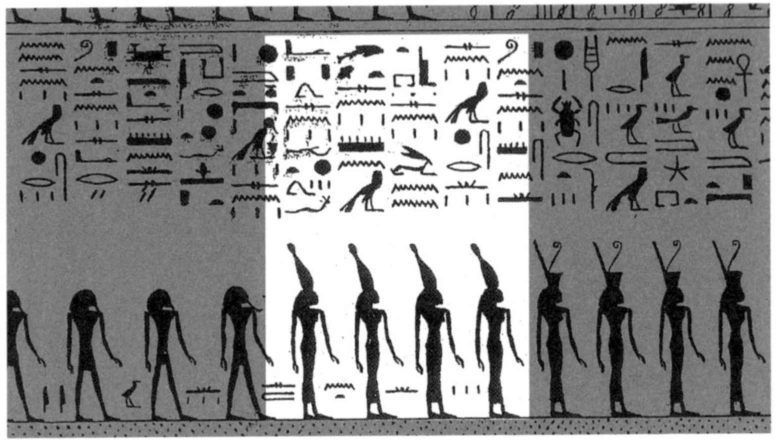

Four goddesses wearing the White Crown: *sṯnwt* (Those who are crowned).

*wnn.sn m sḫr pn*

They are like this:

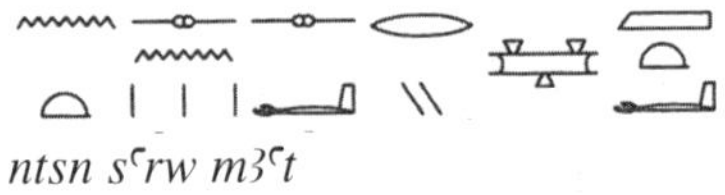

*ntsn sꜥrw mꜣꜥt*

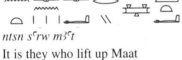

It is they who lift up Maat

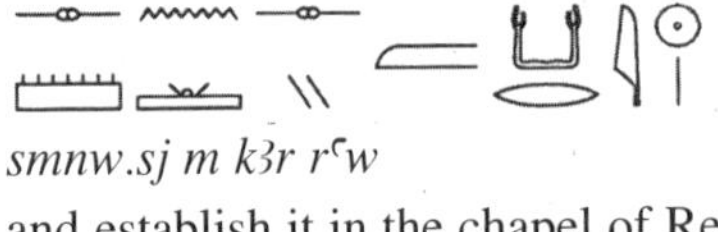

*smnw.sj m kꜣr rꜥw*

and establish it in the chapel of Re,

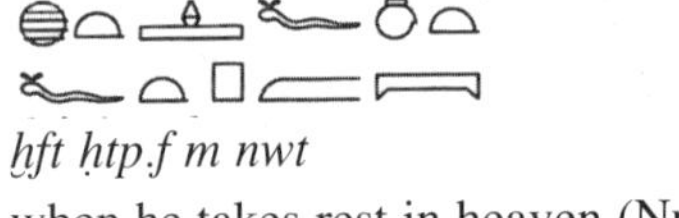

*ḫft ḥtp.f m nwt*

when he takes rest in heaven (Nut).

From the tomb of Pharaoh Ramses V/VI.

*b3w.sn ʿpp.sn ḫtw.f*

Their *Ba*-souls proceed behind him,

*ẖ3wt.sn mnw m st.sn*

(but) their corpses remain in their place.

**97TH SCENE**

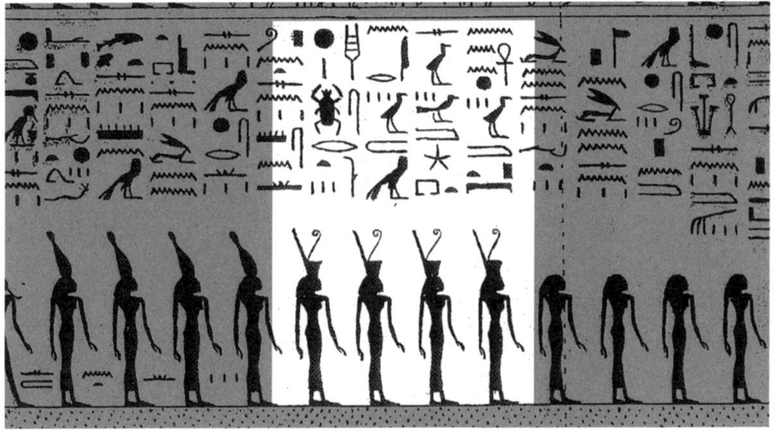

Four goddesses wearing the Red Crown: *ḫnmwt* (Female Khnum-deities).

*wnn.sn m sḫr pn*

They are like this:

*ntsn smnw ʿḥʿw*

It is they who establish the lifetime

*sḫprw rnpwt n jryw ṯmzw m dwꜣt*

and put into being the years for those destined for severe punishment in the Netherworld

*n ʿnḫw m pt*

and for those living in heaven.

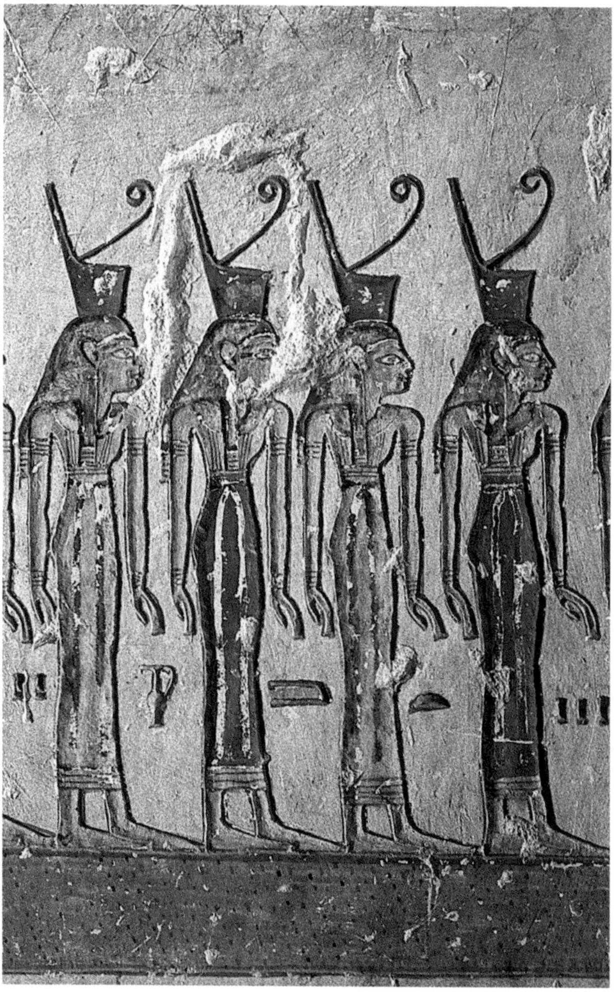

From the tomb of Pharaoh Ramses V/VI.

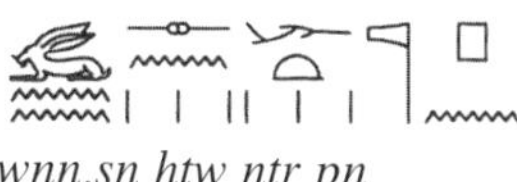

*wnn.sn ḫtw nṯr pn*

They are behind this god.

**98TH SCENE**

Four goddesses without attributes: *j3kbywt* (Those who mourn).

*wnn.sn m sḫr pn m sbḫt tn*

They are like this in this gate:

*ḥ3j.sn m šnjw.sn*

They make mourning tearing their hair

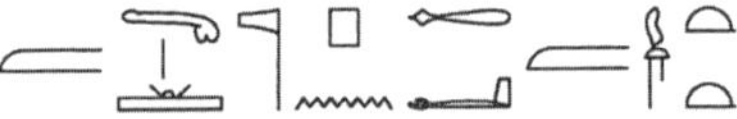

*m-b3ḥ nṯr pn ˁ3 m jmntt*

in front of this Great God in the West.

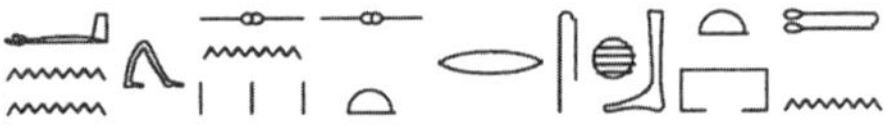

*ˁnn.sn.st r sbḫt tn*

They turn back at this gate,

*n ˁq.sn m ḥrt*

they do not enter the sky.

## 99TH SCENE

Four gods in bowing attitude: *j3wtyw* (The old ones).

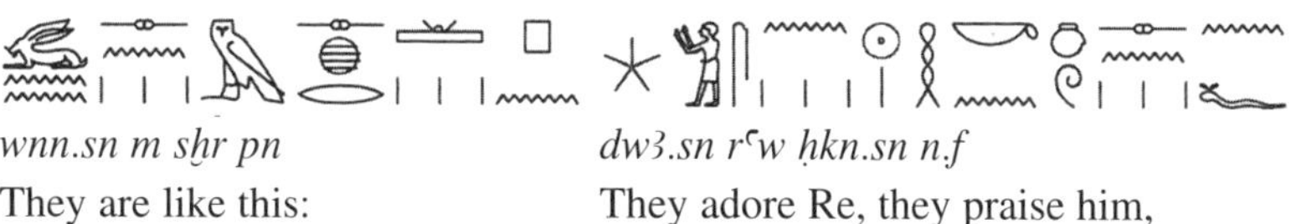

*wnn.sn m sḫr pn*
They are like this:

*dw3.sn rʿw ḥkn.sn n.f*
They adore Re, they praise him,

*sw3š.sn.sw m dw3wt.sn*
and they pay honour to him by their prayers.

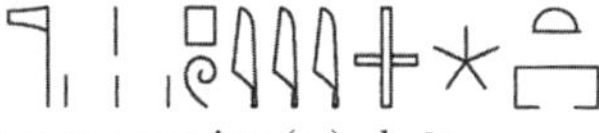

*nṯrw pwy jmy(w) dw3t*
They are the gods who are in the Netherworld,

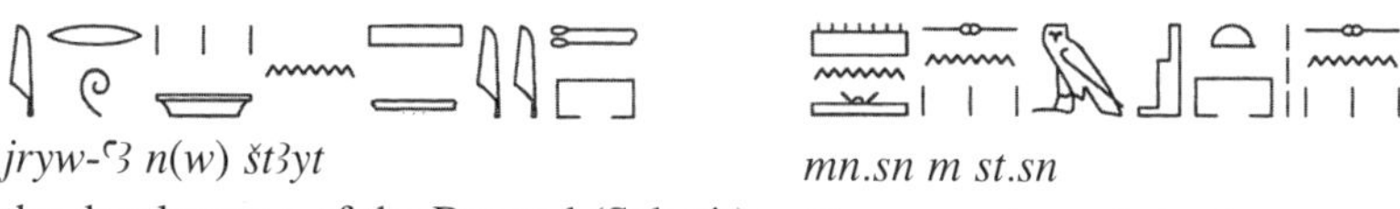

*jryw-ʿ3 n(w) št3yt*
the doorkeepers of the Beyond (Schetit):

*mn.sn m st.sn*
They remain at their place.

### 100TH SCENE

A single, cat-headed god, holding a *Was*-sceptre and a serpent: *mjwtj* (The tomcat-shaped).

*jrj-ꜥ3 pw nj qrrt*

This is the doorkeeper of the cavern.

*mn.f m st.f*

He remains at his place

From the tomb of Pharaoh Ramses V/VI.

From the tomb of Pharaoh Ramses V/VI.

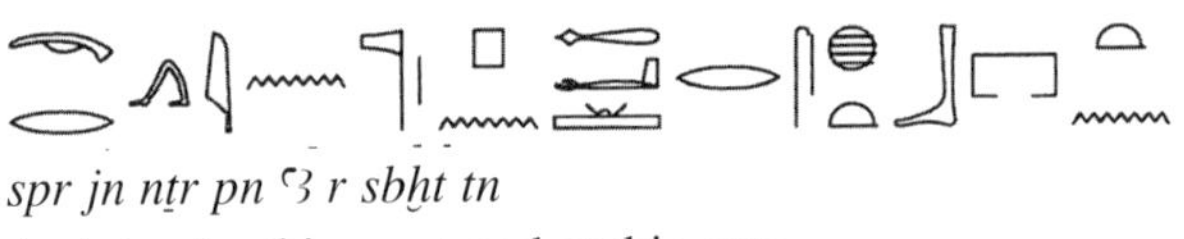

*spr jn nṯr pn ꜥ3 r sbḫt tn*

Arriving by this great god at this gate,

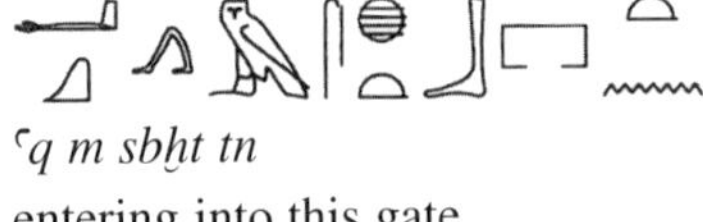

*ꜥq m sbḫt tn*

entering into this gate,

*snsn nṯr pn ꜥ3 jn nṯrw jmyw.s*

praising this great god by the gods who are in it.

Name of the gate:

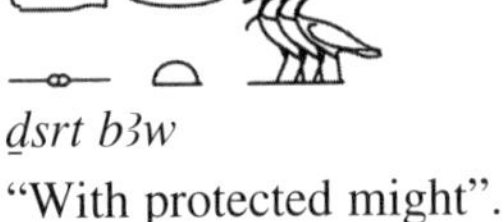

*ḏsrt b3w*

"With protected might".

Upper and lower Uraeus-serpents:

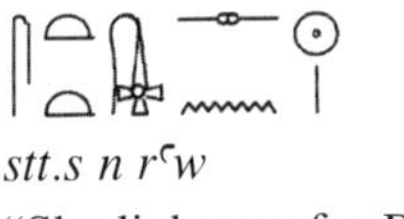

*stt.s n rꜥw*

"She lights up for Re".

Upper guardian:

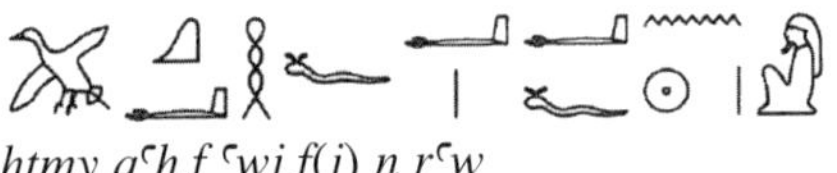

*ḥtmy qꜥḥ.f ꜥwj.f(j) n rꜥw*

"The destroyer". He bends his arms for Re.

Lower guardian:

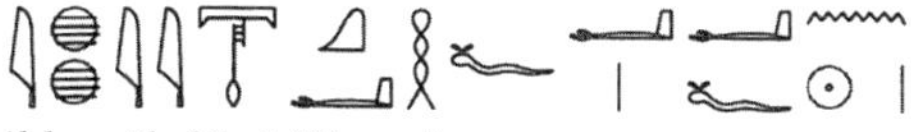

*jḫḫy qꜥḥ.f ꜥwj.f(j) n rꜥw*

"Who is in the twilight". He bends his arms for Re.

Poles with human head:

*ḫprj*

Khepri

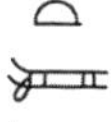

*jtmw*

Atum

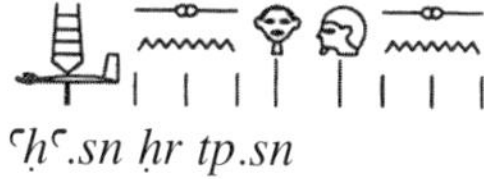

*ꜥḥꜥ.sn ḥr tp.sn*

They stand upon them,

*ḫpr.sn ḥr mꜣwt.sn r sbḫt tn*

they transform upon their staffs at this gate,

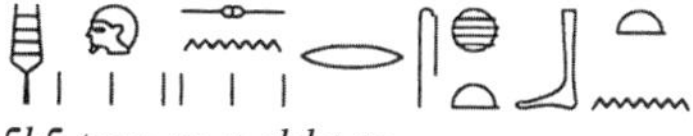

*ꜥḥꜥ tpw.sn r sbḫt tn*

their heads stop at this gate.

Serpent upon the first door:

*sbꜣy*

"Who belongs to the gate".

*wnn.f ḥr ꜥꜣ pn*

He is upon this door,

*wn.f n rꜥw*

he opens for Re.

*sjꜣ n sbꜣy*

Sia says to him "who belongs to the gate":

*wn sbꜣ.k n rꜥw*

«Open your gate for Re,

*zn ꜥꜣ.k n ꜣḫty*

unlock your door for Akhty!

*jw.f prjw m štꜣyt*

He has gone forth from the Shetit,

*ḥtp.f m ẖt nwt*

that he may rest in the womb of Nut.

*ḫtmjn ꜥ3 pn*

Then this door is closed.

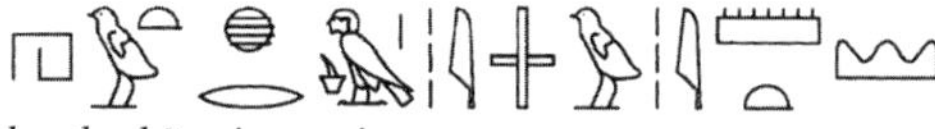

*hwtḫr b3w jmyw jmnt*

Then the *Ba*-souls who are in the West wail,

*m-ḫt h33 ꜥ3 pn*

after this door has been smashed.

Serpent upon the second door:

*pẖry* (var.: *q3by*)

"The encircler".

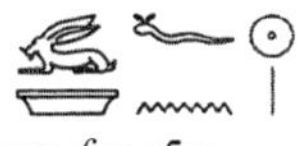

*wnn.f ḥr ꜥ3 pn*

He is upon this door,

*wn.f n rꜥw*

he opens for Re.

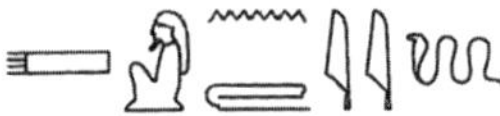

*sjꜣ n pẖry*

Sia says to "the encircler":

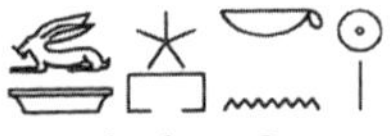

*wn sbꜣ.k n rꜥw*

«Open your gate for Re,

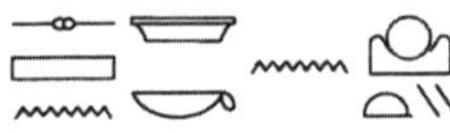

*zn ꜥꜣ.k n ꜣḫty*

unlock your door for Akhty!

*jw.f prj.f m štꜣyt*

He goes forth from the Shetit,

*ḥtp.f m ẖt nwt*

that he may rest in the womb of Nut.»

*ḫtmjn ꜥꜣ pn*

Then this door is closed.

*hwtḫr bꜣw jmyw jmnt*

Then the *Ba*-souls who are in the West wail,

*m-ḫt hꜣꜣ ꜥꜣ pn*

after this door has been smashed.

Two Uraeus-serpents:

*ꜣst*

Isis

*nbt-ḥwt*

Nephthys

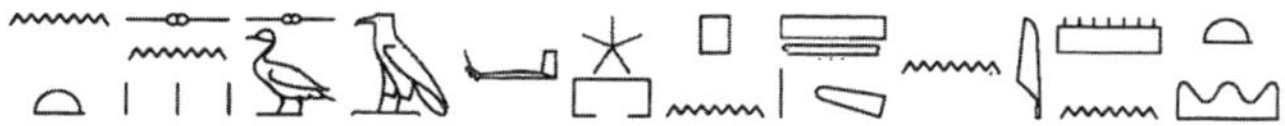

*ntsn zꜣw sbꜣ pn štꜣ nj jmnt*

It is they who guard this mysterious gate of the West.

*ꜥpp.sn ḫtw nṯr pn*

They proceed in the retinue of this god.

## Final Representation

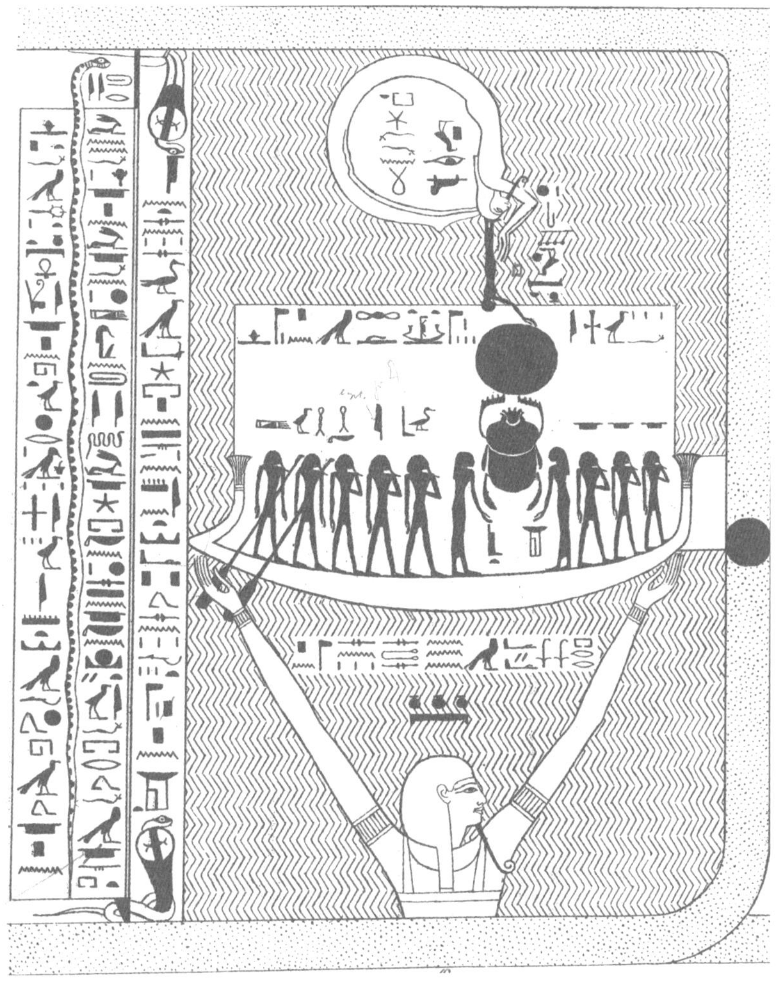

(Osiris:)

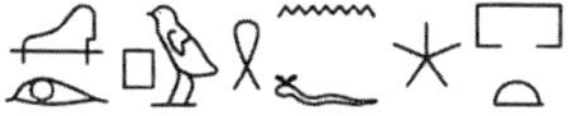

*wsjr pw šnj.f dwꜣt*

This is Osiris. He encircles the Netherworld.

(Nut:)

*nwt pw šzp.s rꜥw*

This is Nut. She receives Re.

(At the solar barque:)

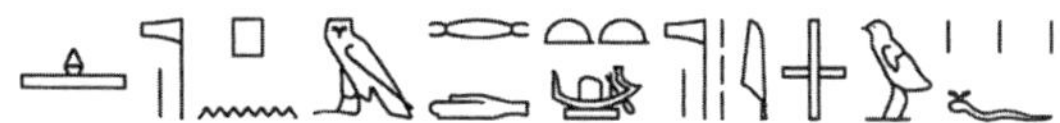

*ḥtp nṯr pn m (m)ꜥnḏt nṯrw jmyw.f*

This god takes his seat in the day-barque. The gods who are in it.

In the solar barque:
(*jryw*)-*ꜥꜣ* doorkeepers - *nbt-ḥwt* Nephthys - *ꜣst* Isis - *gbb* Geb - *šw* Shu - *ḥkꜣw* Magic - *ḥw* Hu - *sjꜣ* Sia

Nun lifting up the barque: *nww* Nun

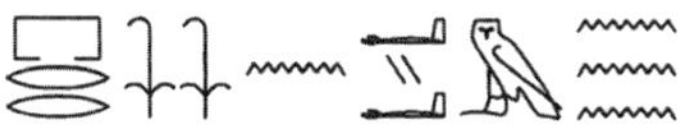

*prr nn nj ꜥwj m mw*

These arms emerge from the water,

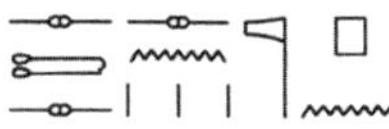

*sṯzj.sn nṯr pn*

they lift up this god.

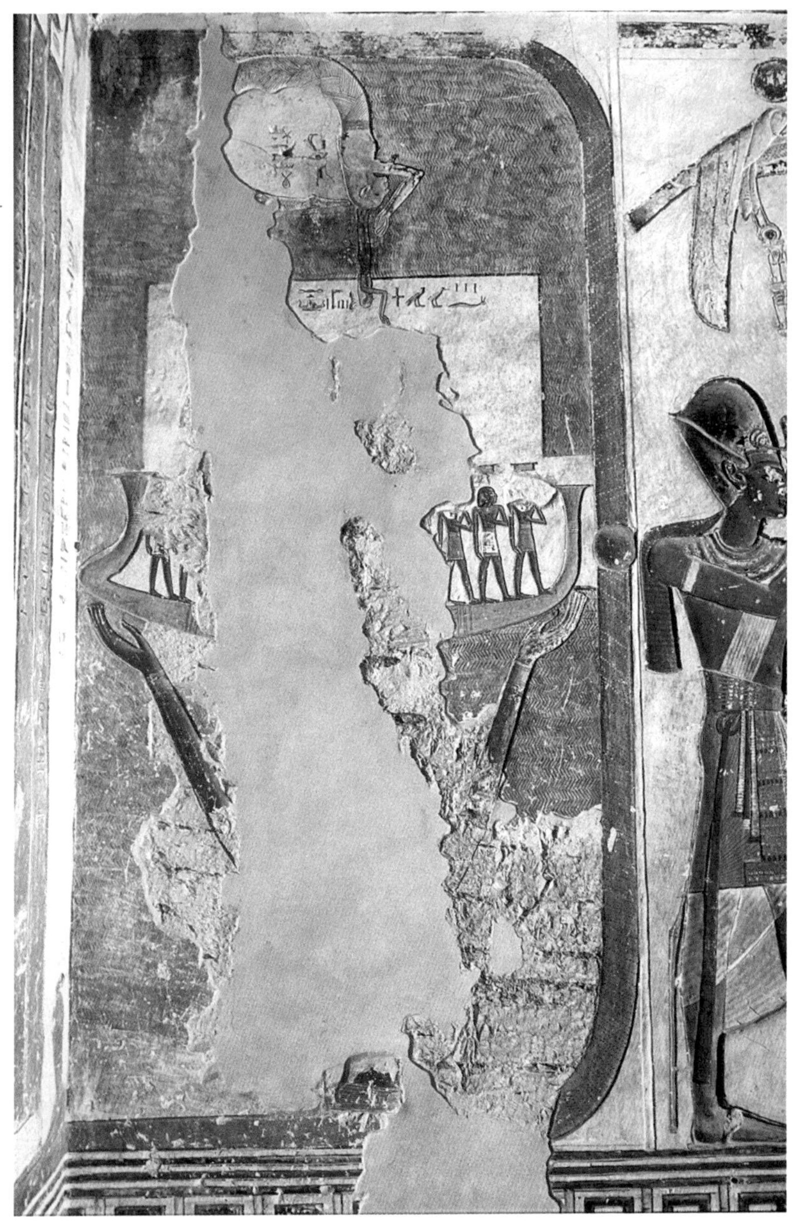

From the tomb of Pharaoh Ramses V/VI.

Papyrus of Anhai in the British Museum (No. 10472).

From the corridor of the Osireion in Abydos.

# 3. Bibliography

Bonomi, Joseph; Sharpe, Samuel: *The alabaster sarcophagus of Oimenepthah I.*, King of Egypt, now in Sir John Soane's Museum, Lincoln's Inn Fields, London 1864.

Hornung, Erik: *Das Buch von den Pforten des Jenseits*, 2 vols, Geneva 1979/1984.

- *Das Grab des Haremhab im Tal der Könige*. Unter Mitarbeit von Frank Teichmann, Bern 1971.

- *The Tomb of Pharaoh Seti I – Das Grab Sethos I*, photographiert von Harry Burton, mit einem Beitrag von Marsha Hill, Zürich, München 1991.

- *Zwei Ramessidische Königsgräber. Ramses IV und Ramses VII*. Mit Beitr. von Susanne Bickel ... [et al.] Reihe: Theben XI. Mainz 1990.

Manassa, Colleen: *The Late Egyptian Underworld*: Sarcophagi and Related Texts from the Nectanebid Period, Part 2: Plates, Wiesbaden 2007.

Piankoff, Alexandre; *N. Rambova ; L.F. Husson*: *The tomb of Ramesses VI. Egyptian Texts and Representations, Vol. I.* Texts, transl. with introductions by Alexandre Piankoff ; ed. by N. Rambova ; Plates, recorded by N. Rambova *;* photographed by L.F. Husson. Bollingen Series 40,1. New York 1954.

Rosellini, Ipollito: „Monumenti del Egitto e della Nubia". Vol I: *Monumenti Storici*, pl CLV/VI Fremdvölker der 5. Stunde. Vol II: *Monumenti del culto*, pl LXVI Gerichtshalle (Ramses VI). Pisa 1832-1834, Genf 1977.

Zeidler, Jürgen: *Pfortenbuchstudien*, 2 vols, Wiesbaden 1999.

# 4. List of Illustrations

Djedher, Louvre D9, in Colleen Manassa (Wiesbaden 2007), pl. 69, 95.

Horemheb by Erik Hornung (Bern 1971).

Merenptah by Theban Mapping Project (Kent Weeks).

Neshutefnut, Vienna I, Kunsthistorisches Museum Vienna, in: Colleen Manassa (Wiesbaden 2007), pl. 3.

Osireion by Theodor Abt.

Papyrus of Anhai, final scene by British Museum (No, 10472).

Ramses I and III by Theban Mapping Project (Kent Weeks).

Ramses IV by Erik Hornung (Mainz 1990).

Ramses V/VI: photographs in black and white by Alexandre Piankoff. (New York 1954) and coloured drawing of scene 33 (5th gate) by Heinrich Carl von Minutoli (1820) in Ippolito Rosselini (1836). Coloured photographs by Theban Mapping Project (Kent Weeks).

Ramses VII by Erik Hornung (Mainz 1990).

Seti I: all schemata, except those of the 6th, 7th and 8th hour are from the alabaster sarcophagus of Seti I by Joseph Bonomi (London 1864). The schemata of the 6th, 7th and 8th hour by Erik Hornung (Geneva 1979/1984). Coloured photographs by Theban Mapping Project (Kent Weeks).

Seti II by Theban Mapping Project (Kent Weeks).

Tawseret by Theban Mapping Project (Kent Weeks).

# 5. General Index

– A –

access 216, 239
acclamation / acclaim 50, 77, 91, 104, 141, 148, 151
adoration / adore 32, 34, 45, 181, 312, 317, 390-1, 420, 443
affair(s) 190, 286
Akh-spirit(s); 41, 104, 129, 149, 152-5, 157, 189, 207, 211, 238, 241, 259, 269, 281, 290-1, 293-5, 298, 302, 320, 328, 333, 338
– Akhfield; *see also region* 153
– are in fear 129
– become / turn into 207, 338
– content 155
– excellent 295
– Foremost of the 123
– hail 291, 294, 338
– of Akhty 293
– of his hour 281
– of the gods 338
– protect 298
– provide for 320
– skilful 290
Akhty; *see also Akh-spirits of* 27, 37, 52-3, 84, 86, 93, 108, 143, 192, 231, 269, 283, 302, 333, 351, 367, 376, 401, 407, 448, 450
– eyes of 381
– hail 142, 155, 297
– moving one 155
– oblations of 217
– offend 45
– Re-(Hor)Akhty 104, 142, 148, 217, 374
Akhu (Blessed) 41
allotment / allot 132, 155, 255
amber 227
Amduat 9
animal; *see baboon; birds; bull; cat; cobra; crocodile; falcon; ibis; jackal; lion; monkey; ram-headed; scarab; scorpion-goddess; serpent*
Anhai, papyrus of 455
Ankh 38, 86, 136, 156, 167, 284
anonymous being / god 262, 347
Anubis 188
Apopis; *see also enemy; evil, Evilface; face, terrible of; rebel; serpent* 82-4, 87, 352, 354, 372, 374-6, 379, 424, 427
– bind / fetter 46, 248, 322, 352, 356, 375
– drive off (away) / fend off / repel / finish off / overthrow / ward off 34, 82, 84, 86, 88, 200-3, 286, 353, 374
– enchant(ment) of 32, 87, 351-3
– evil 47-8, 112, 245, 322, 352, 378
– punish 425
– roaring 365
– voice of 372
– Wicked one 86, 88
Aqen 206-8
arm(s) (extremities) 38, 46, 52, 130, 141, 159, 212, 214, 239, 320, 323, 331, 344, 354, 365, 372, 382, 390-1, 412, 422-3, 424, 453
– bend 52, 91-2, 141, 181-2, 229-30, 267, 299, 301, 331, 403, 405, 446-7
– conceals 214
– firm 159
– hide/hidden 78, 80, 160, 212
– invisible 78
– of Imenrenef 423
– of Nun 412, 422
– open / not 46, 426
– raise 344, 390
– rejoice 130
– stretch 115
arms (weapons); *see spear; knife*
– armed 354, 372, 424
Asiatics 168
attribute, without 32, 35, 102, 178, 256, 278, 296, 308, 342, 344, 356, 433, 436, 442
Atum 44-6, 82-3, 86, 248, 252, 447
authority 331
awe 129
axe, double 391

– B –

baboon(s); *see also monkey* 428
balance (n) 189-90
bank(s) / sandbank 121, 422, 425, 427
barley 69-3, 256-8, 261, 263
– -bread 72
– ears of 68, 73
– of lake 70
– unite with 260
barn 264

barque 8, 20, 38, 71, 74, 77, 78, 84, 114, 158, 210, 246, 277, 282, 316, 319, 348, 355, 384, 396, 400, 402, 420, 422, 453
– boat(s) 340, 375, 379, 384
– crew of; *see also staff* 9
– day-barque 453
– gods / who is in the 200
– oars / oarsman / oarsmen 394-5
– prow 20, 38
– rowing 38, 320, 395
– sail (verb) 49, 363, 385
– solar 380
– stop (verb) 374, 421, 432
– which is in the earth / of the Earth 74-6, 78
basket 238
Ba-soul(s) 34, 46, 48, 76-7, 104, 107-8, 111, 159, 164, 167, 172, 174, 176, 178, 191, 214-5, 217, 222, 225, 227, 232, 244, 287, 291, 293, 308, 310, 312, 315, 317, 321, 324, 329, 345, 356, 363, 406, 420, 429-30, 432-4, 439, 449
– 9 (nine) 312
– 2 (twelve) 164
– (not) in the fire 329
– assist 286
– becomes strong 429
– belongs to heaven 214, 406
– cook 328
– confine 41
– container of 105
– effective 104
– follow Re 430
– glorify 159
– guard 118
– in the West 174, 176, 178, 449
– live 217
– move 222
– of dead 107, 108
– of the Earth 225
– of the West 356
– of this Isle of Fire 315
– proceed 434, 439
– protect 170, 172, 297
– put … to their vegetables 309
– remove 34
– repulse 111
– rests in heaven 363
– satisfy / satisfied 215
– slaughter 191
– soul 47
– strong 165
beds, lying on 294
beer 22, 25, 43, 66, 73, 80, 109, 119, 123, 132-3, 151, 166, 179, 201, 209, 223, 228, 241, 245, 261, 264, 277, 281, 287, 289, 295, 298, 311
– is Djeseret 151
– is wine 245
– of Maat 132
beetle; *see also scarab* 20
bellow 185
belly 313
Benbenhouse 213-4
Beyond; *see also Igeret; Shetit, Netherworld* 37, 49, 64, 76, 114-5, 247, 254, 280, 443
– Foremost of the Beyond 226
bier 218-9, 223, 290, 292, 294
– mummy on 223
birds; *see also falcon, goat, hawk, ibis, ostrich, stork* 70
birth 394, 395, 398, 400
– give 120, 122, 123, 138, 274, 278
– (re)birth 394, 394, 398, 400, 434
– Netherworld has reborn 390
– of (great) god 400
blast (of fire); *see also fire* 85, 112, 227
blessed / blessing; *see also dead* 9, 32, 35, 38, 41, 63, 148, 152, 189-91, 211, 242, 259, 291
blind 268
blood 52, 374
boats; *see also barque, ship* 336, 416-17
bodies / body 22, 24, 62, 68, 71, 315, 318, 328, 349, 372, 377
– 4 (four ) swimming bodies 318
– 12 (twelve) 68
– come forth from 22
– divine 62
– earth belongs to Re‘s body 315
– hidden body 372, 377
– limbs 70, 260
– raise 22, 24
– rest in 349
– swimming bodies 318
bones, put together 220
Book of Protecting Osiris 9, 185
bread 22, 25, 66, 132, 238, 240, 280, 308, 310, 312
– barley-bread 72
– oblations are 80, 109, 123, 133, 166, 179, 201, 209, 223, 228, 241, 264, 277, 287, 289, 295, 298, 281, 311, 315
– offer 310
– of Hu 132

breath / breathe 21, 42, 63, 71, 80, 118, 165, 170, 205, 215, 217, 220, 226, 238, 244, 259, 292, 310, 320-1, 358, 383
brilliance / brilliant 21, 23, 257-8, 381
bull 74, 76, 388, 400
burial chamber 7, 29

– C –

cakes 239, 241, 258, 313
calumny, wicked 48
captive 353
care (for / of) 40, 42, 76, 114, 115, 117
carnage 255
carrier(s) 74, 190, 276
– carrier of the rope 276
– carry Earth 331
– carry Devourer 202, 278
– carry spears 354
– carry stars 384, 412, 419
cat, tomcat 444
catcher, the (god) 344, 346
cattle of Re 169
cavern(s) 37, 89, 159, 276, 394, 402, 430
– doorkeeper of 444
– foremost of the 264
– of the hour 394
– who are in their caverns 314
cavity / cavities 116-7
ceiling 185
census 191
centre 20, 38, 336
chain(s) / enchain 372, 376, 378
chamber, (burial) 7, 29
chapel (of Re) 438
character, hidden 338
charms 347, 350
child 38, 328, 372, 377-9, 390, 420, 424, 426-7
– children 328, 372, 377-9, 424, 426-7
clothing / clothes 294
cloth 21, 24, 41, 126, 129
cobra; *see also serpent* 224-6
coil(s) 20, 84, 200, 202, 206, 208, 209, 276, 278-80, 326
– enter / swallow 204
– forms emerge out of the coil(s) 362
command (noun) 24, 285, 310-1, 350
concealment, conceal 104
condemnation / condemned 48, 85, 174, 176, 250, 254, 255, 378
conduct, rowing of the crew 420
confederates 372
confinement 41
confront 78, 82, 86, 167, 256, 278
consent 252
container of the Ba-souls; *see also basket* 105
content (n), secret 159
cook, Ba-souls 328
corpse(s); *see also bodies; flesh* 48, 212-5, 222, 254, 286, 316-7, 434, 439, 406
– belongs to the earth 215
– burn / destroy 41, 328
– come to his 349
– inspect 179
– remain 434, 439
– rest in 209, 215
council 82, 177, 178, 296, 297, 308, 309
– commands in the 311
– of gods 309
– of judges / who judges 296-8
count 279
court 166-7
cover / uncover 70, 92, 121, 288, 291, 324, 365
creation / create 19, 43, 76, 80, 115, 154, 170, 254, 260, 283, 286, 428
creator, place which raises its creator 115
crew 417
crocodile 354, 399, 418
crown
– crowned (goddesses / head) 432, 438
– red 336, 340, 430, 434, 440
– white 336, 344, 372, 430, 432, 438
cry (n, verb) 44, 121, 205, 399
cutter /cut (off / down) 42, 84, 352, 372, 405

– D –

dagger 50
damage 129, 425
damned; *see also enemies; punishment; judgement* 41-2, 185, 190
– inverted 83
darkness 27, 43, 89, 122, 291, 378, 381
– light enters 63
– primeval 54, 93, 143, 189, 192, 232, 269, 302, 333, 367, 407, 423
– to your face 378
– uncovered 92
day / daily 9, 166, 453
dead 18, 129, 189, 212, 317
– 9 (nine) blessed 82, 191
– blessed 9, 32, 35, 38, 189-91
– deceased 158, 239, 242, 246
– guard 185

– judge 297, 298
– realm of 294, 411
– those of the Underworld 38
decay 394-5
decree 108, 138, 244, 254, 406
deities; *see also divine, the; gods* 9, 22, 24, 40, 42, 157, 440
– 3 (three) 430
– 7 (seven) 38-9, 399
– 12 (twelve) 35, 102
– 14 (fourteen) 38, 350
– who are in it 25, 40, 76, 114, 181, 229, 267, 343, 346
demon 136, 248
depth of Earth / Netherworld 211, 286
descend 427
desert 18, 20-1, 23-7, 44, 169
destine 440
destruction 85, 162, 178, 378
– charge of / head of destruction 131, 136
– destroy 34, 41, 48, 104, 111, 121-2, 176, 204, 243, 282, 321, 324, 328, 352-3, 446
– order destruction 178
– place of destruction 49, 174, 176, 178-9, 185, 191
devourer 141, 199-200, 202, 278-9, 280
dignity 129
direction 23, 372, 401-2
disc (sun disc); *see also sun, disc* 20, 22, 24, 37, 118, 190, 247, 384, 410
dispose of 80, 293, 310, 312, 321
– of barley 261
– of his offering upon earth 321
– of island 312
– of offerings in the West 241
distribute 40, 157
district 245, 363
divider 342-3
divine, the (n) 153, 297, 362
Djam (Was-sceptre) 86, 414-6
Djedher 193, 233
Djeseret, beer is 25, 66, 80, 109, 119, 123, 133, 151, 166, 179, 201, 209, 223, 228, 241, 261, 264, 277, 281, 287, 289, 295, 298, 311
donations 43
done, what you have done; *see also under evil, commit; Osiris; Re* 150, 244, 255, 286, 324
door(s); *see also gate; knife; numbers (first, second etc.); way* 26-7, 53-4, 66, 93-4, 105, 109, 119, 142-3, 192-3, 231-2, 268, 301-2, 332-3, 366-7, 406-7, 448-9
– door-keeper 402, 443-4, 453
– doors in the earth 363
– mysterious 182, 230, 268, 301, 332, 366
– open / unlock 27, 52-3, 62, 93, 143, 182, 192, 231, 269, 302, 333, 363, 367, 407, 448, 450
– close / shut / slam / smash 27, 54, 66, 94, 105, 109, 143, 193, 232, 269, 302, 333, 367, 407, 449
– -way; *see also way* 53, 92, 142, 192, 231, 268, 332, 406
drowning 383
Duat / Duati 20, 92, 138, 148-9, 163, 169, 178, 201, 215, 218
– fields of the 152
– Foremost of the 226
– gods from / in / of the 41, 120, 158-9, 164, 175, 158-9, 218
– head / Ruler of 129, 226
– mystery of 214
– The justified who are in the Duat 35
– way of the 40, 43
duration 105
duty 141, 382
dwellers of netherworld / desert 44, 188, 283

– E –

ears (part of head); *see a. sungod; hear* 205
earth 24, 32, 35, 44, 74, 76, 78, 85, 88, 92, 148, 151, 155, 164, 166, 177, 179, 201, 205, 209, 215, 223-4, 228, 241, 242, 245, 257, 261, 265, 277, 281, 287, 289, 295, 298, 311, 315, 321, 332, 406
– barque of the /in the 74-6, 78
– Ba-souls of the 225
– belongs to Re‘s body 315
– care for 210
– carry / enclose 331
– corpse belongs to the 215
– depth of the 286
– doors in the 363
– god(s) of the 77, 225
– horn of the earth 332
– in the / within the 9, 40, 104, 185, 257, 316-7, 383, 385, 434
– Marvel of the 344, 346
– open / sealed 43, 87, 92
– pass the 64
– -quake / quakes / springs /trembles 76, 91-2, 223
– resting place of the 242
– shrine in the 42
– Wrapped ones of the 78

East 150, 363, 420
– eastern 115, 391, 395, 420, 428
egg 44, 260
Egypt 169, 256
Egyptians 168
elevated 247
emanate 18, 46, 340
embrace 214, 220, 257
emerge 27, 359, 362, 417, 420
– heads emerge out of him 185, 199
– mysteries 279
end 40, 136, 167, 244, 250, 312, 344
enemies / enemy; *see also Apopis; fetter(s)* 44, 46, 49, 88, 104, 112, 128, 130, 137, 176, 17-9, 191, 202, 250, 252, 254-5, 282, 285-6, 322-3, 326, 328, 374
– 2 (two) 248
– 4 (four) 322
– 20 (twenty) 44
– annihilation / destroy / burn 41, 104, 177, 322, 328
– bind 46, 248, 322, 356, 375
– condemn 250, 255-6
– drive away / overthrow / punish 88, 202, 230, 248, 286
– escape 254
– seize 137, 252, 254,
– inverted figures / subversive ones 323, 374
– of Atum / Geb / Horus / Khepri / Shu 248-50
– of Osiris 191, 250, 322
– of Re 202, 248
– put flames into 328
energy, Ka-energies 102
Ennead 50, 52, 84, 92, 141-2, 191, 230, 268, 297, 301, 331
entrance
– (of Netherworld) 40
– enter 27, 42, 50, 54, 91, 94, 140, 143, 150, 179, 181, 193, 204, 208, 229, 232, 267, 269, 294, 299, 302, 330, 333, 339, 346, 362-3, 365, 367, 385, 403, 407, 446
– enter gate 50, 91, 140, 181, 229, 267, 299, 365, 403, 446
– enter sky 358, 423, 442
essence 164, 211
establish 174, 398, 414, 429, 432, 438, 440
– gate 430
– portions 414
– shrine 416
estate(s) 155, 157, 165
evil 47, 48, 112, 245, 322, 352, 378
– afflict / inflict 45, 179
– belongs to you 47
– command 285
– commit / do / evildoers 48, 112, 190, 322, 324, 352
– cry 44
– destroy 243
– Evilface (serpent) 202
– not able to disturb 245
exalt(ed) 185, 188, 189
excellence 292
exist(ing) / existence / being 19, 21, 23, 77, 154
– cease to / extinguish 105, 176, 190, 324
– come into / bring into / put into 24, 169-70, 172, 260, 286, 315, 440
– non-existing / exist not / be not 48, 52, 154, 325, 328
eye; *see also see (not)* 19, 71, 192, 231, 381, 402
– brilliant 21, 23, 170
– burns with his (serpent) 192
– divine 220
– eyes (of Akhty) 247, 381
– filled 21
– inflames with 72
– is shut 268-9
– kindles / shines forth from his 71, 190
– lid 13, 236, 272
– mouth is my 327
– of Re; *see also disc; sun disc* 18-9, 72, 402
– protect /protectress of 188, 190
– remove 21
– sanctuary of 150
– search 172
– seize with 231
– Udjat-eye 255, 402

– F –

face(s) 276, 288, 381, 384-5
– 2 (two) / double faces 336, 391
– darkness to your 378
– burning / fiery / flaming face (serpent) 224, 301-2
– is destroyed 352
– militant 288
– mysterious 381
– of Re 381, 384-5
– opening for 291
– terrible of 376
falcon 38, 168, 274, 322, 336, 356, 383, 405, 416

fasten 206, 357, 363, 377
father 46, 48, 83, 128, 132, 137, 188, 323, 324, 328
fear 129
feed 132
fell 88
fetter(s) / fetterers 44, 46, 162, 199, 323, 324, 372, 374-5, 378-9, 424, 427
field(s); *see also region* 152, 157, 221-2, 256, 260-1, 263, 265
– Akh- 153
– Field of Rushes 155, 157, 165, 222
– of Netherworld 260, 261, 265
fight / fighter 242, 388
finger(s); *see also hand* 254, 426
fire / fiery; *see also flame* 71, 85, 112, 142, 224, 225-7, 326-8, 388
– Ba-soul is (not) in the 329
– Ba-soul of this Isle of Fire 315
– burn (verb) 112, 192
– fiery blast / blaze 71, 85, 112, 227, 328
– fiery face 142, 224
– flame(s) 112, 138, 226, 328
– heat 71
– is water / water is 36, 225
– Lake of Fire 68, 224
– red 136
fist 372, 428
flame; *see also fire* 112, 138, 226, 327-8
– come near to 329
– flaming 62, 126, 301-2
– goes forth 328
– inflames / put flames into 72, 327
– of cobra 226
flesh; *see also bodies; corpse* 38, 88, 114, 158, 210, 220, 246, 282, 316, 348, 422
– hack up 86
– revise 223
– rise up / unite 220
float 318-9
flood; *see also Nun; water* 319, 321, 415
follower(s) 35, 218, 219, 287
– Followers of Osiris 218
– retinue / following 64, 74,78, 116, 132, 191, 244, 253, 356, 388, 432, 451
food; *see also beer; bread; cakes; Djeseret; meat; refreshment; water* 238-40, 256
– generate 256
– sacrificial 22, 25
– take 293
foot 357, 363, 390
– feet 191, 240
force(s), apply 117
foremost 79, 85, 88, 123, 126, 129-30, 132, 182, 214, 226, 230, 258, 260, 264, 301, 317, 331, 366
– of Heaven 317
– of his thighs 79
– of the Akh-spirits 123
– of the Beyond 226
– of the Cavern 264
– of the Duat 226
– of the Horizon 182, 214, 230, 268, 301, 331, 366
– of the Netherworld; *see also Khontamenti* 258, 260
form(s) 164, 262, 264, 283, 317, 337, 362, 405, 436
function 42, 359

– G –

garment, shining 81
gate(s)
– abbreviated form of 26-7
– arrive / enter 50, 91, 140, 181, 229, 267, 299, 365, 403, 446
– Artefact of its Lord 229
– at / in 33, 94, 142-3, 159, 182, 193, 232, 330, 411, 447
– called to 36
– closed 43
– gateway(s) 275, 343, 346, 351, 357, 421
– Glowing one / shining one 267, 299
– He of the 430
– hides / hidden 115, 430
– does her duty 141
– Holy (secluded) one 365
– judge at 296
– leaves 50
– Mistress of Lifetime 160, 181
– Mistress of nourishment 91
– mysterious 451
– nourishes its gods 240
– open / is open 27, 52-3, 93, 142-3, 192, 231, 269, 302, 333, 367, 399, 406, 448, 450
– of Khontamenty 377
– of Shetit 37
– of the eastern horizon 387
– of the God of the Netherworld 430
– protected 182, 301
– rest in 122
– turn (back) 275-6, 342, 345, 351, 357, 421, 430, 442
– unapproachable 230, 268, 332, 366
– way of Nun 275

gate(s; cont.):
– way of the West 343, 346, 421
– with great authority 331
– with high knives 342
– with mysterious initiation 403
– with piercing blaze 50
– with protected might 446
gear, rowing 38
Geb 249, 252-3, 372, 377, 378, 424, 453
glorification / glorify 45, 82, 128, 130
glow, Glowing one 299
go and come (back) 292
go forth 115, 422, 429, 433
goddesses; *see also deity; Isis; Nephthys; Maat; Nut; Sakhmet; Selkis* 182, 372, 397, 438
– 4 (four) 390, 438, 440, 442
– 8 (eight) 418
– 12 (twelve) 120, 396
gods; *see also Akhty; Anubis; Atum; Duat; Ennead; Heka; Horus; Horakhty; Ikeki; Khnum; Nepri; Osiris; Ptah; Re; Seth; Sia; Sopdu; Toth; Zemit*
– 2 (two) 248
– 4 (four) 74, 156, 282, 356, 372, 410, 412, 414, 416, 432-4, 443
– 7 (seven) 38
– 8 (eight) 178, 356
– 9 (nine) 50, 86, 160, 178, 424
– 11 (eleven) 126
– 12 (twelve) 18, 32, 35, 102, 106, 128, 152, 174, 198, 202, 206, 212, 224, 238, 242, 256, 274, 278, 284, 296, 308, 372, 394
– 14 (fourteen) 38, 350
– without power 227
golden, Golden one 250, 255
grain 38, 257, 260
– ear(s) of 68, 73, 256
green 68, 260
greenery 258
ground 155
growth 258
guard (verb); *see also protect* 26, 44, 50, 62, 108, 112-3, 118, 131, 136, 138, 162, 185, 226, 254, 255, 281, 343, 346, 354, 377-8, 411, 451
– 2 (two) 224
– Ba-souls 118
– guardian 26, 50, 52, 91, 141, 181-2, 224, 229-30, 267, 281, 299, 301, 331, 365, 403, 405, 446-7
– jackals guard 108
– life 108
– matters 411
guard (cont.):
– Nehep is guarding 222
– serpent 26
– rope 354
– traps 131, 138
– He who embraces 301
– The roaring one 365
– The blind one 268
– The destroyer 446
– The round one 299
– The Violent (one) 403
– Uniter 229
– Who carries the Earth 331
– Who cuts down 405
– Who devours 52
– Who draws near 141
– Who encloses the Earth 331
– Who uncovers 365
– With burning / fiery face 224
guide 103, 121, 123, 201, 363, 382, 397-8

– H –

hack, up the flesh 86
hail 22, 24, 49, 53, 64, 72, 88, 92, 104, 112, 142, 155, 217, 226, 264, 291, 294, 296, 298, 310, 314, 317, 320, 325, 337, 338, 353, 359, 363, 390, 398
hair 442
hall, great hall (of Re) 44, 48, 255
hand(s) 38, 44, 156, 167, 198, 262, 284, 312, 347, 350, 353, 356, 362, 377, 378, 382, 384, 388, 394, 396, 414, 416-9, 426, 428
– 1 (one) 372, 384, 410, 412, 414, 416
– image which is in their hand 411
– lift up 388
– staff in 424
– tow-rope in 356
head(s) 24, 69, 70, 74, 79, 84, 106, 185, 199-200, 202-4, 226, 238, 242, 247, 274-6, 290, 323, 336, 340, 343, 346, 350, 356, 372, 383, 388, 400, 405, 447
– 2 (two) / double / double-headed 336, 344, 391
– 2 (double) serpent 350
– 4 (four) 274
– 6 (six)-headed 342
– 8 (eight) 344
– cat-headed 444
– crocodile-headed 399, 418
– crowned head (gods) 432
– cut off 84
– emerge 185, 199, 200, 202, 274, 275, 276, 320

head (cont.):
– falcon-headed / falcon heads 38, 168, 274, 322, 356
– human-headed / human heads 68, 202, 336, 344, 350, 383, 400, 405, 447
– in Apopis 204
– in rope 274
– jackal-headed 20, 23, 248, 424
– lion-headed 383
– of an ibis 356
– of antelope 185
– of destruction 136
– of Duat 226
– of Ptah 383
– ram-headed 23, 38, 356, 415
– receive 337
– star above 396, 400
– stops 447
– swallow 343, 346
– reverse 336
– with Uraeus 383
headcloth 21, 24, 41, 126, 128-30
hear 27, 54, 66, 94, 105, 109, 119, 121, 143, 163, 193, 232, 269, 302, 333, 367, 407
heart(s) 128, 159, 181-2, 240, 292, 313
heat; *see fire*
heaven; *see also horizon;* sky 92, 115, 200, 215, 287, 315, 317, 352, 355, 359, 380, 382, 391, 394, 396-7, 415, 427, 438
– Ba-soul belongs to /rests in heaven 214, 363, 406
– drag in / enter 358, 385
– eastern horizon of 395, 428
– Foremost of 317
– heads emerged out of 185
– jubilation in 316
– navigation in 417
– Nut 287, 352, 355, 394, 396-7, 427, 438
– open Netherworld against 423
– sandbank in 427
– separated from 215
– tow towards 380
– who is in / live in 53, 169, 440
Heka 8, 20, 38, 42, 114, 158, 210, 246
help 72, 118
Heqa-sceptre 424
Hereafter; *see also Beyond; Netherworld* 43
hiss 110
honour, pay 443
Horakhty / Re-Horakhty 142, 148, 347
Horemheb 7, 39, 47, 67, 72-3, 81, 95, 103, 107, 112, 119, 186-7, 225
horizon 27, 211, 357
horn(s) 332, 388
Horus 38, 126, 128, 132, 136, 168-9, 172, 322-3, 326, 328, 336, 340, 356, 362, 383, 391, 405, 416, 427
– children / sons of 377, 424, 426-7
– enemies of 250
– engender 325
– of the Netherworld 356, 362
– retinue of 356
– son of 129-30
– who is in the boat 336
– with crowned head 340
hour(s) 42, 74, 280, 374, 382, 396, 417
– cavern of the 394
– comes into being 208
– does her duty 382
– emerges 206, 280
– -god / goddesses 382, 396
– of night 7, 9
– of rest 374
– setting of 208
– who belongs to the hour 382
house, Benben- 212, 214
Hu (utterance) 132, 453
human
– head / -headed 68, 202, 350, 400
– figures / humans / beings 19, 21, 44, 164, 170, 188

– I / J –

ibis, head of 356
Igeret (Beyond) 247, 254, 317
Ikeki 278, 281
illuminate 72, 143, 192, 232, 269, 302, 333, 367, 381, 407
image(s) 7, 68, 216, 356, 383, 411, 423
Imenrenef 423
immerse, who are immersed 318, 320
incense 33, 238
inert, Inert ones 44
initiation, with mysterious 403
inspect (corpse / limb) 179; 426
Isis 451, 453
island / isle 312, 314
– Island of Fire 308, 309, 310, 312, 314-5
jackal (-headed) 20, 23, 106, 108, 248, 424
jaw 327
joy / joyful 64, 256-7
– rejoice (verb) 76, 293
jubilation / jubilate 148, 282-3, 311, 316, 401, 413
judge 283, 285, 296-8
– justify (verb) 35, 89, 177, 189, 324
– oblation is justification 177

judgement (court / hall) 40-1, 166-7, 183, 189, 250, 285

– K –

Ka (-energies / -power) 102, 238-9
Kenset 363
Khentymentef 79
Khepri; *see also scarab* 356, 357-9, 362-3, 447
– enemies of 249
Khnum 38, 415, 434, 440
Khontamenti; *see also Foremost of the Netherworld* 260, 311, 372, 377-8
knee(s), kneeling 20, 23, 383
knife; *see also door(s)* 342, 372, 388, 424-5
– knives 352, 376
knowledge / to know (verb) 9, 64, 148, 292, 329, 395

– L –

lake 68-71, 73, 106-10, 112, 224
– barley of 70
– of Fire 68, 224
– of Life 106
– of Uraeus-serpents 110
– refreshment in / of 36, 244
– rest at 108
– stand upon 120
land / land-measurers 156
– receive land 221
law 35
leaf 26, 50
lean on staff 44, 82, 86, 168, 218, 248, 256, 262, 290, 312, 318, 322
leap up 130
left 429
leg(s) 342, 344, 356
liberate 37
Libyans 168, 172
life; *see also live* 106, 189
– guard 108
– Lake of Life 106
– lifetime 102, 122, 174-6, 178, 188, 389
– living 19, 66, 110, 225, 440
– Mistress of Lifetime 160, 181
lift up 274, 438, 453
light 21, 54, 63, 75, 93, 115, 122, 288
– belongs to you (gods) 21, 288
– enters darkness 63
– illuminate / lighten up / shine/ bring/ throw light into 20, 52, 54, 72, 91, 93, 141, 143, 181, 190, 192, 229, 232, 260, 267, 269, 276, 294, 299, 302, 331, 333, 365, 367, 381, 403, 407, 446
light (cont.):
– in the Netherworld 289
– perceive / see 215, 221, 289
– splendour 209
– twilight 423, 447
limb(s), limbs 70, 220, 260, 426
lion / lion-headed 383
live (verb); *see also life* 19, 36, 66, 85, 88, 118, 122, 132, 205, 225, 244, 358, 440
– gods 211
– in heaven 440
– not 324
Lo 76, 154, 199
loosening 80, 170, 220, 288, 292
lord
– Artefact of its Lord (name of gate) 229
– Lord of the Ennead 298
lying, half-lying 354

– M –

Maat 35-6, 164, 242-5, 297, 438
– beer of 132
– belongs to 36, 244, 297
– carry 242, 245
– examine 243
– give 285
– lives on / from 36, 243
– lift up 438
– oblation is 245
– practise 242
– speak (law of) 35, 164
magician, magic; *see also Heka* 46, 162, 338, 347, 350
magistrates 283-4
manifestation(s) 22, 24, 27, 49, 75-6, 162, 211, 283, 352, 356, 358, 360, 420
master(s) 73, 85, 104, 109, 210, 256-7
– of hours /years 104, 210
– of mysteries 142
– of oblations 85
– of provision 86, 285, 287
– of renewal 73
matter(s), guard 411
matutinal, who greet 418
meal; *see also bread; beer; meat; offering; sacrifice; wine* 133
measuring / measurer 152, 153, 156-7, 175
meat is oblation 118
Mehen; *see also serpent* 37, 158, 246-7, 282, 316, 348, 391, 419, 421-2
– protection in 150
– -serpent 419, 421
– who are in 374
Merenptah 7; 111, 161, 173

messenger, send out 216
might 446
million 172
mistress 91, 160, 181, 221-2
monkey; *see also baboon* 188, 401
– 4 (four) 350
mother, thighs of your 363
mountain 18, 20, 23, 115, 211
mourn (verb) 63, 433, 442
mouth; *see a. breath; throat* 240, 292, 326-8
– of Aqen 207-8
– of Re 358
– of the Uniter 417
– mouth as eye 327
movement 20, 38, 64, 320
– moving one 53
– The removing one (serpent) 120
mower / mowing 263-4
mummy / mummies 62, 68, 170, 220, 223, 288, 292, 326
– 4 (four) 288
– 7 (seven) 326
– 9 (nine) 50, 52, 92, 116, 141, 230, 268, 301, 331
– 12 (twelve) 182, 218, 290
– black 62
– mummiform 50, 74, 206, 248, 383
– mummy-wrapping 170, 220, 288, 292
– resting on his bier 223
mystery / mysteries 182, 212, 214, 276, 279, 282, 290, 319, 324, 391
– be whole in his 349
– carry 212
– embrace 214
– emerge 279
– give birth to 274
– hidden 290
– master of 142
– mysterious 115, 182, 211, 216, 230, 264, 268, 301, 317, 332, 366, 381, 383, 451
– of the Duat 214
– of Re 282, 317, 349
– open Mysterious 268, 301, 332, 366
– protect 217
– shine 276
– surround ... of Re 217

– N–

name(s) 32, 68, 82, 86, 106, 110, 136, 148, 170, 172, 218, 336, 428, 436
– hidden name 33, 423,
– individual name 9, 38
– in your name of 170, 172
– no name / without name 62, 312
navigation / navigate 350, 417
neck 22, 206, 336, 372, 399
Nehep 218, 222
Nephthys 451, 453
Nepri (grain god) / Nepri-Heti 257, 259
net 347, 350
nethersky, He from the 401
Netherworld; *see also earth*
– belonging to the 158, 218
– created / established by Re 254, 314
– open ... against sky 423
– unite with sky 410
– who belongs to the 218
nets 347, 349
night 7, 9, 50
north(ern) 336, 340, 358
noses; *see also breathe* 63, 80
– breath for 71, 165, 170, 220, 292, 320
– without 205
nourishment / nourish 33, 91, 103, 240, 415
Nubians 168, 172
number
– 1st (first) 25, 26, 38, 141, 350, 356, 362, 372, 399, 448
– 2nd (second) 52, 248
– 2 (two) 20, 23, 50, 52, 91, 141, 181, 224, 229, 248, 336, 344, 352, 350, 356, 362, 391, 416-7, 429, 449
– 3rd (third) 38, 92, 249, 350
– 3 (three) 322, 350, 391, 430
– 4th (fourth) 38, 141, 400
– 4 (four) 44, 74, 114, 168, 210, 274, 282, 316, 318, 322, 336, 348, 350, 356, 372, 391, 399, 420, 424
– 5 (five) 424
– 5th (fifth) 424
– 6 (six) 40, 248, 342
– 6th (sixth) 230
– 7 (seven) 38, 74, 248
– 7th (seventh) 250, 268
– 8 (eight) 23, 74, 178, 344, 356, 418
– 8th (eighth) 301
– 9 (nine) 9, 50, 52, 82, 86, 92, 16, 141, 160, 178, 191, 230, 268, 301, 312, 331, 424
– 9th (ninth) 331
– 10 (ten) 110
– 11 (eleven) 126
– 12 (twelve) 7, 9, 18, 32, 68, 106, 120, 128, 152, 164, 174, 198, 202, 206, 212, 218, 224, 238, 242, 256, 274, 278, 284, 290, 296, 308, 342, 372, 394, 396
– 14 (fourteen) 38, 350
– 16 (sixteen) 344
– 20 (twenty) 44

number (cont.):
– 24 (twentyfour) 366
– 100 (hundred) 9
Nun 318, 321, 422, 423, 453
– arms of 412, 422
– cavern of 276
– emerge from 394
– gateway of 275
– Re approaches 415
– who is in the Nun 318
nurse 436
Nut 358, 363, 381, 385, 417, 423, 450, 453
– heaven 287, 352, 355, 394, 396, 397, 427, 438
– womb of 411, 413, 449

– O –

oars / oarsman / oarsmen 394-5
oath 102
oblation(s); *see also offering* 32-4, 71-2, 80, 85, 88, 105, 109, 123, 133, 150, 155, 157, 166, 177, 179, 217, 258
– are/ is bread 66, 80, 109, 123, 133, 166, 179
– destroy 34
– give 37, 43
– is hearing god's voice 163
– is justification 177
– is Maat 245
– is meat 118
– is what is offered upon earth 205
– master of 85
– my … is your … 217
– of Akhty 217
– of Re 85, 88
obscurity 381
odour; *see also stench* 70, 259, 292
offering(s); *see also oblation* 25, 32-3, 36, 42, 43, 71, 77, 85, 88, 103, 105, 108, 150, 222, 238, 240, 258, 282, 293, 321, 398, 415
– apportioning 190
– belong to 34, 36, 71
– bestow 32
– complete 215
– dispose of 321
– food 238-40
– guide 103
– in (this hour) 42
– make 66
– Mistress of Offerings 221
– nourish from 33
– of Re 150
offering(s; cont.):
– of the earth 321
– offer (verb) 33, 398
– offerer (whoever offers/ makes an offering) 73, 81, 85, 88, 105, 109, 123, 133, 150, 151, 155, 163, 166, 177, 179, 201, 205, 209, 215, 223, 228, 241, 245, 261, 265, 277, 281, 287, 289, 295, 298, 311, 315, 321, 329
– present offering 149
– sacrifices 22, 25
oil 292
old one(s) 353, 354, 443
open; *see arms; door; gate; earth; Mysteries; Netherworld*
orbit 314
order (n, verb) 21-3, 46, 78, 133, 178, 285
– destruction 178
– of Re / great god 22, 133
orientation; *see also east, south, west*
– eastern 115, 391, 395, 420, 428
– northern 336, 340
– southern 336, 337
origin / come forth from 19, 22, 24, 122, 155, 157, 172, 204, 28, 328, 358, 414, 423
Osireion 7, 163, 386, 388-91, 456-7
Osiris 9, 85, 88, 126, 129, 130, 153, 189, 191, 240, 243, 259-60, 276, 324, 344, 372, 405, 433, 453
– belong to 226, 258
– bewail 433
– do for 121, 128, 322, 324
– emerges 259
– enemies of 191, 250, 322
– father of 128, 322, 324
– Followers / following of 116, 191, 218
– foremost of the Westerners 85, 88, 126, 129, 130, 132
– Great one 88, 167, 169, 317, 359
– Judgement Hall of Osiris 183
– Osiris Khontamenti 372
– Protecting Osiris 185
– Ruler of the West (?) 219
– satisfy 264
– seclusion of 294
– shrine of 126
– standing on serpent 126
– violate 227
ovation 159

– P –

pain 137

path(s); *see also way* 159, 310, 363
pause 138, 211
peace 405
percipience; *see Sia*
pharaoh, tomb of; *see Djedher; Horemheb; Ramses; Seti; Merenptah; Tawseret; Osireion*
pierce 50, 93
pig 188
pit(s) 139, 224
– fiery 224-7
– unapproachable 226
place 37, 41, 43, 49, 103, 115, 174, 176, 178, 179, 191, 211, 213, 214, 280, 338, 359, 402, 434, 439, 443, 444
– Hidden Place 19, 89
– of destruction 49, 174, 176, 178, 179, 191
– protected 149
– resting place of the Earth 242
– which raises its creator 115
– with lasting nature 211
plant 77, 200, 260, 315, 376
plot(s) 152, 154, 222
poison, who is in his poison 406
pole 20, 23, 248, 249, 250, 388, 447
– 7 (seven) poles 248
– enemies of Atum / Geb / Horus / Khepri / Osiris / Re / Shu 248-50
– gods behind 253
– of Geb 250, 252
– who is precise / terrible / violent 249
– who presses / squeezes 248, 250
– who seizes 231, 248
– with authoritative face 250
portions; *see also field; ration* 190, 240, 414
power 129, 162, 227, 240, 247, 281, 314, 321, 338
– powerful 37, 47, 132, 356, 362, 374, 381
praising / praise (verb) 77, 88, 267, 283, 299, 311-2, 314, 316, 330, 344, 365, 384, 385, 401, 403, 420, 443, 446
– praise great god / Re 88, 283, 311-2, 443
prayer 443
preside (verb) 167
primeval 54, 93, 143, 192, 232, 269, 302, 423
prince 253
procession / proceed (verb) 38, 40, 201, 351, 355, 375, 379, 383, 432, 434, 436, 439, 451
pronounce 166, 250
prosperity 259
protection; *see also guard, guardian* 37, 76, 150, 156, 211
– Book of Protecting Osiris 9, 185
– fight 355
– in Mehen 150
– protect 62, 78, 88-9, 128, 131, 149, 170, 172, 182, 188, 190, 217, 244, 301, 345, 349-50, 446
provision(s) 32, 70, 78, 103, 107, 112, 118, 122, 129, 132, 138, 154, 155, 208
– masters of 86, 285, 287
– provide (verb) 133, 138, 226, 280, 308, 320
prow; *see barque*
Ptah, head of 383
punishment 47, 440
– punish 84, 130, 248, 254, 255, 345, 353, 374, 377, 378, 424-5
– punished ones 41, 345
– punisher /punishress 202
purification / purify 102, 108, 118, 238

– Q / R –

quarrel 44
quarters, four 44
raise/raising 75, 115, 117, 221, 292
– body 22, 24
– gods 117, 221
– oneself 373, 426
ram-headed 23, 38, 356, 415
Ramses
– I 59, 75, 79, 83, 87, 99, 121, 127
– III 197, 209, 217, 221, 227, 239, 243, 246, 251, 257, 263
– IV 30, 31, 34, 43, 55, 94, 101, 109, 113, 131, 139, 149
– V/VI 16, 184, 253, 266, 279, 300, 303, 309, 323, 329, 338, 346-7, 353, 355, 371, 376, 379, 385, 387, 392, 397, 401-2, 404, 421, 426, 431, 435, 437, 439, 441, 444-5, 454
– VII 19
ration (daily / of grain) 166, 260
rattle, rattling one 400
Re; *see also sun, Sungod; will*
– adore 32, 45, 443
– among others 21, 166
– announce 428
– approaches Nun 415
– assigns 63, 118, 414
– attend on 382-3, 387-9, 394
– Ba-soul of / follow 45, 316, 430
– behind 64, 383, 429, 433-4, 439, 441

Re (cont.):
– cattle of 169
– chapel of 438
– decrees 406
– do for 45, 82
– earth belongs to Re's body 315
– enduring 37
– enemies of 45, 202, 248
– entered the sky 358
– eye of 21, 23, 402
– face of 381, 384, 385
– flesh of Re 38, 114, 158, 210, 246, 282, 316, 348, 422
– Foremost of Heaven 317
– goes forth 257, 280, 358, 421, 450
– great image / great of power 314, 383
– guide 121, 397
– hall of 44, 255
– has power over 247
– I am myself 167
– in front of 350, 442
– in the Shetit 113
– in / left the West 148, 151, 433
– join 434
– know 148
– look on 319
– make the way for 426
– manifestation of 27
– Master of mysteries 142
– mouth of 358
– nurse 436
– oblations of 85, 88
– offerings of 150
– open for 26, 53, 93, 142, 192, 231, 269, 302, 332, 366, 406, 448, 449
– opener of the earth 43
– order of 133
– permanent one 104
– proclaim 428
– protects 350
– reaches 111, 160, 252
– Re-Akhty / Re-Horakhty 104, 142, 347
– receive Re 412
– repel the rebel from 201
– restore (to heaven) 215
– retinue of 356, 432
– rich in forms 405
– setting 64
– sky belongs to 315
– splendour of 294
– that which is in 20
– tow / pull 29, 40, 43, 74, 78, 105, 114-5, 139, 158-9, 210-11, 246-7, 275-6, 282, 316-7, 348-9, 356, 359, 362, 380, 384, 396-8

Re (cont.):
– view 49
– with great orbit 314
realm of the dead 294, 411
rear 50, 110
rebel; *see also Apopis* 82, 86, 352
– drive away / back / overthrow / repel / seize 82, 153, 201-3, 252, 374
– ropes of this 426
receive; *see also Re* 33, 115, 152, 221, 263, 312, 340, 394, 396, 398, 412, 425
– heads 337
– knives 425
– oars 394
red 62, 68, 136
– Red Crown(s) 336, 340, 430, 434, 440
refreshment 25, 36, 43, 66, 73, 81, 85, 89, 105, 119, 123, 133, 151, 166, 179, 201, 209, 222, 223, 226, 228, 239, 241, 244, 245, 261, 264, 277, 281, 287, 289, 295, 298, 311, 315, 321
– in / of your lake 36, 244
-(s), take hold of 33, 34, 222
region; *see also field*
– hidden 27, 54, 93, 143, 192, 232
rejuvenation; *see also renewal* 7, 189, 356
remove 102, 324
– Ba-soul 34
– eye 19, 21, 23
– image 324
renewal 9, 73
renown 79
repair 129
replacement 129
respect 164
rest 76-7, 80, 108-9, 122, 160, 167, 190, 209, 214-5, 242, 298, 317, 349, 374, 381, 395, 411, 413, 422, 427, 438, 449
retinue; *see also follower(s)* 64, 78, 132, 244, 253, 356, 388, 398, 432, 451
– of Geb 253
– of this god 388, 451
retreat 132, 199
right 154, 181, 429
rise 83, 118, 150, 339, 344
roof 62, 293
rope(s) 38, 46, 74, 152, 154, 156, 159, 206, 274-6, 278, 336, 354, 356-7, 359, 362, 372, 375, 378-9, 384, 396, 398, 426
– back /hind 336, 340
– carrier of 276
– coil of 208
– double(-twisted) 175-6, 206
– front 336-7, 384
– guard 354

rope (cont.):
– grasp 176, 198, 206, 278, 280, 336, 337, 340, 354, 356, 372, 376, 384, 396, 427
– heads in rope 274
– in finger/hand 426
– in 153
– in their hand 356
– measuring 152, 156
– of rebel 426
– of/in the West 152, 154, 156
– pull 74
– punishing 377
– straight 276
– strong 159
– tie 277
– towing rope (tow-rope) 38, 356, 360, 362, 396, 398
rot 118
round 299, 358
ruler of Duat / West 129, 219
rush, Field of Rushes 155, 157, 165, 222
rower / rowing; *see barque*

– S –

sacrifice / sacrificial; *see also offerings* 22, 25
safety 374
sail; *see also boat; barque; ship* 49, 114, 385
Sais, she of 430
Sakhmet 170, 172, 383
sanctuary 150, 216-7
sand, sandbank 425, 427
scales; *see also balance* 190
scarab / beetle; *see also Khepri* 20
sceptre(s) 405, 405, 415
– Djam-sceptre 86, 414-16
– Heqa-sceptre 424
– Was-sceptre; *see also Was* 38, 372, 399, 405, 414-6, 418, 430, 444
scorpion-goddess; *see also Selkis* 372
seat 153, 208, 414,
seclusion / secluded 108, 211, 244, 294
secret(s) 159, 315
see (not); *see also eye* 212, 216, 429
Sehetepenes 417
Selkis 372, 375
sensible, the Sensible One 38
serpent(s); *see also Apopis, coils* 20, 26, 38, 52, 62, 92, 142, 160, 174, 192, 202, 205, 218, 231, 268, 276, 326, 328-9, 332, 344, 354, 372, 375, 383, 389, 406, 418, 424, 427, 444
serpent(s; cont.):
– 3 (three) Uraeus-serpents 391
– 6 (six)-headed 342
– 10 (ten) 110
– 12 (twelve) 120
– 24 (twenty-four) Uraeus-serpents 366
– burning one / burns with his eye 192, 366-7
– carry 160, 174
– children of the faint one 372, 377-9
– cobra / uraei; *see also Wadjyt* 110; 112
– coiled one / multi-coiled 52-3, 82, 280 326, 450
– deficient one 267
– Devourer 199, 200, 202, 278, 279, 280
– double 344, 350, 356
– Evil Serpent / Evilface 200, 202
– fiery one 326, 327
– Flaming one / with flaming/ fiery face / great flame 62, 66, 126, 142, 301-2, 327, 388
– He with a wise mouth 418
– Horn of the Earth 332
– Khepri 249, 358-9, 362
– lights up for Re 52, 91, 141, 181, 229, 267, 299, 331, 365, 403, 446
– living one 389
– Marvel of the Earth 344, 346
– Mehen 37, 158, 246, 247, 282, 316, 348, 391, 419, 421, 422
– Nehep 218, 222
– of time 174
– Osiris standing on 126
– piercing one 92, 93
– recoiling one 161
– removing one 120
– retain 160
– retreating one 200
– shape of 278
– she who conducts 387
– those in the Earth 383
– those upon the serpent 329
– time as a 120
– uraeus-serpent(s) 50, 52, 91, 110, 126, 141, 181, 229, 267, 299, 331, 336, 365-7, 383-4, 389, 391, 403, 418, 446, 451, 453
– Uraeus-serpent Isis 451, 453
– voice of 111
– Wamemti 372
– who belongs to the gate 448
– who Guards the Desert 26
– who is in his poison 406
– who seizes with his eye 231

serpent(s; cont.):
– who walks 342-3
– whose coils my children are guarding 327
– whose eye is shut / blind 205, 267, 269
– with face of sungod 384
– with (human) head(s) 344, 346, 389
Seth 336, 391
Seti I 7-8, 49, 61, 65, 69, 117, 124, 134, 137, 140, 147, 151, 153, 162, 169, 171, 175, 199, 203, 207, 210, 213, 219, 236, 272
Seti II 157, 165, 167, 177, 179
shadow(s) 111, 214, 292, 295, 349
shapes 276
share(s) (belong to you) 154, 286-7
Shetit (Beyond); *see also Beyond; Igeret; Netherworld* 49, 64, 76, 85, 88, 114-5, 129, 132, 158, 176, 214, 317, 324, 338, 342, 345, 358-9, 363, 448, 450
shine 20, 81, 190, 247, 260, 267, 276, 294
ship; *see also barque* 74-7, 84
shoulder, protected 89
shrine 37, 42, 62-3, 116, 126, 128, 132.3, 247, 416
Shu 249; 453
Sia (percipience) 8, 26, 38, 42, 53, 93, 114, 142, 158, 192, 210, 231, 246, 252, 269, 279, 282, 302, 316, 332, 348, 367, 406, 422, 448, 450, 453
sickles 262-3, 265
sign; *see also Ankh; Djam; scepter; Was* 38, 242, 274
sinners 37
sky; *see also heaven; horizon* 150, 287, 351, 355, 389, 398, 413-4, 421
– belongs to Re 315
– enter the / set foot into 390, 423, 442
– open / unite Netherworld against / with 410, 423
– sandbank in the 425
– travel (in) the sky after Re 391
slaughter(s) 47-8, 191, 372, 352, 425
sleeping ones 218
son (of Horus) 46, 129-30, 377
Sopdu 416
south / southern gods 336-7, 358
space, Hidden Space 269, 302, 333, 367, 407
spear(s); *see also knife* 353-4
spells 258, 292
sphinx 290, 336, 339
spirits; *see Akh-spirits*
– Acclaiming ones who are in the Duat 148
– blessed 148
splendor 113, 118, 150, 209, 294
spring, earth springs 223
staff(s); *see also stick* 38, 40, 44, 82, 168, 218, 248, 256, 262, 290, 312, 318, 322, 424, 447
star(s) 206, 278, 382, 384, 395-6, 400, 412, 418
– above head 396, 400
– carry 412, 419
– make jubilation with 413
– put at their places 401
– who nurses the 400
stench, smell; *see also odour* 343, 346
step(s) 159, 191, 321
stick, forked; *see also staff* 198-200
stone, Benben 216-7
strength / strong 47, 49, 76-7, 130, 159, 165, 292
stride (n) 421
string 200
success 260
sun
– disc; *see also eye of Re; Udjat-eye* 20, 22, 24, 190, 410, 429
– solar barque 380
– Sungod; *see also Re* 7-8, 20, 38, 77, 216, 218, 262, 290, 312, 356, 384
swallow (verb) 120, 122, 188-9, 204, 208, 346
swimmers, who swim 318-20
Syrians 168, 170

– T –

taboo 107
Tatenen 113, 286, 311
Tawseret 306, 313, 319, 325, 327, 337, 339, 341, 343, 345, 359, 361, 386, 429
tears (n) 170
temple 243, 244
thighs 79, 363
Thoth 189, 356
throat, cut off 372
throne(s) 104, 153, 166, 283, 297-8, 402
– assign 283
– enthroned 191, 418
– place on / rest upon 167, 297, 360
time 120-1, 206
– as serpent / serpent of 120, 174
– establish lifetime 174, 398, 440
– rope of 206
torch(es) 37, 71, 388
transfiguration 169
transformation 298, 338, 390, 394-5, 398, 422, 447

traps; *see also net* 131, 136-8
tree, under 205
triumph / triumphant 46, 83, 84, 286
truthful one(s) 165, 167, 244, 245
twilight 423, 447

– U / V–

Udjat-eye 255, 402
unapproachable 226, 228, 230, 268, 332, 366
union
– unite 260, 274, 362, 410
– unite Netherworld with sky 410
– Uniter 229
upside down 83
Uraeus; *see also serpent* 383, 391, 366
vegetable(s) 308, 310, 313-5
venom 427
verdict 285
vessel; *see basket*
voice
– hear (verb) 27, 54, 66, 77, 94, 105, 109, 111, 119, 143, 163, 193, 232, 269, 302, 333, 367, 407
– of Re / god(s) 163
– of serpent (Apopis / Khepri / Uraeus) 111, 358, 372

– W –

wailing / wail (verb) 27, 54, 66, 77, 89, 94, 105, 109, 113, 119, 143, 193, 232, 269, 302, 333, 367, 407, 449
– bewail 255, 433
– lament (verb); *see also mourn* 89
Wamenti 378
Was(-sceptre); *see also sceptre, Djam* 38, 86, 136, 156, 167, 284, 372, 399, 402, 405, 414-6, 418, 430, 444
water; *see also flood; lake; Nun* 25, 36, 66, 68, 70-1, 73, 81, 105, 109, 119, 123, 133, 151, 166, 170, 179, 201, 209, 222-3, 225-8, 241, 245, 261, 264, 277, 280, 287, 289, 293, 295, 298, 311, 315, 318-9, 453
– cool 293
– is fire 36, 225
– is wine 109
– power over 321
– unapproachable 226
way(s); *see also doorway; Duat; path(s);* 40, 43, 160, 317, 352, 397, 426
weakness 378
wearyness / weary one 218, 221, 320
West 43, 149, 153, 201, 286, 346, 420, 422, 451
– Akh-spirits who are in the West 207
– Ba-souls of the 356
– belongs to 286
– Bull of the 400
– Foremost of the Westerners 85, 88, 126, 129, 130, 132
– gateway of the 343, 346, 421
– goddess of the 430
– in the 40, 89, 156, 174, 189, 201, 250, 347, 381, 427, 442, 450
– masters of provision in the 284
– Re has left the 433
– rope of / in the 152, 154, 156
– unapproachable 228
– who crosses the 53
White Crown 336, 344, 372, 430, 432, 438
will, according to Re's 314-5
wind 358
wine 109, 245
wings, winged 387
witch, bewitched 83
witness(es) 45, 48
word, (magic) words 189, 350
world, four quarters of the 44
wrap / (un)wrapping 69-70, 78-80
– mummy-wrapping 170, 220, 288, 292
wrong 35, 37

– Y / Z –

year(s) 104, 389, 398, 440
yellow 62, 68
Zemit 20, 23, 26